D0762995

Clearcutting the Pacific Rain Forest

Richard A. Rajala

Clearcutting the Pacific Rain Forest:
Production, Science, and Regulation

UBCPress / Vancouver

© UBC Press 1998
All rights reserved. No part of this publication may be reproduced, stored in a
retrieval system, or transmitted, in any form or by any means, without prior
written permission of the publisher, or, in Canada, in the case of photocopying
or other reprographic copying, a licence from CANCOPY (Canadian Copyright
Licensing Agency), 900 – 6 Adelaide Street East, Toronto, ON M5C 1H6.

Printed in Canada on acid-free paper ∞

ISBN 0-7748-0590-0 (hardcover)
ISBN 0-7748-0591-9 (paperback)

Canadian Cataloguing in Publication Data
Rajala, Richard Allan, 1953-
   Clearcutting the Pacific rain forest

   Includes bibliographical references and index.
   ISBN 0-7748-0590-0 (bound); ISBN 0-7748-0591-9 (pbk.)

   1. Forest management – British Columbia – History. 2. Clearcutting – British
Columbia – History. 3. Forest policy – British Columbia – History. 4. Forests and
forestry – British Columbia – History. 5. Logging – Technological innovations –
British Columbia – History. I. Title.

SD 146.B7R34 1998   338.1'7498'09711   C98-910179-7

This book has been published with a grant from the Social Sciences Federation of
Canada, using funds provided by the Social Sciences and Humanities Research
Council of Canada.

UBC Press also gratefully acknowledges the ongoing support to its publishing
program from the Canada Council for the Arts, the British Columbia Arts Council,
and the Multiculturalism Program of the Department of Canadian Heritage.

UBC Press
University of British Columbia
6344 Memorial Road
Vancouver, BC V6T 1Z2
(604) 822-5959
Fax: 1-800-668-0821
E-mail: orders@ubcpress.ubc.ca
http://www.ubcpress.ubc.ca

Dedicated to my mother,
to the memory of my father,
and to my wife, Jean

Contents

Illustrations

Acknowledgments

I would like to express my gratitude to Craig Heron, who supervised this work in its dissertation form at York University, for his direction and encouragement. Special thanks go also to the members of my committee, H.V. Nelles, Gordon Darroch, and Joseph Ernst, for their efforts. Peter Baskerville, Eric Sager, Rennie Warburton, and Patricia Roy have fostered my scholarly developments at the University of Victoria.

In researching this book I received much assistance from staff at a number of archives and libraries. I am grateful to all those who made the work pleasant and productive. The British Columbia Forest Service supported this project by granting access to agency records. My thanks to Mary McRoberts for help when it was needed.

Support from the Social Sciences and Humanities Research Council of Canada enabled me to research and write the manuscript.

My greatest debt is to my wife, Jean, whose contributions to this project are too numerous to list.

Abbreviations

ABCPFR	Association of British Columbia Professional Foresters Records
ABTVI	Associated Boards of Trade of Vancouver Island
BCA	British Columbia Archives
BCL	*British Columbia Lumberman*
BCMFR	British Columbia Ministry of Forests O Series Correspondence Files, Ministry of Forests Office, Victoria, BC
BCMLPR	British Columbia, Ministry of Lands and Parks Records
BCNRCL	British Columbia Natural Resources Conservation League
CIF-VISR	Canadian Institute of Forestry, Vancouver Island Section Records
CSFE	Canadian Society of Forest Engineers
DHF	US Forest Service, District Historical Files, RG 95
FC	*Forest Chronicle*
FI	*Forest Industries*
FL	*Forest Log*
IWA	International Woodworkers of America
JF	*Journal of Forestry*
LH	*Logger's Handbook*
MRR	Merrill and Ring Lumber Company Records
NARS-PNW	US National Archives and Records Service, Pacific Northwest Region
NLMA	National Lumber Manufacturers Association

OAR	Oregon-American Lumber Company Records
OHSA	Oregon Historical Society Archives
OSA	Oregon State Archives
OSDFR	Oregon State Department of Forestry Records
OSUSFR	Oregon State University School of Forestry Records
PLTJ	*Pacific Lumber Trade Journal*
PNWLAR	Pacific Northwest Loggers Association Records
PPLC	*Proceedings of the Pacific Logging Congress*
PWFCA	Proceedings of the Western Forestry and Conservation Association
SAF-PSSR	Society of American Foresters, Puget Sound Section Records
SPFDR	US Forest Service, State and Private Forestry Division Records, RG 95
STPTR	St Paul and Tacoma Lumber Company Records
TFL	Tree Farm Licence
TL	*Truck Logger*
TMN	*Timberman*
UBC-SC	University of British Columbia Libraries, Special Collections Branch
UOA	University of Oregon Archives
UWCFRR	University of Washington College of Forest Resources Records
UWL	University of Washington Libraries
WCL	*West Coast Lumberman*
WCLAR	West Coast Lumbermen's Association Records
WFCA	Western Forestry and Conservation Association
WL	Western Lumberman

Clearcutting the Pacific Rain Forest

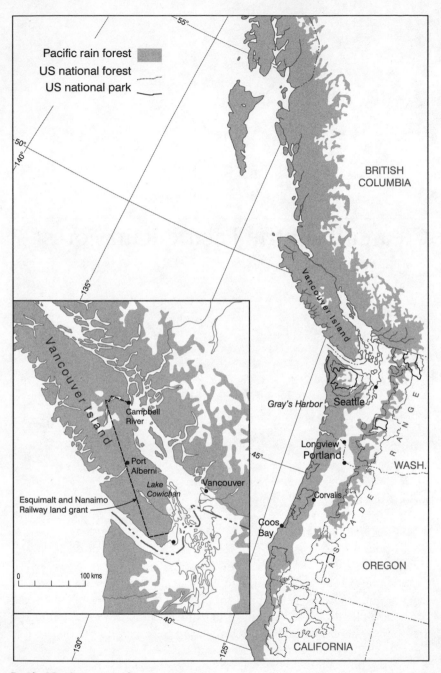

Legend:
Pacific rain forest
US national forest
US national park

55°

BRITISH
COLUMBIA

50°
140°

135°

Vancouver Island

Vancouver Island

Campbell
River

Port
Alberni

Lake
Cowichan

Vancouver

Esquimalt and Nanaimo
Railway land grant

0   100 kms

130°   125°

40°

Gray's Harbor   Seattle

45°

Longview
Portland

Corvalis

Coos
Bay

WASH.

C
A
S
C
A
D
E
R
A
N
G
E

OREGON

CALIFORNIA

Pacific Northwest rain forest

Introduction

West of the Cascade Mountains that divide the coastal and interior regions of British Columbia, Washington, and Oregon, the interaction of heavy precipitation, mild climate, and favourable soil conditions after the ice ages produced one of the earth's magnificent temperate rain forests. The pre-eminent species, in terms of both scale and commercial importance, is Douglas fir. Western red cedar has long been used for roofing and siding, a limited market has existed for Sitka spruce since the early twentieth century, and hemlock became valuable with the development of the pulp and paper industry, but the Douglas fir's combination of strength, light weight, and durability made it ideal for a wide range of construction purposes. For almost a century, the mature Douglas fir, averaging over 190 feet in height and often reaching as high as 250 feet, has served as the cornerstone of state and provincial economies on the north Pacific coast.

Early European settlers would have scoffed at any suggestion that these forests might one day face exhaustion. The California gold rush provided the initial stimulus to their commercial exploitation. F.C. Talbot and Andrew J. Pope brought the entrepreneurial spirit west from Maine in the 1850s, first entering the lumber business in California, then building a large sawmill on Puget Sound in 1853. Within a few years, their Puget Mill Company operation was one of twenty on the Sound serving the California and lesser Pacific Rim markets. During the same decade the future province of British Columbia welcomed New Brunswick's Jeremiah Rogers, Sewell P. Moody from Maine, and Edward Stamp from England. By the time British North American colonies to the east united in Confederation in 1867, Moody and Stamp had established cargo mills on Burrard Inlet that turned out lumber for Australia, Hawaii, South America, and Asia.[1]

These lumbermen had little difficulty gaining control over parcels of what seemed an endless timber supply to feed their plants.[2] In Oregon and Washington, forestland could be acquired by purchase, through manipulation of the Homestead Act, or, after 1878, under the Timber and Stone Act, which enabled prospective settlers to purchase 160-acre claims for $2.50 per acre. Lumbermen quickly turned this legislation to their advantage, paying employees, sailors, and others to stake claims that later enlarged company holdings. Several large tracts were granted to lumbering interests in the colonies of Vancouver Island and British Columbia before the Crown stopped this practice in 1865 in favour of a policy of issuing annually renewable leases. After the united colonies entered Canada in 1871, all of British Columbia's forestland not already alienated became Crown land. Leases continued to be available on easy terms involving an annual rental and royalty payment on timber when cut, and by 1887 the principle of granting cutting rights through leases or licences was firmly established.[3] An important exception was the 1884 grant to coal magnate Robert Dunsmuir, who received two million acres of Vancouver Island's richest timberland in exchange for construction of the Esquimalt and Nanaimo Railway (E & N).

The Douglas fir region's burgeoning lumber industry made only limited inroads into the great forest from the coastline until transcontinental rail systems provided market opportunities essential for the consolidation of industrial capitalism. The arrival of the Northern Pacific Railroad at Tacoma in 1883, the Canadian Pacific Railway at Vancouver in 1887, and the Great Northern at Seattle in 1893 established links to an expanding North American economy while spurring development within the region. Their completion coincided with the onset of timber depletion in the Lake states and centres with a long history of lumbering in eastern Canada. Resource capitalists in those areas saw west coast timber as an ideal field for investment. The westward movement of timber capital began in the 1880s and accelerated in the next decade. Then, in 1900, Frederick W. Weyerhaeuser's purchase of 900,000 acres of forestland concentrated in western Washington from the Northern Pacific Railroad touched off a wave of speculative activity in Pacific coast timber.[4]

The Douglas fir forests of Washington and Oregon drew most of the attention, but operators also turned to British Columbia, especially when American presidents Harrison, Cleveland, and Roosevelt designated large tracts of US forest for inclusion in the National Forest system. Conservative BC Premier Richard McBride threw down the welcome mat in 1905, adopting a new tenure policy that extended the life of timber licences also making them transferable. American lumbermen and speculators eagerly took up cutting rights to the province's timber. Within the E & N belt the Rockefeller interests and Standard Oil assumed outright ownership of huge tracts. One 1910 estimate put American investment in British Columbia's lumber industry at $65 million.[5]

Overproduction, waste, and ruinous competition plagued the new industrial order. Despite a clear trend toward concentration, enough small operators survived to deprive the giants of monopolistic control. Competition was severe both among and within regions, and organizations formed to fix prices and restrict output had little success in controlling the volatile lumber market. Neither the West Coast Lumbermen's Association, created by a merger of several Oregon and Washington trade groups in 1911, nor the British Columbia Lumber and Shingle Manufacturers Association, established in 1903, succeeded in controlling the activities of members during slumps.[6]

Competitive capitalism bred a ruthless, destructive approach to forest exploitation, with lumbermen 'concerned only with getting the best logs out of the woods, milling them at cut-rate costs, and dumping the lumber wherever the market might be soft.' By 1930 the expanse of denuded, barren land in some coastal areas generated predictions of a future timber famine. The Great Depression slowed the rate of cut but during World War II the demand for increased harvests took precedence over regulation to mitigate the social costs of unrestrained logging.[7]

Deforestation on the Pacific coast had reached sufficient proportions by the 1930s to ignite a scramble for timberland by the region's dominant firms and North American pulp and paper interests. Weyerhaeuser and Crown Zellerbach, along with new arrivals such as Rayonier, the St. Regis Paper Company, Georgia-Pacific, and Scott Paper, initiated timber acquisition programs, using their financial power to purchase the mills and holdings of established family-owned companies. This process of consolidation brought an integrated corporate structure to the forest industry, involving all phases of activity from logging and sawmilling to chemical and cellulose production.[8]

Booming construction and wood fibre markets sustained the structure through the immediate postwar decades, producing record cuts and high employment levels that seemed to herald a new era of stability. Over the past two decades, of course, the industry has gone into a decline caused by a host of factors related to the multinational nature of the forest products economy and the onset of what was once unthinkable – the exhaustion of timber supplies. Many firms have begun shifting operations to southern climes to take advantage of plentiful timber, fast growing conditions, and low labour costs.[9]

This book explores the roots of our present crisis by subjecting the process of deforestation in the Douglas fir region of British Columbia, Washington, and Oregon between 1880 and 1965 to critical analysis. I will do so by considering both the technological and managerial structures of forest exploitation and the role of government in regulating the conduct of large corporations. In essence, this amounts to a history of clearcutting, the industry's primary method of harvesting since the mechanization of logging in the late nineteenth century.

Recent years have witnessed heated debate over the fate of the remaining coastal rain forest. Should these stands be preserved or put to the saw –

clearcut or logged selectively? While governments struggle to formulate policies that reconcile the conflict between economic development and environmental regulation, timberworkers ponder an uncertain future. Having already experienced mill closures, unemployment, and dislocation in timber-dependent communities, they find themselves besieged on all fronts. On one side stand the multinational corporations workers depend upon for employment, but whose sophisticated logging technologies have reduced labour requirements. On the other side stands an environmental movement dominated by urban, middle-class interests dedicated to preserving the few remaining pockets of old-growth forest on public lands.

Each contender in the current policy debate draws upon a vision of the past to rally support for a particular position. The environmentalist past is one of wanton ecological despoliation by industry, aided and abetted by state, provincial, and federal governments. Unsubstantiated by serious historical research, the image has sufficient credibility to prevent corporations from countering with a perfectly sanitized version. Rather, executives and their public relations experts admit to past mistakes, but argue that recent reforms now permit logging to proceed in a sustainable, ecologically sensitive manner.

Readers who turn to historical scholarship on the west coast timber industry for insight into the relationship between humankind and nature will find some items of exceptional worth. In the American context, relevant works include Richard White's environmental history of Island County, a model in the field that assesses the ecological impact of early mechanized logging; William Robbin's analysis of the early twentieth century trade association effort to achieve market control through conservation; and a general history of western Washington lumbering by Robert Ficken. Harold Steen's institutional history of the US Forest Service, David Clary's study of the agency's 'bureaucratic culture,' and Samuel Trask Dana's earlier discussion of forest policy collectively provide useful data on national forest management practice, the development of forestry as a profession, and the controversy over regulation of private land that occupied American foresters during the first half of the twentieth century. More recent excellent contributions include Paul Hirt's analysis of postwar national forest management, a history of the Douglas fir bioregion by Robert Bunting that focuses on the nineteenth century, and Nancy Langston's ecological history of the Blue Mountains in eastern Oregon and Washington.[10]

British Columbia's most important industry has drawn relatively little attention from historians, although scholars such as Patricia Marchak, Ken Drushka, Stephen Gray, R. Peter Gillis and Thomas Roach, Mary McRoberts, and Jeremy Wilson have begun laying a foundation of work on policy formation, the timber economy, and the social structure of resource towns.[11] But if a survey of the American and Canadian literature provides the reader with a general outline of development, and some powerful evidence of industry's capacity to shape government policy, it also reveals serious conceptual shortcomings that limit our understanding of the history of deforestation on the west coast. One of the more serious limitations results from the reluctance of historians to probe the relationship between resource and labour exploitation under corporate management. This contributes to studies that consider ecological, technological, organizational, and regulatory processes separately, instead of analyses that emphasize their complex interplay.

Recognition that workers constitute a vital intermediary position in capital's relationship to nature suggests the relevance of Marxian concepts to the study of environmental issues. Although Marx did not ignore nature completely in his work, his primary concern was with the exploitation of workers by owners in early industrial capitalism. In choosing handicraft production as his model, Ted Benton explains, Marx established a weak basis for the subsequent study of environmental degradation.[12]

Hoping to create a closer affinity between socialist and ecological politics, leftist scholars uphold the adaptability of Marxian analysis to the study of environmental problems because of its traditional focus on the dynamics of the production process. R.J. Johnson, for example, calls for recognition of 'the extent to which environmental practices ... are largely determined by the ... mode of production,' which mobilizes land, labour, and technology in the process of wealth accumulation.[13]

The primary value of this appeal lies in the point of entry a focus on modes of production provides for a history of the Douglas fir timber industry – it directs attention to the way that changing technologies, managerial practices, and government interventions shaped the process of deforestation. Seen in this light, it becomes possible to treat the exploitation of natural resources as a narrative concerning a changing mode of production in which corporate leaders are drawn into relations with wage workers, professional managers, and the state, comprising elected politicians and administrative personnel. In short, it is necessary to comprehend the advantages that particular production processes held for business in extracting the maximum value from the labour of employees and the bounty of nature before one can understand precisely what was at stake in the negotiation of forest regulations.

Chapter 1 of this book is devoted to a discussion of mechanization, a process that brought a steady increase in the capacity of logging operators to exploit both workers and nature. After the introduction of steam power in the late nineteenth century, with the exception of the Depression years when market conditions encouraged adaptation of the caterpillar tractor to selective harvesting, logging machinery fostered clearcutting. The main focus is on the technologies associated with overhead logging, a technique introduced in the first two decades of the twentieth century to speed the movement of logs from where they lay in the woods to railway lines for transportation to sawmills. Overhead systems intensified corporate control over the work of loggers, and the post-World War II development of mobile equipment and automatic grapple technology capped industry progress in the creation of a factory-like exploitation process.

Chapter 2 examines the managerial component of industry's factory regime, including the close cooperation between corporate executives and university administrators needed to train individuals in scientific methods of work organization and forest management. Relations between the region's forestry schools and industry commenced in the early twentieth century with the creation of programs in logging engineering, a response to industry's need for comprehensive data on topographic and timber characteristics, essential to the planning of mass production. Closer links were formed in mid-century when deforestation reached sufficient proportions to generate a corporate demand for technical forestry expertise. The schools responded by initiating curricula in industrial forestry, a branch of learning devoted to the accumulation of information on the productive capacity of timberland – information required for investment decision-making.

Having examined the central features of the mode of production in coastal logging, this study will proceed to its major task – an environmental history of clearcutting.[14] Part 2, consisting of Chapters 3 through 6, documents the impact of industry's practices on the regenerative capacity of the Douglas fir forest and the relationship between governments and corporations in policy making. My approach to this subject rests on an attempt to determine how scientific knowledge was used, ignored, or abused in the development of forest regulations.[15] In essence, then, the history of forest practice regulation on the west coast is an ongoing debate about the nature of silvicultural inquiry and the extent to which valid findings would be permitted to inform public policy.

The most pressing forestry problem in the Douglas fir region, after the adoption of overhead logging technologies, was to develop a technique of clearcutting that preserved its extractive efficiencies while providing a basis for natural reproduction of the species. Through most of the period under consideration, operators' interest in conservation did not extend beyond protection of mature timber from fire, and they conducted their logging with regard solely for the balance sheet. Although early research led to the conclusion that clearcutting was in harmony with the ecological characteristics of Douglas fir, and a faulty theory legitimated even its most extreme application during the early twentieth century, the operators' 'high-ball' logging left vast stretches of land stripped of all forest growth.

The research presented here suggests that governments on both sides of the border dividing the Douglas fir region, overwhelmingly dependent upon revenues generated by the timber industry, responded to corporate rather than long-term social or ecological needs in their regulatory initiatives. When the Oregon and Washington legislatures passed forest practice acts in the 1940s, they did so at the behest of trade association leaders anxious to rebut the arguments of US Forest Service chiefs who advocated federal regulation. These same figures controlled the silvicultural content of the measures, sanctioning practices that scientific research on the national forests had determined would fail to produce adequate reforestation.

Even Crown ownership of forestland in British Columbia did not produce a willingness to intervene in the affairs of the corporations that dominated the provincial economy. The adoption of a new Forest Act in 1947 provided these firms with exclusive access to millions of acres of valuable timber, but no effective public control over the method or rate of cut. In the end, despite pressure from a small minority of progressives in the North American forestry profession who saw a need for intervention to perpetuate the resource, the shared preoccupation of government officials and corporate executives with profitable exploitation prevailed over the sort of regulation needed to overcome industry's entrenched tendency to 'mine' the Douglas fir forest.

A few remarks on the limitations of this book are necessary. First, it devotes more attention to the activities of the region's largest companies than to small operations. This approach is dictated in part by the nature of available sources, but is also justified by the fact that major corporations comprised the industry's most innovative sector in technology, in management, and in moulding relations with government. Second, the study concentrates on Douglas fir – appropriate in that this species' commercial importance made it the principal subject of scientific investigation and regulatory action.

Finally, a note on the time period covered in this book. The rationale for terminating the study at 1965 is to avoid becoming entangled in the modern debate about forestry issues. Since 1970, the entire structure of corporate exploitation described here has come under attack from environmentalists and native peoples, the latter attempting to assert claims to traditional territory.[16] I intend to undertake an analysis of environmental regulation in the Douglas fir region in future, but the present study is concerned with the relatively narrow range of business, professional, and government interests that dominated resource politics prior to the rise of the environmental movement. The reader will discover, however, that I have pushed slightly beyond my closing date of 1965 in the initial two chapters, allowing discussion of important recent developments in the technology and management of logging operations.

Part 1
Machines, Managers, and Work

Introduction

The nature of work is currently generating enormous interest as the introduction of computer-based technologies and competition in the global economy create rising levels of unemployment. The titles of some recent books – Jeremy Rifkin's *The End of Work,* David Noble's *Progress Without People,* and *Vanishing Jobs* by Osberg, Wein, and Grude – convey a sense of the harsh realities facing workers today. The impact of technological change in the workplace is, of course, far from a new subject of inquiry. Viewing the consequences of the first industrial revolution first-hand, Karl Marx predicted a day when automation would render workers superfluous to industrial production.[1]

Historical scholarship on the transformation of the workplace received a major stimulus in 1974 with the appearance of Harry Braverman's *Labor and Monopoly Capital.* Braverman's seminal text has inspired an outpouring of labour process research, a tradition that constitutes the primary influence on my treatment of the technological and managerial structures of work in west coast logging. For Braverman, the introduction of machines and the techniques of scientific management could be attributed to capital's all-consuming desire to wrest control of the workplace from skilled craft workers. At the heart of his analysis is the concept of labour power. 'What the worker sells and the capitalist buys is not an agreed amount of labour,' Braverman writes, 'but the power to labour over an agreed period of time.'[2]

Accordingly, employers have mechanized the workplace and adopted sophisticated managerial practices to effect the transformation of labour power into work on their terms. Machines are seen to have 'the function of divesting the mass of workers of their control over their own labour.' Frederick W. Taylor's organizational philosophy of scientific management, which Braverman terms 'the explicit verbalization of the capitalist mode of production,' serves the same end by separating the conception of work from its execution. Together, he argues, these strategies have given employers complete control over the design of work and the pace of production. Effectively deskilled, workers perform routinized, regimented tasks devoid of intellectual content.[3]

Braverman's depiction of the 'degradation of work' under monopoly capitalism has drawn the ire of a second generation of labour process analysts. Chris DeBresson, for example, asserts that he fell victim to a naive acceptance of managerial ideology, which represents 'a manager's impossible fantasy' rather than the reality of workplace relations. Others have suggested that Braverman not only overestimates the extent of deskilling; he also failed to recognize the creation of new highly skilled occupations.[4] These arguments are rooted in what the second generation perceives as Braverman's most grievous error: his conscious disregard of class consciousness and class struggle. Individual and collective resistance, students on both sides of the Atlantic argue, plays a critical role in structuring the labour process. From this dialectical perspective the history of work represents less an inevitable 'consolidation of untrammelled capitalist power' than a dynamic process exhibiting complexity, counter-tendencies, and possible contradictions.[5]

The critique of Braverman's determinism has produced a vastly more nuanced view of workplace change, but this has come at a price. Studies of specific industries addressing a wider range of variables, including the influence of product and labour markets in determining both the rate and nature of change, have rendered the creation of a satisfactory theory of the labour process less plausible. Instead of a unitary process of change driven in accordance with capital's compulsion to enhance capital accumulation by achieving the formal subordination of workers, there emerges a multiplicity of labour processes, each structured historically by factors that may transcend the workplace. The most promising path out of this conceptual morass has been suggested by Sheila Cohen, who argues that critics have misunderstood Braverman's thesis. 'Braverman's primary concern was not with "control" or even deskilling,' she writes, 'but with the specifically capitalist logic which *constructs* these tendencies.'[6] Exploitation, not control, is the 'central dynamic' of capitalist production. The exertion of control by capital is thus one technique to achieve efficiency in production, which in turn is a means to intensify the rate at which workers are exploited.

Cohen's conceptualization of the labour process as the site of exploitation revives the question of efficiency, which serves as the central explanatory concept in this analysis of technological and managerial change in the coastal logging industry. How have logging operators defined efficiency, and in what ways have machines and management strategies served the interest of timber capital in the exploitation of both workers and the resource? I hope to demonstrate that the industry's concept of efficiency drew heavily on that of the factory, a model offering operators a high degree of control in their relations with loggers through mechanization and a rigid division of labour.

The fundamental importance of class forces is most apparent in the development of extractive technologies, which brought a progressive reduction in labour requirements, less reliance on physical and conceptual skills once considered essential to the industry, and a consequent loss of autonomy as loggers found themselves increasingly subject to the discipline of machine-pacing. True, technological sophistication involved the emergence of highly skilled occupations, but these invariably enhanced capital's control over the collective labour process.

West coast logging's industrial revolution began in the late nineteenth century with the displacement of oxen and horse teams by the steam engine, achieved real significance with the adoption of overhead logging systems early in the twentieth century, and received further impetus from the introduction of the internal combustion engine during the 1930s and postwar decades. Although environmental factors and product and labour markets played a part in the industry's record of technological progress, each innovation was judged primarily in terms of its capacity to advance operators toward their goal of a factory regime in coastal logging.

Another equally significant but less conspicuous dimension of the operators' factory regime had its roots in the scientific management movement of the late nineteenth and early twentieth centuries, and involved a group of technicians trained in universities to collect and organize data considered essential to efficient resource exploitation. Anxious to erect a managerial structure equal to the scale and technological complexity of the industry, operators in the early 1900s arranged for degree programs in logging engineering to be created within the region's forestry schools. These institutions were originally organized to train foresters for employment in public resource agencies, and they responded eagerly to the opportunity to gain a foothold in the region's dominant industry.

The engineers functioned largely in an administrative capacity, providing data on timber and topographic conditions necessary for efficient mobilization of men and machines in the exploitation of huge corporate holdings. But by the time of World War II, looming timber shortages and the emergence of a more integrated corporate structure prompted executives to turn again to the universities, this time for the production of industrial foresters. Professionals in forest management were needed to assess the value of timberland for firms engaged in acquisition programs, to coordinate harvesting with the demands of a more complex product market, and to provide data needed to formulate long-term operating policies.

This focus on the objective features of work in the coastal logging industry represents an unfashionable departure from the current trend in labour process study, which exhibits a great emphasis on constructing a sufficiently dialectical theory.[7] My justification for this approach involves two positions that require some defence. First, in North America, capital's right to set the technological and managerial structure of the workplace has, on the whole, been accepted.[8] Challenges to this power have met with little success. As I have argued elsewhere, the individual and collective resistance by west coast loggers to their conditions of employment in the early twentieth century generated important changes in working and living conditions. There is no evidence to suggest, however, that their opposition to dangerous and oppressive technologies had a similar outcome.[9]

Second, although the Industrial Workers of the World were critical of logging methods that displaced workers, preliminary findings indicate that the International Woodworkers of America (IWA) has not been hostile to technological innovation. A 1955 editorial in the *British Columbia Lumber Worker* asserted 'industrial workers ... know that it is impossible to arrest technological progress. They know that it would not be in their best interests to try.' The IWA would attempt to ensure that 'automation is made to provide greater abundance and leisure' but counsel no Luddism.[10] Although the historical record reveals that loggers shared far less faith in technological progress than the above statement implies, their hostility to certain systems of exploitation has not prevented their introduction. In his study of the American industrial relations system, Howell Harris concludes that organized labour is 'more a reactive than an initiating force in the process of social change; a weak institution in a powerfully organized capitalist society.'[11] This assessment has equal, if unfortunate, relevance in the realm of technological and managerial change.

In the end, the corporate search for efficiency in west coast logging achieved remarkable if not absolute success in subordinating workers and nature to the imperative of capital accumulation. Even in manufacturing enterprises, where industry is able to bring the factory system to its pinnacle of efficiency, reservoirs of craft control are left intact. But if, in 1965, coastal logging retained its reputation as an industry in which workers toiled free of the more strict control achieved in processing plants, this image reflected past better than present realities. By then loggers had almost as much in common with contemporaries in various factory settings as their forebears in the western woods.

1

The Forest as Factory: Technological Change in West Coast Logging, 1880-1965

The earliest logging on the west coast required no external power source, as trees could be cut so that they dropped directly into rivers, lakes, or inlets, which provided ease of transportation. Although the hand logger plied his singular craft along the British Columbia coastline well into the twentieth century, once the timber standing in close proximity to water bodies had been cut, logging evolved into a three-stage process.[1] Trees are first felled and bucked into logs, then they are 'yarded' to a central point or 'landing,' from where they are transported to a mill for processing into lumber or pulp.

Prior to 1930, falling and bucking underwent little change. By the 1880s the crosscut saw was in use for both procedures, and hand methods prevailed until the introduction of the motorized chain saw in the 1940s. Innovations in yarding involved the replacement of oxen and horses by the steam engine or 'donkey' during the last fifteen years of the nineteenth century, followed by the transition from steam-powered ground-lead yarding to overhead systems of logging in the 1900-20 period. The final stage, transportation of logs out of the woods, was accomplished first by driving logs down rivers during the winter freshets. During the 1880s the logging railroad appeared on Puget Sound, a technology that was introduced to the British Columbia industry in the next decade. In the mid-1920s there were seventy-nine logging lines in the province, totalling over 700 miles of track.[2]

By 1930 the basic foundation of industry's factory regime was intact, a structure of technological control over loggers and nature that underwent further refinement in subsequent decades with the introduction of the internal combustion engine to all phases of logging. The chain saw, diesel yarder, logging truck, and caterpillar tractor brought new levels of mobility, flexibility, and productivity to the exploitation process, enhancing the validity of the factory analogy. Logging technology reached new heights of sophistication with the development of the portable steel-spar, and timber capital culminated its impressive record of innovation during the 1960s when the automatic yarding and loading grapple completely mechanized these procedures.

Timber harvesting takes place in isolation from urban manufacturing centres, which have drawn the lion's share of attention from labour process analysts.[3] In the field of forest history, Ian Radforth's fine study of northern Ontario logging stands virtually alone as a scholarly analysis of the social processes that shaped the techniques of exploitation. With the exception of Alfred Van Tassel's 1940 study of mechanization on the west coast and Ken Drushka's recent book on British Columbia logging, the industry in this region has been ignored by students of technological change. Popular historians have asserted the importance of large timber and rough terrain in moulding logging methods, but their descriptive efforts have not been matched by a corresponding passion for analytical rigour. Academics who have studied prominent lumbermen, companies, and the character of the lumber industry commonly devote a few pages to the development of logging machinery and systems, but here again generalizations about the imposing natural obstacles faced by those engaged in harvesting the resource have sufficed.[4]

In short, an overwhelming environmental determinism has dominated our thinking about technological change in west coast logging. Van Tassel, for example, interprets mechanization as a response to changes in the characteristics of the resource and its setting. 'New machines and methods,' he writes, 'have been developed to meet changes in conditions of accessibility and size of timber.'[5] Explanations based solely on the environmental imperative lack credibility on two counts. First, they carry the implicit and extremely dubious assumption that had conditions remained constant no impetus to technological change would have existed. Second, they ignore what I will argue is the independent variable in structuring innovation: the class relationship.

Production technology is introduced in the workplace to enhance the ability of owners and managers to achieve efficiencies and increase the value available for appropriation by enterprises.[6] Recognition of this characteristic of the labour process is vital in deciphering technology in resource extractive industries, where the corporate relationship to the natural environment can so easily obscure the relationship between owners and workers. This is not to suggest that the condition and accessibility of the staple can be ignored. Rather, it is necessary to view the forest as the arena within which the relationship between logging operators and loggers is played out. Timber capital sought domination over nature not as an end in itself, but to secure control over production. One MacMillan Bloedel manager hinted at this dynamic in 1970, stating that 'changes in topography and conditions have only a minor influence on new methods ... compared to economic factors.' Industry's real objective in the design of logging machinery was 'to reduce manpower requirements.'[7]

The epitome of labour process control is the mechanized factory, a model that has inspired the development of logging systems in the west coast industry. Much of the intellectual energy of innovators has been focused on the yarding procedure, the most labour intensive phase of logging, and the one most dependent upon the physical and conceptual skills of loggers to cope with the variable conditions of the coastal environment. Yarding, remarked J.J. Donovan, vice-president of the Bloedel-Donovan Lumber Mills, 'more than any other part of the organization, makes or mars the work of a day.'[8] Offering the greatest incentive for innovation, yarding would yield the most dramatic advances in technology.

Logging operators confronted real obstacles in their efforts to emulate the factory mode of production. Unlike their counterparts who headed manufacturing enterprises, they had to organize workers and machinery within the constraints laid down by nature. Rough terrain, dense timber stands, underbrush, and the need to shift operations frequently to gain access to timber contributed to a chaotic productive context that bore little resemblance to the ordered setting of the factory. 'The work of the logger is never the same,' observed Grays Harbor operator and equipment manufacturer Frank Lamb at the inaugural Pacific Logging Congress in 1909, 'each tree grows in a different location, each behaves a little differently in the handling. Fixed rules of procedure are of little use, every proposition, every location, every camp, every day's work, even every log is a separate engineering proposition.'[9] Thirteen years later Minot Davis, director of logging operations for the Weyerhaeuser Timber Company, articulated an explicit contrast of manufacturing and resource extraction. 'In a factory,' he wrote, 'once the character of the product is determined, the machinery tried out, and the organization completed, the working conditions are practically uniform from day to day. In the woods, conditions are seldom the same from day to day.'[10]

In this industrial context, the strength, agility, and 'working knowledge' of loggers was paramount, but mechanization offered a means to subdue nature and workers by subjecting both to the machine. The skill embodied in human labour power was an unsatisfactory if necessary source of profit, one manager pointed out to a group of young logging engineers and foresters at the University of Washington in 1915. 'While a logger can go to the manufacturer and buy a machine to do a certain amount of work,' J.D. Young observed, 'in purchasing labor the proposition is far different. Here there is an element of uncertainty which makes the progressive logger unhappy.' Young's precise characterization of the employment relationship captures much of the dynamic behind mechanization. Operators and their managers, like A.C. Dixon of Oregon's Booth-Kelly Lumber Company, would indeed find it 'more satisfactory to have the smaller crew and the machine rather than the larger crew and no machine, even if there should be no variation in cost.'[11]

Logging to 1890: Hand Tools and Animal Power

Prior to the 1940s, when Pacific coast operators succeeded in mechanizing their falling and bucking operations, this first stage of logging was accomplished with simple hand tools. When Emil Engstrom worked as a head faller in 1910, he and his partner performed their task with a nine-foot crosscut saw, two long-handled falling axes, a sledge hammer, wedges, a bottle containing oil to cut through the pitch, and two springboards.[12] The head faller examined the tree to determine its 'lean,' observing the surrounding area so that it would drop without breakage. Falling a single tree might take several hours of strenuous, coordinated labour, involving considerable judgment and physical strength. Alfred Moltke's recollection provides a description of the procedure:

> We chopped springboard holes in the sides of the trees about five feet above the ground, cut a couple of lengths of two-by-eight rough lumber, about five feet long. On one end we shaped the board sort of round, and on one side nailed a horseshoe with the toe cleat facing up, away from the board.

Hand fallers pose on springboards after having made an undercut on a Douglas fir at the intersection of skidroads at Cowichan Lake, Vancouver Island.

The new boards, called 'springboards' were stuck in the holes we had chopped in the sides of the tree, then getting up on these boards we started to saw the under cut on the side we wanted the tree to fall. After we had sawed for about a half hour, we would be in the tree about a foot or fourteen inches. Removing the saw from the cut, we chopped the wood from above the cut, starting about a foot above the saw cut, and when we had finished we had made the 'undercut.'

Now we would swing the boards we were standing on to the back of the tree, so we could start sawing the back cut. As the average tree was six or seven feet in diameter, even that far above the ground swell of the tree, the job of cutting the back cut used up most of the day.[13]

When the tree began its descent, the men scrambled off the springboards and ran in the opposite direction of the fall. Dropping a tree over a stump or log could result in breakage, lost timber values, and consequent unemployment. 'You had to save your timber,' recalls Edwin Meece, 'if you didn't save your timber you didn't last long.' Proficient falling played a critically important part in a successful logging operation. The faller, observed R.D. Merrill of the Merrill and Ring Lumber Company in 1917, 'is the most important man in the woods ... as one tree broken by a good faller would mean a loss greater than two or three days wages.'[14] After the tree lay on the ground the bucker 'bucked' it into lengths, working individually with a crosscut saw,

A bucker makes an undercut in a Douglas fir log at Industrial Timber Mills' Cowichan Lake operation on Vancouver Island, 1935.

axe, wedges, and an eight-foot marking stick. Judgment and dexterity was required here too, as the bucker considered the requirements of the market and determined the location of defects that might affect the log's value.[15]

When the cutting crews had moved on, loggers faced the most problematic stage of log transportation – moving them from their position in the woods to the skidroad. These costly paths into the forest might extend up to a mile from the waterfront. After the route was chosen and cleared, crews using picks and shovels graded the roadway. In rough terrain workers constructed bridges to achieve a level surface. Logs or 'skids' were then placed across the length of the skidroad. Where conditions necessitated curves, placing the skids closer together and elevating them slightly on the inside of the bend prevented the log from rolling off. Skidroads were the initial technique devised by coastal operators to achieve a measure of control over the forest environment, and the limited power supplied by oxen and horse teams required engineering to exacting specifications by specialized crews or contractors. 'It is in the placing of the skids,' wrote one observer, 'that the utmost skill is required.'[16]

Skidroads offered a means of neutralizing some of the instability of coastal terrain, but in moving logs to the roads, operators depended wholly upon the abilities of loggers. Ten logs, remarked journalist Louise Wall, could be hauled down the skidroad with less effort than was needed to move a single log out of the bush.[17] Expressed in terms of the relationship between employer control and worker skill, the early logging operator was utterly reliant upon the judgment and experience of his crew to overcome the chaotic productive setting. The yarding of each log represented an individual problem to be solved. No two logs could be dealt with in exactly the same manner; procedures varied in accordance with the size of the log, the terrain, and the behaviour of the team. Control rested with the loggers rather than an engineered harvesting system.

Axemen first prepared each log for yarding, bevelling or 'sniping' its lead end and removing the bark and knots from one side. Swampers cleared windfalls and other debris along a path leading to the skidroad. The task of manoeuvering the log fell to the teamster and hooktender, the dominant figures in oxen and horse logging operations. While the team was 'prodded, sworn, and cajoled' into position by the teamster, the hooktender attached a complex arrangement of rigging involving cables and pulleys or 'blocks' to the log and adjacent trees or stumps to increase pulling power and manoeuvrability. 'A considerable amount of rude science,' remarked Wall, 'is required to accomplish this without accident or waste of time.' An experienced hooktender had the choice of several different block and tackle holds to negotiate the log to the skidroad. One arrangement called the 'luff,' recalls Lloyd C. Rogers, helped the team to generate thirty-six times its normal power. After several logs had been yarded to the skidroad, they were

A crew pauses before rolling logs into water after oxen have pulled the load over a skidroad. The teamster on right holds his goad stick, used to prod the animals.

coupled with chains into a 'turn' and hauled to water by the roading team, usually consisting of six or seven yoke of oxen or an equal number of horses.[18]

Along with the hooktender, the teamster exerted control over the pace of the operation. Coordinating the efforts of up to fourteen oxen to form a cohesive pulling unit required the bull puncher to 'know each bulls' characteristics' and develop a special accord with the lead oxen so the team would act in unison on his commands and gestures.[19] One logger recalls that 'driving ox teams was an art,' and John Reavis, who observed a bull team operation in 1899, wrote that the occupation required 'great skill and nerve.' 'It was nothing uncommon,' claimed pioneer Grays Harbor lumberman George Emerson, 'for the bull puncher to be the turning point between the success and failure of a logging enterprise.' Albert Drinkwater, a British Columbia horse logger, has articulated the distinctive nature of logging with animals. 'There is something about a horse that isn't an engine ... a horse won't work for everybody the same. He'll work for one man and he'll pretend to pull for the other one ... the horses themselves became ... part of the man that drove them.'[20]

Special skills and a personal rapport with the team combined to give teamsters a high degree of control over the production process and a corresponding power in their relations with logging operators. Competition for their services appears to have been fierce. One contractor who supplied logs to the Port Blakely Mill Company complained in 1878 that a rival's offer of a

Horse-logging crew at Cowichan Lake, Vancouver Island. The log has been sniped and barked to ease its passage.

higher wage 'would be the means of him getting a good teamster from me.' George Emerson also recalled the teamster's tendency to 'quit at a moment's notice and shut down the camp.' The teamster's power, reflected in his position at the peak of the wage structure and propensity to take advantage of competitive bidding by operators, would provide capital with one motivation for adapting the steam engine to coastal logging.[21]

Steam Power and the Attack on Worker Control

In 1899 the *Pacific Lumber Trade Journal* reported that oxen might be found in a few Pacific Northwest camps, logging horses were still 'much in demand,' but the trend toward steam-powered donkeys for yarding was now well under way. The Victoria Lumber and Manufacturing Company probably introduced the first steam donkey to British Columbia around 1892. Until the second decade of the twentieth century, the predominant method of yarding with steam power involved the extension of a cable from the hauling drum of the donkey to a log, the log then being dragged to the landing along the ground. The essential components of a donkey consisted of a vertical boiler, an engine, and a winch mechanism mounted on an iron or steel frame, the entire apparatus normally resting on a wooden sled to facilitate moving. The earliest machines were adaptations of hoisting engines used as pile drivers or for loading cargo on ships. In 1882 John Dolbeer,

One of the first steam donkeys in British Columbia at the Victoria Lumber and Manufacturing Company's Camp 2 at Chemainus, Vancouver Island, ca. 1902. This Dolbeer relied on a line horse to return the rigging to the next log selected for yarding.

a California lumberman, received a patent for his side-spool 'Steam Logging Machine,' the first engine designed specifically for Pacific coast logging. The following year Dolbeer patented an 'Improved Logging Engine' featuring a vertical spool or capstan, in all likelihood the first donkey used by operators in the Pacific Northwest and British Columbia.[22]

The traditional explanation for the adoption of steam-powered yarding emphasizes timber depletion. According to Van Tassel, as 'the timber line receded before the logger's axe' operators took to the donkey because of the longer distances involved. More recently Robert Ficken has argued that the donkey 'made it possible to move logs over longer distances, at a more rapid pace.' It is true that yarding with oxen was limited to a distance of about one mile. Sol Simpson informed the Port Blakely Mill Company in August of 1888 that his team was 'too slow on a long road in hot weather' to haul beyond this distance.[23] Horses were faster on the longer hauls, but the railroad provided the real answer to increasing hauling distances. A contractor advised the same company in 1885 against construction of a skidroad near Skookum, Washington, because 'the road would soon be so long as to take up all the profits and it would soon have to be abandoned for a railroad.' A more fundamental weakness of the timber depletion interpretation is its failure to recognize that steam donkeys first came into use yarding logs to the skidroad; from this point horse teams took over. Longer hauling distances, then, cannot account fully for the introduction of the steam donkey.[24]

Mechanized logging offered logging operators a range of advantages: increased control over terrain, faster yarding at lower costs, and a fractional reduction in their reliance on the skills of loggers. Oxen and horses tired quickly in the hot summer months, and rain and snow frequently forced a curtailment of animal-powered operations. Freezing conditions offered little relief as the hard ground necessitated constant shoeing of animals, a laborious, time-consuming procedure. Although steam power lessened vulnerability to coastal weather, rain and muddy conditions continued to hinder these operations.[25]

There were, in addition, costs associated with animals that the mechanized operator did not have to meet. Unlike machines, oxen and horses required training, aged quickly, and had to be fed even when not working. The animals themselves were not inexpensive. Sol Simpson paid $1,400 for seven yoke of oxen in 1889, and the Percheron and Clyde horses that replaced oxen in his camp for a time cost as much as $500 each. Steam donkeys offered the possibility of higher yarding speeds, required no training, and needed no feed when idle. All of these factors could figure into a company's decision to purchase a donkey. A Brunette Sawmill Company manager informed a shareholder in 1896 that he had sold the firm's ageing logging cattle, which were 'eating their heads off,' and went on to advise the purchase of steam donkeys 'as the cattle is too slow to log to any advantage.' Moreover, he pointed out that 'the fuel is on the ground ... and when we shut down for the rainy season all the expense could be shut off.'[26]

While it is difficult to attach relative weights to the various factors, at least one operator associated mechanization with a diminution of the control exerted over production by the teamster. In recalling the high wages paid to teamsters and their propensity to quit on short notice, George Emerson remarked that 'the elimination of the bull puncher by the introduction of steam was the greatest step forward ever made in the logging business.'[27] Significantly, Emerson hails the displacement of the teamster rather than elimination of the animals. The occupation of donkey engineer demanded mechanical expertise and judgment, but the new skills were more easily acquired than those of the teamster, and the latter's personal rapport with the team no longer figured into the equation.

Operators initially used manilla rope to draw logs to the landing under steam power, but flexible steel cable know as 'wire rope' proved superior. In operation, the chokerman, working under the direction of the hooktender and his assistant, the rigging slinger, put a loop of wire rope called a choker around the log. These chokers were then hooked to the haul-in line. After the chokermen and rigging slinger were in the clear, the donkey engineer engaged the yarding drum, starting the log to the landing. In addition to the engineer, donkeys required wood buckers and firemen to fuel the machines, and a spool tender to take the turns of cable off the capstan as the log advanced. After the log reached the landing, a worker fastened the cable to the line horse and guided the animal to the next log selected for yarding.

Shortly after the Dolbeer came into use in the coastal woods, engines made by eastern manufacturers of hoisting equipment, such as the Lidgerwood and Mundy, appeared, although they were poorly adapted to the huge coastal timber.[28] During the 1890s, coastal machinery companies recognized the market potential of the expanding logging industry and began producing machines designed to meet regional demands. The initial donkeys produced by these manufacturers generated higher speeds than the Dolbeer, due in part to the introduction of the horizontal yarding drum, displacing the spool tender. Mechanization of yarding advanced further with the development of the two-drum donkey, eliminating the line horse. Instead of the animal plodding back to the next log with the mainline, a smaller 'haulback' line was taken from the second drum and strung through a series of blocks to the end of the setting, then around its perimeter to the donkey. This innovation accelerated the yarding procedure; now when the log reached the landing and was detached from the mainline the donkey engineer simply reeled in the haulback line, returning the mainline and rigging to the crew in the woods.[29]

The introduction of steam power and subsequent development of more powerful and sophisticated logging donkeys had a significant impact on the nature of loggers' work, but did not revolutionize the harvesting process. The pace of production still hinged upon the speed of yarding to the head of the skidroad, a procedure in which technological control remained negligible. Timber capital continued to depend upon the abilities of loggers to cope with an ever-changing productive setting that bore no resemblance to the factory floor. Log preparation, involving sniping and barking, was a necessity, and swampers continued to clear a path to the skidroad. Negotiating the log's passage over rough, stump-covered terrain remained a tortuous affair. The limited power supplied by early donkeys necessitated frequent application of auxiliary rigging by the hooktender. 'Upon his alertness and ability to keep the logs moving without loss of time,' wrote an observer, 'depends largely the profit in logging.'[30]

No matter how powerful the donkey, when the log approached one of the blocks through which the mainline ran, yarding ceased while the chaser unhooked the choker, removed it from the block and reattached it to the mainline, allowing the log to pass. Vertical spools fastened to stumps, called stump rollers, later came into use to guide the mainline in place of some of the blocks. Although use of these rollers increased output, hang-ups as the

Steam-powered ground-lead logging on the west coast of
Vancouver Island.

log progressed still required frequent changes in choker holds to roll the log
away from stumps, remaining timber, and other obstructions.[31] R.V. Stuart
described ground-lead logging as 'the most frustrating and irritating business that you could imagine.' Stuart went on to recall the 'turmoil' of
ground-lead logging: 'The yarder would haul a log ... some 1,500 feet if it
had room to do it, but the stumps were so thick on the ground that it probably wouldn't haul it more than fifty feet on the first lap, they had to change
the choker and go another fifty feet. There was a lot of jumping back and
forward.'[32] In short, the initial application of steam power to logging failed
to achieve the stability of the factory setting, where the technological structure of the workplace sets the pace of production. The yarding of each log
continued to represent a complex problem requiring a coordinated effort
by the yarding crew.

The limitations inherent in ground-lead logging should not, however, obscure the fundamental transformation that occurred during this period. Both the superiority of steam donkeys over oxen and horses and the expansion of the coastal lumber industry created a permanent market for the products of equipment manufacturers, forging a relationship between the engineering staffs of these concerns and timber capital. The process of technological innovation would henceforth become 'self-reinforcing and cumulative,' with the profits of both timber companies and the manufacturers of logging machinery linked to the introduction of cost-saving technologies.[33] Concepts arising from what Washington Iron Works' Francis Frink termed a 'sharing of ideas' among operators, their master mechanics and superintendents, and the equipment producers then developed, the latter serving as the medium through which recent advances in science met industry demands. Periods of slack demand encouraged innovation – operators confronted with depressed markets sought ways to reduce operating costs, and engineering staffs had time to devote to research and development.[34]

Timber corporations and machinery manufacturers shared a common desire to increase productivity. Power was the key to ground-lead logging, and the introduction of compound-geared donkeys reduced the need for loggers to apply rigging to manoeuvre the log around minor obstructions. Increases in engine cylinder size from seven to nine inches brought additional power, and the Willamette Iron and Steel Works 'Mogul' yarder, introduced in 1906, featured cylinders eleven inches in diameter. Machinery manufacturers attempted to satisfy demands for faster yarding by increasing the diameters of mainline and haulback drums. Slow line speeds meant that 'a large and expensive crew are not required to put forth their best efforts to keep the engine busy.' Increasing the size of the haulback drums accelerated the return of rigging to the woods, a measure designed to 'keep the yarding crew constantly on the jump.'[35]

The power and line speeds of more sophisticated steam donkeys and cable yarding systems gave loggers their initial experience of machine pacing; the productive apparatus itself began to dictate the rate of task performance. A related consequence of timber capital's new ability to exert control over the environment involved a subtle diminution of loggers' skills, as the power of the large donkeys made obsolete some of the rigging expertise formerly needed to increase energy and avoid obstructions.[36] Changes in the wage structure reflected the shift in control over production. The teamster had earned the highest wage in the logging crew, but his replacement the donkey engineer now stood second to the hooktender.[37] Donkey operation required judgment and skill, but the power for logging was now generated by a machine operator moving a lever upon command.

Mechanization also presented the opportunity for increased managerial control through implementation of a more rigid division of labour. Firms purchased extra donkeys and rigging, hiring special rig-up crews to establish the productive system in advance of logging. When loggers completed one setting or breakdowns interrupted production, they moved to a new area with minimum disruption. The new division of labour possessed an additional benefit: workers employed on the rig-up crew were 'not such high-priced labour.'[38]

Finally, machine yarding brought a sharp increase in the dangers associated with logging. The tremendous pressure exerted on wire rope, shackles, and blocks caused breakage, creating a more hazardous workplace. Evidence of how loggers responded to the introduction of steam power is fragmentary, but it appears that the new technology was not welcomed. Francis Frink admitted that mechanization was 'resented in some camps.' One Humbolt County operator recalled in 1921 that local loggers refused to accept the two Washington Iron Works donkeys he purchased in 1906, forcing him to import crews from another region. Loggers at a Vancouver Island camp took a similar stand; here too, the owner had to secure replacements willing to work with the new machines.[39]

As the industry moved overwhelmingly to steam at the turn of the century, loggers had little choice but to accept the new technology or leave the industry. Loggers' resistance to mechanization did not present an insuperable obstacle to corporations in their efficiency drive, but the impact of steam-powered ground-lead logging should not be exaggerated. Even the most powerful donkeys did not free operators from their dependence upon the conceptual and physical skills of the hooktender and crew to negotiate each log to the landing in an environment marked by instability and uncertainty.

Overhead Logging: The Flying Machine and the Factory Regime
The overhead yarding methods that came into use in the coastal woods after the turn of the century can be grouped into two main categories: skidder systems, involving the suspension of cables and rigging from two spar trees; and high-lead logging, which features a single spar tree. Although the numerous systems varied widely in operation, each represented a fundamental advance over the laborious ground-yarding method by allowing logs to be pulled to the landing while partially suspended from overhead cables.

Overhead yarding was first employed in Michigan in about 1886, and by the middle of the next decade the Lidgerwood skidder system had come into common use throughout the midwest and cypress swamps of the southern states. On the Pacific coast, Oregon's Bridal Veil Lumber Company first used an overhead system in 1901 to swing logs from landing to railroad. The initial direct overhead yarding was accomplished the following year by the Lamb Lumber Company at Hoquiam. The Kerry Mill Company at Kerriston, Washington, introduced the Lidgerwood skidder to the coastal region that same year. In 1903 the Lidgerwood Company established an office in Seattle, and shortly thereafter acquired the patents to Lamb's cableway system.[40]

Illustration of the high-lead and overhead skidder systems from a 1934 equipment catalogue.

Developed for yarding smaller timber, the initial Lidgerwoods used in the Douglas fir region experienced frequent breakdowns. But in 1912 the firm began advertising a tree-rigged skidder designed specifically for coastal conditions. By this time many of the largest firms in the west had adopted the Lidgerwood system, and within a few years other northwest producers, such as the Willamette Iron and Steel Works, Washington Iron Works, and Empire Manufacturing Company in Vancouver, began marketing their own skidders.[41]

The Lidgerwood system featured a cable suspended between two spar trees. Through a complex system of lines and blocks, a carriage was drawn back and forth between the skidder at the landing and the rigging crew. When it reached the chokermen, they hooked the chokers to the 'in-haul' line. The engineer then applied power, raising the logs off the ground, and yarded the load to the landing. A complete arrangement could be obtained for about $30,000 in 1914, and less expensive alternatives were available, such as the MacFarlane and North Bend systems, developed and patented by innovative operators.[42]

The high-lead provided a simpler way to achieve a similar effect. Loggers passed a mainline through a block atop a single spar tree, then through a series of blocks around the perimeter of the setting and attached it to the haulback line. The high-lead provided less elevation and an effective yarding distance of about 600 feet, allowing a group or 'turn' of logs to pass over obstructions as they came to the landing. The origin of the high-lead is unclear. One manager suggested in 1916 that the technique had been introduced at two coastal camps about a decade earlier, but came into widespread use only in the previous two years. By 1915 the method was in 'very general use' on the coast along with the increasingly popular skidder systems.[43]

The accepted wisdom concerning the transition to overhead methods portrays lumbermen responding to the problem of handling large timber on increasingly difficult terrain as logging progressed inland.[44] Although the complaints voiced by operators about the higher costs of logging on rough ground provide support for such an interpretation, a close reading of the data casts doubt on environmental explanations. After the Merrill and Ring Lumber Company's logging superintendent reported favourably on the operation of the Kerry Mill Company's skidder in October 1908, Merrill and Ring secured its first Lidgerwood the following month – one of the few yet on the coast. The first six months of operation proved a 'huge success,' and by 1911 the company had three such units.[45] We might expect to find Merrill and Ring executives stressing environmental factors in their discussions of the new technology, but R.D. Merrill reported to the 1911 Pacific Logging Congress that the skidders were working on 'level ground' and that 'only experience would show how well it would do on rougher conditions.'

It could be argued that Merrill referred to an initial trial period, but as late as 1916 the company's secretary-manager Tiff Jerome informed another firm that the Lidgerwoods were logging on 'comparatively level ground.'[46]

Other coastal operators implemented skidder systems under similar topographical conditions. The Ballard Lumber Company installed a new Lidgerwood on 'comparatively level ground.' When R.W. Vinnedge introduced his North Bend system at the 1913 Congress, he bemoaned the passing of the easy logging chances or 'shows' but referred to the terrain at his operation as 'slightly broken, but on the average good.' Finally, H.B. Gardner

Lidgerwood skidder system, or 'flying machine,' in operation on holdings of Comox Logging and Railway Company, Vancouver Island.

concluded in 1916 that the Lidgerwood reached its peak of efficiency 'where the ground is not too rough.' While the system functioned well on level ground or up-hill hauls, one could not expect satisfactory performance 'on rough ground.' The sole exception to this pattern was the English Lumber Company, which set up a Lidgerwood on 'very rough, steep ground.'[47] The 1916 Pacific Logging Congress, devoted primarily to discussion of high-lead yarding, elicited a similar range of reports. F.C. Riley of the Bloedel-Donovan Lumber Mills explained that the system suited yarding up-hill or on 'reasonably level ground,' and James O'Hearne, manager of the English Lumber Company, recommended high-leading for timber 'standing on the level or where it can be yarded up a slight incline.'[48]

Clearly, then, the environmental interpretation fails to provide a satisfactory account of the adoption of overhead logging methods. In ignoring the importance of the class relationship, students of the industry have neglected a vital factor of which operators, themselves, were all too conscious. When timbermen explained their embrace of the new technology, they emphasized the inherent superiority of these systems, citing increased productivity, the elimination of positions on the yarding crew, and a reduction in the degree of control exercised by skilled workers over the pace of production.

The balance sheet reflected the fundamental superiority of overhead logging. Over a two-year period the Merrill and Ring Lumber Company's skidder production cost was one-third less than with the ground-lead operations conducted concurrently. Comparisons of the high-lead system with ground yarding reflected similar savings.[49] In order to comprehend this quantitative gain, however, it is necessary to focus on the dynamics of the production process. Because aerial systems permitted longer yarding distances, over 2,000 feet in extreme cases, railroad construction costs declined. In addition, cable and rigging had a longer life, as the constant jarring and shocks experienced in ground-yarding were reduced in frequency and severity. But the fundamental advantage of these systems lay in their capacity to restructure timber capital's relationship to the environment, and in consequence, with workers.

So long as yarding took place in direct contact with coastal terrain, ultimate control over the process had rested with loggers. By permitting logs to be yarded while partially suspended, overhead systems brought corporate command to a new level, manifested in lower direct labour costs. As log preparation had become unnecessary, companies dispensed with the services of swampers, snipers and barkers; these men embarked on an 'eternal vacation.' More reflective of the shift in the character of class relations was the operator's unprecedented ability to transform the potential of human labour power into work. R.D. Merrill boasted that the Lidgerwood moved logs through the air at two to three times the speed permitted by ground yarding, and rigging returned to the crew at an accelerated pace. The haulback speeds on Frank Lamb's early cableway system doubled that of the ground yarder. Machine pacing, the essence of the factory system, had come to coastal logging.[50]

In ground yarding, Lamb explained, an experienced crew working on level terrain might bring in an average of thirty logs per day, but under the overhead system no time was lost preparing yarding roads and swamping, and 'the time consumed in placing and throwing lines in and out of lead blocks and in blocking logs away from obstructions is devoted to hauling logs.' For Lamb, R.W. Vinnedge, and other operators, overhead logging represented a 'solution to the yarding problem,' marking the end of the 'necessity for an endless shifting of chokers and pulling of lines to permit one, and seldom over two logs to bore a tortuous path through acres of stumps and debris.' Vinnedge's North Bend Lumber Company could now transport up to six logs to the landing at one time, 'with seldom a stop after the go-ahead whistle.'[51]

As the new technology eliminated much of the discontinuity that plagued ground-lead logging, routinization diminished timber capital's reliance on traditional skills. Machinery manufacturers and operators may have been prone to exaggeration, but their testimonies reflect an undisguised enthusiasm over the deskilling of loggers. Lamb pointed out that his system required only two 'high priced men,' the hooktender and donkey engineer. The line horseman, chaser, and riggingman were replaced by 'cheaper men.' Overhead methods, declared another writer, diminished the control exerted by the hooktender, 'upon whose caprices hangs the day's output.' These claims are borne out by the recollections of Sid Smith, a veteran British Columbia logging manager. According to Smith, the high-lead system undermined the authority of hooktenders and 'took away the necessity of having good chokermen and rigging slingers.'[52]

The development of multi-gear donkeys capable of higher speeds contributed to a further acceleration in the pace of yarding operations. Manufacturers had met with limited success in their efforts to design a two-speed engine for ground yarding because of a tendency for the log to stop during the gear change, causing heavy shocks to equipment. Overhead logging eliminated this impediment, and in 1917 the Willamette Iron and Steel Works introduced the first unit that supplied power for the initial pull and a second gear to permit higher speed after suspension of the load.[53]

By the early 1920s demand was heavy for the two-speed machines being manufactured by the region's equipment companies and priced around $10,000. Operators eagerly invested in these donkeys, as a Willamette permitted line speeds of 750 feet per minute with a turn of logs. A model manufactured by Vancouver's Albion Iron Works, concluded logging engineer H.H. Baxter in 1924, if 'crowded to capacity,' provided much higher production than a less sophisticated unit.[54]

Faster yarding speeds led to a change in logging methods. In a procedure known as cold decking, donkeys yarded logs into a huge pile or 'cold deck.' From this point they would later be swung to the rail landing by a large skidder, reducing railroad construction expenses and permitting more intensive use of labour power. The Oregon-American Lumber Company purchased two of these geared machines in 1923 and a third the following year, rather than extend a railroad spur on their operation.[55] By 1927, Oregon American managers decided that the remainder of the company's conventional donkeys had become obsolete because the skidder and its large crew were not working to full capacity. 'With the distance necessary to yard,' argued superintendent C.E. Davidson, 'it is impossible to keep the skidder busy ... on account of the slow line speed of the yarder.' He estimated that the most advanced two-speed donkey would increase skidder production by at least two rail cars per day. Company officials authorized the purchase, then another in 1928 after experiencing double the anticipated production increase.[56]

The efficiencies provided by overhead logging did create a new aristocrat of the woods – the high rigger. This worker's task was to climb the chosen spar tree, taking the limbs off along the way. After reaching the appropriate height, somewhere between 75 and 150 feet, he topped the tree. The necessary blocks and cables were then raised into position on the tree and attached. Finally, after guy-lines had been fastened to surrounding stumps, logging could commence.

No photographer's visit to a coastal logging operation was complete without a shot of a high rigger at work, an image that dominates the perception of work in the western woods. The occupation of high rigger, while perhaps not as dangerous as other less glamorous jobs, seems to represent the courage and rugged individualism associated with the industry. The image is not without its irony, however, for the high rigger functioned to establish and maintain the harvesting system that ensured operators unprecedented efficiency in the logging labour process. Conceptualized in this way he occupies a position analogous to that of the skilled maintenance worker in a manufacturing plant. Companies were eager to add another skilled worker to their payroll because the benefits – higher output and less reliance on the skills and initiative of loggers of the yarding crew – far outweighed the expense.

But the high rigger had no immunity from the social and economic pressures that created the occupation. Firms with holdings sufficient to ensure long-term existence began exploring the suitability of the Lidgerwood portable steel-spar skidder, which had been in use in the midwestern and southern lumbering regions for some time. Rigging ahead was cost-efficient, but required additional donkeys, rigging, and a special crew headed by the high rigger. An advantage of the steel-spar skidder mounted on a railroad car was

High rigger tops a spar tree in preparation for logging.

rapidity of movement, eliminating the expense of extra equipment and workers. Because blocks remained fixed to the spar, only the sky-line and guy-lines had to be reset and the tower raised when the machine arrived at a new setting.[57]

R.D. Merrill expressed an early interest in the steel-spar skidder, capable of being moved in a three- to four-hour period, instead of the day and a half required to shift the tree-rigged Lidgerwoods then in use. Other firms noted the attraction of this feature. An Oregon-American Lumber Company manager pointed out that with the steel-spar 'you have practically no rigging ahead to do ... when you finish one setting you can go to another and go to work.'[58] Late that year Merrill sent the firm's logging superintendent to Minnesota and Louisiana to watch the machines at work. The superintendent returned 'very favorably impressed' with their performance, but for unknown reasons the company did not proceed with the purchase immediately.[59]

Lidgerwood steel-spar skidder mounted on rail car.

The Lidgerwood company began advertising its steel-spar skidder for coastal use in 1914, and by the mid-1920s several of the largest firms had purchased these units. The machines, costing approximately $50,000 in 1923, reportedly achieved hauling speeds of up to one thousand feet per minute, with an advertised daily maximum output of 250,000 feet. The steel-spar skidder represented an extension of the control inherent in aerial logging, freeing companies from the necessity of locating railroads and logging tracts in accordance with the position of natural spar trees or the expense of raising them at appropriate points. This enabled operators to devise logging plans with 'only the natural contour of the section to be logged' in mind, setting the skidder at points 'to which the timber will come out easiest.'[60]

How did loggers respond to the introduction of overhead harvesting systems? Fragmentary evidence suggests that many workers shared a hostility toward overhead logging. The high speed at which logs and rigging now travelled not only brought a higher level of regimentation to the labour process, it also made logging one of the most hazardous of industrial operations. Loggers at the Merrill and Ring camp expressed their resistance in the usual fashion, by quitting. Although very satisfied with the performance of their skidder obtained in 1909, the company immediately experienced 'trouble in keeping a crew.' Finnish loggers were the most adept at operating the new system, but finding it 'almost impossible to keep Finns' the firm began hiring them for railroad construction work to maintain a supply of replacements for work on the skidder. This new employment policy failed, however, and Tiff Jerome reported that the superintendent was 'working in some white men on the skidder' in hopes of eliminating the Finnish loggers.[61]

The Merrill and Ring experience was not an isolated one. Comox Logging and Railway Company managers found it 'an extremely hard job to get men to tackle the skidding machines.' The English Lumber Company's manager told delegates at the 1910 Logging Congress that the only shortcoming associated with the firm's new skidder was 'the aversion the men felt to working around the machine.' Loggers at Weyerhaeuser's Yacolt operation in Washington had a similar reaction to the introduction of the high-lead system about 1915.[62] How widespread was the resistance to overhead logging? Further research hopefully will provide more insight on this critical issue, but given the paucity of sources it will be difficult to reconstruct workers' response with any degree of certainty. The few references gathered to this point indicate that many loggers did not greet the new technology with enthusiasm.

Further research might also clarify the relationship between the introduction of new techniques and the labour militancy that erupted in the western woods under the leadership of the Industrial Workers of the World (IWW) during this period. Wobbly speakers and the *Industrial Worker* made frequent reference to the increased level of exploitation that the 'flying machines' brought to woods work.[63] At this point, however, it is an open question as to how the IWW's technological critique related to grievances rooted in hours of work and camp conditions. These were shared concerns, affecting loggers equally, while the response to the introduction of new technology would have been influenced by one's place in the division of labour.

Certainly, there is no evidence to suggest that the examples of resistance to overhead logging cited here slowed the adoption of these systems throughout the industry. While the loggers' individual and collective protest against squalid living conditions in the camps and dawn to dusk work days resulted in gains on both fronts during the second decade of the twentieth century, they had no success in resisting the instruments of production that determined the structure of their labour.

Although these systems represented a partial attainment of the factory regime, harvesting remained marked by discontinuity, and the pace of production depended to a considerable extent upon the physical and conceptual skills of loggers. Overhead systems did allow tracts to be logged profitably that would have defied ground methods, and here the ability to avoid and overcome 'hang-ups' was critical. 'If not for the ever present human element to contend with,' Washington operator R.W. Vinnedge complained in 1922, 'the skidder system would yard as many logs on rough as smooth ground.' Moreover, the new technology placed a high premium on the ability of a crew to function as an organic production team. Logging, Frank Lamb observed in 1909, 'calls for a high order of teamwork,' and operators such as R.D. Merrill were well aware of the importance of having 'men in the crew that are accustomed to working together.'[64]

Nevertheless, by 1930 the impact of technological change on the skills of loggers is clear, if difficult to quantify. Certainly the yarding of each log represented less of a problem to be 'solved' by the yarding crew than it once had. High-lead logging 'isn't exactly an assembly line,' wrote journalist and historian Stewart Holbrook in 1938, 'but it's all routine.' Logging operations had indeed come to resemble 'a giant factory without a roof.'[65]

Refining the Factory Regime:
The Small Machine, Light Rigging, and Small Crew Era
By 1930 coastal logging operators had succeeded in erecting a rudimentary factory regime with their overhead systems. No subsequent innovation would effect such a fundamental restructuring of the corporate relationship to workers or the productive environment. Operators and machinery manufacturers were far from satisfied, however, and over the coming decades new technologies increased both the scale and intensity of the exploitation process. During the 1949-62 period alone, the productivity of British Columbia loggers jumped 103 percent, while employment in the industry

declined by one-quarter.[66] The key to this gain lay in the application of the internal combustion engine to falling and bucking, yarding, and log transportation, permitting the chain saw, diesel yarder, and motorized truck to replace the crosscut saw, steam donkey, and railroad in the majority of large operations. In addition, the caterpillar tractor provided operators with a valuable, multi-purpose logging unit. During the 1950s the self-propelled tire or track-mounted steel-spar came into widespread use, and with the subsequent introduction of the automatic grapple, corporations achieved full mechanization of yarding and loading procedures.

Students of forest history have acknowledged the role of power saws, tractors, and steel-spars in stepping up the rate of cut and opening previously inaccessible timber to harvesting, but environmental determinism has contributed to a confusion of consequences with objectives. The real value of modern machinery was its capacity to enhance and refine the factory regime in west coast logging. One dimension of this process is easily understood. Power saws, for example, boosted the productivity of fallers, and one need look no further to explain their appeal. Less obvious is the way the mobility of the new generation of machinery reinforced corporate control over resource exploitation, permitting a more technologically structured flow in production.

The transition from railroad to truck logging symbolized the new emphasis on mobility. The massive twenty-ton skidder with its complex rigging system, unsurpassed as a log producer once in place, was cumbersome. Its size, weight, and crew requirements militated against frequent moves to secure optimum yarding conditions – moves that would tie up a twenty-man crew for a few days. Railroads, expensive to build and limited to moderate gradients and curvature, did not in all cases permit landing locations that facilitated efficiency in yarding. This discontinuity, determined by the need to continually shift operations as land was cut over, constituted a major barrier to the realization of a truly mass production factory regime.

Modern portable machinery did not eliminate the disruption associated with natural resource extraction, but ease and rapidity of movement did enable operators to realize the full potential of overhead yarding systems in two ways. First, less time was devoted to moving equipment from site to site, and shorter yarding distances equated to less idle time during the cycle. Paralleling this more intensive use of labour power was a subtle but equally important reduction in operators' reliance upon the ability of loggers to cope with rough terrain, where natural obstacles to technological control were most imposing. Mobility permitted more frequent repositioning of machinery to take advantage of topography, negating to some degree the environmental instability that had placed such a premium on the conceptual and physical skills of loggers. By adopting a lighter power source, by placing machinery on wheels or caterpillar tracks, and by integrating multiple functions in a single self-propelled unit, operators gave real meaning to the factory analogy.

The introduction of the power saw between 1930 and 1950 brought falling and bucking operations into step with the mass production character of the coastal logging industry. Operators had long expressed frustration at their inability to mechanize these procedures. Indeed, in 1917 the *Western Lumberman* wondered how long the crosscut saw would continue to 'form an armour that cannot be pierced by the scientific brains of the age.' Saws powered by electricity, compressed air, and gasoline motors were demonstrated at the 1919 Pacific Logging Congress, but none exhibited the necessary combination of portability and durability. Congress secretary and *Timberman* editor George Cornwall urged operators to establish a research fund throughout the 1920s, but with no apparent success.[67]

Nevertheless, by the middle of that decade T.D. Merrill felt that mechanized falling was the most important challenge facing the industry. He offered to support the endeavours of E.P. Arseneau, who had developed a mechanical saw for cutting small trees, if the inventor would devote his energies to the design of a unit suitable for the region's timber. In 1927 Arseneau demonstrated a saw for the British Columbia Loggers Association, but his wheel-mounted device was too unwieldy. Not all operators shared Merrill's sense of urgency; Oregon-American Lumber Company management decided against giving 'any nutty inventors or theorists permission to experiment in our woods' when an Oregon man asked for an opportunity to test his creation.[68]

Although operators in the pine and redwood forests experimented with the drag saw, essentially a wheel-mounted crosscut saw and gasoline engine, by the early 1930s Douglas fir operators saw more potential in the chain saw. The Reed-Prentice Corporation's Wolf saw, and the Dow, produced by a California firm, seemed promising, and in 1936 a Pacific Logging Congress committee composed of lumbermen and mechanical engineers began studying the available options. That same year the British Columbia Loggers Association imported a Dow product and a German manufactured Stihl chain saw for tests at Bloedel Stewart and Welch's Franklin River camp.[69]

The company selected the Stihl for further development, and worked the saw to identify shortcomings. Managers maintained close contact with the factory in Germany, leading to a 1937 visit from a Stihl engineer to gather data for necessary modifications. Late the next year five redesigned models were in use at the operation, and Donald J. Smith and Company had become local agents for Stihl. This firm then acquired the Stihl patent and marketed the saw throughout the Douglas fir region under the 'Timberhog' name. When Reed-Prentice acquired Smith's company in 1940, operators were cheered by the prospect of mass production, which promised lower

Two-man falling crew makes an undercut with early power saw, ca. 1945.

prices and improved distribution of parts. A 1941 Pacific Logging Congress survey revealed that 31 percent of responding firms had experience with power saws, and by the end of the decade at least a dozen makes were on the market.[70]

The output of falling crews increased dramatically with the new technology. During the early 1940s Bloedel, Stewart, and Welch fallers increased production by a third, enabling the company to achieve a 25 percent reduction in the size of cutting crews. The availability of magnesium after World War II contributed to further productivity gains. Early saw models weighing well over a hundred pounds required two loggers to operate, but lighter materials, such as magnesium, made one-man operation possible. The greater power-to-weight ratio of later units permitted chain saw bucking, banishing the crosscut saw from the industry.[71]

Higher productivity provided firms with sufficient incentive to purchase power saws, but the advanced age of cutting crews contributed to industry's interest in mechanizing these procedures. Most fallers and buckers, executives claimed, were ageing European immigrants. Those employed by Weyerhaeuser at Vail, the Long-Bell Lumber Company's Ryderwood camp, and the Oregon-American Lumber Company's Veronia operation averaged between forty-two and fifty years of age in 1940. Young North American-born workers, according to some reports, were not attracted to these arduous

occupations, suggesting that the labour shortages Ian Radforth has identified as an important factor in the mechanization of northern Ontario's postwar logging industry may have played a part in the popularity of chain saws
on the west coast.[72]

On the other hand, operators had long sought to mechanize these procedures, and their pursuit of labour-saving technology during the Depression
years casts doubt on an explanation that rests too heavily on a labour market interpretation. Certainly acute labour shortages during World War II
would have increased the appeal of power sawing, but this had been an
objective since the introduction of overhead logging systems created a significant disparity between the output of falling and yarding crews.

Industry claimed that fallers received the new technology with open arms.
Older men in particular, asserted the *Timberman*, looked forward to less
strenuous labour and longer working lives. But one manager reported in
1941 that 'the noise, and smoke, and dust together with a very unfamiliar
machine made most of our crew antagonistic toward the power saw.' Workers and their young unions also had reason to fear technological unemployment. British Columbia's Federation of Woodworkers, soon to
participate in formation of the IWA, recognized a threat to cutting crews
when a power saw was demonstrated at the 1936 Logging Congress. Confirming the union's suspicions, one firm replaced eight sets of hand fallers
with two power saw crews. In many instances workers simply refused to use
the machines, and according to the Congress's 1941 poll, just over 50 percent of firms met opposition from crews when introducing the saws.[73]

This resistance from older hand fallers undoubtedly figured in the establishment of informal apprenticeship programs to train workers with no woods
experience as power saw operators. By 1940 Bloedel, Stewart, and Welch
had trained over a hundred such men. Jack Challenger, the firm's falling
and bucking supervisor, described the typical trainee as a husky Saskatch-
ewan farm boy who had come west looking for work. British Columbia
firms even gained government support for this enterprise as World War II
wound down. In 1944 cooperation between companies, the Canadian Vocational Training Branch, and the Department of Veterans Affairs resulted
in the establishment of a power saw program in Nanaimo that produced
over two hundred graduates in three years of operation. The *West Coast
Lumberman* urged American operators to follow this example, but it is unclear if they did so.[74]

Union opposition to the power saw increased during the 1940s as firms
went to the piecework system. Even more disturbing was the trend toward
worker ownership of these machines, which contributed to the emergence
of a large number of independent falling contractors. Ultimately, however, the IWA made no attempt to 'set back the clock hands of progress' by

attacking the technology, and its protests against piecework had little support from power saw operators whose earnings rose during the postwar
years.[75]

Mechanization of falling and bucking boosted the productivity of workers engaged in these occupations. The internal combustion engine proved
equally valuable to operators in improving efficiency in moving logs from
woods to mill after 1930, providing a power source for tractors, donkeys,
and trucks. The caterpillar tractor, or 'cat,' received its first use in the coastal
industry during World War I in selective logging of spruce required for air-
craft construction, and was better suited to the smaller timber and gentler
terrain of the pine forests east of the Cascades. By the early 1930s, however,
the development of more powerful engines and stronger frames made logging with cats a practical alternative to cable yarding in the Douglas fir
region.[76]

Low labour requirements, speed, and agility were the chief advantages of
these units. Whereas a large skidder featured a crew of over twenty loggers,
three or four men could operate a cat show. 'Each unit requires only a small
crew to operate it,' University of Washington logging engineer Russell Mills
wrote, going on to assert its capacity to maintain 'a constant total output
under varying conditions.' Moreover, since no elaborate rigging systems
were needed, logging commenced soon after the machine arrived at a designated site. 'We can kick it off a car anyplace and it will move ... and be ready

Caterpillar tractor, equipped with arch, hauls logs to landing at Ladysmith
operation of Comox Logging and Railway Company, 1937.

to log in a day, whereas a steam donkey requires from three days to a week to make such a move and be ready for logging,' explained one manager.[77]

Large firms used tractors to best advantage by integrating them with skidder systems to increase the productivity of the latter. The manufacture of units equipped with yarding drums enabled the Long Bell Lumber Company to high-lead timber from the fringes of settings, accumulating logs into piles. These 'cold decked' logs were then yarded to the landing by the large skidder. By providing a ready supply of logs and shorter yarding distance for the skidder, this procedure kept its crew busier than if it had operated in isolation.[78]

Lower railroad development expenses provided another benefit. Prior to using tractors to complement skidder logging, the Weyerhaeuser Timber Company laid out railroad spurs at one-mile intervals. The skidders drew logs in from a maximum distance of 2,000 feet on each side of the spur. By assigning tractors to haul logs from a central area between spurs to an accessible location for the skidder, Weyerhaeuser set its lines two miles apart. Expanded output for the large yarding units along with the saving in rail construction costs, which might reach $10,000 per mile, more than compensated for the investment in tractors.[79]

Slack demand during the 1930s contributed to the widespread adoption of these mobile logging units. Traditionally operators had cut costs by pushing for greater output per man, but as the Comox Logging and Railway Company's Robert Filberg observed in 1934, sheer productivity did not suffice when the market failed to absorb the logs and lumber turned out by industry. Tractors, unlike traditional cable logging systems, permitted operators to harvest timber selectively, an advantage when prices for lower grades no longer justified removal of hemlock.[80]

Selective logging of high-quality Douglas fir generated controversy among foresters, but as J. Kenneth Pearce wrote in 1935, operators hoped to realize 'the economic advantages of a flexible mobile operation.' Instead of logging all the timber along a railway spur and picking up the track for use elsewhere, they could 'afford to take only the settings of highest conversion value ... then move on to like areas tapped by other roads, leaving the marginal settings on the first road to be logged at some future date.' Whether used in selective or clearcutting operations, the tractor's low labour requirements and mobility were welcomed. Although they were less effective on steep terrain or rain-soaked ground, under appropriate conditions many believed 'cats' to be 'the most economical way to log' even after World War II created a booming wood products market.[81]

The gradual replacement of the steam engine by gasoline- or diesel-powered donkeys presented operators with rewards of a similar nature. A topic of discussion at the 1917 Logging Congress, the first application of the internal combustion engine to yarding came in 1921 when Bloedel-Donovan

Lumber Mills persuaded the Skagit Steel and Iron Workers to construct a small gas donkey for logging patches of fallen cedar. Steam power remained the choice for long-distance yarding, but during the 1930s small, manoeuvrable gasoline or diesel machines gained increasing use where timber values did not warrant heavier steam equipment.

Some firms had already converted from wood to oil as a fuel for steam equipment, and the internal combustion engine provided additional labour-saving advantages. No workers were required to cut wood or fire the engine, or to service extensive pipe systems that conveyed water from lakes or streams. In 1939 the Oregon-American Lumber Company calculated that dispensing with the services of firemen, wood sawyers, splitters, and water pump tenders would bring a daily saving of $40 per machine.[82]

As with tractors, diesel yarders were often utilized to supplement large steam skidders and reduce railroad construction costs. The Merrill and Ring Lumber Company obtained an early model in 1928 when logging progressed into rougher terrain. 'Where we are now,' Thomas Merrill explained to his brother Richard, 'the cost of railroad building is very high and the quantity is not large enough to justify building our railroads close together, as we have been in the habit of doing.' The purchase of a light diesel donkey to yard scattered timber from the edge of a setting to a central cold deck provided more logs for the skidder while lightening the investment in rail lines.[83]

The development of diesel engines capable of generating over 300 horsepower led to the eventual disappearance of steam-yarding machines. The most sophisticated models were capable of bringing in logs from a distance of 2,000 feet at high speeds, and weighed only half as much as a comparable steam engine, reflecting the trend toward less labour-intensive, mobile operations. Introduction of the automatic transmission during the 1940s made frequent gear changes unnecessary. In permitting constant yarding at 'the highest speed at which a load can be handled' some of the 'human element' in donkey operation vanished, boasted one manufacturer. By 1941 only 15 percent of the companies in western Oregon relied exclusively on steam donkeys, and wartime labour shortages accelerated the adoption of diesel machinery.[84]

Displacement of the railroad by the motorized, pneumatic-tired logging truck as the primary means of log transportation during the 1930-50 period represented the most significant expression of industry's new accent on mobility. Introduced initially during World War I in conjunction with spruce logging operations, trucks mounted on solid rubber tires were used by small operators during the 1920s to carry loads short distances along plank roads. But it wasn't until development of the pneumatic tire, more powerful engines, and improved braking and suspension systems that truck logging attracted the interest of major firms.

Historians have interpreted this change in technology as yet another adaptation to more difficult terrain forced by the need to access timber at high elevations. Trucks, Donald MacKay writes, 'could go places railroads could not go.'[85] While correct at a superficial level, this explanation exhibits the usual flaw associated with environmental determinism. Trucks indeed surpassed railroads in reaching timber, but equally important in industry's calculation was the advantage they held for improved efficiencies in yarding.

The market catastrophe of the Great Depression encouraged firms to contemplate truck transportation. Roads could be engineered and constructed at lower cost than rail lines, and the truck's flexibility made it possible for operators to focus on high-value timber. The technology also fostered expansion of the 'gyppo' system, which saw large firms hire independent contractors to log isolated tracts. Gyppos received a fixed rate for logs delivered to the mill or railroad, absorbing the lion's share of risk and supervisory responsibilities.

By the end of the 1930s many Pacific Northwest corporations had begun integrating the motor truck into their existing rail systems, joining its ability to negotiate steeper terrain at low cost with the economies of scale of the traditional technology. Logs were trucked out of the woods from various sides to transfer points, loaded quickly onto cars, and railed to the mill. Canadian Forest Products Ltd. constructed one of British Columbia's last industrial lines on Vancouver Island in 1957 in conjunction with a feeder

BC Forest Products' logging truck approaches reloading site for transfer of logs to the firm's railway at the Harris Creek operation on Vancouver Island in the early 1950s.

system that combined 'the flexibility of truck logging with the economy of long distance railroad transportation.'[86]

Viewing truck logging in the context of its impact on the yarding procedure brings the method's relationship to the factory regime into focus. Lower road costs and agility enabled operators to shorten yarding distances and neutralize environmental obstacles. As Robert Filberg recalled, managers had more freedom to 'put the logging unit into the timber.' A US Forest Service engineer explained the advantage with greater precision: these transportation systems made it possible to locate yarding equipment 'in more strategic position, thus reducing the cost of bringing logs to the landing.' As a consequence the practice of cold decking declined in favour of direct yarding to roadside.[87]

The new generation of mobile logging equipment gave corporations an opportunity to achieve more continuity of output by decentralizing operations. The breakdown of a large skidder unit might cripple production for an extended period, whereas numerous tractor and diesel donkey sides could be dispersed over a wider area. When Filberg's Comox Logging and Railway Company opened up a new Vancouver Island tract in the 1930s, executives opted to commence truck hauling, anticipating no cost advantage when compared to rail transportation. Instead, they premised their decision on the expectation of 'steady and even production' afforded by working a larger number of yarding units manned by smaller crews.[88]

These considerations dominated when St. Paul and Tacoma Lumber Company officials contemplated the introduction of logging trucks in 1947. After comparing the financial consequences of extending their railroad or penetrating a tract by truck road, engineer Warren Tilton reported that the lower construction cost of the latter option would be offset by the additional mileage required to accommodate the shorter yarding distances permitted by diesel or gas donkeys to be utilized in association with trucks. Tilton, nevertheless, recommended the conversion to secure the benefits of optimum yarding conditions and faster movement of production and repair crews.[89]

Frank Hobi, a veteran coastal operator hired by St. Paul and Tacoma to report independently on the proposition, came to the same conclusion. Hauling by truck would permit 'more cat logging, more one-donkey logging and the use of lighter machinery and rigging.' Moreover, he elaborated, 'the various stages of the operation are more independent of each other and smaller unit crews can be used. The operation is much more flexible and adaptable to high and low peak production and can be readily moved so as to stay in desirable species to meet market demands.' Convinced, the company's board of directors approved conversion of one operation to truck logging, the other having too little timber remaining to justify a large investment.[90]

Another Washington firm, the Kosmos Timber Company, also converted to truck hauling during this period. The firm first arranged for University of Washington logging engineering instructor J. Kenneth Pearce to have his senior class compile a cost analysis while on field trips to that operation in 1948 and 1949. Pearce reported that continuation of the company's rail line into a new tract was the least costly method of log transportation. Despite this finding, he recommended the change on the grounds of efficiencies in logging that outweighed anticipated higher trucking expenses.

Calculating advantages in labour control, Pearce argued that trucks permitted closer oversight of widely scattered crews: 'the saving in travel time of superintendents, foremen ... etc., would increase the efficiency of their supervision, and consequently, the efficiency of the operations they supervise.' In the event of equipment malfunction mechanics reached the site more quickly, reducing 'the idle time of crews,' which would spend less time travelling to and from logging sites. The instructor went on to cite more rapid movement of injured workers and fire suppression crews, and the ease of salvaging timber left to meet requirements of the state's Forest Practices Act, but his main thesis detailed the advantages trucks held for improved efficiency.[91]

By 1950 timber corporations presided over an exploitation process that differed significantly from the massive skidder and railway operations of the 1920s. Fewer loggers laboured to produce an equivalent amount of wood in these clearcutting operations, and the mobility of the new machines encouraged their integration to ensure continuous output. After witnessing a Crown Zellerbach operation in Oregon featuring tractors and diesel donkeys moving logs to truck roads, a writer noted that yarding and loading crews were no longer 'waiting on the train crew and charging up expensive running time without production.' The absence of bottlenecks resulted in 'steady maximum production.' Coastal logging, a superintendent wrote, had entered 'the small machine, light rigging and small crew era,' promising more intensive work for loggers through a reduction in the discontinuities associated with the older generation of machinery.[92]

The Portable Spar Tree and Chokerless Concept

The industry's search for speed and mobility, so well represented by the machines previously discussed, next found expression in the development of self-propelled, portable steel-spars. A 'logical refinement to the flexibility of truck logging,' the steel-spar was the first fundamental innovation in overhead logging since the introduction of the Lidgerwood system. With it, operators added another element to the factory regime, further heightening their technological dominion over loggers and the forests where they toiled.[93]

The initial advance toward the fabrication of a complete mobile logging unit sprang from industry's desire to speed-up the process of loading logs onto trucks. Traditionally logs had been loaded on rail cars with the aid of horizontal booms attached to the spar tree. Since cars arrived at the landing in long trains, loading crews alternated between bouts of frantic activity and idleness. These systems were poorly adapted to servicing trucks which arrived individually, with more intermittent opportunities for loading. Moreover, logs arriving at the landing threatened the safety of loaders.[94]

J.W. Baikie, a pioneer British Columbia truck logger, expressed displeasure at the sight of yarding crews standing idle while loaders completed their task, then the latter waiting for logs to place on the next truck. An Oregon manager complained of 'the loss of time, excessively large crews, interrupted production and skyrocketing loading costs' involved with the use of traditional systems. In their place, operators called for one capable of handling logs coming into the landing 'in such a manner that the production is never interfered with,' simultaneously allowing the loaded truck to be dispatched without undue delay.[95]

The preloading system, enabling workers to construct loads in advance on a structure of 'false bunks,' provided one solution. Upon arrival at the landing the driver backed his trailer under the load, secured it, and departed. Developed during the 1940s by several timber companies, preloaders reduced waiting time for trucks and kept loading crews continuously engaged. One manager advised training new workers in this procedure rather than using 'old hands' who were 'not too happy about the greater output expected of them.'[96]

The adaptation of mobile track-mounted excavation shovels to load logs provided a second means to improve the productivity of yarding and loading operations by separating the functions. First used to excavate railroad grades, diesel-powered shovels equipped with boom attachments were being utilized in the pine region during the 1930s, and over the next decade came to be recognized by Douglas fir operators as 'the most economical and efficient method of loading logs.' Able to service multiple landings, these self-propelled units allowed operators to reduce the size and number of loading crews. Further, they arrived 'ready to load logs,' thus dispensing with the time and expense of rigging up spar tree systems. Anxious to 'get along with less men ... and increase the efficiency of our operation,' the St. Paul and Tacoma Lumber Company purchased shovel-loaders in 1950.[97]

Coastal logging and equipment firms quickly recognized the potential these machines had for conversion to yarding. By the 1940s few suitable areas remained for the 'cumbersome, complicated and expensive' tower skidders of the railway era, and operators hoped to develop a truly mobile logging unit.[98] They first adapted the shovel loader to yarding functions, then collaborated in the development of all-purpose portable logging machines, a process of innovation that culminated in the diesel-powered steel-spar yarder.

The Washington Iron Works 'Trakloader' and Skagit Steel and Iron Works series of 'Mobile Loggers' appeared during the late 1940s and early 1950s, equipped with boom extensions that facilitated short distance yarding to roadside. Capable of travelling up to 20 miles per hour, these machines could be driven into position and stabilized with guylines and could commence logging in short order.[99] MacMillan Bloedel's system of 'access logging' utilized their mobility to best advantage in areas of gentle terrain and low timber volumes. A Trackloader or Mobile Logger with two or three chokermen and a chaser worked along temporary roads, a technique that appealed because of 'smaller crews ... reduced road costs and the elimination of unproductive rigging time.'[100]

Efficient as the new machines were, under most conditions only the donkey rigged to a spar tree provided the lift necessary to carry logs over environmental impediments at distances of more than a few hundred feet. Progress toward development of the portable steel-spar began in the years after World War II, when an expanding pulp and paper market encouraged operations to take a second look at the wood remaining on cutover lands as a source of fibre. Lumber companies entered into agreements to supply pulp and paper concerns with formerly unmerchantable logs and chunks, usually hiring contractors to conduct these activities.

Since the quantity of wood did not justify the expense of rigging a spar tree, even if such were available, firms such as Crown Zellerbach, Weyerhaeuser, and MacMillan Bloedel constructed portable 're-logging' units consisting of a short mast assembly capable of being mounted upon or towed by tractors and trucks. The Isaacson Logging Tower, manufactured by the Isaacson Steel Works in 1945 for the Soundview Pulp Company, was one of the first produced for sale to the industry.[101]

None of these arrangements featured the required combination of height, strength, and portability to be applied to logging of virgin timber, but equipment manufacturers took up the challenge early in the 1950s. Washington's Priest Logging and Equipment Company led the way in 1953 with its sled-mounted 'Porta-Spar.' The Berger Engineering Company's 'Porta-Tower,' similar in design, appeared in 1957, and by the end of the decade self-propelled models mounted on wheels or caterpillar tracks were available. The S. Madill Company of British Columbia became that province's major producer, and licensed an American firm to manufacture its product for that market after securing patents.[102] Small operators seemed the most frequent early purchasers, perhaps because they lacked the financial resources to follow industry giants in employing specialized rig-up crews. But during

Portable steel-spar positioned for yarding at BC Forest Products'
Cowichan Lake operation.

the 1960s large firms converted almost entirely to steel-spars for their main
logging operations.[103]

Environmental factors played a part in industry's adoption of this technology. As operations advanced into higher elevations timber values declined and large settings suitable for logging from a single landing were
encountered less often, along with trees possessing the requisite height and
strength to serve as spars. This forced rig-up crews to raise a tree in the
proper position for efficient yarding, a complex procedure that required
three or four days. But just as changes in the character or accessibility of
timber fail to account fully for previous innovations, neither do they explain the enthusiasm with which corporations greeted the steel-spar. The
profits to be derived from more intensive use of labour power and the resource rather than conditions of nature dominated in the calculus of industrial capitalism.[104]

The need to shift equipment constantly to access timber constituted the
chief barrier to uninterrupted production in coastal logging in the 1950s, as
it had at the beginning of the century. The two or three days devoted to
rigging a standing spar tree at each new setting moved British Columbia's

Baikie to conclude in 1956 that industry must find a way to 'retain a system of high leads and at the same time get away from the stationary spar tree.' The diesel-powered wheel- or track-mounted steel-spar complete with yarding drums could be moved to a new location, the spar raised, and guylines strung out in a matter of hours. 'Every day,' Baikie asserted, 'looks the same on your production sheet.'[105]

Baikie, who purchased one of the first Madill spars, undoubtedly overstated the case. But there is no disputing the rewards that operators reaped. One British Columbia contractor estimated that his portable spar resulted in an additional thirty days of logging per year, time formerly devoted to rigging up sites. Large firms quickly eliminated crews previously needed to establish cable systems in advance of logging. As one example of this trend toward 'more production with less men,' a MacMillan Bloedel camp dropped a six-man rigging crew after converting to steel.[106] The most notable casualties were the high riggers, now a 'vanishing breed' whose skills continued to be useful on occasion. 'Nowadays you can't find anyone who knows a damn thing about rigging a spar tree,' grumbled one manager in 1974.[107]

Steel-spars represented a major advance in the continuum of innovation begun with the introduction of the first steam donkeys. Skill obsolescence, associated with a further tightening of capital's control over production, accompanied mechanization – a development that should come as no surprise. Freed from the necessity of rigging imperfectly positioned spar trees or the expense of raising one at the appropriate location, operators enjoyed a new-found capacity to 'take better advantage of the lay of the land for more efficient logging.'[108]

To an unprecedented extent, corporations mobilized machinery in a manner that reinforced technological control over workers. 'The possibility of locating the spar at exactly the right place,' Weyerhaeuser manager Alden Jones explained in 1965, 'is a big advantage.' Operator and manufacturer Reid Priest equated steel-spar mobility with the power to 'get close ... and speed up the system of getting chokers on the logs.' Hailed by lumbermen, more rigorous machine pacing would hardly have been welcomed by yarding crews working on more mountainous terrain. Pondering the high rate of turnover among chokerman, British Columbia's Bill Moore acknowledged in 1970 that 'the rigging crew's work has speeded up over the years while the going gets tougher for them.'[109]

Although it goes just beyond the time frame of this study, a few words on the most recent element in industry's factory regime in west coast logging are appropriate. By the mid-1960s corporations had accomplished much in mechanizing the exploitation process. 'If some of our old time loggers could see our modern machines and view our methods of today,' remarked Pacific Logging Congress president Nils Hult, 'they would be amazed at the simplicity with which everything seems to be accomplished.' But in one critical

Steel-spar yards logs to landing for Trakloader to place on truck trailer
at BC Forest Products' Cowichan Lake operation in 1961.

respect logging remained virtually unchanged. Regardless of the speed at
which the cable logging system rushed logs to the landing, the journey did
not begin until a nimble, quick-witted chokerman first attached the rigging. 'Since the first logs were brought in behind the oxen,' wrote a
Weyerhaeuser manager, 'there has always been a need for tong setters or
choker setters.'[110]

That mechanization had not yet penetrated to the heart of the procedure
was no minor consideration, since the task of setting chokers consumed 70
percent of each yarding cycle; the remainder of the time being under the
control of the yarder engineer in pulling logs to the landing and running
chokers back out to the crew. 'What's all the speed needed for,' asked Bill

Chokermen at work readying log for yarding to the landing.

Moore in a 1971 critique of complex and expensive machinery, 'when you've got green chokermen stumbling around in the bush for ten minutes trying to untangle the jet speed chokers.'[111]

The introduction of the automatic grapple to yarding during the late 1960s represented, according to one manager involved in its development, 'the greatest breakthrough in the history of the industry, elimination of the need for human hands to attach tongs or cables to logs in the brush.' The grapple first proved itself as a device with enormous labour-saving potential in loading. Invented by a Crown Zellerbach superintendent in the late 1940s and manufactured by the Berger Engineering Company, the grapple powered by compressed air, hydraulics, or cables reduced the loading crew to a single man at the controls of a machine. The operator simply dropped the grapple over a log, closed it by manipulating a control in the cab, lifted the log to 'heel' against the boom, and lowered it onto the trailer. Loading by hand may have been faster, J. Kenneth Pearce observed, but this innovation freed companies from the need 'for a man on the ground to set tongs, and a man on the load to release them.'[112]

Excited about the prospect of applying this 'step in the direction of automation' to yarding, Weyerhaeuser and the Skagit Corporation initiated a cooperative project to integrate the grapple with overhead logging systems.

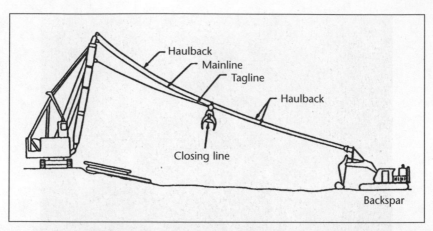

The grapple-yarding system.

In British Columbia, Crown Zellerbach's Nitinat operation on Vancouver Island pioneered in the development of grapple yarding. By the mid-1970s the technique was in widespread use with both steel-spars and specially designed mobile cranes. Under ideal conditions the grapple decimated logging crews, requiring neither chokermen nor a chaser to release logs at the landing. Instead only two workers, a machine operator and a spotter, with perhaps a third man to move lines carried out the procedure.[113]

Communicating by radio when the engineer's vision was obscured, the spotter 'talked' the grapple into position. Once the grapple was in place the operator closed the instrument around the log, raised it, and engaged the yarding drum, depositing the log at the landing by opening the grapple. 'There is no question of the advantage of the concept,' declared a MacMillan Bloedel manager, 'when you consider that two men can produce as much or more wood as six or seven men on a choker unit.'[114]

There is evidence that young men were not flocking to entry-level chokerman positions during the 1960s, contributing in some measure to grapple yarding's appeal. Over the previous decades many firms had disbanded their camps or industrial villages, using buses to transport loggers from nearby towns to the woods. Some linked this process to a decline in the number of males who followed their fathers into logging. Expanding educational opportunities in colleges and universities may have had a negative effect on industry's labour supply as well. Additional research on labour market structure is needed, but corporations took aggressive action to attract workers to logging during the 1960s. British Columbia's Council of Forest Industries hired a career counsellor for liaison with secondary schools, and in 1965 succeeded in having a training program for choker setters established at the province's Nanaimo Vocational Institute. Oregon operators received government funding for a similar course at North Bend.[115]

Modern grapple yarder bringing in a log at Canadian Forest Products'
Woss Lake operation on Vancouver Island.

To place too much emphasis on a labour market interpretation of grapple
yarding would obscure the technique's status as a logical culmination of
nearly a century of innovation directed toward replicating the factory mode
of production. No longer, a Weyerhaeuser industrial engineer pointed out,
was output 'influenced by the speed at which the chokerman can work.'
The new system contrasted favourably with traditional overhead methods,
in which machine operators experienced 'regular delays while the crew is
setting chokers and the chaser is unhooking.' As a result of this new 'steady
out-and-back operation,' engineers experienced stress and fatigue, while firms
enjoyed a substantial reduction in logging costs. At Crown Zellerbach's
Nitinat division, grapple yarding costs in 1968 were 62 percent lower than
high-lead units working with full crews.[116]

The introduction of grapple yarding techniques marked a triumph for
corporate timber capital; the 'chokerless concept' realized the full potential
of overhead logging. Output per man-hour, which had doubled between
1950 and 1968, received another boost.[117] Grapple technology was indeed
a breakthrough, but on rough terrain chokermen continued to find work
with the region's corporations. Where nature threw up its most difficult

challenges, the 'extreme variation in a multitude of factors affecting operating conditions' dictated reliance upon human labour power. Despite the grapple's failure to provide 'the final solution for all yarding problems,' it possesses the potential for future development into a fully mechanized logging system, and research to achieve this objective continues.[118]

Technology and Labour Process Theory

This study has approached mechanization from a Marxian perspective, which views work as a 'relationship of power.' Human labour power, like any other commodity, was to be obtained only in the necessary amounts, cheapened as much as possible, and pushed for all it was worth. The vision of the factory drove the process of technological change that culminated in the introduction of grapple yarding.[119]

The relationship between corporations and loggers was structured in part by competition between units of capital, product markets, and environmental factors. But lumbermen shared with other capitalists what David Noble terms 'an ideological faith in the inevitable efficiencies of reduced skill requirements.'[120] Competition in the marketplace proved no barrier to cooperation among firms in what can only be described as a unified drive to bring the efficiency of factory methods of work organization to coastal logging. Operations may have taken place in relative isolation, but after the inaugural Pacific Logging Congress in 1909, employers and managers had an annual forum for discussion of mutual managerial concerns. Although some voiced complaints at the absence of systematic research and development, by the early twentieth century the industry had entered the mainstream of North American industrial capitalism in its approach to technological innovation.[121]

Timber corporations made great strides in emulating the factory mode of production, but executives continue to bemoan the fact that 'the logger exerts a large influence on the volume of production because the man, not the machine, is the controlling factor in the woods.' An operations research enthusiast remarked in 1973 that the forest remained a 'hostile environment defined by a large number of variables,' which sets logging apart from the 'relatively controlled environment' of manufacturing plants.[122]

It would be an error, then, to suggest that coastal loggers have been utterly subordinated by sophisticated technologies. But it would be a distortion of equal magnitude to underestimate the change in workplace relations wrought by the process of innovation that concluded with grapple yarding. The rigging skills that had once been the vital component of any logging operation were undermined as functions shifted from workers to machines. This progressive narrowing of the task range and discretionary content of occupations, and outright elimination of so many others, confirms the essential thrust of Braverman's degradation of work thesis.[123]

It must be noted, however, that the mechanization involved some un-pleasant, and perhaps unforeseen, consequences for timber capital. In plac-ing their faith in multi-function machinery, employers have become increasingly dependent upon the remaining workers who operate these mar-vels. Technological sophistication came at a price, both in terms of initial expense and the 'implicit penalty of unrealized potential.' The key to effi-cient logging lay increasingly with the 'men who know how to use the modern machinery,' asserted Bill Moore in 1964. Thus, the loading grapple eliminated that crew, but industry analysts noted an unacceptable reliance upon 'the skill and knowledge of the operator.' On the other hand, manag-ers found it easier to evaluate the performance of a single machine than the cooperative effort of a crew. The hive of activity once associated with load-ing logs gave way to a repetitive cycle that lent itself 'very nicely to stop-watch study.'[124]

This concentration of functions in logging equipment warrants a qualifi-cation, rather than a repudiation, of Braverman's deskilling thesis. As Paul Thompson argues, reduction of physical labour should not be confused with skill upgrading. Workers at the controls of grapple technology exerted enor-mous influence over the pace of production, but industry had always shown a willingness to accept the creation of a skilled occupation to achieve tighter control over the collective effort of workers. Such was the case with the high rigger in overhead logging, whose duties diminished the skills of the yarding crew, before the steel-spar in turn rendered his position redundant.[125]

With the new generation of machinery, corporations made obsolete much of the remaining reserves of traditional knowledge responsible for west coast logging's distinctive occupational culture. However, although the overall impact of technology on skill is clear, it is difficult to quantify. True, mod-ern machines required proficient operators, but many of the industry's time-honoured physical and conceptual skills, along with the collaborative labour once needed to extract timber from the coastal environment, were only memories held by retirees. At the end of this period of study, nature still constituted a formidable obstacle to achieving a factory regime, but if Stewart Holbrook was correct in describing a high-lead operation as a 'giant factory without a roof' in 1938, the grapple yarder brought his analogy into sharper focus.

2
Managing the Factory Regime: The Emergence of Logging Engineering and Industrial Forestry, 1880-1965

The preceding discussion of mechanization argued that the corporate search for efficiency produced more intensive control of workers. Part 2 of this study will examine operators' use of these technologies and how they interfered with the process of forest renewal, the scientific research into the ecology of Douglas fir, and the role of governments in regulating harvesting practices. Before entering the arena of resource politics, however, the managerial component of industry's factory regime will come under analysis. Scholars have devoted little attention to the operational management of these enterprises.[1]

This chapter documents the impact of both technological innovation and changes in corporate structure on the development of logging engineering and industrial forestry as technical occupations, on the relationship between timber capital and universities in the production of expertise, and on the function of forest professionals in the assertion of managerial control. A diverse body of literature exists to inform such an endeavour. Historians of the 'organizational school,' for example, offer a broad perspective on the rise of large bureaucracies and the role of experts in directing business affairs.[2] The work of Alfred D. Chandler is particularly relevant, in that technological change is considered central to the emergence of managerial hierarchies necessary to coordinate the mass production and distribution activities of large firms. Chandler's functionalist orientation, however, leaves little room for consideration of management as a tool of power and social control.[3]

Braverman's analysis of scientific management, or Taylorism, provides a more appropriate starting point. Formulated by Frederick W. Taylor, the fundamental principle of scientific management was that all planning and design work be removed from the shop floor and concentrated within the engineering ranks, depriving craft workers of their knowledge of production. In depicting management as a relationship of power, Braverman offers valuable insight, but his focus on craft work neglects the vast majority of workers who, as Szymanski points out, 'never had either all around knowledge of, or basic control over the production process.' This critique is relevant to the forest industry, which, aside from hand logging, has involved a collective and relatively well-defined division of labour. Moreover, the logging labour process places operators in a relationship with nature as well as workers, a subject neglected in traditional Marxist analysis.[4]

The application of formal technical and scientific knowledge to forest exploitation on the Pacific coast has followed two distinct but related lines of development. During the late nineteenth and early twentieth centuries the concentration of holdings and introduction of railroad and overhead logging technology generated a demand for industrial engineering expertise. As the expanded and increasingly complex exploitation process came to exceed the organizational capacities of industry's existing managerial structure, forward-looking operators approached the region's universities, requesting the establishment of programs to train experts with skills in logging engineering.

Close collaboration between industry executives and administrators in the forestry schools at the University of Washington, Oregon State University, and University of British Columbia produced degree programs in logging or forest engineering at these institutions between 1912 and 1921. West coast logging thus exemplifies two related phenomena associated with the development of industrial capitalism: the effort of industrialists to introduce tight administrative control over their enterprises, and the emergence of a more complex division of labour involving a formally educated stratum of employees assigned to harness science and technology to business objectives. As agents of authority, the logging engineers functioned primarily to facilitate the planning process, gathering and organizing data on the physical character of tracts to permit the formulation of rational, cost-efficient harvesting schemes.[5]

Engineering knowledge declined in importance in mid-century with the replacement of railroads by trucks, but as new technologies with less exacting requirements threatened the logging engineers, industry experienced a demand for technical forest management expertise, previously valued only by federal, state, and provincial resource agencies. Industrial forestry emerged as a distinct branch of professional endeavour as a consequence of timber depletion, a booming postwar wood products market, and an increasingly diversified, integrated industrial structure that generated a need for more complete knowledge of the productive capacity of forestland.

The integrated corporate giants that dominated the industry approached the universities again during the 1930-50 period, this time calling for personnel with the ability to conduct timber inventories, estimate the productivity of forestland, prepare management plans, and negotiate access to public reserves. In tandem with an engineering concept of efficiency devoted to deployment of technology, the new dimension of forest management concerned itself with the understanding and manipulation of natural processes. As firms contemplated depletion of the regional resource inventory and strove to maximize long-term returns on investments in holdings and production facilities, industrial forestry satisfied the demand for knowledge of corporate lands as a source of immediate as well as future profit. Together, the logging engineers and foresters comprised a stratum of educated labour for the managerial component of industry's factory regime, providing superiors with the technical information necessary to 'reduce uncertainty in the process of decision-making.'[6]

Logging as an Engineering Science
The operational management practices of forest industry firms have escaped rigorous analysis by scholars. For their part, historians of urban manufacturing industries have documented the introduction of Taylorism in the factory setting, but this focus on structures of control and authority at the workplace has not been matched by a commensurate attention to the production of technical expertise essential to the development of modern management. Analysis of the relationship between industrial capital and educational institutions is of particular importance for this study because of the North American conservation movement's influence in establishing the forestry profession's foundation in public land management. This orientation placed value on the classic elements of forestry as a natural science: the relationship of tree species to soil, climate, and light; and their reproductive and growth characteristics.

Founded to turn out professionals for public service, forestry schools in the American portion of the Douglas fir region shifted their emphasis in response to the early twentieth century managerial crisis in coastal logging. Although foresters and logging engineers shared a utilitarian view of the forest and a conception of efficiency that dictated a central role for the expert, the education of the latter took its cue from industry's need for technical assistance in the organization of exploitation rather than resource conservation and renewal.[7]

In the United States the linkage between professional forestry and the federal government was forged in the late nineteenth century. Concerned over the unregulated disposal of timberlands by the Department of Interior, naturalist Franklin B. Hough presented a paper to the American Association for the Advancement of Science in 1873 that prompted a resolution urging the creation of a commission to study the forestry problem. Subsequently appointed to conduct an inquiry, in 1877 Hough recommended that Congress adopt the Canadian practice of selling only cutting rights, a system that would permit the government to regulate logging practices and retain possession of productive timberland.[8]

In 1881 a Division of Forestry was established in the Department of Agriculture under Hough, but control of the federal lands remained in the Department of Interior. The federal government's involvement in timber management began in 1891 when passage of the Forest Reserve Amendment conferred presidential power to withdraw lands from the public domain for designation as forest reserves. By the end of 1892 President Benjamin Harrison had withdrawn over 13 million acres, and his successor Grover Cleveland created additional reserves totalling over 21 million acres concentrated in the west. Western opposition stalled the movement, but Congressional passage of the Pettigrew Amendment in 1897 asserted the federal government's right to designate reserves for the protection of timber and watersheds. Most importantly, the Forest Management Act of that year granted the secretary of Interior the power to regulate use of the reserves, a precondition of commercial exploitation.[9]

Between 1897 and 1905 a division of the Department of Interior's General Land Office administered the reserves, developing fire prevention and suppression, timber sale, and tree planting programs. The Division of Forestry, headed since 1886 by Bernard E. Fernow, supplied technical advice. Fernow, a German-trained forester who had emigrated to America in 1876, oversaw the division's early research into dendrology, tree planting, and the physical properties of wood. By the time Fernow left the Division in 1898, William G. Robbins asserts, he had 'established the scientific basis for federal forestry,' and provided the foundation for a cooperative relationship between that organization and the lumber industry.[10]

Fernow's departure had a double significance. First, he resigned to become director of the first formal North American school of forestry at Cornell University, establishing the prerequisite for professional stature – a university-based institution for the transmission of knowledge to students. Second, he was succeeded by the dynamic Gifford Pinchot, who pushed forestry to prominence in the early twentieth century conservation movement. Three years later Pinchot's division achieved bureau status, and he realized one of his chief ambitions in 1905 with the transfer of control over the forest reserves, renamed as National Forests, to the Department of Agriculture. Federal forestland thus came under the management of the newly titled US Forest Service. In order to gain support from western congressmen for the transfer, Pinchot had advocated that the reserves not be withheld from commercial exploitation. Forest Service policy with regard to their development followed a philosophy of 'conservative use,' meaning that timber would be sold in accordance with demand, and cutting regulated to prevent waste, protect young growth, and ensure regeneration.[11]

Pinchot also moved aggressively on other fronts during this period, hosting a 1900 meeting in Washington, DC, that led to the formation of the Society of American Foresters (SAF), an association confining active membership to 'professional foresters of achievement.' The same year Pinchot's family provided an endowment for the new Yale University School of Forestry. Within the next few years, centres of professional training opened at universities in Michigan, Maine, and Pennsylvania. A national conference on forestry education held in 1909 set out a standardized curriculum, placing heavy emphasis on silvics, silviculture, forest management, and mensuration.[12]

The profession in Canada developed along similar lines despite some important differences in natural resource policy. Unlike the United States where private ownership was the rule, the principle of public control over timber and other resources gained early acceptance in Canada. Under the terms of the British North America Act of 1867, the provinces gained jurisdiction. Although the federal government retained control over the natural resources of the prairie provinces until 1930, by the time of Confederation the governments of Ontario, Quebec, and Nova Scotia had established administrative branches that oversaw the leasing and licensing of cutting rights on forests that remained in Crown ownership. Judson F. Clark became the first forester in provincial employ, leaving the United States to take a position with Ontario's forest administration in 1904.[13]

When British Columbia entered Confederation in 1871, the new province opted for Crown ownership of its forestland. Exceptions included timber already alienated, a belt of land forty miles wide transferred to the federal government for construction of the transcontinental railroad, and the E & N grant on Vancouver Island. In 1912 a Forest Act created a Forest Branch under professional leadership within the Department of Lands. Yale graduate H.R. MacMillan was appointed chief forester, and within two years twenty foresters had entered government service to supervise a timber sale program operated on the US Forest Service model.[14]

The federal state in Canada played a much less influential role in forestry issues than to the south, where US Forest Service management of the national forests gave that agency a prominence never achieved by its Canadian counterpart. John A. MacDonald's Conservative government established the first federal forest reserve in the prairie region in 1884, and five years later the ruling Liberals created the position of chief inspector of timber and forestry in the Interior Department's Timber and Grazing Branch. Responsible for the leasing of Dominion lands for timber production, this organization shared authority with the Forestry Branch, later the Canadian Forestry Service, which oversaw protection and cutting on the federal reserve system.[15]

In both national contexts, government responsibility for scientific resource management inspired programs for the education of foresters. Bernard Fernow presented the first forestry course in Canada at the Queen's University School of Mining in 1903, becoming Dean of the University of

Toronto's new Faculty of Forestry in 1907, the nation's initial professional curriculum. The following year Fernow became president of the newly organized Canadian Society of Forest Engineers (CSFE), which like the SAF, restricted active membership to individuals with technical training. By 1911 Laval University in Quebec and the University of New Brunswick also offered degree programs in forestry.[16]

In the American west, where the vast acreage of the national forests was concentrated, forestry education began in the first decade of the twentieth century. Individual courses had been offered during the 1890s at Oregon State University's Department of Botany and Horticulture and in the Department of Natural Science at the University of Washington, but formal professional-grade instruction began in 1905 at Oregon State with the introduction of an official course of study in a new Department of Botany and Forestry. The University of Washington founded a School of Forestry in 1907 and six years later the Oregon State program achieved this status. Early graduates of these institutions were equipped with technical skills geared directly to the requirements of the US Forest Service. 'The success of any school of forestry,' Oregon State School of Forestry Dean George Peavy wrote in 1910, 'will depend to a considerable degree on the esteem in which it is held by that institution.' Neither state governments in the region nor the timber industry had progressed beyond rudimentary systems of fire protection as the sole criterion of forest management at this time.[17]

The establishment of forestry education in the American far west coincided with growing concern among lumbermen over the organizational implications of their emerging factory order. Two related factors generated the industry's early twentieth century managerial crisis: the concentration of holdings that accompanied the movement of resource capital to the region, and the mass production technologies introduced to extract and transport timber from woods to mill. The owner or manager of a small operation featuring animal hauling or a single steam donkey was able to formulate an effective logging plan simply by walking over the tract in question, perhaps consulting the rough topographic notes compiled by the 'timber cruiser' who had estimated the quantity and quality of timber prior to purchase. The setting out of yarding roads and landing locations was accomplished by forming a 'mental picture' of the tract, and deciding upon the basis of this conceptualization the most efficient means of organizing the exploitation process. Adequate for planning small operations, this 'rule of thumb' method of management failed when applied to tracts ranging in size from 20,000 to 100,000 acres.[18]

The adoption of railroad technology further undermined the effectiveness of traditional practice, as lumbermen expanded the scope of logging to achieve the economies of scale that the construction, operation, and maintenance of these systems demanded. By 1898, for example, the Simpson

Logging Company had roughly 800 loggers toiling at eight camps along eighty miles of railroad. In the early, less extensive operations, one operator lamented, the owner or manager 'was able to keep in close personal touch with all the details of the work.' But with a number of production sites spread over a wide area it had become impossible to maintain these 'close relations.' In addition, the planning and construction of rail systems required engineering expertise. Operators turned to civil engineers to lay out their mainline railroads, while foremen or superintendents sometimes performed the less exacting task of spur-line location. Unfortunately, the civil engineering knowledge essential to railroad development did not always fulfil industry requirements. Many engineers who were experienced in laying out permanent passenger and freight systems simply applied these principles to logging lines, which had relatively short lifespans, accepted more severe grades and curves, and in general required less exacting construction standards. Cost-conscious operators criticized the work of civil engineers when it exceeded their needs.[19]

The civil engineers' performance also suffered because of their ignorance of coastal logging methods. Few of these individuals, observed one operator, possessed 'any idea what a logging operation is.' More than simply a transportation system, the railroad served a function analogous to the structural layout of a factory, dictating the conditions under which the crucial yarding phase was conducted. As one logging engineer wrote, railroads must be planned to achieve 'harmony with the rest of the operation.' A British Columbia consulting engineer expressed an essential rationale of his profession in a letter soliciting employment. 'The development of any sized tract of timber,' wrote C.S. Roray, 'requires the service of an engineer thoroughly familiar with the best modern methods of logging as well as merely technical knowledge to lay out railroads.' Operators, then, had to balance their desire for low construction costs against the need for a planning procedure that maximized efficiency by providing optimum yarding opportunities. 'All our plans,' Oregon-American Lumber Company manager Judd Greenman explained to one of the firm's directors, 'depend very largely on a clear understanding of railroad development.'[20]

Entrusting this work to a logging manager or foreman could prove equally unsatisfactory because of an inverse ratio of logging to engineering knowledge. Expensive errors in railroad construction might result from the lack of formal training. Moreover, time devoted to plotting future operations detracted from their primary responsibility – supervising logging crews. 'It is only an exceptional crew that does not turn out more work when they know the boss is close at hand,' claimed E.T. Clark, a pivotal figure in the early history of logging engineering.[21]

By 1910, what Daniel Nelson has termed 'the foreman's empire' was crumbling under the pressures of technological and structural change in the logging industry as in other sectors of the North American economy. Operators had learned that factory methods of exploitation demanded a more elaborate managerial structure – one capable of performing the function of planning and coordinating the flow of production as well as exercising supervisory authority over workers. They turned to the region's universities to secure the required technical expertise.[22]

In this effort to reorganize the internal structure of their firms, operators participated in a broader process of integrating the educational apparatus of the state with the corporate economy. During the early twentieth century, David Noble observes, 'the efforts of industrial leaders to reshape educational institutions into a valuable industrial resource ... coincided with university efforts to extend the services they rendered.' The engineering profession was central to this new relationship; the number of American institutions with degree-granting powers grew from 17 in 1870 to 125 in 1915, and 21,000 engineers graduated between 1901 and 1910. In Canada, engineering developed in a comparable fashion, drawing away from the British tradition of apprenticeship training and moving into the universities.[23]

On the west coast, operators set the wheels in motion by organizing the Pacific Logging Congress in 1909 to communicate their specific needs to universities. The creation of courses in logging engineering was one of the 'underlying motives' in the Congress's formation, and its 'supreme object' would be to 'direct and mould the form of instruction' to fulfil operators' demand for personnel able to provide comprehensive representations of industrial holdings. On the occasion of the inaugural meeting, Congress secretary George Cornwall noted the existence of 'a growing field on the Pacific Coast for young men with a knowledge of engineering, both civil and mechanical, who will devote their time to a study of ... logging requirements, with a view of being able to present in an intelligent and practical manner a working plan for opening up and logging a tract of timber.' Grays Harbor lumberman Frank Lamb echoed the need for 'detailed topographical plots' to provide an 'accurate birds'-eye view' of forestlands. Although the appropriate cost of new planning procedures was in dispute, operators agreed on the necessity of thorough topographic investigation prior to railroad construction. 'The time has come,' said J.J. Donovan, a prominent Washington lumberman, 'when you must know your ground if you are going to log at least expense.'[24]

Administrators at the American forestry schools, concerned about declining US Forest Service recruitment as the agency filled its personnel requirements on the coast, welcomed the opportunity to meet industry's managerial requirements. University of Washington College of Forestry Dean Frank Miller took the initiative in 1909, obtaining Regional Forester E.T. Allen's approval for W.T. Andrews to conduct lectures in timber cruising, mapping, log scaling, and 'lumbering in general.' Later that year Miller, Andrews, and faculty members developed a short course in logging engineering attended by about ten students in 1910.[25]

The following year the College of Forestry restructured its curriculum, establishing a four-year Bachelor of Science program in logging engineering as an alternative to the existing field in technical forestry. An additional year of study qualified students for a Master's degree. Yale forestry graduate E.T. Clark, construction superintendent for the Standard Logging and Railway Company, was appointed instructor. Clark prepared by touring operations during the summer of 1911 to 'investigate the different methods used and secure advice from the leaders of the industry.' With a clear understanding of their views, he devised a curriculum embodying five 'governing principles.'

First, there would be detailed study of engineering concepts, enabling graduates to conduct land surveys, locate logging railroads, make cost estimates, and supervise construction projects. A thorough knowledge of logging machinery and systems comprised a second essential component. Courses in mathematics, English, physics, chemistry, and geology provided students with a 'broad college training.' Fourth, the engineers received sufficient technical forestry instruction to understand 'the general laws of the growth and management of forests.' Finally, this foundation of theoretical knowledge was to be combined with practical experience through summer work assignments and the senior field trip, involving a two-month stay at a large operation to prepare a topographic map, cruise estimates, and logging plan for a specific tract.[26]

Operators and educators soon came into conflict over the nature of education in logging engineering, the latter defending the theoretical content of instruction considered essential to professional status against industry's demand for 'practical' training, but at the outset harmony prevailed. The faculty received 'many practical suggestions' from lumbermen, and Dean Hugo Winkenwerder, appointed to the post in 1912, intended to 'have the course criticized by the practical men of the [logging industry] and revised in accordance with suggestions from these men.' The appointment of an advisory committee in 1916, comprising Donovan, the Weyerhaeuser Timber Company's George Long, and James O'Hearne of the English Lumber Company, provided operators with official status in curriculum development and revision. That same year, University of Washington president Henry Suzzallo informed the West Coast Lumbermen's Association of his determination to make the College of Forestry the 'right hand of the lumber industry' by turning out engineers rather than foresters. Winkenwerder extended this policy to student recruitment, advising candidates to 'enter work which will lead to positions with private corporations.'[27]

The general health of the industry between World War I and the early 1920s provided plenty of employment opportunities for his graduates although, as Winkenwerder confessed to J.P. Weyerhaeuser, they were 'at first accepted with some misgivings' by certain operators. The high demand for engineers in 1920 prompted Winkenwerder to inform fellow educator Raphael Zon that 'we have been having more calls from the lumber companies for men in this line than we have been able to supply.'[28]

In Oregon, logging operators and officials at the Oregon State University School of Forestry followed the example set in the neighbouring state. 'The logging people are showing some interest in us,' Dean George Peavy informed Winkenwerder in 1912, 'and I am going to do my best to see to it that they don't forget we are on the map.' The following spring Peavy conveyed industry's hopes to the university president, and a Pacific Logging Congress committee participated in developing a course of study in logging engineering first offered in 1913. The presence of George Cornwall on the university's Board of Regents undoubtedly helped speed adoption of instruction designed 'to meet the peculiar requirements of the timber business.'[29]

The Oregon school, like the University of Washington, offered two distinct lines of professional education: the original forestry program emphasizing training in 'the reproduction, protection, and care of the forest' leading to Forest Service employment; and the new venture designed to develop expertise in 'the harvesting of the mature crop.' His policy in the latter endeavour, Peavy declared, would be to 'keep in close touch with the leading lumbermen of the state to the end that it may meet as fully as possible their special needs.' In 1916 the demand for 'high grade instruction' led to John Van Orsdel's appointment to the faculty. As a manager, civil engineer, and partner in the region's first logging engineering consulting firm, he possessed the desired blend of practical experience and technical knowledge. By 1916, then, Oregon and Washington operators had succeeded in placing their industry squarely in the mainstream of American industrial management, moving George Cornwall to proclaim 'the distinct place of the logging engineer in mechanical science.'[30]

Progress on the Canadian side of the Douglas fir region, where the University of British Columbia did not open until 1915, came more slowly. As early as 1912 the British Columbia Loggers Association appealed to the government for engineering training based upon the Washington model. In 1917, university president F.F. Wesbrook received a similar request from the Pacific Logging Congress and BC Forest Club, but World War I and a shortage of funds delayed introduction of a forestry department until 1920.[31] Instruction followed the utilitarian disposition of the American institutions. 'The forestry problems of British Columbia are largely of an engineering nature,' declared instructor H.R. Christie, who visited the University of Washington College of Forestry in 1920 to gain insight into that curriculum. Only after a thorough grounding in mechanical and civil engineering subjects did students proceed to a fifth year consisting exclusively of forestry studies, qualifying for a Bachelor of Applied Science.[32]

Forestry education in British Columbia was thus, at the outset, 'designed chiefly to train men for engineering work,' Christie advised a colleague in 1924. Faculty member Malcolm Knapp, a University of Washington graduate, expressed concern in 1929 with the concentration of graduates in the province's Forest Branch; only one-third had secured employment with logging companies. This state of affairs reflected both the preoccupation of the provincial state with the administration of industrial activities on public lands, as well as the influx of engineers from the University of Washington who took positions with major firms operating within the E & N belt.[33]

With the establishment of the University of British Columbia Forestry School, the educational apparatus of provincial and state governments on the north Pacific coast had been harmonized with the timber industry's operational specifications. Professional instruction at these institutions emphasized the efficient exploitation of old-growth timber. 'During the period of liquidating ... our virgin stands,' an educator later commented, 'something different from orthodox European forestry education was needed.' The curricula in logging engineering provided technical knowledge 'specifically for American conditions.'[34]

Although this development shifted the focus of forestry education, the state, industrial capital, and the profession each shared a preoccupation with creating centralized decision-making structures. The training of what Winkenwerder termed 'specialists in the harvesting of the forest crop' was entirely consistent with the spirit of the early twentieth century conservation movement, which Samuel P. Hays has characterized as seeking 'rational planning to promote efficient development and use of all natural resources.'[35] Moreover, as Carroll Pursell has shown, 'the concept of efficient utilization of natural resources was ... basic to the thought and practice of the engineer.' In combining a modicum of forestry knowledge with a primary focus on engineering expertise, educators extended the influence of their profession by aligning with the region's dominant sector of industrial capital. Decades passed before the deforestation accomplished under the factory regime generated a use for the science of forestry on corporate lands; in the interim, efficiency was defined solely in extractive terms.[36]

The logging engineers' primary functions lay in three areas: topographic mapping, railroad projection, and overhead yarding system layout. With railroads and skidders absorbing a significant portion of operating budgets, firms required more accurate and comprehensive data than was provided by the traditional timber cruise. Engineers provided a new basis for rational management by depicting topographic features and timber stand characteristics on detailed logging plan maps. 'The topographic map is the backbone of the whole scheme of logging,' an early University of Washington engineer advised one operator – 'upon it, if reliably constructed, one can build the entire fabric of the operating details.' E.T. Clark advertised his graduates' mapping abilities to the industry, explaining that an accurate conceptual representation was essential in showing 'possible routes for the [railroad] lines, in determining proper spacing of the lines for the most efficient yarding distance, in deciding upon future extensions of lines, and for getting the line in a location in which it can be most cheaply constructed and at the same time give the best grades and curves.'[37]

Not only did firms seek to balance their desire to minimize railroad construction costs against the need to obtain favourable yarding conditions, overhead systems themselves required consideration of several technical variables. 'Proper location of railroad skidders,' stressed Judd Greenman in 1926, necessitated preparation 'to determine proper yarding distance and compute the proper deflection on overhead cables for maximum carrying capacity.' West Fork Logging Company owner L.T. Murray suggested that intensive planning in the selection and arrangement of skyline settings equalled railroad location in importance.[38]

Most of the largest firms in the Douglas fir region began to invest in this kind of engineering during the early twentieth century. The Merrill and Ring Lumber Company contacted John Van Orsdel in 1911 to inquire about the mapping of holdings on the Olympic Peninsula. The Weyerhaeuser Timber Company, Long-Bell Lumber Company, Puget Sound Mills and Timber Company, and Bloedel-Donovan Lumber Company also had their lands mapped during this period. Weyerhaeuser projected the logging of their timber in southwest Washington for a one-hundred year period on a large map, assigning different colours to areas to be logged in each decade. By 1934 the company had surveyed 110,000 acres, marking contours at ten-foot intervals.[39]

The Oregon-American Lumber Company contracted a large mapping project out to the Portland logging engineering firm of Thomas and Meservey Inc., whose engineers prepared a topographic survey on two scales: one a detailed study of 'the different possibilities of actually logging the area'; the second a comprehensive overview of the entire property 'so that a minimum of mileage is needed to serve the tract ... with the least possible grades and construction cost.' An examination of the map in 1929 alerted manager Judd Greenman that the neighbouring Hammond Lumber Company owned lands vital to his firm's railroad extension plans. 'One glance at the tracing is sufficient to indicate that we need the Hammond lands to get at our own,' Greenman informed a director. 'The physical conditions in this territory are simply that Hammond controls the passes necessary for development of the country.'[40]

Forest industry giants in British Columbia, such as the Alberni-Pacific Lumber Company, Empire Lumber Company, Campbell River Timber Company,

Forest engineers Harold McWilliams and Jim Hoar pause
while conducting a preliminary railway survey for
Bloedel, Stewart, and Welch Ltd. in the upper Nimpkish
Valley on Vancouver Island.

and Capilano Timber Company, faced similar problems and accordingly either hired engineers or secured the services of one of the province's several consulting concerns. A typical map prepared for Bloedel, Stewart, and Welch illustrated prospective railroad grades, landing locations, and timber types.[41]

By 1930 the collaboration of operators and forestry school educators had produced a cadre of professionals with the capacity to bring rational management to coastal logging operations. Maps that displayed cruise figures in relation to topographic features allowed projections to be made, profiles to be compared, and preliminary estimates to be formulated. 'The one big feature,' proclaimed an enthusiast, 'is that the comprehensive plan is laid out ... before a dollar is spent in operation.' The operator would 'have his holdings in his office and cease to rely upon the sole judgement of men ...

in the field.' Managerial control was indeed centralized, but the natural environment of the coastal region defied precise representation. One operator remarked in 1923 that it was 'impossible to get a map sufficiently accurate to eliminate the necessity of having to comb that land day by day.' Weyerhaeuser chief engineer Walter Ryan agreed that the contour map was 'just a guide for the engineer in making his final analysis ... in the country.' Consequently, the development of logging plans continued to involve considerable fieldwork, with engineers plotting preliminary locations of railroad routes and landings on paper before making final determinations in the woods.[42]

Outweighing the limitations of this process in importance, however, was the operator's enhanced ability to maximize efficiency in the mobilization of workers and technology. In keeping with the principle of Taylorism, the engineers gathered the data necessary for owners and managers to organize mass production in the woods. Those who took advantage of this expertise enjoyed greater control over all phases of logging. Operational plans could be approved before implementation, and superintendents possessed a means to monitor the performance of foremen, now relegated to the bottom of the managerial hierarchy. 'This redistribution of work,' wrote University of Washington graduate Joseph Morgan, 'makes for efficiency in all departments of the operation. The superintendent really superintends, the foreman sees that his crew produces the maximum results.'[43]

The role loggers played in the planning of operations prior to logging's industrial revolution is, regrettably, unclear. Certainly they were firmly excluded from this function after the arrival of the engineers, who themselves expressed frustration at their lack of autonomy within management ranks.[44] For their part, loggers laboured under three levels of control associated with the industry's factory regime. First in importance were the technologies of mass production, which determined the objective character of work, supplemented by the personal supervision of foremen. The introduction of Taylorist methods of management, analyzed here, created or at least widened the gap separating their manual labour from the conceptual duties performed by managers and the new cadre of efficiency experts.

Analysts are correct in cautioning against uncritical acceptance of statements that depict management under such arrangements as unproblematic. For example, when Crown Zellerbach's Harold Goodrich concluded a description of his firm's methods at the 1944 Western Forestry and Conservation Association (WFCA) meeting by declaring that 'when the logger moves in, he goes in and logs just the way it was planned,' the executive provided a valid perspective on the separation of conception and execution, which Braverman identifies as the key feature of industrial capitalism. If Goodrich's declaration is overly simplistic and merits some scepticism, it nevertheless captures the essence of modern logging management.[45]

Industrial Forestry: The New Process of Fact Gathering

Over the 1930-65 period, the relationship between the timber business and universities in the Douglas fir region entered a new phase as a consequence of the emergence of industrial forestry as a distinct technical occupation. The remainder of this chapter will be devoted to analyzing the economic and political factors that created a place for foresters within the private sector, the response of their educational institutions to this opportunity, and the techniques professionals used in securing and processing the data essential to the corporate brand of forest management. Like the engineers who preceded them, foresters served industry primarily in an information-gathering capacity.

Prior to the 1940s few employment opportunities existed for foresters in industry on the west coast. In 1919 the SAF's North Pacific Section organized a committee to promote the practice of forestry on private lands beyond fire prevention, but another two decades would pass before industry responded to the profession's overtures. On both sides of the forty-ninth parallel the abundance of timber encouraged most operators to 'cut and run' rather than invest in a second crop. 'The average small lumberman of the coast has about as much regard for his forest as a commission man has for his produce,' remarked E.T. Clark in 1922.[46]

Professional prospects were little brighter among the largest firms. By 1928 only Weyerhaeuser, the Long-Bell Lumber Company, and the Crown Willamette Paper Company had established forestry departments. Although the latter two constructed nurseries to produce seedlings for small-scale planting programs, foresters in the employ of these giants were occupied primarily with the classification and appraisal of cutover lands and supervision of fire protection plans. According to the Long-Bell company's John B. Woods, corporate forestry might involve the negotiation of US Forest Service timber sales, building public goodwill, and land analysis, but rare was the opportunity to 'develop and maintain adequate timber supplies.'[47]

The first glimmer of hope for foresters anxious to penetrate into the Pacific Northwest industry came in 1929 when the Oregon legislature passed an act providing for classification of cutovers as reforestation lands. The legislation fixed annual taxes for lands dedicated to the growing of a new crop at five cents per acre, with a yield tax to be paid at the time of harvest. Washington state followed with similar legislation in 1931. Designed to encourage operators to hold their logged-off lands, the reforestation acts failed to generate much in the way of systematic timber growing. Some firms assigned engineers or foresters to map cutovers in order to qualify for the low assessment, but most continued to practice liquidation. During the 1930s, county governments found themselves taking possession of vast stretches of barren, tax-delinquent land.[48]

As the timber industry struggled through the severe early years of the Great Depression, unemployment among graduates and declining enrolment at forestry schools prompted some to suggest that the profession should become more closely attuned to the needs of lumbermen. The University of California's Emanuel Fritz called for educators to 'sit down with the private forest industries to get acquainted with them and solicit a more sympathetic attitude toward university training as a foundation for developing their officers.' When Hugo Winkenwerder rebuked him for ignoring the University of Washington engineering program, Fritz replied that the northern institution was 'the only forestry school able and competent to train men for the lumber industry.'[49]

Referring to those activists within the profession currently campaigning for federal regulation of private cutting practices, Fritz went on to relate to Winkenwerder his frustration at foresters who conveyed the impression that they were 'gifted by God to lead the world away from the clutches of the sinful lumber industry.' This crusading posture contributed to the difficulty educators experienced in securing employment for graduates who should have been scattered throughout the industry 'doing everything from setting chokers to piling lumber.' Once these foresters made their way into administrative positions, Fritz argued, 'even if they never had any use for the silviculture they learned they will at least have a sympathy for it and will be inclined ... to institute what we look upon as logging reforms.'[50]

Passage of the National Industrial Recovery Act (NIRA) generated optimism among American foresters that the opportunity to gain a foothold in corporate management had arrived. Signed into law by Franklin D. Roosevelt in 1933, the legislation encouraged trade associations to draft Codes of Fair Competition that created legal industry-wide price fixing and production limitation schemes. The timber industry code, which will come under more thorough analysis in Chapter 4, included Article X, a conservation clause pledging operators to cooperate with federal and state authorities in the development of less destructive logging practices. The measure, Fritz declared, was a potential 'catalyst for bringing foresters and lumbermen together.' Others shared this hopeful outlook. 'If I read the Code properly,' wrote one University of Washington graduate, 'each operator will have to carry not one, but several trained foresters to properly carry out the provisions of the Code.'[51]

Industrial self-regulation under the NIRA, as will be shown, failed as an agent of both recovery and conservation. Neither did the legislation open the door to private employment for foresters. The Joint Committee on Forest Conservation of the West Coast Lumbermen's Association and Pacific Northwest Loggers Association, responsible for Code administration on the west coast, did hire Russell Mills as divisional forester from his post as instructor in logging engineering at the University of Washington. Five additional professionals were employed by the Joint Committee to oversee the logging and fire protection practices of coastal firms between April 1934 and May 1935, at which time the United States Supreme Court ruled the NIRA unconstitutional. Although the Joint Committee decided to continue its administration of Article X on a voluntary basis after the NIRA was struck down, employing a few professionals, there is little evidence to suggest that this period witnessed any significant movement of foresters into industry. With the exception of Norman Jacobson, hired by the St. Paul and Tacoma Lumber Company to head a new forestry department, and perhaps a few other appointments, engineers continued to fill the technical demands of corporations on the American side of the Douglas fir region.

Opportunities within the public sector did increase markedly for a brief period after Roosevelt's election. Congressional approval of the Civilian Conservation Corps in 1933 created a huge demand for foresters to supervise the young unemployed men who planted trees, constructed fire lookout towers, and built roads and firebreaks as part of the federal government's forest conservation effort. Five new American schools of forestry opened in the 1930s, and as enrolments jumped nationally, foresters worried that supply would soon exceed demand. But for the moment, at least, prospects for the profession were brighter. In the spring of 1935 Winkenwerder informed a foreign colleague that 'forestry is booming here in the States due to President Roosevelt's recovery program and we receive many more requests for trained foresters than we can begin to fill.' By 1938, however, the New Deal had lost much of its impetus, and retrenchment in federal agencies again raised the spectre of widespread unemployment. The Joint Committee on Forest Conservation described the outlook for increased employment of graduates as 'pessimistic' that year. With under 20 percent of American foresters employed by corporations, educators were more anxious than ever to develop a professional base in industry.[52]

Over the next two decades, changes in the structure of the resource economy provided foresters with the opportunity they so eagerly awaited. By the time World War II brought the Great Depression to an end, many firms faced shortages of old-growth timber. Land acquisition programs, a healthy market for forest products, and increased dependence on public timber generated a demand for technical forestry expertise that invigorated the relationship between universities and industry. 'Never was the time better,' observed Norman Jacobson in 1941, 'for the university to step right out and really cooperate with business.' Educators on the west coast agreed that these were 'days of maximum opportunity' for their schools.[53]

Operators first set out the terms under which they would welcome foresters into the private sector. J.P. Weyerhaeuser, the St. Paul and Tacoma Lumber Company's E.G. Griggs, and Peter Schafer of the Schafer Brothers Logging Company warned the SAF's Puget Sound Section in 1944 that opportunities for members existed 'only where and as long as they can sell and keep sold forestry practice as economics permits.' Industry representatives also stressed that a mere shuffling of foresters trained for government service into their ranks did not meet their needs. 'The college courses in technical forestry,' remarked a trade association forest engineer, 'are not designed to make students useful in private industry.'[54]

Despite operators' dissatisfaction with their training, an increasing number of University of Washington graduates entered the field of industrial forestry during the early 1940s. Anxious to gain an understanding of corporate expectations, administrators assigned J. Kenneth Pearce to survey executives. Pearce concluded that graduates possessed insufficient understanding of 'the complex economic structure in which industry functions.' He also reported unhappiness among lumbermen with the 'one-sided theories learned on campus [that] were not conducive to loyalty to one's employer.'[55]

At Oregon State, Dean Walter F. McCulloch revamped the forestry program in 1947. During his tenure as Oregon's assistant state forester, McCulloch had heard graduates criticized as 'dilettantes rather than men hardened to the stern realities of forest economics.' Accordingly, the institution developed a new forest management curriculum oriented less toward 'classic theoretical applications to public forests' than to 'workable principles of managing both public and private forests.' A new course in industrial forest administration, mandatory for all management majors, ensured that even those destined for state and federal employment would learn to 'appreciate the problems faced by the industry.' Finally, forestry students received encouragement to take business courses.[56]

The logging engineering curriculum at Oregon State underwent revision as well, to take advantage of expanding opportunities in the layout and administration of logging plans on public lands. Firms operating on the national forests, for example, found it useful to have their own experts to negotiate the terms of timber sale contracts with Forest Service staff. The most forward-looking corporations began making a marginal commitment to natural restocking of timberlands at this time, and passage of the 1941 Oregon Forest Conservation Act and 1945 Washington Forest Practices Act to head off the threat of more meaningful federal regulation encouraged the employment of engineers with a modicum of forestry knowledge. Thus, Oregon State University administrators increased the forest management component of engineers' education and renamed the department to Forest Engineering to reflect 'the change from logging only, to present day industrial forest management.'[57]

In 1947 Walter McCulloch reported that it had finally become profitable for corporations to employ foresters to 'evaluate, acquire, and manage accessible cutover lands.' His claim that they also participated in the planning of cutting operations falls largely into the category of wishful thinking, but graduation figures illustrate the rise of industrial forestry. Oregon State University's 1949 senior class totalled 84 students: 56 in forest management, 12 in forest engineering, and 16 in forest products. Of the total, 31 joined federal forest agencies, an equal number found positions with firms, and 10 began careers with the Oregon State Department of Forestry. By this time about 125 industrial foresters were employed in Oregon, more than 200 over the entire American side of the Douglas fir region, and a further 75 worked for some forty consulting concerns.[58]

The 1950s brought further expansion in the new branch of the forestry profession, with large integrated firms providing most of the openings. One company alone had forty-seven forest management positions, and at one point in the 1960s Weyerhaeuser employed fifty-nine University of Washington forest professionals. Along with Crown Zellerbach, Georgia-Pacific, and the St. Regis Paper Company, Weyerhaeuser regularly contacted universities to secure the services of graduates equipped to 'apply under field conditions the academic principles, practices and theories of land management, forest protection, and harvesting methods.'[59]

In British Columbia industrial forestry developed under similar conditions at roughly the same pace, receiving an additional boost when the provincial state adopted a sustained-yield program in 1947. Instruction at the University of British Columbia retained its engineering focus until the mid-1930s, with a majority of the thirty-one graduates between 1923 and 1933 finding employment with public agencies. The Forest Branch's F.D. Mulholland saw little reason for optimism in the midst of the Depression. 'Whether there is any advance for forestry in this province remains to be seen,' he reported to an Empire Forestry Association member.[60]

Concern over forest devastation peaked during the late 1930s, however, as Chief Forester Ernest C. Manning followed US Forest Service leaders in campaigning for more effective regulation of logging practices. Although the agitation failed to produce meaningful reforms, it probably contributed to awareness of the University of British Columbia's shortcomings as a centre of forestry training. In 1936 Dr. Percy M. Barr, a former Forest Branch researcher then teaching at the University of California, was appointed to review the program and propose changes.

Barr concluded that instruction at the university was 'not broad enough to meet the needs of the industry,' and recommended that forest engineering 'be abandoned as an exclusive approach to professional forestry employment.' He proposed a major revision, involving an expansion of the curriculum to provide three paths to a Bachelor's degree in Forestry. With the implementation of Barr's plan the next year, students had the choice of three options, spending four years in one of the departments of Botany, Economics, or Commerce before a fifth year of study devoted to advanced forestry subjects in the Department of Applied Science. The training of forest engineers remained unchanged, with graduates receiving a Bachelor of Applied Science degree.[61]

The revamped University of British Columbia program integrated forestry education more closely with the changing nature of the resource economy, but within a decade, depletion of the province's forests led to the adoption of a new tenure system and further modification of the curriculum. British Columbia's 1944-45 Royal Commission on Forest Resources provided the key stimulus to industrial forestry, leading to 1947 legislation that permitted the amalgamation of Crown timber and private land into sustained-yield units to be operated by corporations under government supervision. The relationship between state and industry in the introduction and management of the new Tree Farm Licences will be discussed in Chapter 6; here I wish to confine analysis to the impact of this development on professional prospects and education.

A number of firms employed foresters soon after the announcement of the royal commission, both to demonstrate their commitment to resource stewardship and take advantage of technical expertise in dealing with the inquiry. Many hired professionals after the commission's deliberations to prepare applications for the new tenures. As early as 1945 the Forest Service's F.D. Mulholland noted 'the increasing number of university [trained] foresters who are working with industry.' After the amendment of the Forest Act, Chief Forester C.D. Orchard reported that qualified men were 'much in demand,' and most would have agreed with Thomas Wright that 'industrial forestry now has its greatest opportunity.' By 1955, twenty-two Tree Farm Licences had been awarded, most to large integrated firms required by law to employ at least one member of the Association of British Columbia Professional Foresters, the professional registration body established shortly after passage of the new Forest Act.[62]

Testimony at the royal commission made it clear that the calibre of professional education at the University of British Columbia, which concentrated advanced forestry subjects in a single fifth year of study, no longer met the needs of either government or industry. 'Interests here,' Orchard informed an American colleague, 'are very much concerned about the type of training the university has been giving and ... are very much interested in having it improved.' Forestry Department head John Lierch testified that facilities were inadequate, urging that the department be raised to faculty status. Royal Commissioner Gordon Sloan recommended in his 1945 report that the university act on Lierch's proposal.[63]

The following year the administration approved a plan submitted by Lierch, implemented in 1947, that established Bachelor of Science options in Technical Forestry, Forest Business Administration, and Chemical Wood Products. Students in all fields began courses in basic sciences and forestry during the second year of study. The Technical Forestry option was designed to train professionals in silviculture and forest management for careers in government service and industrial forestry. Those in Forest Business Administration would enter 'the business end of the forest industries.' Forest Engineers continued to graduate with a Bachelor of Applied Science degree, but received additional instruction in silviculture.[64]

By 1950, when forestry achieved faculty status at the university, the province's largest firms sponsored four teaching positions, and within five years industry funded half of the ten chairs of instruction. As in the Pacific Northwest, graduation figures reflect the growing corporate demand for forest professionals. The institution granted double the number of degrees between 1949 and 1952 as in the school's previous history, and 52 percent of the graduates found employment in industry. Perhaps more significant is the ratio of engineers to those with Bachelor of Forestry degrees. Although 85 engineers graduated between 1950 and 1952, only 30 such degrees were issued during the 1953-64 period. Meanwhile, there were 634 graduates in the three Bachelor of Science options between 1950 and 1964. In 1962 the forest engineering program was dropped because of the difficulty in meeting professional standards for forestry and engineering in a single degree, leading to the establishment of a Forest Harvesting option in the Faculty of Forestry.[65]

The increasingly pronounced 'corporate identity' of forestry education throughout the Douglas fir region is directly attributable to changes in the character of the timber economy. The Pacific coast was the continent's last logging frontier, and forest depletion had reached sufficient proportions to prompt land acquisition programs among those firms with plans for future operation. The growing importance of pulp and paper contributed to the new pattern of control. Pulp plants demanded huge capital expenditures, and firms contemplating the erection of integrated logging, sawmilling, plywood, and fibre enterprises sought to consolidate holdings to ensure long-term survival.[66]

Resource scarcity and corporate integration, in short, generated a new managerial context in which executives required precise information concerning 'the location, extent and productive capacity' of private timberland.[67] The primary responsibility of the corporate forestry department, wrote one forester, was 'to be prepared to advise top management ... about its timber growing lands and the forest resources on them.' Another described his role as 'collecting, analyzing, synchronizing and reporting the silvicultural aspects of forestry information.' For William B. Greeley, secretary-manager of the West Coast Lumbermen's Association, this 'process of fact gathering' lay at the heart of industrial forestry.[68] Foresters also supervised planting activities, protection plans, and engaged in a good deal of public relations work. But as will become evident in Part 2, they had marginal influence on the conduct of logging, which continued to be ruled largely by engineering rather than silvicultural principles.

Weyerhaeuser pioneered in utilizing the skills of industry's new efficiency experts to produce technical information for more systematic land management. In 1936 that firm's directors ordered a survey of cutover areas prior to rendering a decision on whether property taxes should be paid. A report based on this field study in conjunction with Forest Service data prompted directors to authorize payment of back-taxes on productive lands rather than allow reversion to county ownership. By 1939 the company employed six foresters, two forest statisticians, and numerous summer crews at Longview, and operational maps indicated the type and degree of forest cover, logging history, and fire hazard status.[69]

During the 1940s the skills of foresters in land and forest evaluation came into widespread demand. Postwar expansion of the construction industry, particularly in home building, along with further development of the wood-fibre and plywood industries led to a marked rise in stumpage prices, which stimulated interest in small tracts of private timber as well as logged-off land. The Simpson Logging Company began acquiring cutover land adjacent to its Mason County holdings in 1938. Anticipating approval of the 1944 Sustained-Yield Management Act, allowing creation of cooperative units combining national forest timber and private land, the firm then initiated a land classification project. Logging Superintendent George Drake explained to Hugo Winkenwerder that the Simpson proposal to the US Forest Service made it necessary to do 'more intensive and detailed cruising' than past practice. In 1946 the investment paid off with formation of the Shelton Cooperative Sustained-Yield Unit, the only one of its type, giving the company exclusive access to a portion of Olympic National Forest timber. During the next decade Simpson became a major player in the scramble for timberland, purchasing the holdings of the Schafer Brothers Logging Company at Grays Harbour before expanding into Oregon and northern California.[70]

The St. Paul and Tacoma Lumber Company's new forestry department was equally active in providing data for long-range planning. By 1939 Norman Jacobson and his staff had surveyed and typed the firm's logged-off lands, illustrating the age classes of young growth as the basis of a logging plan to the year 2008. In 1950 Jacobson began preparing an annual analysis of timber designed to depict the raw material supply available to the company's plants for five and ten year intervals. Three years later St. Paul and Tacoma president Corydon Wagner instructed Jacobson to compile a single large map amalgamating data on the species, age classes, and degree of stocking of cutover lands, providing a comprehensive overview of the operation.[71]

Integrated firms with multiple, diverse manufacturing plants became the leaders in systematic land management, assigning foresters to compile inventories that presented information on potential products, growth rates, and the status of second-growth stands. In 1950, for example, Weyerhaeuser's Longview logging operation supplied raw material for three sawmills, two pulp mills, and a plywood plant and planing mill, in addition to wood briquette and bark reduction facilities. In British Columbia the 1951 merger of Bloedel, Stewart, and Welch Ltd. and the H.R. MacMillan Export Company into MacMillan Bloedel produced a huge organization with control over 747,000 acres of timberland, six sawmills, two pulp mills, two plywood mills, two shingle mills, and a plant for conversion of cedar waste into fuel logs, all fed by six logging operations. The Crown Zellerbach corporation erected a similarly integrated structure. By 1957 pulp mills at Ocean Falls and Elk Falls, a sawmill and plywood plant at Fraser Mills, and a Richmond box factory utilized logs from the firm's numerous logging sites. For the integrated firm, observed H.R. MacMillan executive Don McColl, 'successful management control depends upon reliable facts concerning all details of the timber and ground' to achieve 'reduction of waste and disposal to the best market advantage.'[72]

As an average stand might produce lumber, plywood, and pulp products, these corporations required accurate data to coordinate logging plans with forest and market conditions. After the formation of the Shelton Cooperative Sustained-Yield Unit, the Simpson Logging Company instituted a monthly accounting of the type, species, and quality of logs arriving at its sawmills, plywood mills, and sash and door plant. By 1951 Thomas Wright, who replaced John Liersch as dean at the University of British Columbia and later joined Canadian Forest Products Ltd., had identified the age classes of timber held by that firm in the Nimpkish Valley on Vancouver Island and compiled this data in growth and yield tables. 'I believe this information will be very useful in helping to determine the sequence of cutting in our old-growth stands,' Wright informed a government forester. 'We have already formulated some general long range management plans which are influenced in a considerable degree by the age and thriftiness of the standing timber.'[73]

The definition of operating units in accordance with natural boundaries enabled managers to exert greater control over all phases of their current and future operations. These were 'comparable to farm fields, factory departments or railway divisions,' asserted Percy Barr. Like the factory manager who maintained a balance between semi-manufactured goods, inventory, and shipments, the industrial forester sought to 'maintain a balance between timber growth, growing stock, and cut of saw logs.' While there is no doubt a good deal of hyperbole in such statements, it seems clear that managerial efficiency came to take on a new meaning in the coastal forest industry during this period, as executives strove to maximize current revenues in a more complex industrial structure and place their firms in a strategic position for the second-growth economy.[74]

Since the 1930s, increasingly sophisticated techniques for forest professionals to utilize in accumulating information for engineering and forest management purposes have become available. Two of the most significant involve the application of aerial photography and computers to analyze the topographic and biological characteristics of industrial timberlands. The science of photogrammetry has accelerated the rate at which forest inventories and topographic maps can be compiled and integrated into logging plans. Computers have served in a similar fashion, providing rapid and accurate data processing. Research by universities, public agencies, and industry in the development of biological and financial models for guiding investment decisions, and digital terrain simulation programs for the planning of logging operations represent more recent efforts to apply computer analysis to forest exploitation.

First utilized for forestry purposes in Quebec in 1919, aerial photography proved less useful on the west coast because of dense tree cover on mountainous terrain. Operators in the Douglas fir region expressed interest in the technique during the 1920s, but it wasn't until the following decade that it came into practical application by the BC Forest Branch and Pacific Northwest Forest Experiment Station in forest inventory work. Foresters at the latter research institute concluded that aerial photography possessed great potential in timberland analysis, but required further refinement.[75]

Nevertheless, prior to and during World War II, firms such as Weyerhaeuser, the West Fork Logging Company, the Hawley Pulp and Paper Company, and the H.R. MacMillan Export Company found aerial photographs useful in obtaining a 'general picture' of their timberlands and logging operations. The development of the science of photogrammetry for military purposes during the war, featuring the use of stereoscopic instruments to measure distances and plot contours on photographs or maps, dramatically increased the utility of aerial photographs for operational planning. The introduction of the Multiplex plotter after the war was a key to the development of the procedure. By 1948 the Kendall B. Wood engineering firm of Portland had purchased one of these instruments designed to transfer information from aerial photographs to topographic maps.[76]

The initial stage in this process involved fieldwork to determine the elevation of dominant topographical control points and identify appropriate flightlines. Photographs taken during the flight were developed and aerial mosaics of the area created. Crews then returned to the field to mark these points on the photographs, which were then returned to the office where projectors providing a three-dimensional image enabled the Multiplex operator to plot topographical information from the pictures onto the final product, a large contour map. The Wood Company conducted mapping projects for the Long-Bell Lumber Company, Crown Zellerbach, and Rayonier, among others, and between 1947 and 1949 photographed over

500,000 acres of Pacific Northwest timber holdings. In 1948 a major air survey firm established an office in Vancouver, bringing this managerial aid to British Columbia.[77]

The University of Washington's Gordon Marckworth described the 1940s as a period of 'phenomenal' progress in aerial photography and interpretation. During the next decade this method of mapping became standard practice in the region. According to J. Kenneth Pearce, engineers found photogrammetric maps 'indispensable in their work in planning the layout of logging operations.' Even in cases where large-scale logging plan maps were not created, technicians viewed images under a stereoscope to locate topographic features that influenced road construction, landing location, and setting boundaries. At the very least, one engineer observed, they 'give us an idea about the adaptability of each show for different kinds of logging.'[78]

Professionals found aerial photographs useful in the preparation of forest inventories. Although compilation of accurate volume per acre statistics proved impossible, the images enabled foresters to make gross estimates of timber density and species composition. On large holdings, aerial photography provided a fast and inexpensive method of obtaining an overview and identifying areas requiring more intensive investigation. Thus, wrote the head of a Vancouver air survey firm, 'it remains only for the forester to examine those productive areas in which he is interested.' Here was one source of the technique's popularity – a reduction in the amount and expense of fieldwork. A study at the University of British Columbia's Experimental Forest demonstrated that mapping by air cost $.60 per acre, over one dollar less than traditional ground methods. Firms attracted by the prospect of 'reducing the cost of field examinations of the larger areas' accepted the sacrifice in accuracy. A Rayonier engineer explained to Pearce that a multiplex map depicting a portion of that firm's holdings was 'perhaps insufficient for the best logging engineering needs,' but 'the speed and a $.65 to $.75 per acre cost will compensate for the difference.'[79]

Forestry schools and government agencies responded quickly to demand for training programs in air photo interpretation. By 1947 the University of Washington had begun devoting attention to the subject in advanced forest management and logging engineering courses. Shortly thereafter the Oregon State University School of Forestry and the Pacific Northwest Forest and Range Experiment Station jointly sponsored the first annual five-day short course in air survey methods. Twenty-five forest professionals attended the inaugural session, including personnel from British Columbia's Powell River Company. The University of Washington initiated a similar course in 1952, drawing a large number of industrial representatives.[80]

Aerial photography enhanced timber capital's planning process, providing a cost-efficient means of preparing maps with 'all possible detail plotted for operational uses.' But while the technique was a valuable asset, forestry and engineering problems continued to require considerable field analysis. The development of orthographic photography in the 1960s allowed for more accurate measurement of horizontal distances, but mapping conducted on this basis could not overcome the problem of dense forest cover, preventing precise determination of topographical conditions. 'Although today's maps are marvels of representation,' admitted engineers attending a 1974 planning seminar, 'there is no substitute for going over the ground and actually looking.'[81]

The forest industry's experience with the use of computer technology began during the latter 1950s, producing a similar record of qualified success. Digital computers received their original application in the compilation and analysis of inventory data. In 1957 the prominent Portland consulting firm of Mason, Bruce, and Girard contracted for access to the facilities of International Business Machines (IBM) in that city to increase the speed and accuracy of timber volume calculation. Data gathered in the field was recorded on sheets, turned over to IBM, and transferred to punch cards for rapid processing. Professionals became increasingly alert to the advantages the computer offered for application to a range of technical procedures. After attending a University of British Columbia programming course in 1959 one forester concluded that 'any forester ... who has some occasion to engage in statistical analysis, mensuration studies, milling studies, production studies and forest finance calculations, operations research problems, etc., is well advised to avail himself of the opportunity to learn programming for digital computers.'[82]

During the 1960s the Simpson Logging Company, Crown Zellerbach, MacMillan Bloedel, and the St. Regis Paper Company established their own IBM facilities for forest inventory analysis. The development of a program for analyzing lumber recovery data by a researcher at the Pacific Northwest Forest and Range Experiment Station extended the computer's usefulness, and Simpson's Industrial Engineering Group applied this principle to the creation of a system routing various sizes and grades of logs to different plants for maximum recovery of value in the form of plywood, lumber, or chips.[83]

By the late 1960s many forest management activities within public agencies and major corporations were being conducted in a 'computerized atmosphere,' placing pressure on older professionals to upgrade their skills. 'All foresters,' W.F. McCulloch suggested, 'should know enough to appreciate ... computer possibilities and limitations in the field of forestry operations.' Particularly intriguing were the efforts of researchers to develop computer models capable of simulating forest growth, enabling foresters to calculate future yields under various management options. Such a study was initiated at the Oregon State University School of Forestry in 1961, and the University of British Columbia's J.H.G. Smith undertook research along this line later that decade. Inadequate biological and economic data hindered these projects, but in 1968 Weyerhaeuser began using computers in systems analysis to forecast forest management options. Weyerhaeuser vice-president Harry Morgan boasted that the integration of biological and financial models enabled the firm to 'measure the investment required for each of our biological alternatives and to forecast the potential return on that particular investment.'[84]

In the engineering field, public forest agencies utilized computers for the rapid calculation of survey coordinates and analysis of road construction problems in the early 1960s; then in 1970 Hewlett Packard began marketing a program that heralded the arrival of automated planning in logging system layout. Although just beyond the study's time-frame, it is worthwhile analyzing this modern approach to logging engineering. Researchers at the Pacific Northwest Forest and Range Experiment Station devoted considerable effort to the development of computerized timber harvest design methods. 'No other single advance has revolutionized forest engineering to the extent of desk-top computing facilities,' wrote one US Forest Service engineer. 'An entirely new approach to logging planning is possible.'[85]

Interactive software for digital terrain simulation generated a scale perspective of timber tracts on a computer's display screen, and the potential for an office-based planning procedure. Survey coordinates and contour data gathered in the field were entered to create a three-dimensional representation of the area. The engineer then selected prospective landings and setting boundaries that conformed with the characteristics of available logging equipment and terrain. After choosing a particular landing location and entering the technical specifications of a yarding system, such as spar height, maximum yarding distance, and the necessary line deflection, the technician instructed the program to project appropriate setting layouts, finally plotting various options on the topographic map.[86]

Weyerhaeuser and MacMillan Bloedel cooperated with universities and public forest agencies in the development of these systems, and by the 1970s software packages were available 'to analyze a variety of logging engineering problems from the office.' Although the early programs presented 'powerful applications' in planning, computing system requirements and the shortage of trained personnel limited their use. Moreover, two University of British Columbia researchers reported in 1976 that the data base provided by the contour map was 'not sufficiently accurate' to permit the solution of engineering problems from the office. The purpose of the digital terrain simulation model, they concluded, 'is not to produce final plans but rather to reduce the large number of alternatives to a few most promising ones that will be selected and modified after comprehensive ground checking.' The engineer's most important qualities, MacMillan Bloedel's manager of engineering and development remarked, were still 'a pair of sturdy legs, good eyes and good wind' in addition to a detailed knowledge of logging systems.[87]

Despite the innovations generated by the corporate search for administrative control over the conduct of forest exploitation, managerial efficiency has not attained the precision possible in the factory setting. Aerial photography and computerized data processing provide technically advanced planning procedures, while environmental concerns have increased the number of variables demanding consideration by forest professionals. Operational management in the logging industry has become more sophisticated since the first university-trained engineers entered the woods, but representations of coastal forestland remain inexact.[88]

Scientific Management and the Forest Industry

The managerial component of industry's factory regime involved the production of expertise under the terms of a mutually beneficial relationship forged by corporations and administrators of the region's forestry schools. The engineers and foresters who emerged from the universities comprised a formally educated stratum of employees possessing technical knowledge needed for efficiency in the exploitation of workers and nature. Conflict over the character of their training and the degree of influence they wielded in management existed, but no one disagreed with C.D. Orchard when British Columbia's chief forester declared that one of the state's primary responsibilities was to provide industry with 'competent technically trained personnel.'[89]

Future work hopefully will probe more fully into the occupational and professional world of these engineers and foresters than has been possible here. This study has attempted to demonstrate that their essential function, in common with other white-collar workers, was to assemble and process information demanded by directors and executives. From the early topographic maps and forest inventories to the recent computerized planning procedures, university graduates have applied their talents to furnishing data for investment decisions. Engineers played a more direct role in the exertion of control over workers than foresters, whose understanding of natural processes became valuable as a direct result of the deforestation accomplished under the factory mode of production in logging.

Harry Braverman and Alfred D. Chandler have, from quite different perspectives, depicted management as a relatively unproblematic process. Braverman's analysis of Taylorism emphasizes the subjugation of labour by capital through the separation of conception and execution in work. Chandler devotes little attention to relations of power between employers and workers, focusing instead on the development of managerial structures to coordinate activities within the firm. For both, the identification of inefficiency is followed closely by the imposition of procedures that bring managerial control to new heights. According to Braverman, scientific management separates craft workers from their knowledge of production, awarding capital with control over the labour process. Chandler's managers triumph over the market through integration of raw material supplies, processing, distribution, and marketing functions in the large multi-unit enterprise.

My analysis of management goals and structures in the coastal forest industry draws more heavily upon the insights provided by Braverman and the neo-Marxist school of labour process analysis than Chandlerian organizational theory, but attempts to avoid the determinism of both by recognizing the difficulty of imposing centralized administrative controls over an extractive process that must constantly shift its base of operations in a complex and unstable natural setting. Management in the Douglas fir region continues to require constant scrutiny and surveillance at the point of production. But the ever-present obstacles to managerial efficiency should obscure neither the steady increase in corporate control, nor the societal implications of a division of labour featuring a 'middle level' of educated professionals situated between the executive ranks and production workers.[90]

A brief glance back at logging engineering as it reflects the impact of scientific management on North American business practices and social organization clarifies these issues. Although Frederick W. Taylor himself had no direct contact with the industry, a fundamental tenet of his management philosophy, that the conceptualization of work should be the domain of trained engineers, manifested itself in response to the complexities of mass production. The logging engineer, declared American forester Judson Clark in 1915, was a 'specialist' whose responsibility was to determine 'the method of operation best suited to any combination of stand and terrain ... leaving the less difficult task of operation to cheaper men.' The new divide between the labour performed by educated professionals and manual workers also drew the approval of Weyerhaeuser's Minot Davis, who hailed the creation of a 'considerable and essential difference' between those who planned operations and the workers who executed these plans.[91]

Scientific management, Daniel Nelson suggests, had marginal influence on the nature of work because of the piecemeal manner in which industrialists introduced reforms. More recently, Paul Thompson and David McHugh argue that Taylorism should be seen as an element of a broader movement toward systematic administration 'implemented in a variety of forms and ... in a selective manner' rather than a 'coherent and total package.' They go on to assert the existence of 'a widespread, if uneven, diffusion of key aspects of Taylorist practices in industrial societies during the early twentieth century.' My analysis of managerial change in the west coast logging industry confirms this perception, and lends support to Judith Merkle's conclusion that Taylorism has had 'a profound and permanent impact on American industrial management.'[92]

Engineers and foresters occupied a similar position in the managerial ranks, with a few of the most able and ambitious making their way up the career ladder to executive status at the head of logging and land management departments. But one element of the knowledge these experts possessed posed an implicit challenge to the corporate concept of efficiency. Foresters, and to a lesser extent engineers, held sufficient understanding of forest growth and renewal to satisfy public as well as private needs if permitted to exercise this expertise. Unfortunately, the factory regime in coastal logging did not easily accommodate conservation principles. Ultimately, the challenge of making science relevant to the conduct of corporate forest practice became a matter for government action, a subject explored in Part 2 of this book.

Part 2
Clearcutting, Conservation, and the State

Introduction

The second and final part of this account shifts analysis from the class relationship embedded in the industry's factory regime to the arena of resource politics, integrating the study of clearcutting as a method of timber exploitation, the accumulation of knowledge concerning the technique's impact on forest renewal, and the relations between industry and governments in the regulation of forest practices. The goal is to contribute to an understanding of North American natural resource industries by situating the policy-making process in its technological and scientific context, complementing the excellent scholarship on forest administration by Robbins, Nelles, Gray, Hirt, Langston, Wynn, and Parenteau.[1]

Closely associated with the New Left historiography of the American progressive era, the corporate liberalism model of business-government relations emphasizes the capacity of firms to shape public policies in pursuit of market stability.[2] This tradition also has much in common with the orthodox Marxist depiction of the state in capitalist societies as a simple tool of big business. More recent neo-Marxist thinking questions the instrumentalist assumption that governments invariably act to the benefit of private enterprise. Rather, these analysts assert that the state, consisting of administrative managers and elected politicians, exhibits a 'relative autonomy' in its relationship to the capitalist class.[3]

In serving the interests of capitalists as a whole, this theory assumes, state personnel must have the freedom to act in ways that particular business interests may find objectionable. Even in the promotion of economic development – the most important function of any government – divisions within ownership ranks prevent agencies from satisfying the demands of all. A more significant source of autonomy derives from the state's role in legitimating the inequality inherent to class-based societies. Some policies may offer an opportunity to promote capital accumulation and legitimation simultaneously, but frequently the potential contradiction between these objectives dictates some sacrifice of one to the other.[4] This tension is particularly evident in the case of environmental regulation, which poses a challenge to the corporate mode of production, requires expenditures directors would typically reject, and often runs counter to the state's commitment to economic growth.[5]

Application of the relative autonomy model to the study of welfare and collective bargaining reform by national governments has proven insightful, but its relevance to the workings of regional levels of government – be they state or provincial – seems less certain.[6] This account of forest practice regulation supports a conception of British Columbia, Washington, and Oregon as 'client states.'[7] Highly dependent upon the revenues generated by resource corporations for financial health, they tended to define the public interest in terms of the corporate interest. In subordinating genuine conservation to the encouragement of investment in the forestry sector, governments proved incapable of achieving more than an endorsement of forest practice standards already observed by leading firms. 'Legislation has always followed practice,' one manager explained in 1953. 'The forest laws of the western states and British Columbia have been created to conform with practices which the most forward-looking members of this industry had previously adopted.'[8]

The history of government intervention in the Douglas fir region between 1880 and 1965 breaks down into three periods, dominated throughout by conflict over the nature of scientific knowledge and the attempt to have minimal requirements for restocking forestland introduced in cutting practice regulations. Largely the domain of public resource agencies, research was permitted to inform public policy only if it accorded with the wishes of corporate and government leaders whose shared preoccupation with capital accumulation prevented meaningful integration of science and forest law. As sociologists of science have observed, in order to achieve legal status scientific knowledge must become linked to the power of dominant economic and political interests.[9] A divided forestry profession provided another obstacle to the enactment of the sort of legislation needed to limit the destructiveness of industry's factory regime. The profession's militant minority pushed unsuccessfully for reforms to reconcile the conflict between private and public interests, against the wishes of the moderate majority who held that the state should confine itself to a cooperative role in fire control and stabilization of the timber economy.

The period to 1930 witnessed the emergence of clearcutting as the dominant mode of production, the initiation of research into the ecology of Douglas fir, and the establishment of cooperative relations between government and industry. Small openings created by the ground-lead method of logging exposed cutover land to sunlight, creating optimum regeneration conditions for this shade-intolerant species. The perception of these forests as decadent and unproductive contributed to foresters' enthusiasm for clearcutting, equating rapid removal with good forest management. While the US Forest Service made provision for natural restocking on the national forests, on corporate holdings in the Pacific Northwest and British Columbia's mix of public and private lands, operators' interest in forestry did not extend beyond protecting mature timber from fire. Early twentieth century state and provincial forest policy in the west committed public funds to fire protection, but imposed no silvicultural controls.

The introduction of overhead logging technologies encouraged continuous clearcutting, undermining the forest's regenerative capacity. Although a fallacious theory of Douglas fir regeneration legitimated the practice, during the early 1920s American lumbermen faced a challenge to their property rights when Gifford Pinchot campaigned for federal regulation of private timberlands. However, assisted by Chief Forester William Greeley, industry successfully manipulated the political process to ensure that federal funding in support of state fire protection programs was not accompanied by logging practice controls.

British Columbia experienced no equivalent of the early American regulation debate, but by 1930 researchers on both sides of the border had identified the operators' use of sophisticated, mass production technologies as a major factor in the failure of the rapidly expanding area of cutover land to take on a second crop. Professional and public awareness of the role technology played in the creation of barren lands set the stage for a challenge to the efficiencies of the factory regime in the Douglas fir region during the decade.

One source of the clearcutting critique originated with operators themselves. When lumber demand collapsed with the onset of the Great Depression, many in Washington and Oregon adapted the caterpillar tractor to logging, selectively extracting only the high-quality Douglas fir from their holdings. Similar economic concerns prompted the US Forest Service to develop a model of selective timber management and experiment with selective logging on national forest timber sales. Its advocates perceived the method as a cure for overproduction and a basis for eventual conversion to sustained-yield forestry, but the agency's silviculturalists remained firmly committed to clearcutting, seeing in the traditional technique a mechanized equivalent to fire – nature's way of clearing the land for a new Douglas fir forest.

While western foresters grappled with the economic and ecological implications of tree selection logging, Depression-era leaders of the US Forest Service took their cue from Franklin D. Roosevelt's New Deal, joining with other reformers in a revived campaign for federal regulation. The president secured Congressional approval for a wide-ranging approach to recovery, featuring industrial self-regulation to bring disorganized, chaotic sectors of the economy under control. Presidential and Forest Service pressure resulted in the incorporation of a conservation clause in the agreement governing the timber industry, but trade association control over its drafting and enforcement ensured that the forest practice rules posed no threat to efficiency in corporate resource exploitation. However, Forest Service leaders continued to press for regulation after the US Supreme Court struck down the New Deal experiment in regulation. Thus, by the outbreak of World War II, executives in the west had determined that industry's best defence against federal restrictions on clearcutting lay in a program of symbolic state legislation.

British Columbia operators also withstood the reform impulse with no infringement on their managerial prerogatives. With most of the timber under provincial ownership, resource policies were developed with no threat of federal interference. But perhaps to a greater extent than in the American context, the clearcutting critique reinforced support for the selective alternative. From the political left and a range of civic groups in both urban and rural centres, conservationists called for an outright ban on overhead logging systems. Chief Forester Ernest Manning concluded that selective logging warranted study rather than enforcement, then launched a campaign to achieve a moderate reform of clearcutting practices. His proposal gained sufficient public support to produce amendments to the Forest Act, but government's preoccupation with revenue over conservation prevented the introduction of regulations requiring operators to reserve timber as a seed resource for restocking clearcuts.

The Douglas fir industry's factory regime emerged intact from the policy debates of the 1930s. Over the next twenty-five years the region's corporate and government leaders exhibited a firm commitment to its protection and enhancement. Oregon and Washington operators proved very adept at working with local legislatures, shaping the content and passage of state forest practice acts in an effort to demonstrate the irrelevance of proposals for state administration of federal silvicultural standards. That these 'seed tree' acts owed more to political considerations than a genuine corporate commitment to conservation is evident when viewed in their scientific context. Research on the national forests by US Forest Service silviculturalists left no doubt that their provisions would not foster adequate restocking under most conditions.

Dominant firms in the Pacific Northwest states initiated land acquisition programs and relied increasingly on the national forests to ensure a long-term timber supply. Public ownership in British Columbia restricted the amount of timber available for purchase there, a decisive factor in the provincial state's adoption of a sustained-yield policy in 1947. According to Chief Forester C.D. Orchard's vision, BC Forest Service approval of cutting and reforestation procedures on Tree Farm Licences would ensure a melding of the public and private interest. However, evidence accumulated quickly that his faith in large-scale private enterprise was misplaced. Management plans bore only a casual resemblance to what occurred in the woods, government foresters commented frequently on the constant vigilance required to keep logging practice on the tenures at acceptable standards, and mill requirements carried more weight in the determination of allowable cuts than did sustainability.

Internal criticism of corporate conduct on British Columbia's Tree Farm Licences grew in volume as advances in artificial reforestation techniques and a late-1950s slump in the wood products economy encouraged firms on both sides of the border to reject cutting practices that fostered natural reforestation in favour of continuous clearcutting. Although industry's new plantation style of forest management was based upon expectations of higher profits to be derived from more intense resource exploitation, the introduction of expanded planting programs to restock massive clearcuts allowed executives to advertise the modern factory regime in coastal logging as a culmination of scientific progress in the harvesting and renewal of the timber crop.

The continuous clearcutting associated with the plantation model emerged with no interference from state and provincial forest law. Crafted from the start by industry and government leaders to enhance rather than challenge the corporate concept of efficiency, regulation in the Douglas fir region never intruded upon operators' freedom to utilize technologies as dictated by class, market, and environmental factors.

3
Clearcutting, Forest Science, and Regulation, 1880-1930

Between 1880 and 1930 the development of steam-powered logging systems created a factory regime with important consequences for the workplace relationship; equally significant was the influence of technological change on forest science, cutting practice, and business-government relations during these years. Patterns established during this formative period continue to structure human interaction with the forest west of the Cascade mountains, and an awareness of their emergence is essential to an understanding of modern forestry issues.

This period in North American forest history is associated with the emergence of a movement devoted to conservation of the continent's natural resources. Unstable markets, overproduction, and intense competition created a wasteful and migratory pattern of logging. The conservation movement devoted itself to curtailing this destructive style of exploitation, but the rhetorical crusade against rapacious corporate power masked a more fundamental devotion to the principles of scientific management. Conservation, Samuel Hays has shown, was given a very specific definition by the aspiring professionals and business interests that dominated the movement in the United States. In essence, the term came to mean not preservation but 'rational planning to promote efficient development and use of all natural resources.'[1]

Such a technocratic vision promised to elevate experts in land use to new levels of influence just as it met the needs of large corporations capable of providing the 'efficiency, stability of operations, and long-range planning inherent to the conservation ideal.' Thus, foresters and lumbermen in the United States could agree on the wisdom of creating forest reserves and awarding jurisdiction to Gifford Pinchot's US Forest Service in 1905 because these policies met mutual objectives. Foresters gained administrative control over millions of acres of timberland, while owners with large holdings welcomed the prospect of market stability, which withdrawal from purchase might achieve without sacrificing long-term access to public supplies. That the national forests also appeared to represent a triumph of the 'people' against private interests only increased their appeal to American progressives during an era of widespread suspicion of corporate power.[2]

The conservation movement in the Canadian context exhibited a similar preoccupation with scientific resource management. Unlike in the United States, however, where decisions concerning land were overwhelmingly a private matter, in Canada public ownership and control of natural resources by the provinces was the rule. The question of private versus public ownership, so central to the American experience, was not present to energize the Canadian movement. Rational management of Crown lands seemed to be a simple administrative matter, requiring only the establishment of professionally staffed agencies to supervise resource companies in the public interest.[3]

British Columbia appeared at the cutting edge of progress in 1912, when the province adopted a comprehensive Forest Act and established a professional bureaucracy to oversee cutting on the Crown forests. But as in Ontario, New Brunswick, and Nova Scotia, public ownership of most of British Columbia's resource base did not 'necessarily imply a more systematic pursuit of conservation programs.' The province's lumbermen, many of whom also operated in Washington and Oregon, succeeded in shaping public policy to their own needs.[4]

This feature of business-government relations in the resource sector west of the Cascades becomes abundantly clear when the scientific and administrative history of clearcutting is analyzed. During this period foresters began to grapple with the question of how the coastal forest should be managed to maintain its productivity. Central to the professional foresters' mandate, as they understood it, was the design and regulation of cutting methods to secure natural regeneration.[5] Shortly after the turn of the century clearcutting gained legitimacy as the appropriate harvesting technique for the old-growth Douglas fir forest.

Although scientific findings supported the adoption of clearcutting on public lands administered by the US Forest Service and British Columbia's Forest Branch after its creation in 1912, foresters' support of the procedure can also be attributed to their acceptance of certain economic and technological realities. By the time these resource agencies took on the task of administering lands under their jurisdiction, coastal operators had already begun utilizing steam-powered cable logging systems on their properties, technologies poorly adapted to any other practice than clearcutting. From the outset, foresters recognized that logging on public lands must conform with the technologies that had been developed solely in accordance with a corporate concept of efficiency that gave no consideration to resource perpetuation.[6]

Just as the imperative of intense forest and labour exploitation shaped technology, the central focus of forestry science was to accommodate the productive requirements of changing modes of production.[7] Initially foresters responded positively to the introduction of mechanized logging; the limited clearcuts created by ground-lead donkey operations fit well with the ecological characteristics of Douglas fir. Although the expectation that logged lands would provide a second growth of valuable commercial timber with little interruption drew upon flawed research that sanctioned unregulated clearcutting, the production of scientific evidence concerning the negative impact of mechanized logging had no immediate impact on government policy.

By the early 1920s abundant evidence existed that lands were not restocking at the anticipated rate. Overhead systems of logging, foresters discovered, had calamitous results for the regenerative function of the Douglas fir forest when utilized in the typical 'high-ball' fashion. Ruinous to young growth and capable of totally denuding huge expanses of timberland, this technology was found to be much more destructive than earlier ground-lead methods.[8] To that point the social and ecological implications of research findings had relevance primarily for management of the American national forests. On private lands in that country and on British Columbia's mix of Crown grants, leases, licences, and, after 1912, timber sales, governments exerted no control over the actual conduct of logging operations to secure reforestation. Firms employed no foresters, conducted their logging operations solely in accordance with the principles of engineering efficiency, and defined 'forestry' as fire prevention.

American operators took a strong interest in the regeneration issue during the 1919-24 period, however, when a debate raged over the regulation of logging practices on private timberland. Chief Forester Henry S. Graves initiated the dispute in late 1919, proposing a national forest policy that would see industry benefit from federal funding for protection of corporate holdings from fire in return for compliance with cutting regulations adopted at the state level. Even as Graves vacated his post the proposal was eclipsed by a more radical campaign for direct federal regulation headed by former Chief Forester Gifford Pinchot.

Activated by this threat to their property rights, forward-looking timbermen cooperated with new Chief Forester William B. Greeley in the formulation of a scheme to introduce innocuous regulations at the state level along with federal funding of state fire prevention systems. When it became apparent that Pinchot's legislative package lacked Congressional support, industry's tolerance for even a mild program of state control evaporated. Always sympathetic to the economic woes of lumbermen, anxious to maintain friendly relations with his agency's clientele, and basically hostile to the sort of government activism that cutting control would require, Greeley then orchestrated a joint Forest Service-industry effort to muster federal support for greater protection of private timberlands from the threat of fire. This collaboration resulted in the Clarke-McNary Act of 1924, providing federal funding for state fire control programs with no accompanying interference in operators' cutting practices.

Over the course of the 1920s, research conducted on the reproductive traits of Douglas fir in conjunction with cutover land surveys revealed the severe ecological consequences of unregulated clearcutting in the Pacific Northwest and British Columbia. As the decade drew to a close, foresters recognized that the reckless application of modern technologies of timber extraction posed a threat both to the forest and the existence of communities dependent upon the resource.

Mechanization, Clearcutting, and Early Forest Administration

Forest administration of a very loose sort began in the Douglas fir region with the establishment of the American forest reserves during the 1890s, shortly after the steam donkey came into widespread use. Prior to coastal logging's industrial revolution, forest exploitation had relatively little negative ecological impact. Bull and horse team operations were small in scale, selective in nature, and did not affect the reproductive functions of the old growth forest to any great extent. The constraints of primitive technology and a limited market dictated extraction of only the highest quality timber located in close proximity to a waterway or sawmill. Logging alongside streams damaged their banks and the techniques of river driving had serious, sometimes catastrophic consequences for salmon habitat, but the slow pace of such operations inflicted only minor damage on young growth and those mature trees that did not justify the arduous, time-consuming tasks of falling and removal. Abundant timber remained to produce seed, and foresters who studied these areas in later decades concluded that team logging left the forest in 'good producing condition.'[9]

The adoption of the steam-powered ground-lead system to supply expanding continental and Pacific Rim markets began the transition from selective logging to clearcutting. The steam donkey increased the pace, scale, and, scientists later determined, environmental degradation associated with coastal logging. While less destructive than the aerial systems that supplanted ground-leading, cable yarding with powerful steam donkeys tore up the forest floor, knocked over immature timber, and left an enormous amount of debris that increased the likelihood and intensity of fire. But the trails over which logs travelled suffered the heaviest damage, and logging was confined to relatively small areas open to reseeding from adjacent stands.[10]

With steam-powered logging entrenched as the established mode of production on private timberland west of the Cascades, American foresters accepted both clearcutting and the technology that fostered the practice when they contemplated appropriate logging methods on the region's forest reserves. This represented a fundamental departure from cutting standards on the eastern reserves, where horse logging was the norm. There foresters marked specific trees above a certain diameter limit for cutting, reserving the remainder for future growth and seed distribution. This selective approach to harvesting conformed with terms of the 1897 Forest Management Act, which stated 'for the purpose of preserving the living and growing timber and promoting the younger growth on national forests, the Secretary of Agriculture ... may cause to be designated and appraised so much of the dead, matured, or large growth of trees found upon such national forests as may be compatible with the utilization of the forests thereon.'[11]

On the west coast, a range of factors encouraged foresters to reject this technique. The most basic of these related to the dynamics of donkey logging. Capable of yarding huge timber over rough terrain, the technology imposed an indiscriminate rather than surgical approach to forest exploitation. On the mature forests of western Washington and Oregon, forester Burt Kirkland explained in 1911, logging methods necessary to remove the heavy old-growth timber did not 'permit the saving of young growth.' Silviculturalist Thornton Munger also recognized that where steam logging was practiced, 'any other system than clearcutting is practically impossible.'[12] Operators had adopted the donkey for use on private lands, and to bar the technology from the public forests would have equated to a policy of preservation. Given the utilitarian character of the US Forest Service, which in 1905 took over administration of the reserves, now called national forests, such an outcome was unthinkable. In fact, Chief Forester Gifford Pinchot sought to generate greater revenues by increasing annual cuts, provided that logging proceeded in accordance with silvicultural principles.[13]

In other regions foresters who considered the steam donkey incompatible with the goal of forest renewal opposed its introduction, but without the support of those on the northwest coast. In 1909 the Washington, DC, head office of the Forest Service asked the regions if timber sale contracts should include a clause prohibiting purchasers from replacing horses with steam technology where it would prove destructive. Region Six forester E.T. Allen responded that 'conditions west of the Cascades ... do not demand any prohibition of steam logging.' Assistant Chief Forester E.E. Carter concurred that 'in your District steam logging is the only practical method and is desirable on most sales on the west side of the range.'[14]

Foresters' enthusiasm for steam-powered clearcutting on the coast is attributable to more than difficult terrain, huge timber, and the pragmatic acceptance of modern technology. They also had a scientific rationale for their willingness to embrace the existing mode of production. Research on the ecological characteristics of Douglas fir began in 1901 with two seasons of fieldwork by E.T. Allen. In 1903 Allen presented his report on the region's most important commercial species, making the key observation that Douglas fir reproduced best on 'open ground,' where it received exposure to sunlight. The worthless hemlock, by contrast, thrived in dense shade under the canopy of the mature forest. The discovery that Douglas fir was 'intolerant' of shade established clearcutting as the proper silvicultural technique in these forests. To secure regeneration of the species on the public lands, Allen concluded, foresters should 'cut everything which can be utilized and clear the ground for a healthy young seedling growth.'[15]

Allen also noted that fir seeds germinated most readily on a seedbed of exposed mineral soil. Burned-over areas featured an abundant growth of Douglas fir seedlings, but where the layer of organic material that coated the forest floor remained intact, hemlock and cedar dominated. Slash burning was appropriate, therefore, both to reduce the fire hazard and to clear the layer of 'duff,' exposing the mineral soil that provided fir with its best opportunity for establishment. Although the silvicultural merit of slash burning became a matter of debate by the early 1920s, Douglas fir's status as a shade-intolerant species has provided foresters with an enduring scientific rationale for clearcutting.[16]

Foresters' perception of the west coast rain forest as over-mature and decadent, and therefore an obstacle to sustained-yield management, provided a final justification for clearcutting. Sustained-yield theory was premised on the attainment of a balance of annual cut with growth on a designated area. Only in this way, the credo held, could a constant flow of forest products and employment levels be maintained. From this perspective, proper policy on the Olympic and Snoqualmie National Forests, where 90 percent of the timber appeared to be stagnant and unproductive, was to liquidate the old-growth and replace it with vigorous young stands.[17]

By the second decade of the twentieth century, then, a consensus had been forged among professional foresters that clearcutting was the appropriate harvesting technique west of the Cascades. 'From the knowledge which we have of the best method of cutting in the types found in the Washington National Forest,' observed one forester in 1908, 'it is certain that clearcutting ... will be practiced in most sales in the future.' Kirkland agreed that 'some clearcutting method should always be used.' On the Olympic National Forest, W.H. Gibbons declared in 1910, 'clearcutting must be permitted.'[18]

The decision to adopt the same methods for national forest timber as operators practiced on their adjacent private lands had two important consequences. First, management procedures were greatly simplified. Under a selective system technical staff appraised and marked individual trees for cutting, but in the Douglas fir region foresters needed only to designate cutting boundaries and perhaps reserve a small number of trees to provide seed for the restocking of cutovers. A second, equally important result was to focus much of the scientific research conducted by resource agencies on the ecological impact of clearcutting. It soon became evident that the transformation of clearcutting from simply a cost-effective means of removing the old-growth forest into the first stage of a system of timber management, as foresters liked to describe it, would be difficult. More problematic yet would be the task of having the knowledge acquired on the national forests implemented on private lands, where logging was heaviest, and carried out with no regard for reforestation.

Silvicultural research had fallen within the mandate of the US Forest Service since the organization's days as the Division of Forestry. In 1903 Gifford Pinchot placed Raphael Zon at the head of a newly created Section of Silvics. After investigating the European system of experimental stations in 1908, Zon advocated the establishment of a similar arrangement in America. Time passed before Zon saw his plan implemented, but some progress resulted from Pinchot's decentralization of national forest administration. When the agency established the Region Six administrative area to oversee the Pacific Northwest national forests in 1908, F.E. Ames took charge of silviculture at the Portland headquarters. Yale graduate Thornton T. Munger arrived the same year to begin a long career in Douglas fir research and administration. Observation of timber sale areas was the primary means of gathering data on the reproductive character of Douglas fir at this early stage.[19]

The Forest Service employed the seed tree method of securing reproduction on initial sales. Individual trees were reserved from cutting, serving as a source of seed for the reforestation of cutover areas. Foresters quickly noted the failings of this regeneration technique. On one 1906 sale in Washington's Wind River valley almost all the trees reserved for seed distribution were lost within two years, 'either killed by fire when the slash was burned, or uprooted by winds.' This left the site with a negligible opportunity for restocking, prompting Arthur Wilcox to propose that seed trees be left in one- to five-acre groups on knolls or ridges. Blocks of well-rooted timber reserved in these locations would be less vulnerable to blowdown and slash fire damage, and in a superior position to distribute seed over the cutover area.[20]

Some of the region's high-ranking foresters advocated a more technologically oriented silvicultural system, involving absolute clearcutting followed by artificial regeneration. In a 1908 report on the Washington National Forest, Burt Kirkland acknowledged that the agency's reliance on some form of seed tree method of natural reforestation must continue for the immediate future, but in his estimation the more efficient policy would be to cut all of the merchantable timber and rely on broadcast seeding to restock sale areas. E.T. Clark had arrived at the same conclusion while analyzing management options for the Snoqualmie National Forest.[21]

Clark was pessimistic about the capacity of scattered seed trees to reforest cutovers, primarily because of the likelihood of blowdown loss. He had a more positive evaluation of strip or patch cutting, involving logging in discrete blocks. Since early estimates suggested that the winged Douglas fir seed carried up to 1,000 feet in favourable wind conditions, limiting cutovers to this width would permit seed blown in from either side to restock the area. Moreover, this method meant 'cheaper logging,' the prime attraction of total clearcutting. Disadvantages included the strong possibility of blowdown along the edges of uncut timber and high development costs, since construction of two rail lines was necessary, one for the initial cut and another to log the second crop. Worse, any technique demanding the reservation of timber for reforestation tied up forest capital for long periods, delayed restocking, and did not guarantee a uniform new stand.

Real silvicultural and economic efficiency, Clark maintained, lay in a program of absolute clearcutting. Planting or seeding cutovers would produce a perfectly even-aged stand of the desired species and require 'no restriction on logging.' Harvesting on the national forests would be 'as cheap as in unregulated cutting' provided that the Forest Service did the necessary research in methods of artificial regeneration and established adequate nursery facilities.[22]

Kirkland and Clark carried the professional forester's faith in science and technology to its logical conclusion in these proposals for management of the national forests. Separating the processes of resource exploitation and renewal completely, and conducting each without regard for the other, fostered optimum efficiency in both. Reliance upon natural reforestation involved the introduction of silvicultural considerations into logging operations, leaving valuable timber in the woods, and delaying the establishment of a new forest. The superior procedure, they reasoned, would see the old-growth stands cut clean and replaced immediately with a new forest engineered to meet future needs.

So committed were the region's foresters to this technocratic vision that they introduced clauses in timber sale contracts stipulating that purchasers furnish labour to assist with planting denuded areas. This requirement seemed particularly appropriate in the case of mixed stands where scattered Douglas firs co-existed with hemlock and 'other species of distinctly inferior quality.' Restocking such an area to the desired species by natural methods required reservation of the valuable firs, eliminating the sale's value to purchasers. Leaving hemlock seed trees would produce a new stand of that species, a policy Chief Forester Henry S. Graves described as 'such poor forestry and such poor business administration that it should not be considered.'[23]

The attempt to require purchasers to participate in artificial reforestation may have been sound silviculture, but the US Department of Agriculture's solicitor found no legal basis for such a practice. The 1897 Forest Management Act authorized the Service to enforce regulations 'naturally incidental to the cutting,' such as seed tree reservation and slash disposal, but artificial reforestation exceeded this authority. West of the Cascades, Regional Forester George Cecil explained in response, 'the only practicable method of cutting is to remove all the merchantable trees, leaving the area as clean as possible without attempting to preserve any of the younger growth or seedlings.' By its very nature clearcutting violated the terms of the Forest Management Act, Cecil pointed out, as the method failed to 'preserve the living and growing timber upon the areas cut over.'[24] Artificial reforestation was thus 'incident to the cutting' and therefore within the discretion of the secretary of Agriculture. Persuasive as the argument may have been from a management perspective, it did not carry the day. W.B. Greeley, in charge of the Washington, DC, Office of Forest Management, recognized the merit of clauses providing for the assistance of the purchaser in planting but did not pursue the matter.[25]

The decision placed the responsibility for restocking the region's national forests exclusively on the Forest Service. With over 7 million acres nationally requiring artificial regeneration, Greeley declared that on the Pacific coast the natural method should be the goal, 'even if at a sacrifice of the best silviculture from the standpoint of the cost of establishing the new crop.' Although the stumpage value of seed trees might exceed the expense of planting or seeding, the timber cost the Forest Service nothing and should be used to secure a second growth. Moreover, the Service lacked the facilities to adopt a large-scale artificial regeneration program on the west coast. Experiments in direct seeding had only just begun in 1909, and a nursery opened at Wind River, Washington, for seedling production the following year. Funding problems, difficulties in obtaining sufficient quantities of seed, and fungi that caused a high rate of seedling mortality all constrained the US Forest Service's early restocking effort in the west.[26]

Lacking both the legal mandate and facilities to employ artificial reforestation on the national forests of the Douglas fir region, the agency relied on natural methods. This, in turn, demanded study of the reproductive characteristics of Douglas fir, thus permitting inclusion of the appropriate silvicultural clauses in timber sale contracts. But as Thornton Munger put it in 1910, foresters in the Pacific Northwest had 'hardly begun to discover what our problems are, much less to solve them.' One year later the Forest Service initiated a research program, establishing an 80-acre plot on a sale area in the Wind River valley. Seed trees were measured and tagged, and reproduction plots were laid out to accumulate data on seed tree survival, the distance of fir seed dissemination, and factors influencing germination and seedling development. The Wind River nursery became the site of a small field research station under director J.V. Hoffman in 1913, two years prior to the creation of the Service's Branch of Research.[27]

These developments did not reflect any deep anxiety over the impact of steam logging on the forest's reproductive capacities. The demand for public timber remained weak, and among both foresters and lumbermen the threat fire posed to the virgin forest was of much greater concern. Indeed, the fire menace inspired the major timber holders of Washington and Oregon to initiate collective action aimed at the creation of publicly funded regulatory schemes for the protection of corporate properties. Devastating fires during the summer and fall of 1902 prompted George Long, western manager of the Weyerhaeuser Timber Company, to lead a legislative campaign that produced a 1903 Washington fire law. Inadequate funding and poor organization rendered ineffective this measure that made the state commissioner of public lands the ex-officio state fire warden.

Timbermen used their strength in the Washington legislature to secure passage of a 1905 Forest Protection Law that repealed the 1903 legislation, creating a board of forest commissioners with the authority to appoint a state fire warden and deputy wardens. Only $7,500 was appropriated to support the fire control program, however, and in 1906 Long and a few other timber owners contributed funds to employ wardens on a temporary basis. Still dissatisfied with the level of state support, early in 1908 Weyerhaeuser and other large timber holders organized the Washington Forest Fire Association. The 138 original members assessed themselves a penny an acre to employ men who patrolled 2.6 million acres of forestland.[28]

Events followed a similar course in Oregon, where *Timberman* editor George Cornwall played a lead role at Salem. The governor repealed a 1903 act that created a board of forest commissioners and fire protection districts on the grounds that lumbermen themselves should bear the costs associated with protection of their property. A 1905 law empowered county courts to appoint fire rangers at owners' expense, then in 1907 Oregon timbermen gained partial victory with legislation establishing a State Board of Forestry and public funding for wardens' wages. As in Washington, however, appropriations and organization were inadequate. Two years later lumbermen from across the Pacific Northwest created the Western Forestry and Conservation Association (WFCA), a regional lobbying and public relations organization. Former Forest Service employee E.T. Allen became the WFCA's executive director, the first of many foresters to pass easily from public to private employment in the west. Following the establishment of the WFCA, in the spring of 1910 prominent Oregon lumbermen organized the Oregon Forest Fire Association and began to press for improved protective legislation.[29]

The inadequacy of cooperative fire programs in the Pacific Northwest became evident that summer when fires burned over 3 million acres of forestland in Washington, Oregon, Idaho, and Montana. The conflagration generated general western support in the Senate for the 1911 Weeks Act, allowing federal cooperation with states for protection of private timberland on the watersheds of navigable streams. States wishing to gain eligibility for federal funds were required to have a functioning fire protection agency and match federal expenditures. Oregon's lumbermen had already moved to increase public protection of their timberlands. The 1911 legislature enacted a new forest law authorizing employment of fire wardens and established a fire season requiring burning permits for campfires. New rules required operators to dispose of slash and to equip their steam-powered logging equipment with spark arrestors. Francis A. Elliot became Oregon's first state forester at the same time, holding that position until 1930. Washington state similarly upgraded its forestry laws after the 1910 fires. By 1913 both states had qualified for the maximum Weeks Act allotment, and in 1917 Washington followed Oregon's lead in enacting a compulsory forest patrol law.[30]

Timber capital had sufficient influence within the western state legislatures to ensure that fire protection laws met, but did not exceed, the standard of the 'more responsible and progressive' owners. There was, of course, no possibility that funds from state coffers for the safeguarding of private lands would be conditional upon adherence to cutting practice regulations. But to the operators' great consternation, this notion emerged briefly in federal politics during the progressive era. Dismissed as chief forester by Republican President William Taft in 1911 for his opposition to Secretary of Interior Richard Ballinger's willingness to open public lands in the west to development, Gifford Pinchot joined with ex-president Theodore Roosevelt in proposing greater government control of American corporations. Western lumbermen were appalled when Pinchot began advocating that they be compelled to conduct their operations in accordance with federal regulations designed to end destructive logging. Happily, from their perspective, Roosevelt's bid to recapture the presidency failed and the issue slipped from the political agenda until 1919 when revived by Chief Forester Henry S. Graves and Pinchot.[31]

Just what form forest practice regulation in the southern part of the Douglas fir region might have taken had Roosevelt been successful is a matter for conjecture. Prior to the 1920s, as previously noted, foresters expressed little concern about the relationship between logging and reforestation in the west. Virgin timber supplies were still abundant, and a consensus prevailed that a new Douglas fir forest would quickly take the place of the old as donkeys cleared the land of its centuries-old stands. Foresters hoped that operators would adopt a rudimentary silvicultural system on their lands to ensure reforestation, citing the US Forest Service's national forest practices as an example to emulate. In his 1911 WFCA publication *Practical Forestry in the Pacific Northwest*, E.T. Allen noted that since winds carried Douglas fir seeds over a mile in distance, firms need only leave a few scattered seed trees to practice sound silviculture.[32]

Thornton Munger offered a more conservative estimate that same year, holding to the forester's rule of thumb that seed would be spread twice as far as the height of a tree. Thus, 350 feet seemed to Munger to be 'just about the right distance for us to assume that Douglas fir seed will be distributed thoroughly under all conditions in all directions from a seed tree.' Early Forest Service management policy was to reserve two or three seed trees per acre. Under the ground-lead system of logging, it required little or no explicit attention to reforestation to leave this amount of defective or 'conky' timber to reseed cutovers. Early mechanized logging, then, seemed entirely compatible with the goal of forest renewal. 'The obtaining of reproduction after logging,' Munger concluded in 1911, 'is a simple problem and does not entail any decided modifications of present logging methods.'[33]

In British Columbia, which experienced a timber boom of remarkable proportions after Richard McBride's Conservative government opened the province to speculators and timber capitalists in 1905, knowledge of forest conditions was negligible. During the two years the government's transferable twenty-one-year special timber licences were available, interests staked out over fifteen thousand square miles of Crown land. Much of this timber went to American lumbermen who, while generally supportive of the creation of the national forests in the Pacific Northwest, sought to seize control of as much timber as possible in British Columbia when the reserves curtailed access to the resource in that country.[34]

By 1909 politicians and lumbermen alike recognized the need for rational administration of the province's disorganized mix of leased, licensed, and private Crown-grant land. Operators who had expanded their timber holdings north from Washington and Oregon, aware of the benefits to be derived from state involvement in forestry affairs, hoped for government action to secure perpetuity of tenure, improved fire protection, and price stability. Accordingly, timber interests supported McBride's decision to call a royal commission to investigate the forestry situation.[35]

Those who submitted opinions on cutting regulations to the Fulton Commission generally argued that fire, not logging methods, posed the greatest threat to forest perpetuation. One Department of Lands and Works official conceded that damage inflicted to young growth made steam-powered operations 'a much greater menace to the forest than team logging,' suggesting rules to protect immature timber might be appropriate. More reflective of contemporary thinking were the comments of land surveyor Noel Humphreys, who expressed confidence in nature's capacity to provide a second crop after logging given adequate fire prevention. Provincial Timber Inspector R.J. Skinner, more concerned about economics than conservation, advised against adopting 'ill-judged or unnecessary obligations and restrictions' that might impair the profitability of enterprises.[36]

Skinner's reflections on the regulation issue matched those of the BC Loggers Association. The province's major operators feared that the 'theoretical might predominate over the practical,' and prompt the commissioners to recommend controls damaging to their competitiveness. With lumbering interests having a prominent place on it, little chance existed of the commission issuing radical proposals, and its report reflected the goals of a 'continental conservation movement dedicated to the promotion of large-scale corporate enterprise and the application of scientific management.' Recommendations included the establishment of a forestry department to enforce utilization and slash disposal rules, competitive bidding, and placement of all forestry revenues into a forest protection fund. An appendix to the report presented a statement of practices followed by the US Forest Service on the national forests of the Douglas fir region, but the commissioners had little to say about the impact of logging on regeneration. 'Effective re-afforestation,' they concluded, 'depends upon effective discouragement of waste.'[37]

Passed with the support of lumbermen, the 1912 Forest Act created a Forest Branch within the Department of Lands to collect revenue and administer a Forest Protection Fund jointly supported by government and industry. The new timber sale program featured contracts specifying utilization standards and slash disposal obligations, but demanded no reservation of seed trees. Unfortunately, the new bureaucracy gained very little authority on temporary tenures issued prior to 1912. Although operations on the 1,500 square miles of land under lease and 14,000 square miles of licensed timber were in theory subject to any regulations issued under the act, cutting went largely uncontrolled. On these lands the Forest Branch sought to prevent illegal cutting of adjacent public timber and to collect rental fees and royalties for the provincial treasury. Completely beyond the influence of the Forest Branch were 6,000 square miles of timberland under private ownership. On Crown-grant lands, including the enormous two million acre E & N Railway grant on southeastern Vancouver Island, operators had a free hand to exploit the resource without challenge to their property rights.[38]

Overhead Logging, the Seed Storage Theory, and the First American Regulation Debate

The organization of state and provincial forest administrations coincided with the transition to overhead methods of timber exploitation. High-lead and skidder systems necessitated complete clearcutting. While isolated patches of young growth and defective trees might survive on high-lead settings, almost total devastation of huge areas accompanied use of sophisticated aerial systems. In either case, operators cut timberland clean to permit rapid shifting of lines and unimpeded passage of logs to the landing. Most small or unmerchantable timber that escaped the falling crews was knocked over and uprooted during the yarding operation, a consequence of the high speeds at which logs and rigging travelled under the power generated by enormous skidders.[39]

It became apparent very quickly that national forest management practice would require adjustment to cope with the destructive effects of the new technology. After a 1916 timber sale inspection, R.Y. Stuart reported that 'the use of high lead logging has presented difficulties in ensuring reservation of individual trees or groups of trees for seed purposes.' The problem was not insurmountable but forest officers should become 'more aggressive' in seeing that seed trees survived logging. Above all, they should stress operators' contractual obligation to reserve designated seed trees on national forest timber sales, and should engage in advance planning to encourage compliance.[40]

Foresters, however, voiced no general protest against overhead logging at this time. One major source of continuing complacency was the 'seed storage' theory propounded by J.V. Hoffman, director of the US Forest Service's Wind River field station. Although never accepted wholeheartedly and proven to be without foundation in the 1930s, Hoffman's interpretation of Douglas fir reproduction legitimated unregulated clearcutting and by extension provided coastal operators with a scientific rebuttal to use against advocates of cutting practice regulation.[41]

Hoffman's theory had its genesis in 1913, when he discovered young growth on vast areas burned over eleven years earlier during the 1902 fires that swept through southwestern Washington. As yet no accurate data on Douglas fir seed flight had been compiled, but the presence of what appeared to be even-aged seedlings two or three miles from timber suggested that the reproduction originated from seed that had survived the fire, stored in the forest floor. Hoffman advanced a startling new theory: Douglas fir seed had the capacity to retain its vitality for long periods, perhaps up to eight years, while stored in the 'duff' or layer of organic material coating the forest floor. The seeds germinated, he argued, when exposed to sunlight after logging or fire removed the forest canopy.[42]

The theory found immediate acceptance in British Columbia, where Ontario forester C.D. Howe was engaged in the first scientific investigation into the province's coastal forest resource in 1915 for the Dominion government's Commission on Conservation. After conducting regeneration surveys and discussing the issue with Hoffman, Howe accepted the 'probability of dense stands of Douglas fir arising from several seed crops accumulated in the soil.' As he explained to the BC Forest Club, this feature made close attention to seed tree reservation unnecessary. Regeneration could be obtained simply by clearcutting, conducting a light slash burn immediately after logging, and preventing subsequent fires.[43]

Hoffman's attempt to prove the validity of his hypothesis involved placing healthy seed in containers, burying these in the forest floor and testing the germination quality of the stored seed at regular intervals. Unfortunately, while the seed germinated as expected after one year, results thereafter were negative. According to Leo Isaac, the researcher responsible for discrediting Hoffman's work, the latter then abandoned the experiment, attributing the germination failure to damage caused to the containers by rodents, exposing the seeds to air while in storage. 'There was no basis for that conclusion,' Isaac recalled, 'he just explained away his theory in that manner.'[44]

Although Hoffman's research fell far short of validating his hypothesis, he published a number of papers between 1917 and 1924, all advancing the comforting but dubious notion that vast quantities of dormant but viable Douglas fir seed lay in the forest floor awaiting only a logging operation to spring to life. 'When the forest is removed by fire, or by cutting,' he claimed in 1920, 'the stored seed is left under favorable germination conditions and immediately responds to the stimuli. The result is an immediate replacement by the species which occupied the ground.' One had only to conduct a mild slash burn before seeds germinated to assure a new crop. Slash burning after germination would destroy the seedlings, placing the entire reforestation burden on seed trees.[45]

Even within the US Forest Service some greeted Hoffman's work with a degree of scepticism. On timber sales it remained standard practice to reserve two or three seed trees per acre, suggesting a reluctance to rely exclusively upon stored seed as an agent of regeneration. Assistant District Forester Fred Ames expressed this ambivalence in 1920, informing a representative of the Oregon Chamber of Commerce that protecting logged-off lands from fire appeared to be more important than cutting methods in securing reforestation. 'There is abundant seed stored in the ground that will escape the slash fire and start a new forest,' Ames wrote, before going on to describe this idea as a hypothesis requiring further research. In a 1922 report on Douglas fir management, Thornton Munger, never a supporter of the seed storage explanation for reproduction, wrote that investigations at Wild River had 'demonstrated quite conclusively that most of the seedlings which spring up after logging come from seed cast by the virgin forest in the few years before cutting, had been stored in the cool duff, escaped injury from the slash fire and responded to the sunlight on the bare, burned-over, logged-off land.' But Munger followed with a qualification, stating that most of the seed 'apparently germinates the first summer after the timber is felled.'[46]

The uncertainty that prevailed among foresters concerning the effect Hoffman's research should have on national forest management held little interest for operators. On private forestland, producing well over 90 percent of America's wood products, logging continued with exclusive regard for the balance sheet. In the timber-rich Douglas fir region, the corporate concept of efficiency did not extend beyond technological and engineering sophistication to encompass consideration of forest renewal. During World War I this single-minded approach to natural resource exploitation meshed nicely with the national goal of full production for military purposes, but the return of peace brought a revival of interest in conservation.

Late in 1919 Henry S. Graves, Pinchot's successor as chief forester, ignited a five-year controversy by setting out a proposal for an American forestry policy. Unfortunately Graves' initiative coincided with the postwar disintegration of the progressive movement, attributable in part to the withdrawal of middle-class support for government intervention in economic affairs. Although progressives continued to wield considerable support in Congress during the 1920s, the Republican administrations of Warren G. Harding and Calvin Coolidge provided a strong counterweight against regulation of American business.

In essence, Graves recommended that timbermen receive greater public support in protecting their lands from fire in exchange for adherence to cutting regulations. The solution to the forestry problem on private land required public assistance, the chief forester declared, but federal funds should be conditional upon the adoption of logging methods to 'leave the forest in a productive condition.'[47] The Graves scheme proposed an ambiguous mix of cooperation and regulation involving the federal government, states, and timbermen. The initial requirement was Congressional approval of a bill authorizing the secretary of Agriculture to cooperate with individual states in the formulation of forest protection and cutting plans. Costs would be shared between the federal government and the states, with the legislatures of the latter qualifying for federal funds by enacting measures providing for fire control and logging regulation.

The entire network of local legislation would be enforced through the US Constitution's commerce clause, prohibiting interstate shipment of forest products cut in violation of state law. As a further enticement to operators, states would be urged to revamp their taxation systems. Instead of the annual assessment on timberland, which owners held responsible for their practice of allowing land to revert to counties for non-payment of taxes after logging, states should defer the tax on timber until cut. Once relieved of this burden, the argument went, owners were sure to retain and care for their holdings in expectation of the second harvest. On the whole, then, Graves seemed to place the federal government in a supervisory role, with the states serving as the 'active agents for carrying the plan into effect.'[48]

William Robbins maintains that the chief forester's scheme 'appealed to progressive trade association leaders,' but enthusiasm on the west coast was muted. Hugo Winkenwerder drew on his association with operators to warn Graves of their resistance to any regulatory initiatives. 'The lumbermen of this region are less conservative than those of any other section of the country,' he advised 'and it will be a harder battle to get something started here than in any other section of the country.' The Forest Service should abandon this misguided attempt at compulsion, and follow the traditional method of educating operators to the financial advantages of forestry. St. Paul and Tacoma Lumber Company president Everett G. Griggs described the Graves proposal as entirely too 'theoretical,' a serious denunciation indeed. A national forest policy should be established through cooperation between the Forest Service and the 'practical operators' who struggled against high taxes and operating costs. Private forestry would become a reality, Griggs maintained, when governments relieved lumbermen of the tax burden that compelled timber liquidation.[49]

American foresters with direct ties to industry accepted the need for a comprehensive national policy, but along with their employers criticized the regulatory features of the policy suggested by the chief forester. Royal S. Kellogg, formerly a Forest Service employee now working in a public relations capacity for the pulp and paper interests, argued that it was 'neither practical nor expedient to compel the practice of forestry on private lands.' Attempts to use the interstate commerce clause of the Constitution to prohibit the use of child labour had twice failed, Kellogg pointed out, and Graves' program was certain to be found unconstitutional. Perhaps more to the point, federal coercion would 'alienate and render hostile' the owners of timberland. In the final analysis, growing timber for profit was too lengthy and uncertain a process to attract private capital, hence any policy of compulsion was doomed to failure. Kellogg and National Lumber Manufacturers Association (NLMA) forest economist Wilson Compton had no doubt that the public should bear the entire cost of reforestation.[50]

Among the vast majority of foresters still confined to public employment, Graves' blueprint for reform generated considerable controversy, prompting SAF president Frederick C. Olmsted to appoint a Committee for the Application of Forestry. Any hope for a unified stance on the regulation issue by the forestry profession collapsed when Gifford Pinchot assumed leadership of the committee, which issued its report in November 1919. The document warned that devastation of private forests had plunged America into the early stages of a timber famine, and recommended strict federal regulation of operators' logging practices. A commission consisting of the secretaries of Agriculture and Labour and the chairman of the Federal Trade Commission should be authorized to 'fix standards and promulgate rules to prevent the devastation and provide for the perpetuation of forest growth and the production of forest crops on privately owned timberlands for commercial purposes.'[51]

In its insistence upon federal regulation, the Pinchot report posed a more serious threat to operators' managerial prerogatives than the moderate Graves plan. Industry progressives might be induced to accept state control in exchange for greater federal fire protection funds because of the influence they wielded in local legislatures. But the SAF report, if implemented, would see Forest Service administration of 'compulsory nation-wide legislation' drafted in Washington, DC, where control over the regulatory process was not assured. Accordingly, lumbermen denounced the former chief forester's proposal. To the charge that silvicultural knowledge was insufficient to permit the formulation of practical cutting guidelines, Pinchot replied that foresters knew enough to begin protecting forestland from devastation.[52]

Now faced with a choice between the status quo and two regulatory options, the forestry profession threatened to split along ideological lines. An SAF referendum ballot produced a 94 to 61 vote in favour of federal regulation, but made no provision for members to register support for control at the state level. A majority favoured that option when SAF members voted at the society's 1920 annual meeting. William B. Greeley also appeared to approve of regulation exercised by the states when he became chief forester after Graves left the Service to teach at Yale University early in 1920.[53]

A third group, numbering among its ranks educators and consultants to industry, had no sympathy for any governmental regulation of logging operations. Chief among these was David T. Mason, a Yale graduate who had worked for the Forest Service from 1907 to 1915, then become a professor at the University of California, now beginning an influential career as a consulting forester in Portland. For Mason, lower taxes, fire protection, and industrial stability were the key preconditions for forest conservation, and he became the major proponent of the sustained-yield model as a cure for overproduction.[54]

Greeley and Pinchot, however, were the main protagonists in the debate leading to passage of the 1924 Clarke-McNary Act. Initially Greeley attempted to downplay their differences, expressing agreement with his former chief on the need for an extension of governmental power. He nevertheless doubted the constitutionality of Pinchot's recommendation, arguing that progress would be achieved more quickly through state regulation with the federal government providing funds and leadership.[55]

For his part Pinchot was adamant that the influence wielded by lumbermen over state legislatures, especially in the west, would render any regulation adopted by those bodies purely symbolic. Moreover, the forestry problem was national in scope, transcended state borders, and required direct action by the federal government. 'To scatter control among the States,' he asserted, 'would be to subdivide and distribute it among numerous comparatively weak and frequently changing hands.' Burt Kirkland had his own reservations about state regulation in the Pacific Northwest. Washington, for example, might enact conservation laws that raised operators' costs, leaving those in Oregon free to exploit a competitive advantage in the marketplace.[56]

Pinchot reserved his most bitter commentary for foresters such as Mason, who expressed faith in operators' willingness to embrace forestry voluntarily given greater economic stability and a helping hand from government in fire protection and taxation reform. An early 1920 publication containing this message drew Pinchot's contempt. 'Mr. Mason, I fear,' he remarked, 'still lives under the spell of flattery and lip profession which held the rest of us so long.' Then, in a veiled reference to E.T. Allen, Pinchot noted that Mason's article 'follows closely the arguments advanced by the lumberman-forester who guards so efficiently the interests of the organized lumbermen in the Northwest.' Such rhetoric could only divide a profession troubled for the first time by ideological issues.[57]

The forestry debate began making its way into the political arena in May 1920 when Senator Arthur Capper of Kansas introduced a resolution directing the secretary of Agriculture to investigate the timber situation in the United States. In his June report Greeley urged that the federal government involve the states and operators in a cooperative and 'realistic' program of fire protection and reforestation. Backed by federal support, the states should enact complementary legislation to strengthen fire protection, begin the task of reforesting private lands, and introduce tax reforms. In the chief forester's mind the primary cause of forest devastation was fire; action on destructive logging practices could wait. 'It is my position,' he explained to district foresters in June, 'that the problem of forest devastation is three-quarters a problem of preventing fire; that the immediate thing to be done is to bring the fire hazard in our forest regions under control; [and] that other measures of reforestation such as the regulation of cutting may well wait until we have gotten the fire menace under control.'[58]

At this early date, however, regulation of logging by the states held a place on Greeley's agenda, if only as a long-range goal. In one essay he went so far as to class forestlands as public utilities, subject to whatever controls were necessary to maintain their productivity. But the key to progress lay in the public approaching timbermen 'in the spirit of assistance rather than of regulation.' As beneficiaries of nominal land taxes and increased government expenditure on the fire problem, owners would reciprocate by adhering to equitable cutting, slash disposal, and fire protection measures.[59]

Greeley's report met with the hearty approval of forward-looking operators. The *Timberman* praised the chief forester's emphasis on local, as opposed to federal, control. Pinchot, meanwhile, succeeded in having the essentials of his committee's recommendations presented to Congress in a bill submitted by Capper. Greeley responded quickly; with industry's backing he had Bertrand Snell present to the House of Representatives his scheme of federal funding for those states that required owners to maintain the productivity of their lands. Some measure of public control was necessary, Greeley conceded, but he could not accept Pinchot's position that 'direct police action by Uncle Sam is necessary to bring about decent treatment of our forests.' Rather, the federal government should assume a cooperative role, leaving to individual states the 'measures of regulation affecting the private owner of land which are found to be necessary.'[60]

The Capper and Snell Bills presented operators with a choice between federal regulation and what Greeley termed the 'encouragement of local initiative.' Recognizing that state control posed no significant threat to their interests, and might counter the more ominous Capper measure, prudent industry leaders threw their support behind the Snell proposal in the Congressional hearings that took place over the next three years. Trade association officials organized the National Forestry Program Committee in December 1920 to present industry's case. Royal S. Kellogg of the American Pulp and Paper Association chaired the organization, with the WFCA's E.T. Allen serving as its 'master strategist.' The latter warned western operators that if the Capper Bill triumphed, an 'army of federal employees' would descend upon their lands to penalize those who failed to comply with harsh regulations.[61]

Allen, David Mason, and Greeley testified as professional experts before Congress in 1921, all expressing their preference for local control and stressing that measures to prevent and suppress fire should take priority over regulation of cutting practices. Pinchot challenged them on both points, arguing that lumbermen supported the Snell Bill only because they had confidence in their ability to control state legislatures. This was particularly so in the western states, he charged, which held the bulk of the nation's timber supply and where corporate interests dictated public policy with ease.[62]

After 1921, Pinchot's successful gubernatorial campaign in Pennsylvania detracted from his role in the forestry debate. As his major rival slipped temporarily from centre stage, Greeley experienced troubles of his own. Although the NLMA backed the Snell Bill, lumbermen, especially in the South, were far from unanimous in accepting the principle of state regulation. The *Timberman* suggested that fear of the odious Capper proposal would create sufficient unity to ensure passage of Greeley's brainchild, but the chief forester later recalled that he struggled during this period 'to keep lumbermen in the cooperative tent.'[63]

Greeley struggled to hold the alliance together when he arrived on the west coast late in 1922 to present his case to the WFCA's annual meeting. He began by assuring the audience that his was a practical approach to the reforestation question, recognizing the difficulties imposed by high taxes, compound interest, and the ever-present risk of fire. Nevertheless, operators should accept the public's right to insist that 'in the process of converting valuable natural resources on these lands into cash reasonable provision for a future growth of timber must be made and its cost absorbed as part of the logging operation.' His 'fair and reasonable' program of regulation would make all operators in the region equal in the market, allowing them to pass the expense of reforestation on to consumers. In return, operators could count on the public fulfilling its obligation to bear part of the burden through financial cooperation in fire protection and taxation reform. Finally, they could look forward to controlling the regulatory process. Statutes would merely declare that private lands be maintained in a 'reasonably productive condition,' with the drafting of specific rules left to forest boards. Industry representation would guarantee that such boards dealt with the issue in a 'reasonable and practical way.' Surely, Greeley suggested, this arrangement was an attractive alternative to the 'arbitrary, impractical, long-range or political type of forest regulation' sure to emanate from Washington, DC.[64]

Greeley then turned to the issue of what regulation might involve in the Douglas fir region. Ignoring concern that had been expressed about the adequacy of management practices on the national forests, and basing his conclusions upon a rather questionable reading of silvicultural research findings, he informed his audience that their cutting practices required no serious modification. Hoffman's seed storage theory, already the subject of considerable scepticism, justified his assurance that the capacity of Douglas fir to reproduce from stored seed would 'usually obviate the necessity of reserving stumpage for reseeding purposes.'[65]

The chief forester's commitment to pacifying western operators is evident when his statements are seen in the context of Thornton Munger's report on the minimum practices required to maintain forest productivity, written earlier that year. On private lands in the Douglas fir region, Munger observed, the present system of overhead logging provided 'absolutely no intentional measures to secure ... reforestation.' 'Whatever reproduction takes place,' Munger concluded, 'is in spite of present methods, not as a result of them.' Although the researcher attributed the operators' apathy to reforestation to economic and political factors requiring public action, he urged them to follow the Forest Service in leaving a couple of trees of marginal value on each acre when this could be accomplished 'without inconveniencing the logging.' Given Greeley's willingness to ignore data that pointed to the need for regulation, it is difficult to avoid the conclusion that any controls imposed by the states under his stewardship would have been meaningless, as Pinchot had charged.[66]

The issue, in any event, was rapidly becoming academic as support for the Snell Bill waned. Many lumbermen had endorsed it only as a hedge against Pinchot's proposal, which seemed increasingly unlikely to be passed by Congress. Certainly Hugo Winkenwerder gave the Forest Service program little chance of success on the Pacific coast. Although the professor's perception of the Snell Bill as a threat to his own legislative initiatives in the state of Washington coloured his analysis, he was perhaps not too far off the mark when he described Greeley's attempt to use 'police power' to achieve silvicultural objectives as misguided. 'Your proposal,' he argued, 'has not a ghost of a chance if left for a solution to the legislatures of these western states.' The region's operators had a deeply ingrained suspicion of foresters, and they tended to 'bristle up' when threatened with conservation measures that promised no return.

On the other hand, the lumbermen had shown a willingness to regulate themselves when such action served their own interest, as in the case of earlier legislation providing for protection of corporate timber holdings. Operators had begun to recognize the value of their lands, Winkenwerder advised, and the time had come to press for the extension of protection to cutover areas. Greeley's proposal had no hope of success, and would merely damage hopes for improved fire legislation in the state. 'Let us not try to do the whole thing at once,' he pleaded, 'but step by step without unduly arousing the suspicion or enmity of those most concerned.' Foresters should intensify their educational efforts, convince lumbermen of their sound business judgment, and when a majority had been won over legislation would follow bringing the recalcitrant minority into line with industry standards.[67]

Still hopeful of having the Snell Bill passed intact, Greeley maintained that while education must remain a high priority, operators should also be alerted to their public obligations. 'I want to see the lumbermen of the country use their opportunity to lead this thing into practical channels,' he replied, 'rather than sit back and wait for a steam roller.' In truth, very little separated Greeley and Winkenwerder. Both chose the path of accommodation over confrontation, seeking to gain the confidence of timber capital by bringing the profession's aspirations into line with the operators' definition of forestry progress. As the professor put it, foresters must endeavour to overcome their reputation as idealists 'lacking in the fundamentals of business.'[68]

The chief forester's willingness to conform with the economic and political objectives of American timber owners soon became apparent. With opposition to the regulatory dimension of the Snell Bill on the rise, E.T. Allen recommended that this objectionable feature be dropped. Greeley agreed, and regulation of logging vanished from the Forest Service political program. Henceforth he made no further reference even to inoffensive state controls. Federal aid to increase protection of private timberland from fire, always Greeley's main goal, remained as the dominant feature of his policy proposal.[69]

Greeley's opportunity to shape a policy based exclusively on the cooperative principle came early in 1923. With both the Snell and Capper Bills stalled, the US Senate established a Select Committee on Reforestation, chaired by Oregon's Charles McNary. Selected as the committee's expert counsel, Greeley later confessed to 'packing the stand' at the nationwide hearings with lumbermen and foresters who cited fire as the only impediment to reforestation. Timber growing was a viable commercial enterprise,

Greeley himself testified, given sufficient public funding for fire control and taxation reform. Meanwhile in February, Congressman John D. Clarke introduced a revised version of the Snell Bill, purged of its noxious reference to state regulation.[70]

At the committee's west coast hearings, Hoffman's seed storage theory figured prominently when opponents of regulation expressed themselves. In a report printed by the WFCA and endorsed by federal, state, and private agencies in the west, E.T. Allen declared that natural regeneration of commercial species was 'exceedingly swift and certain unless destroyed by fire.' Recommended practice in the Douglas fir region was to clearcut, burn the slash, and 'let the seed stored in the ground sprout.' Good forestry, Allen argued, 'coincides with common logging practice.'[71]

Other foes of federal regulation within the profession shared a disinclination to convey in their public statements any of the uncertainty that surrounded the Hoffman theory. Anxious to support their corporate clients, both George Peavy and Hugo Winkenwerder placed their professional and institutional stamp of approval on current logging practices during the regulation debate. Peavy's 1922 state publication on Oregon's forest resources presented the seed storage hypothesis as proven scientific fact. That same year Winkenwerder informed a public official that existing methods were perfectly adequate from the standpoint of regeneration. 'All we need to do,' the educator pronounced, 'is to burn the slashings the first year after logging, then rigidly protect the area from all future forest fires and Nature will pretty nearly do the rest.'[72]

The chief forester left the Pacific Northwest hearings in a hopeful frame of mind. Firms such as Weyerhaeuser, the Merrill and Ring Lumber Company, and L.T. Murray's West Fork Logging Company had declared an interest in retaining and reforesting their cutover lands, he informed Regional Forester George Cecil. Promising signs abounded that 'private timber growing in the Douglas fir region as a deliberate policy of the land owner will gradually come about.' Forest Service men should be 'vigorous promoters' of this trend, and work on an individual basis with the most sophisticated operators. Cecil assured Greeley that his staff would step up efforts to spread the 'gospel of sustained yield and good silviculture.'[73]

Greeley was equally pleased with the Select Committee's report, a document that followed faithfully the cooperative line of argument advanced by the chief forester and timber industry. Not surprisingly, the legislators laboured under the assumption that in the Pacific Northwest, at least, cutting methods played 'but a minor part' in the creation of devastated forest lands. When Congress passed the Clarke-McNary Act on 7 June 1924, the chief forester's victory over Pinchot and the regulationists was complete. The legislation increased federal funds to states whose fire control programs met accepted standards, allowed the secretary of Agriculture to match state expenditures in the establishment of nurseries, and provided for enlargement of the national forest system. Other sections of the act authorized a study of state taxation policies and a survey of the nation's timberlands.[74]

Passage of Clarke-McNary ended the first great American regulation debate on terms entirely satisfactory to timber capital. Private forestlands would be more secure from fire, and expansion of the national forests held out the promise of a more stable lumber economy. The 'practical forester,' as Greeley's biographer characterized his subject, had played a key role in setting American forest policy on a 'cooperative' course that focused exclusively upon fire as the cause of forest devastation. The movement to introduce silvicultural objectives into the conduct of logging practices lost momentum, not to re-emerge until the end of the decade. For the time being, as Regional Forester Christopher M. Grainger explained in 1925, the US Forest Service would confine itself to assisting firms in progressing 'through internal evolution toward their new function of land management.'[75]

Looking back on his triumph with pride, Greeley maintained that the legislation 'cleared the air of controversy and launched an era of goodwill and joint effort.' Historians have generally evaluated Clarke-McNary as an important accomplishment, achieved thanks to Greeley's pragmatism. For William Robbins, on the other hand, the events leading to the act's passage demonstrate the power of American lumbermen to mould public policies that served the corporate rather than the general interest. On balance, Robbins provides the most convincing treatment by documenting the activities of trade associations and directing some attention to the role of foresters in legitimizing a cooperative approach.[76]

Absent from either interpretation, however, is analysis of the intersection of the scientific and policy-making processes. While it would be naive indeed to expect the regulation issue to be determined purely on a scientific basis, it is nevertheless worthwhile to consider the impact of such knowledge in the realm of resource politics. Through this sort of inquiry it is possible to provide additional insight into the relationship between resource agencies and industry, to clarify what was at stake in the regulation debate, and to assess with greater precision the impact of legislation. In this case, it would be incorrect to suggest that Greeley and his allies in the forestry profession deliberately distorted the scientific record. But in their determination to maintain harmonious relations with lumbermen and achieve some progress in the fight against fire, they were not above presenting as conclusive a theory that many in Greeley's own agency found suspect – one that was of minimal importance in shaping management practice on the region's national forests and that would soon be discredited entirely.

Silvicultural Research and the Reforestation Crisis
The Clarke-McNary Act's status as a signal achievement in American forest

policy becomes dubious when it is evaluated within the context of subsequent developments. By 1930 researchers had exposed the fallacy of Hoffman's seed storage theory and discovered that a reforestation crisis loomed in the most heavily logged areas of the Douglas fir region. In the process they came to a much better understanding of the impact of logging practices on reforestation. Taken together, these findings pointed to one conclusion: unregulated clearcutting with modern overhead logging systems posed a threat to the perpetuation of the forest and the timber economy.

The regeneration issue dominated forestry research on the Pacific coast during the 1920s. In British Columbia the Forest Branch was 'very weak scientifically' in its formative years, and seventeen of the twenty-four foresters in public employ in 1914 enlisted for military service. After World War I, the agency's George McVickar identified a pressing need for study to provide data for logging regulations. Howe's 1915 report, 'hardly complete or definite enough to form the basis of any action,' remained the only source of information on the province's forest resource. Chief Forester Martin Grainger supported the proposal, and McVickar apparently assessed regeneration on some timber sale areas in the Vancouver Forest District in 1921.[77]

The following year J.L. Alexander received an assignment to investigate the relationship between logging and reforestation in British Columbia's coastal forests. In 1922 he established a few sample plots to determine the amount and distribution of seedlings after logging and provide an informed estimate on the distance of seed dissemination. Initial results of this work, aimed at determining whether seed trees should be reserved on timber sales, indicated that the effective range of seeding from a 175-foot Douglas fir approximated 350 feet and raised questions about the wisdom of slash burning to encourage reproduction of this species.[78]

By this time a growing number of foresters on both sides of the border attributed the growing expanse of barren land, at least in part, to the extensive clearcutting practiced by operators. In his 1922 'Minimum Requirements Report' Munger had urged operators to adopt US Forest Service methods, but, even on the national forests, cutover areas often appeared in an 'unsatisfactory silvicultural condition,' prompting demands for greater care in timber sale management. British Columbia's Chief Forester P.Z. Caverhill also felt that the relationship between logging methods and the process of forest renewal required attention. 'There is a growing feeling,' he informed C.D. Howe in 1923, 'that the high-lead system of logging is responsible for large areas of cut-over land not restocking.' Prohibition of these methods was out of the question, of course, because of their widespread use and engineering superiority, but the Branch needed to 'ascertain the technical measures, necessary and practical, to ensure perpetuation of our timbered areas.'[79]

J.L. Alexander's early work suggested that most sites would restock quickly after logging 'even where present methods of logging are used,' provided that fires were controlled. Another Branch forester went so far as to deny the existence of devastated forestland. 'Nature reclothes all,' G.E. Stoodley informed P.Z. Caverhill. 'It is only a question of the time element.' But even optimists knew that the creation of larger contiguous areas of logged-off land would impede natural reforestation. Still confident at the end of 1924, Caverhill assured the minister of Lands that reproduction after logging was 'ample to assure a new forest' at no cost to the government. Planting, on the other hand, would involve considerable expense. In fact, the chief forester's statements to colleagues, elected officials, and the public were uniformly reassuring to 1928, suggesting that political considerations played no less a role in shaping the presentation of research findings in British Columbia than in the American context.[80]

The data that informed such pronouncements in British Columbia was hardly substantial, given the low priority assigned to research within the Department of Lands. Alexander remained the Branch's only silvicultural investigator until 1924, leading future Chief Forester E.C. Manning to criticize the meagre resources devoted to science. 'As it is now,' he observed, 'everyone has a hand in it whenever we can get a little time off from our routine work.' Continuing the present half-hearted effort would carry a high price to be paid in 'useless experiments, wrong conclusions based on ignorance or insufficient data ... resulting in money spent in adhering to regulations which are later found not to be practicable.' Percy Barr was assigned to research in 1924, but Caverhill's recommendation that experiment stations be established went unheeded for the time being. Progress of a bureaucratic sort came in 1927 when Barr became director of the Forest Branch's new Research Division.[81]

In the southern part of the Douglas fir region, funding from the US government permitted a slightly more serious commitment to silvicultural study. In 1925 the budget allotted $26,000 for establishment of the Forest Service's Pacific Northwest Forest Experiment Station at Portland. Thornton Munger was appointed director of the new facility, with the small Wind River station becoming a fieldwork centre. An advisory council chaired by Weyerhaeuser forester C.S. Chapman, consisting of representatives of the Forest Service, BC Forest Branch, universities, and a number of prominent operators, served to guide the station's research projects along practical lines. This period is also noteworthy for the arrival of Leo Isaac, who replaced J.V. Hoffman at Wind River after the latter's resignation early in 1924. Isaac would dominate the field of Douglas fir silvicultural research for the next thirty years.[82]

US Forest Service Wind River Experimental Forest Headquarters and Nursery, Washington, 1935.

The establishment of the experiment station at Portland occurred as scepticism over Hoffman's seed storage theory gained strength. If correct, Munger and others queried, why did so much of the land fail to restock as it should? And on some sites the most likely source of reproduction seemed to be wind-blown seed. Although the US Forest Service had devoted moderate attention to the study of Douglas fir regeneration for over a decade, the rapid rate of deforestation created a new sense of urgency for data to guide the development of cutting practices. 'We have come to a point where evidence is demanded from which to base sound conclusions,' Munger declared. Only when foresters knew more about seed production, dissemination and survival, and germination and seedling establishment would they be in a position to 'devise the method of securing a seed supply, of burning the slashing, and of handling the tract thereafter in a way that will assure quick and sufficient reproduction on every type of soil and climate.'[83]

With the furore over logging regulation a memory, the WFCA's E.T. Allen felt safe in calling for a reassessment of the seed storage theory in 1925. In the previous year, that organization had initiated a cooperative survey of 130,000 cutover acres belonging to seven member companies, and they discovered that the Douglas fir seedlings were not even-aged, as would be expected if seeds stored in the ground had germinated simultaneously when exposed to sunlight. Rather, they ranged in age, suggesting that these areas had restocked over time as a result of wind-blown seed. 'The whole theory of fir reforestation seems to require revision,' Allen advised.[84]

His colleagues, Munger included, counselled patience; additional research was required. Caverhill confessed to *Timberman* editor George Cornwall that foresters in his Branch had 'for some years not been fully convinced of the seed storage theory.' He wanted to proceed with caution, however, at least in part out of concern over 'the effect upon the public mind' of repeated shifts in forestry science and practice. J.L. Alexander shared his chief's conviction that the issue demanded more study. In October 1925, after examining approximately 1,000 cutover areas in the coastal region he could not yet definitively rule out stored seed as a factor.[85]

Leo Isaac conducted the experiments that finally discredited Hoffman's theory. Beginning in September 1925, he began replicating his predecessor's germination tests. Fresh seed was collected, examined for soundness, and embedded at various depths in containers of forest soil. These were placed in rodent-proof enclosures under a mature timber stand and on an adjoining logged area. The intent, as Isaac explained, was 'to simulate as nearly as possible the natural storage of seed as it falls from the cone and is worked into the soil or duff by rodents, falling debris, rain, or logging.'[86]

The procedure called for Isaac to take up a container from each test site annually for four years, test the seed for germination, and thus determine if Douglas fir seed survived on the forest floor for longer than a single year. Alexander, performing a similar series of investigations in British Columbia, reported in late 1926 that reliance should not be placed on stored seed to restock cutover lands. When a Long Bell Lumber Company executive requested an opinion early the following year Alexander replied that stored seed was 'relatively unimportant when compared to wind disseminated seed.' Isaac's work pointed to the same conclusion. Seeds taken up the first year germinated, a very few the second, but none thereafter.[87]

The American silviculturalist held off publishing his findings until sure of his evidence. Aware of the consequences for Hoffman's reputation and reluctant to 'destroy an established theory if it had any foundation of fact in it,' he repeated the germination tests three times. A brief research note appeared in 1931, indicating that Douglas fir seed had a one-year life span on the forest floor before decaying. It wasn't until 1935 that his 'Life of Douglas Fir Seed in the Forest Floor' appeared in the *Journal of Forestry*, invalidating Hoffman's theory. As many foresters had long suspected, no accumulation of Douglas fir seed crops awaited removal of the forest canopy; the reforestation of clearcuts must arise from seed trees or adjacent timber.[88]

Isaac's seed dissemination studies produced results more quickly. This was not a new field of investigation; foresters had been stationing seed traps at intervals from banks of timber for years to gain insight into the range of seed flight. But Isaac brought new precision to the inquiry in 1926 by staging a series of experiments involving the release of seeds from a home-made box kite over snow-covered ground in the Maupin valley of eastern Oregon.

The researcher loaded an oatmeal carton with seed and attached it to the kite, sending the arrangement up to various heights. After measuring wind velocity, he released the seeds by pulling a trip-wire. His team, at one point including A.E. Pickford of the BC Forest Branch, then traced the distance and pattern of seed flight, shifting a frame over the area and counting the seeds until reaching the limit of distribution.[89]

The tests indicated that under average conditions foresters could expect Douglas fir seed dissemination up to one-quarter mile from a bank of green timber in sufficient quantity. When caught by a rising air current over a warm slope seed might travel much farther, however, providing a probable explanation for the reproduction that had prompted Hoffman to advance his theory. Pickford's investigation of seed traps in British Columbia supported these conclusions. On the national forests in the Douglas fir region, the US Forest Service immediately instituted changes in the spacing of seed trees to conform with Isaac's finding that natural seedfall to a range of 1200 to 1350 feet would provide adequate coverage of timber sale areas.[90]

The determination that reproduction originated from wind-blown seed, coupled with Isaac's dissemination data, gave government agencies new insight into the ecological character of Douglas fir. As a consequence, foresters were better equipped to adjust clearcutting practices to secure natural regeneration, and they were more aware of the pressing need to do so. Meanwhile, related projects and ongoing examination of sample plots suggested both the scale of the reforestation problem and the extent to which modern logging practices contributed to the growing expanse of barren land.

Even on the national forests where the US Forest Service supervised cutting to ensure restocking, existing management techniques underwent reappraisal. A study of seed tree survival initiated in 1925 confirmed the doubts foresters had harboured about this silvicultural practice. In 1930, Isaac reported that 42 percent of the seed trees reserved on sale areas had been lost, the majority to windfall. By this time foresters knew that Douglas fir seed crops varied widely; seed production was prolific in some years, moderate or nonexistent in others. Thus, seed trees that did not survive for a long duration might contribute little or nothing to the restocking of a cutover area. These findings implied that the traditional Forest Service practice of leaving two seed trees per acre was inadequate, prompting trials involving their reservation in groups or strips in locations to maximize wind-firmness and lessen damage from logging or slash fires. Foresters were particularly optimistic about the benefits of logging on a staggered-setting basis, a method providing both fire breaks and a seed supply if they restricted cut-blocks to a reasonable size.[91]

Mounting evidence also confirmed that the faith originally placed in slash burning as an agent of Douglas fir restocking had little basis. Indeed, studies disclosed that in some conditions the practice did serious damage to soil.

Intense burns reduced soil to a red ash that exhibited little capacity to absorb water. Such areas dried out rapidly in hot weather, reducing the moisture available to seedlings and inhibiting their survival. Moreover, in destroying the 'duff' layer of organic material, burning deposited high quantities of nutrients in the surface soil. Seedlings on these sites developed shallow root systems, increasing vulnerability to summer drought.[92]

Studies designed to determine what conditions favoured Douglas fir germination added an important dimension to the growing body of silvicultural knowledge, contributing further evidence of unregulated clearcutting's negative impact. Douglas fir's intolerance of shade had traditionally been, and would remain, the primary scientific justification for clearcutting. But tests recorded higher germination rates on sites that received some shade protection. A moderate amount of shade proved especially beneficial for seedlings on severe sites. On unshaded mineral soil surfaces an 80 degree air temperature might generate ground temperatures of 140 degrees, sufficient to cook the seedling stem. Particularly on south-facing slopes, where exposure to the sun was most intense, 'the effect of shade in favoring seedling survival is striking,' a 1928 Pacific Northwest Forest Experiment Station research note concluded.[93]

Definitive evidence of the ways in which the conduct of clearcutting retarded or prevented new growth developed when foresters scrutinized private cutover land. In his 1927 report *Timber Growing and Logging Practice in the Douglas Fir Region*, Thornton Munger presented a bleak summary of US Forest Service restocking surveys in western Oregon and Washington. Approximately 40 percent of the logged-off land was barren, with much of the remaining 60 percent bearing an incomplete stand. Moreover, much of this reproduction had become established under early systems that were 'more favorable to natural reforestation than modern logging methods.' Long-Bell Lumber Company forester John B. Woods admitted in 1927 that his firm logged so much land each year that the fringes of standing timber could not be expected to scatter seed over more than half of the cutover.[94]

Work of a similar nature carried out by foresters in British Columbia pointed to an emerging regeneration crisis in that province. Alexander had initiated a history map study of ten major operations on Vancouver Island and the lower mainland in 1924, with the intention of making annual examinations of these areas to determine the rate of reforestation. Although the project had lapsed, in 1928 Percy Barr was authorized to update the maps. Defining 1,000 seedlings per acre as satisfactory restocking, Barr and Eric Garman estimated that 60 percent of the cutover lands failed to meet this standard. Logging and fire, the Forest Branch's 1928 annual report explained, had created extensive denuded areas too far removed from seed sources to restock. To this point the Branch had made no effort to reserve seed trees, even on timber sales where it possessed strong authority. 'Personally,' Caverhill informed Christopher Grainger in late 1927 while arranging an inspection of US Forest Service sale areas, 'with the high-lead method of logging I can hardly visualize how these trees are protected during the yarding operation, especially if they are left in any regular or systematic manner.'[95]

A survey of early sales in the Vancouver Forest District left little doubt that mass production overhead logging techniques were more destructive than earlier methods. Logged between 1915 and 1919, most of these small areas averaged approximately 200 acres, and featured an abundance of seed trees. On the whole, then, the cutovers exhibited optimal opportunities for natural reforestation, resulting in satisfactory restocking on 75 percent of the area. This contrasted sharply with the situation Barr discovered on lands logged recently. 'On these large operations very few seed trees have been left,' he explained, 'and most of these have been destroyed in fires subsequent to logging.'[96]

In a 1930 *Forest Chronicle* article Barr and Eric Garman set out in explicit terms their understanding of the relationship between changes in technology, logging practices, and reforestation. In logging selectively, oxen and horse loggers left plenty of seed trees and did little damage to remaining timber and saplings. Slash accumulations were minimal, and protected by trees and undergrowth, did not become dangerously flammable. Forest

A portion of Capilano Timber Company clearcut at North Vancouver, 1922.

reproduction became much less certain with the adoption of the steam donkey. Utilization was more intensive, and greater damage inflicted upon young growth. The amount of debris left behind increased significantly, creating a more favourable environment for fire. Nevertheless, timber not selected for cutting remained to produce seed, and fires were usually restricted to comparatively small areas exposed to reseeding from adjacent stands.

The unrestrained application of high-lead and skyline systems of logging in the years around World War I shattered any residual harmony existing between the processes of forest exploitation and renewal. Clearcuts became much more extensive, and yarding with high-speed heavy equipment levelled the young growth that had survived earlier methods. A vastly increased amount of slash was left exposed to the sun and wind. The intense fires that inevitably swept through such cutovers destroyed not only the fresh seed present on the ground, but also any remaining timber. Moreover, the two silviculturalists observed, clearcutting on the coast was 'conducted on such a large scale and at such high speed that the operations of a single company may cover several hundred acres during a year.' Much of the cutover land was thus 'too far removed from marginal stands to receive any seed.'[97]

The Political Economy of Clearcutting
By the end of the 1920s, silvicultural researchers held the operators' use of

BC Forest Branch Green Timbers Forest Nursery near New Westminster, 1940.

steam-powered cable logging systems responsible for regeneration problems in the Douglas fir region. In British Columbia the Forest Branch's Green Timbers Tree Nursery opened in 1930 to produce seedlings for about 50 percent of the logged areas on the coast that required planting. By this time the US Forest Service had planted over 30,000 acres on the national forests of Washington and Oregon. But foresters and political elites on both sides of the border believed that reforestation of all lands denuded in the future would be far too costly. Natural regeneration would secure a new forest at nominal expense to the public, if only operators adopted slight modifications to their clearcutting practices.[98]

Precisely how to transform clearcutting into a sound silvicultural system had been the subject of considerable research in the Douglas fir region. Foresters had dispelled some myths, gained a sense of the scope of the problem, but arrived at no definitive conclusions. They were, however, better equipped to study the reforestation question as governments, awakening to the need for reliable information and increased support for research. In the United States, passage of the 1928 McSweeney-McNary Act provided greater funding for US Forest Service programs, and the following year Percy Barr finally obtained authorization to establish a permanent experimental station at Cowichan Lake on Vancouver Island.[99]

There remained a good deal to learn about Douglas fir silviculture. Nevertheless, on one level such initiatives were promising, reflecting a recognition that effective public policy required a foundation of accurate scientific

BC Forest Branch Cowichan Lake Experiment Station, 1937.

data. On the other hand, the resolution of the first American regulation debate had demonstrated conclusively that knowledge was a necessary but not sufficient precondition of rational forest management. American lumbermen, with the assistance of a Greeley-led US Forest Service, had withstood one challenge to their 'right' to exploit the forest without regard for regeneration. In British Columbia, where most of the forestland had not been alienated, the illusion of enlightened administration held through most of the 1920s despite the fact that the timber interests of that province had 'succeeded in penetrating the administrative process in order to shape public policy to their private needs.'[100]

In specific localities throughout the Douglas fir region, the devastation wrought by reckless logging began to cause concern. On Washington's Grays Harbor district, along with certain parts of Puget Sound, the exhaustion of private timber supplies loomed. The situation in British Columbia was not yet so alarming, but some residents of lumbering communities within Vancouver Island's E & N Railway belt criticized industry's lack of regard for sustainability and the absence of government controls.[101]

Foresters in leadership positions on both sides of the border acknowledged the problem, but as the decade of the 1920s drew to a close in anything but a roaring fashion for the lumber industry, they expressed no real enthusiasm for firmer government control of logging. In British Columbia the Forest Act gave government the authority to regulate exploitation on Crown lands, but officials were reluctant to impair the competitiveness of firms through any measure that might increase logging costs. In any case, 50 percent of the provincial cut came from Crown-grant lands, primarily from large operators within the E & N belt. Reluctant to place those logging on public lands at a disadvantage with these operators, the government allowed unregulated practices on the E & N belt to become the provincial standard. 'With regard to Crown Grants,' Chief Forester Caverhill informed an Ontario colleague in 1929, 'public opinion has not yet reached the point where interference with the free use of private lands will be countenanced.' Public opinion notwithstanding, the collective voice of the province's lumbermen carried weight with politicians.[102]

The prospect for government control of destructive cutting in the Pacific Northwest states was equally unpromising. Industry dictated the activities of the state forestry departments of Washington and Oregon. 'The size of their appropriations, their personnel policy, and probably at times their existence is largely dependent upon the lumbermen,' Regional Forester Grainger noted. A change in the leadership of the US Forest Service in 1928 heralded a more aggressive policy for that agency. Greeley's departure that year to become executive secretary of the West Coast Lumbermen's Association brought R.Y. Stuart to the head of the Forest Service.[103]

Early on, Stuart requested regional foresters to review the agency's policy of cooperation in bringing about better forest practice on private lands. Willing to take the Forest Service along a more confrontational path than his predecessor, Stewart received little initial support from Grainger on the west coast. The latter replied that 'probably the greatest need of the fir region at present is a seed supply,' but saw no merit in replacing the Service's cooperative philosophy with one emphasizing compulsion. 'I cannot see any angle to the problem out here that cannot be better approached from the cooperative base,' he advised the new chief. Improvement in practices on private land in the west, as elsewhere, would come only when owners perceived 'a sound economic reason for protecting it and getting the most out of it.'[104]

By 1930, then, the Douglas fir region's most influential foresters were not yet prepared to adopt a more assertive stance toward operators. Anxious to avoid confrontation with operators, and undoubtedly aware of the profession's impotence in the face of the power wielded by their potential clients, those on the west coast remained quiet. In any case, the 1920s was not a propitious decade for stringent government regulation of business in the wider political economy. In the United States, Herbert Hoover's Department of Commerce cooperated with trade associations in their effort to eliminate market competition and inefficiency. In Canada, too, provincial and federal politicians followed a policy of partnership with business interests in fostering economic development.[105] Just over the horizon, however, loomed a collapse in the world economy that would create a more favourable context for state intervention in economic and social affairs. This, in tandem with the emergence of widespread public and professional criticism of the operators' conduct in exploiting the region's most important natural resource, set the stage for a new challenge to timber capital's factory regime in the western woods.

4
Depression-Era Forestry in the Pacific Northwest: Selective Logging, a New Regulation Debate, and the State Option

The Depression decade of the 1930s stands as a critical period in the history of logging and forest practice in the Pacific Northwest. The adoption of new technologies, revival of the regulation issue, and a brief experiment in federally sanctioned industrial self-government made these chaotic and hectic years for operators, foresters, and indeed, the historian interested in developing a coherent narrative of these complex themes. But for all of the decade's hustle and bustle, its key theme, viewed from the perspective of the forest, is continuity rather than drastic change. When World War II erupted late in 1939, the factory regime stood intact and had incorporated a market-driven version of selective logging. Operators, meanwhile, sought to preserve the efficiencies of clearcutting against federal encroachment behind a defensive barrier of state forest practice legislation.

Against the backdrop of crisis in the world capitalist economy, unregulated clearcutting came under technological and political challenges during the Great Depression. Operators, ironically, triggered the first by adopting the caterpillar tractor to log timber selectively in an effort to reduce labour costs and cope with restricted markets. Foresters were unanimous in deploring the practice, which left slash and trees of poor quality intermingled on partially cut stands, but some considered tractor technology to hold the potential solution to the evils of extensive clearcutting. The Forest Service itself, amidst considerable internal controversy, developed and propagated a system of selective timber management as a cure for overproduction and an initial step in the conversion to sustained-yield forestry.

For silviculturalists, both the operators' selective logging and the Forest Service's model contradicted the scientific legitimacy accorded clearcutting as the best practice for coastal forests. The resulting intra-agency conflict pitted the Pacific Northwest Forest Experiment Station's Thornton Munger, who placed his faith in clearcutting reforms, against Regional Forester C.J. Buck, who saw in selection a remedy for the waste and regeneration problems associated with the tradional practice. By the end of the decade selective logging advocates and opponents alike recognized the need for research to resolve the cutting practice debate, and Leo Isaac was busy accumulating data that subsequently supported some of the reservations silviculturalists had expressed about the new method.

Operators themselves had to treat the selective logging issue with caution when it intersected with the revitalized campaign for regulation of logging on private land. Exhibiting the reform sentiment that flourished during the Depression period, progressives within the forestry profession again took up the crusade against a forest policy based exclusively on the cooperative principle. Their hopes for an end to the destructive logging permitted under the Clarke-McNary Act received a boost when the presidential election of 1932 brought Franklin D. Roosevelt to the White House. Roosevelt's political ideology defies easy explanation, but he shared his cousin Theodore's concern for conservation and his New Deal platform seemed sufficiently inclusive to accommodate restrictions on the property rights of timber owners.

Presidential influence was, in fact, responsible in part for inclusion of a conservation clause in the timber industry's Code of Fair Competition, adopted in accordance with the 1933 National Industrial Recovery Act (NIRA). But Article X, drafted and administered by trade association leaders in keeping with the NIRA's philosophy of industrial self-regulation, was recognized by conservationists as a dead letter long before the Supreme Court declared the legislation unconstitutional in March 1935. With the NIRA's demise, the regulation campaign took on new life under the leadership of Chief Forester Ferdinand Silcox, who added his agency's voice to the chorus demanding imposition of federal controls to curtail forest devastation. For the remainder of the decade, Silcox and his successor, A.H. Clapp, pressed to have the public assistance granted to industry made conditional upon operators' adherence to cutting standards formulated at the national level and administered by the states.

The establishment of a Joint Congressional Committee to inquire into the status of American forestry shifted the regulation debate back into the political arena. Douglas fir lumbermen responded by mounting an aggressive public relations campaign and lobbying effort, emphasizing both advances made under self-regulation and the need for a stronger public commitment to make forestry a profitable investment. Forest Service data suggest that the progress claimed by operators was illusory, and the agency's submissions to the Congressional Committee made a strong case for a national plan of silvicultural controls to increase the productivity of forestland.

Finally, aware of Forest Service plans to legislate restrictions on the practice of clearcutting, and concerned that federal regulation would become a reality later if not sooner, Douglas fir trade association leaders sought to effect a permanent pre-emptive solution. They turned to their state legislatures, initiating the process of drafting, sponsoring, and garnering support for forest practice acts passed in Oregon and Washington during the next decade.

The Selective Logging Problem, a Second Regulation Crusade, and FDR Comes to Washington, 1930-32

When the New York stock market crashed in October 1929, the American lumber industry was no stranger to depression, having been outproducing demand for the previous three years. On the west coast, heads of forty of the largest lumbering enterprises had attempted to gain lasting control over the market by merging their firms, a scheme that failed only when Weyerhaeuser refused to provide the timber necessary to ensure the conglomerate's long-term viability. Troubled by competition from British Columbia producers in the eastern seaboard market, Pacific Northwest operators also worked with marginal success to have tariff barriers erected. Unanimity was difficult to achieve, however, as those with investments in British Columbia and mill owners dependent on log shipments from that province opposed tariff restrictions. The Smoot-Hawley tariff of 1930 imposed a minor duty on lumber, leaving Canadian logs and shingles free to enter the American market.[1]

Conditions worsened in the first two years of the Great Depression. Lumber production in Washington dropped from 7.3 billion feet in 1930 to just over 2 billion in 1932, and throughout the Douglas fir region mills and camps sat idle. Government assistance in the form of President Hoover's mid-1931 order that the Forest Service curtail timber sales and a 1932 increase in the duty on lumber helped, but not enough to save many operations. One measure of distress in the timber economies of Oregon and Washington was the rate at which forestland reverted to public ownership because of tax delinquency. In four counties alone over 51,700 acres reverted during 1932.[2]

Hoover's Timber Conservation Board, created at the behest of the NLMA in late 1930, raised hopes among lumbermen that a mechanism for market control was at hand. An advisory board dominated by industry luminaries, including Greeley and Mason, recommended measures to bring order to the lumber market. Given the influence that trade associations wielded in the Board's activities, it came as no surprise that its July 1932 report expressed industry's usual demand for increased federal funding of fire prevention and timber acquisition programs, and property taxation reform by the states. Another recommendation, more reflective of the gravity of the situation and timber capital's openness to more drastic measures, anticipated Roosevelt's National Industrial Recovery Act by advocating federal supervision of production control.[3]

The Hoover administration's preoccupation with the 1932 election campaign prevented action on the Timber Conservation Board report.

Meanwhile, operators in the Douglas fir region experimented with a technological solution to the problem of overproduction while they presented their case for further government assistance. The adoption of the caterpillar tractor, and to a lesser extent light, mobile yarding equipment, reflected in the extractive realm the same logic that industry exhibited in its efforts to rationalize the national timber economy.

The atmosphere of 'doubt and despair' that pervaded the Douglas fir lumber industry in the early 1930s bred a receptivity to new methods of forest exploitation. With prices down to pre-World War I levels and demand for lower grades of logs and lumber almost nonexistent, the progressive clearcutting dictated by complex, labour-intensive skidder systems came into question. A more selective approach, made possible by the tractor, seemed to hold the only hope of salvation. Oregon-American Lumber Company manager Judd Greenman conveyed this sentiment to Charles S. Keith in December 1931. Currently idle due to bankruptcy, Greenman wanted to

Selective logging operation in a fir and cedar forest at
Snoqualmie Pass, Washington.

reopen but asserted the futility of doing so under traditional operating methods. All logging for the foreseeable future in the Douglas fir region, he declared, would 'be on a basis that involves only the best trees and only the best of the tree.' Many open-market loggers and integrated firms ran only by practising a tree or 'show' selection system. Selective logging might not generate profits under existing conditions, Greenman advised, but it did 'enable the operator to minimize his direct losses by permitting him to pay at least part of his shutdown overhead expense.'[4]

Operators' willingness to consider more precise techniques accorded with and may have been inspired by arguments certain foresters had begun advancing in the latter 1920s. University of Washington student Axel Brandstrom was an early proponent of the financial advantages to be derived from concentrating harvesting activities in areas of maximum value. Even high-lead and railroad technology permitted a form of 'area selection' he wrote in a 1927 article, advocating that operators remove only mature high-quality timber certain to yield a profit.[5]

Although financial considerations dominated Brandstrom's writings, he also devoted some attention to the silvicultural superiority of economic selection. As an alternative to the traditional plan of operation, to 'strip off all timber growth over a large area, leaving behind a desolate scene of complete destruction,' he proposed a series of limited clearcuts capable of being reseeded by surrounding trees. Only stands containing merchantable timber would be liquidated, providing both profit and a means to ensure 'perpetuation of the productive capacity of the forest.'[6]

Burt Kirkland, now a University of Washington professor, and consulting foresters David Mason and C.L. Lyford were other selective logging advocates. Like Brandstrom they appealed primarily to operators' pecuniary interests, presenting selection as an alternative to the clearcutting that flooded the market with unwanted lumber. Citing the work of his student Brandstrom, Kirkland pointed out in 1930 that under 25 percent of Pacific coast stands yielded returns under present conditions. Focusing on cutting only this timber and holding the remainder for future logging would cure overproduction and establish a foundation for continuous operation. Mason advertised his firm's forest valuation services to operators interested in making a conversion to sustained-yield management by taking timber fit for immediate harvest and reserving young growth.[7]

The association of selective logging with improved forest practices made for interesting reading in professional and industry journals, but many foresters remained sceptical. All hoped to see clearcuts reduced in size to permit natural reforestation, but the silvicultural consequences of individual tree selection by tractors were unknown and a matter of complete indifference to most operators. To the extent that the technique justified high-grading of the forest with no regard for slash disposal or future stand composition it might prove to be a curse rather than a blessing. William Greeley admitted that conservation played no part in the tractor's appeal to industry, but argued that if the practice contributed to market stabilization, increased profits, and reservation of timber, operators would have an incentive to retain their lands for future operation.[8]

With some foresters suspecting that the term 'selective logging' merely provided a convenient disguise for a new style of liquidation, informed discussion of the topic was difficult to achieve. Selection might mean anything from removal of individual trees, to a heavier cut of mature timber, to a series of clearcuts. 'One can hardly be sure what a man has in mind when he speaks of selective logging,' Assistant Regional Forester Fred Ames complained. One thing was clear: tractor logging on private lands in the Douglas fir region had no resemblance to the classic selection system of forest management that saw the periodic harvesting of the oldest, largest, diseased, or defective trees to achieve an even distribution of age classes throughout the forest.[9]

On the other hand, Ames found it difficult to imagine a worse outcome than followed from the 'typical clearcutting of extensive areas without any provision whatever for regeneration.' Even on the national forests of the region his agency had achieved only 'variable results' from the reservation of seed trees either singly or in strips and blocks because of blowdown loss and slash burning damage. Foresters should keep an open mind, then, and consider selective logging a 'development deserving encouragement.' Ames and others perceived some merger of the principles of selection and clearcutting as the most intriguing option. Logging small scattered settings would preserve the known benefits of clearcutting for the reproduction of the shade-intolerant Douglas fir, would expose cutovers to seed disseminated from surrounding timber, and would reduce problems associated with burning huge areas of slash.[10]

Sufficient interest in the potential of selective logging to remedy the ills of the Douglas fir industry existed at Washington, DC, to bring Kirkland and Brandstrom to the staff of the Pacific Northwest Forest Experiment Station in 1931. Although Director Thornton Munger had serious doubts about the silvicultural merit of the technique, and may even have attempted to block the appointments, he advertised the new research project as 'having greater possibilities for radical betterment of forest practices than almost anything else we are doing.' But from the outset, economic considerations outweighed conservation in the studies conducted by Kirkland and Brandstrom. Their research addressed the facility's primary mandate in the Depression context: 'to find ways by which the demoralized business of forestland management and exploitation may be reorganized on a better and more stable basis.'[11]

The Forest Service's own ability to generate revenue figured in the appeal the new technique held for officials. National forest timber sales had declined, and the agency felt considerable pressure from coastal lumbermen who wanted the cutting of public timber curtailed completely. Logging on a select basis might improve the general health of the lumber economy while increasing revenues to an agency struggling under reduced budget allotments. The region's national forest supervisors felt strongly enough at the end of 1931 to recommend that the method be given thorough tests. Brandstrom had already conducted time studies of the Simpson Logging Company's tractor logging operation, and 1,000 acres of old-growth Douglas fir in the Columbia National Forest were reserved to apply his findings in the appraisal of stumpage values.[12]

During the summer of 1932 Chief Forester R.Y. Stuart visited the west coast, devoting considerable attention to the subject of selective logging. He inspected the Crown Willamette Paper Company's operation at Youngs River, Oregon, the site of a logging cost study by Brandstrom. After shutting down its steam operation, that firm experimented with tractors, characterized by Brandstrom as the 'modern mechanical replica of the old bull team.' Stuart came away 'very impressed ... with the opportunities presented through application of selective logging methods in the Douglas fir type,' and instructed Regional Forester C.J. Buck and Ames to work with Experiment Station staff in trials of the method on prospective timber sales.[13]

Brandstrom's *Analysis of Logging Costs and Operating Methods in the Douglas Fir Region*, published in June 1933, was the first tangible result of the Forest Service's research into the economic advantages of selection cutting. Summarizing his work on a wide variety of operations, the forester calculated that logging selectively with trucks and tractors cost $2.00 per thousand feet less than conventional clearcutting. Brandstrom also presented his findings to operators at a series of conferences throughout the region.[14]

Already, however, some within the agency's ranks had reservations about the new process. Recognized as being of obvious benefit to operators in maximizing returns on their own holdings under certain conditions, its impact on the long-term productivity of forestland could not be ignored by the Forest Service. Simplicity was the great virtue of clearcutting, both in terms of exploitation and protection. Slash disposal on clearcut areas was an inexpensive matter of broadcast burning. But in stands logged selectively by tractor, slash volumes might be too great to burn without destruction of residual timber. Also, silviculturalists feared that in the common case of mixed stands containing a significant proportion of hemlock, removal of Douglas fir would allow the shade-tolerant, inferior species to dominate the future forest.

These concerns led O.F. Ericson to conclude early in 1933 that tree selection was appropriate where scattered over-mature trees could be extracted without damaging neighbouring timber, but in stands featuring an even distribution of all age and diameter classes the technique warranted application 'only to the extent that the fire menace can be controlled.' Even Regional Forester Buck, one of the more ardent selective logging advocates, advised Stuart that slash disposal and fire protection problems required further study before the agency recommended the method to operators.[15]

While foresters in the west struggled to come to terms with the management implications of new technology and cutting practices, reformers within the profession resurrected the campaign for federal regulation. Two years after Gifford Pinchot ended his tenure as governor of Pennsylvania in 1927, he penned a foreword to George Ahern's *Deforested America*, a critique of corporate forest exploitation that accused the US Forest Service under Greeley of complicity in the destruction of the nation's private timberland. Greeley and Ahern, formerly chief forester of the Philippines, went to the SAF's 1929 annual meeting and attracted the support of a small band of colleagues.

They issued a direct challenge to the profession in the April 1930 issue of the *Journal of Forestry*. A 'Letter to Foresters,' signed by Ahern, Pinchot, Robert Marshall, E.N. Munn, Ward Shepard, Raphael Zon, and William Sparhawk, described American lumbering as a 'tragedy of waste,' one accepted and condoned by foresters. The profession must finally recognize that owners would not practice forestry voluntarily, and resist being 'lulled into inaction by a lack of faith in the possibility of remedying the evil.' Only federal regulation in conjunction with a vast expansion of the national forest system would end the devastation and raise foresters' usefulness to the nation.[16]

Robert Marshall reached a wider audience with his 1930 pamphlet, *The Social Management of American Forests*, published by the League for Industrial Democracy. The forest industry should be operated for the welfare of all, Marshall argued, including workers who endured miserable living standards, a lack of family life, and hazardous working conditions. Stripping the case for government control of cutting to its essentials, he described forestry as having meaning only if in 'harvesting the present crop, provision be made that the same land bear another crop of timber.' Abundant evidence existed to demonstrate the failure of cooperation in achieving even a minimal standard of forestry. Cooperation, Marshall noted, 'has brought out several beautifully illustrated conservation magazines. It has resulted in many eloquent talks before school children, womens' organizations and rotary clubs. It has produced a great many lachrimose promises and wild assertions, but it has not resulted in any appreciable practice of forestry.'[17]

Meeting industry's demand for fairer taxation and permitting the formation of combinations for control of production would not suffice, he continued. Forestry demanded that immediate profits be sacrificed to invest in practices producing no return for many years, a delay lumbermen had no intention of enduring. Because private enterprise was incapable of engaging in real resource stewardship, social ownership of forestland was the only solution, but as an interim measure the federal government should use its power to regulate activities on interstate streams and create a Forest Service branch with authority to levy fines against operators who violated cutting laws.[18]

Foresters who hoped to maintain the profession's friendly relationship with timber capital criticized the reformers' faith in the interventionist state. R.S. Kellogg declared that such 'propaganda' had no rightful place in a scientific organization such as the SAF, and would succeed only in fostering dissension. The society's president, Franklin Reed, noted the absence of business foresters among the signatories of the 'Letter,' decried its 'religious zeal,' but observed that since forestry was both a cause and a business, idealists and pragmatists alike had a place within the profession. Respondents to the 1931 report of the SAF's Committee on Forest Policy endorsed regulation, but by the states rather than the federal government.[19]

The relationship between practice and policy became a subject of more than theoretical interest when New York Senator Royal S. Copeland introduced a resolution calling for a study of American forest resources. The Pacific Northwest Forest Experiment Station submitted a 1932 report in response to a headquarters request for information on measures required to end forest devastation. 'Economic selection by area' was recommended as the appropriate cutting method for the Douglas fir type. In general, this meant that second-growth, low-value, mature timber or inferior species should be left to provide seed and discourage extensive slash fires that often escaped to destroy reproduction on adjacent areas. Tracts of uniformly valuable timber should be logged in alternate blocks, or strips of timber left at strategic points. In stands where values varied and clearcut widths exceeded 1500 feet, the reservation of low-grade or defective timber would have a positive effect on regeneration.[20]

The report went on to acknowledge the expense involved in requiring operators cutting on a liquidation basis to leave merchantable timber temporarily, but pointed out that those cutting for a sustained yield would merely experience a delayed return. It recommended regulation by the states, which had constitutional authority to specify the manner of cutting and protection measures, with the federal government making satisfactory standards a condition of financial assistance. The cost to operators must be recognized, however, and the imposition of logging regulations must be 'accompanied with the financial help to carry out the requirements.'[21]

The Copeland Report, compiled by Forest Service staff in Washington and titled *A National Plan for American Forestry*, appeared in March 1933. A mild document, it criticized timbermen and laid primary blame for the nation's forest problem on private ownership but issued no clarion call for regulation. Instead, the agency emphasized the benefits of intensive management of an expanded public forest system. Lumbermen applauded this prescription, which disappointed left-wingers in the forestry profession such as Ward Shepard. He approved of the report's depiction of the 'failure of private-ownership,' but expressed regret at its failure to propose a 'vigorous, aggressive, and direct attack on forest destruction' through federal regulation of cutting practices.[22]

Uncertainty and confusion prevailed within the American forestry profession during the first three years of the Depression, and nothing had been resolved by early 1933. Foresters in the Pacific Northwest detected no improvement in traditional clearcutting practices, but could not embrace its most radical alternative – individual tree selection – because of the many unanswered questions surrounding the technique's application in Douglas fir stands. No less troubling was the revitalized regulation issue, which divided the profession and strained relations with operators. Both industry and the Forest Service continued to reel under the impact of the Depression. Certain that the only solution to the economic malaise lay in the re-election of Herbert Hoover's Republican administration, lumbermen were disappointed when the vast majority of voters responded favourably to Franklin D. Roosevelt's vague promises of a New Deal for the American people in late 1932. Roosevelt's election created apprehension among operators, hope for workers and the unemployed, and set the stage for a brief, dramatic attempt to stimulate recovery through government sponsored industrial self-regulation.

Industrial Self-Regulation and Article X: Forestry under the NIRA, 1933-35

Like his cousin Theodore, the new president was a conservationist of some conviction, but restoration of confidence in the American economy topped his list of priorities. After a flurry of moves designed to stabilize the financial and monetary structure, Roosevelt turned his attention to industrial revitalization. Business leaders, anxious to ensure that recovery policies met the needs of their enterprises, flooded Washington, DC, with proposals. David Mason, now general manager of the Western Pine Association, expressed the widespread conviction within trade association circles that antitrust laws should be relaxed, permitting firms to achieve market stability through cooperation in production and price control schemes.[23]

The NIRA, passed by Congress on 16 June 1933, gave the American business establishment much of what it had requested. Intended to have a two-year existence, the legislation suspended antitrust laws, legalizing cartel arrangements within major industries. Termed 'codes of fair practice,' these agreements allowed producers to collaborate openly in setting prices and restricting output. In essence, writes Kim McQuaid, the NIRA's intent was to 'place dominant industrial trade associations in charge of a nation-wide restructuring of the peacetime United States economy.' But corporate executives were not Roosevelt's only constituency, and negotiations to secure Congressional approval ensured that the bill was not crafted solely in accordance with their demands.[24]

Along with a desire to avoid fostering monopoly, the Democratic president and his 'brains trust' hoped to increase the purchasing power of working people and gain the support of trade union leaders for the recovery plan. Thus, industrial codes included minimum wage, maximum hours, and child labour standards. Finally, and least palatable to all but the most sophisticated corporate liberals in oligopolistic sectors, the NIRA's Section 7-A extended to workers in mass production industries the right to organize and bargain collectively through representatives of their own choice. General Hugh S. Johnson headed the National Recovery Administration (NRA), responsible for the development and enforcement of codes.[25]

Members of the NLMA agreed upon a draft of the Lumber Code in late May, approved by the West Coast Lumbermen's Association at a series of June meetings. The region's logging operators organized the Pacific Northwest Loggers Association at this time to prevent mill owners from ignoring their interests. Later in June a delegation drawn from these organizations attended meetings in Chicago for further negotiations, where representatives decided that the regional trade associations would administer the code. Conservation was absent from the agenda of the NLMA's Emergency National Committee, charged with drafting the final document for submission to the NRA. But foresters like Shepard, Earle Clapp, and Raphael Zon argued for inclusion of regulations in the code as a *quid pro quo* for industry receiving the right to circumvent antitrust laws. Secretary of Agriculture Henry Wallace, Chief Forester R.Y. Stuart, and Roosevelt himself agreed that some provision to end destructive cutting should be included. Anticipating the president, William Greeley had already advised western lumbermen to 'beat him to the draw' by drafting a conservation clause.[26]

The former chief forester, Wilson Compton, David Mason, and Laird Bell of the Weyerhaeuser Timber Company prepared the initial draft of what became Article X, industry's concession to Roosevelt's wish that the code address conservation. The Forest Service countered with a more substantive version, and negotiations produced a compromise accepted by the president on 19 August 1933, putting a New Deal stamp of approval on the entire Code of Fair Competition for the Lumber and Timber Product Industries. Thus, in addition to placing wage, hour, production, and price standards under the control of the Lumber Code Authority's regional divisions, the document committed operators to cooperate with state and federal agencies in carrying out 'such practicable measures as may be necessary ... for the conservation and sustained production of forest resources.'[27]

The specific measures required to give some substance to this pledge were to be worked out at conferences during the winter of 1933-34. In the interim Stuart died, elevating Ferdinand A. Silcox to leadership of the Forest Service. A forester of 'relatively radical views' with a background in industrial relations, Silcox was 'every inch a New Dealer' in Greeley's estimation. He and others in the agency who saw an opportunity to foster improved practices on private lands soon became distressed at the influence wielded by industry representatives in the Article X negotiations.[28]

The final conference produced agreement on a program for submission to the Lumber Code Authority that included the usual items on industry's wish list: expanded federal and state forests; higher tariffs; more public support for forest protection, reforestation, and marketing; modification of taxation systems; and credit agencies similar to those established to assist farmers. Lumbermen, in return, agreed to an amendment to the Lumber Code known as Schedule C – Forest Conservation Code. Approved by Roosevelt on 23 March 1934, the amendment gave regional trade associations the additional task of developing and enforcing rules of forest practice that were to include 'practicable measures to be taken by the operators to safeguard timber and young growing stock from injury by fire and other destructive forces, to prevent damage to young trees during logging operations, to provide for restocking the land after logging if sufficient growth is not already present, and where feasible, to leave some portion of merchantable timber (usually the less mature trees) as a basis for growth and the next timber crop.'[29]

On the west coast, the West Coast Lumbermen's Association and Pacific Northwest Loggers Association created a Joint Committee on Forest Conservation to formulate rules for the Douglas fir region and employ personnel to administer Article X. The Joint Committee's voting members came exclusively from industry, including George Drake of the Simpson Logging Company, E.T. Clark, now manager of the Loggers Association, Don Denman of the Crown Zellerbach Corporation, and Weyerhaeuser's C.S. Chapman. Advisory members, with no voting privileges, were the managers of the Washington and Oregon forest fire associations, the state foresters, Regional Forester C.J. Buck, and Thornton Munger. Only the latter two had any degree of independence, and having confined them to a strictly advisory function, lumbermen would dictate the terms of the code's conservation clause with no interference from foresters who might wish to introduce meaningful restrictions on their operating methods.[30]

With absolute control over the rule-making process, operators and their technical advisors succeeded in drafting a series of vague, flexible provisions that posed no challenge to traditional liquidation techniques. Young growth and trees reserved as seed sources were to be protected 'as far as practicable' or 'so far as feasible' from logging damage. As a general standard, clearcuts were to be no further than a quarter-mile from reserved timber of sufficient quantity that it might 'reasonably be expected to furnish an adequate source of seed.' Where operators practised extensive clearcutting and no suitable seed trees survived, they were urged to break up such areas, 'as far as practicable,' with strips or patches of timber in the form of 'marginal long corners' between settings, trees along creeks or ridges, or by logging in alternate blocks. As a final insurance of flexibility, the operator could submit a management plan best suited to his individual operation.[31]

The Joint Committee also expressed a cautious endorsement of selective logging as appropriate to the Douglas fir region 'under certain conditions.' Operators were handling this issue with care by this time. Industry supported the agency's research endeavours, utilized the method when it provided greater profits than clearcutting, but wanted to prevent advocacy of selective cutting from becoming linked to the still-simmering regulation campaign. So when Brandstrom presented a paper touting the advantages of selective tractor logging to the Pacific Logging Congress late in 1933, operators emphasized that topographic and weather conditions ruled against general application of his system. Judd Greenman expressed this change in sentiment. Formerly convinced that selective logging offered the only hope for profitable operation, he now worried about government enforcement of the method. Brandstrom's report merely supplemented Forest Service propaganda for a technique that was 'fine from the conservationists' standpoint but not so hot for the poor operator.'[32]

Nothing in the Article X rules drafted by the Joint Committee obligated Douglas fir region operators to anything beyond the normal conduct of logging. As the *Timberman* noted, there was no intention to 'invoke any radical changes in logging methods overnight.' Progress in the application of commercial forestry would come through 'a slow process of education rather than by statute.' Although small operators disliked the expense involved in upgrading their equipment to comply with the fire control provisions of Article X, industrial self-regulation of cutting practices was largely symbolic.[33]

Industry's determination not to allow conservation to interfere with the pursuit of profit became abundantly clear when advisory member C.J. Buck pressed for the adoption of more specific rules. The regional forester argued that the Committee should commit Douglas fir operators to the reservation of two seed trees per acre, a measure the Forest Service had found inadequate on the national forests, but one that would have represented a definite improvement upon the Article X standards. The Committee refused to consider the proposal. 'To make this anything like a requirement,' C.S. Chapman replied on behalf of his associates, 'would seem to us unnecessary in many instances and depriving the provision of the flexibility that must exist in rules of practice for the Douglas fir region.' The existing rules were 'entirely sufficient to meet the situation,' and would be sent to Washington, DC, for approval as drafted.[34]

Having quashed that annoyance, the Joint Committee engaged the important matter of choosing administrative personnel. As the Long Bell Lumber Company's J.D. Tennant explained to an associate early in the recruiting process, forestry training alone would not suffice; industry required a man with logging experience to ensure a 'practical application of Article X as well as a theoretical application.' E.T. Clark and George Drake saw in Russell Mills, a 1922 University of Washington logging engineering graduate now teaching that subject at his alma mater, the necessary blend of diplomacy, ability, and practicality. Mills, a 'calked boots logger' with considerable experience in industry, became forester for the Code Authority's West Coast Lumber and Logging Division in May 1934. The Committee then hired three district foresters to work under Mills. Kenneth Murdock was assigned to the Eugene area, Warren Tilton to the Puget Sound–Grays Harbor district, and Erwin Rengstorf was responsible for instructing Columbia River operators.[35]

Mills's first report, submitted in July, suggests that the forestry staff devoted most of their attention to fire control matters rather than cutting practices. Although 125 companies provided general slash disposal and restocking outlines, only five, all Weyerhaeuser affiliates, had presented complete cutting plans for the coming year. That firm began leaving strips of defective or out-of-the-way timber in 1932 to better confine slash burns, a procedure that no doubt shaped the Article X provisions. On the whole, Mills informed his employers, operators were 'taking steps toward bringing their woods operations into line with provisions of the Rules of Forest Practice.' Thus far none had objected to the rules 'as either impractical or unfair.'[36]

Industry was regulating itself to leave cutover land in the 'best possible growing condition,' lumbermen and their spokesmen claimed while appealing for government to fulfil its promises of financial cooperation. In March 1935, just two months before the Supreme Court struck down the NIRA, Mills reported further progress. Thanks to the cooperation of the fire associations and state foresters, 95 percent of the Douglas fir operators had met the requirements for fire suppression equipment and planning. He admitted to encountering 'certain difficulties' in the introduction of restocking measures, but gave his superiors a positive evaluation of this new phase of commercial forestry. Thirty of the largest operations had submitted management plans that, according to Mills, equalled reforestation provisions on national forest timber sales.[37]

Then, in May 1935, the US Supreme Court ruled that the NIRA was unconstitutional, ending the New Deal experiment in government sanctioned industrial self-regulation. Lumbermen shed no tears at the dismantling of their code, which failed completely to impose order on the diverse, competitive timber economy. Violation of price standards and production quotas was commonplace, and the NRA's lack of enforcement powers reduced the code to 'something of an open joke,' writes Robert Ficken.[38]

As for Article X, little evidence exists to support David Clary's contention that it produced significant reforms in industry's logging practices. Given the widespread disregard for other features of the code, it is difficult to imagine wholehearted adherence to its conservation component. Even if we suppose that operators demonstrated a temporary and very uncharacteristic devotion to conservation during the NIRA period, the rules of forest practice were in effect for too brief a period to have influenced the conduct of logging appreciably. Russell Mills noted in March 1935 that most of the logging done during the previous year had been planned without regard for reforestation, so it had been 'difficult or impossible to fit restocking provisions into the old plans' as effectively as would be the case in future.[39]

The New Deal experiment in industrial self-government brought no real advance in silviculture on private lands in the Douglas fir region. Industry's control over the drafting and enforcement of the Article X provisions ensured that the Lumber Code's reference to conservation had little or no impact on the actual conduct of logging, either selective or clearcutting. The brief interlude was significant, however, in providing major operators with concrete evidence of the value of self-regulation in the fight against federal controls.

The Road to State Regulation, 1935-40

The demise of the NIRA revived the regulation controversy, but with an important difference in the array of forces. For the remainder of the 1930s, Chief Forester Silcox and his successor, Earle Clapp, placed the US Forest Service at the forefront of the campaign for cutting practice regulation. Pacific Northwest trade association leaders first sought to counter this threat by extending their administration of the Article X rules on a voluntary basis. But by decade's end, worried that the advocates of regulation would eventually triumph, far-sighted Douglas fir lumbermen accepted the need for a permanent solution that achieved public legitimacy without sacrificing the advantages of self-regulation. The result was the initiation of the process that produced forest practice legislation in the states of Oregon and Washington during the 1940s.

This period is also noteworthy for the ongoing, complex debate over selective logging. It is evident that some, both in and out of the Forest Service, continued to perceive selection as the solution to many of the region's forestry problems. Most silviculturalists had no such faith, adhering to the principle of clearcutting as the appropriate system. This implied no support for clearcutting as practised on private land, but rather a conviction that tree selection logging created insurmountable slash disposal problems, reduced the species quality of stands, and resulted in little additional volume growth. Nevertheless, operators had some justification for fearing that regulation, in some minds, meant nothing less than a prohibition of clearcutting.

Silcox did not wait for the Supreme Court ruling to bring his agency's influence to bear on the regulation debate. In January 1935, amidst growing doubts about the code's constitutionality, he shocked the SAF meeting with a paper entitled 'Foresters Must Choose.' Industry's administration of Article X was a farce, he charged, providing neither a mechanism for public approval of forest practices nor a system of inspections to ensure compliance. Issuing a direct challenge to the profession, the chief urged his audience to embrace a commitment to the social ideals of community stability, employment, and balanced resource use. Each forester must 'choose whether he will align himself with those who would continue, in spite of past failures, to leave the exploitation of our forests and the destinies of many communities to the mercy of selfish, private interests, or with those who aim to bring about a permanent use of our forestland, with due consideration for the welfare of the people.'[40]

Professional self-interest played a part in Silcox's appeal. If foresters remained aloof from the social and economic problems associated with forest exploitation, he warned, they would soon find themselves reduced to the status of 'mere technicians.' Most of those in attendance found these proposals too radical, and no doubt many agreed with lumberman George Jewett's characterization of Silcox's thinking as 'distinctly socialistic.' The chief forester continued to express his dissatisfaction with industry's performance until the Supreme Court's decision in the Schecter case struck down the NIRA in May. Douglas fir operators were well aware that the regulation campaign now had the nation's most powerful forester at its head when the experiment in industrial self-government ended.[41]

The trustees of the Pacific Northwest Loggers Association and West Coast Lumbermen's Association acted with their usual sagacity in June, extending the life of the Conservation Committee to continue administering the Article X rules on a voluntary basis with a reduced staff of two foresters. Among its post-code objectives were stable forest ownership, additional public assistance in the protection of private timber from fire and disease, and promotion of the 'orderly and profitable utilization of forest resources.' The Committee also pledged to encourage the maintenance of lands in good productive condition, but its central task was to keep the industry 'free from unnecessary regulation' that might impair the competitiveness of the region.[42]

Public relations, rather than forest practice instruction and inspection, seems to have occupied the Committee's skeleton staff of foresters. They prepared news releases, newspaper stories, and material for radio broadcasts, all designed to place the industry in a 'fair light.' Trade association foresters David Mason and John B. Woods assured Silcox that voluntary compliance with the Article X rules was high, nationally, reflecting industry's commitment to high standards of management. The chief forester attended the WFCA's December 1935 annual meeting, and heard testimonials about the operators' 'genuine and increasing interest' in commercial forestry.[43]

Silcox arrived on the coast just as dissension over selective logging in the Douglas fir region came to a head within his agency. Toward the end of 1934, Regional Forester C.J. Buck had conveyed to Forest Service headquarters his concern over the tractor logging carried out on private lands, and recommended the initiation of a Civilian Conservation Corps (CCC) experimental project to gather data necessary for improvement of the selection system. Apparently excited by the technique's potential superiority over clearcutting, he then took more dramatic action, informing national forest supervisors that the development of tractor and truck technology merited a radical change in timber sale policy to selective harvesting.

Buck foresaw a number of benefits to be derived from lighter cutting procedures that retained a portion of the forest canopy, including preservation of soil fertility, since less slash burning would be necessary, improved utilization, and an accelerated return of logged areas to productivity. For the immediate future, then, regional policy was to introduce selective logging on an individual and small-group basis using tractors along with 'carefully controlled short distance high lead logging on scattered small settings.' Eliminating any doubt about his intentions, he alerted supervisors that 'the possibility of applying this system must be considered in connection with every application for National Forest timber.'[44]

Buck's directive drew a mixed response from the chief forester's office. Assistant Chief E.E. Carter agreed that the availability of CCC men might present the Forest Service with an opportunity to do its own selective logging tests, but suggested that mature, even-age stands of the shade-intolerant Douglas fir were an inappropriate setting to demonstrate the technique's silvicultural value. It was a 'basic silvical fact' that openings in the canopy of mixed stands were necessary to assure reproduction of that species. Nevertheless, he had no objection to trials in 'carefully selected places' to determine the potential of selection in the region. Backtracking hastily, Buck assured Carter that he intended only to alert supervisors to the possibilities of the method so that it would receive the 'best opportunities possible for successful realization.'[45]

In response to Carter's subsequent request for a clarification of the region's policy, Buck emphasized the necessity of developing an alternative both to extensive clearcutting and the 'zero-margin' tractor operations that removed all timber capable of yielding a profit with complete disregard for the silvicultural condition of the partially logged forest. Modification of the tractor system to restrict the cut to under 20 percent of stand volume might provide a solution, but experimental cuttings on this basis were required 'to demonstrate to the industry the practicality of handling cutting operations in this manner.' The scientific results of a CCC project would be of great value in determining future timber sale policy and silvicultural practice in the Douglas fir region.[46]

Nothing illustrates the conflict and confusion that prevailed within the Forest Service over the new method better than the process leading to publication of Burt Kirkland and Axel Brandstrom's *Selective Timber Management in the Douglas Fir Region*. The report presented a detailed argument favouring the use of trucks and tractors to harvest timber 'in the order of economic and silvicultural desirability.' In these technologies, they argued, operators now possessed 'practical operating tools for intensive selection by individual trees and small groups,' providing a basis for sustained-yield management. Early construction of an extensive, permanent road network to access all parts of a property was the key to their system, permitting an initial heavy cut of financially mature trees to defray road costs, followed by a series of light cuts at short intervals tailored to market demands.[47]

Publication of the Kirkland-Brandstrom proposal, Leo Isaac recalls, was a 'stormy procedure.' From the outset, foresters' perception of industry's selective logging as a silvicultural disaster coloured their response to the proposed management system. The most fundamental opposition appears to have come from the Experiment Station, with Munger urging that the submission's economic appeal not be permitted to obscure its silvicultural deficiencies. He collaborated with Isaac on a lengthy critique of the manuscript, arguing that partial cutting in old-growth Douglas fir stands would lead to dominance of shade-tolerant species, which thrived in the uneven-aged forest.[48]

Foresters at the Regional Office questioned a range of issues, finding the manuscript's authoritative tone particularly objectionable. Fred Ames censured Kirkland and Brandstrom for their casual dismissal of clearcutting, and pointed out their failure to address the probability of blowdown losses or discuss the rate of growth that might be expected on selectively managed stands. B.E. Hoffman speculated that the report's denunciation of clearcutting might succeed, not in persuading operators to take up the rigorous selective management system, but instead in popularizing their market driven tractor-logging practices that foresters found so disturbing.[49]

Buck's summary of his office's position on the manuscript reveals the extent to which this latter concern shaped professional opinion. He began by expressing his commitment to 'an aggressive policy of selective logging,' but described the document as written 'too much in the vein of promotion or propaganda.' Given the host of silvicultural or management questions raised by the method, the gravest danger was that operators would 'seize upon the statements and advocacy of selective cutting ... as a justification for continuance of the present-type zero margin selective logging.' Such operations produced a much heavier cut than recommended by Kirkland and Brandstrom, invariably leaving cutover lands in 'deplorable condition.' Their system would almost certainly be of great value on private lands, he explained, but publication should be delayed until completion of further experiments.[50]

A revised version of the manuscript, in which Kirkland and Brandstrom acknowledged the need for trial and experimentation, failed to overcome all of Buck's reservations. Still worried that the report legitimated the operators' selective logging practices, he urged the inclusion of a statement 'so definitive and so explicit that there will be no possibility of industry using this bulletin as a justification for systems of liquidation cutting which inevitably leave the forest in an extremely dangerous condition.'[51]

When *Selective Timber Management* finally appeared in January 1936 the document's language was much less definitive than earlier drafts. The authors acknowledged the need for further research and took pains to distinguish their system from the operators' 'high-grading' methods. They gave greater recognition to area and group selection as appropriate cutting procedures, and less to individual tree logging. A foreword by Chief Forester Silcox stressed the preliminary character of the data and described selective timber management as a 'working hypothesis' that might not be applicable in all conditions.[52]

By the time the agency had reconciled all the conflicting views sufficiently to allow publication of the manuscript, even foresters optimistic about selective logging recognized that operators' use of the tractor to extract specific trees represented no improvement over clearcutting. The exclusive concern for profit maximization negated any potential either system may have held for resource conservation. But clearcutting had a history of legitimacy, and many foresters had resigned themselves to all but the most glaring abuses that occurred under the technique. Cutting clean yielded returns under all but the worst financial conditions, permitted easy disposal of slash, and in theory at least, provided a basis for renewal of the most valuable commercial species.

Selective logging, on the other hand, raised a multitude of new and disturbing questions. For protectionists such as the Washington Forest Fire Association's Charles Cowan, fire hazard abatement stood as the most pressing immediate problem. Broadcast burning was impossible, and the alternative, piling brush for spot burning, was labour intensive and expensive. Future stand composition remained Thornton Munger's greatest concern. As he explained to British Columbia's Chief Forester Ernest Manning, removal of quality Douglas fir timber left a 'residue stand of inferior species, understory trees, and defective trees.' Admittedly, clearcutting on private lands had produced 'a pretty sorry mess,' but Munger felt strongly that this failure was neither 'the fault of the system nor that from now on must results be so bad.'[53]

Unlike Munger, who exhibited a faith in the eventual reform of clearcutting, Buck continued to view selection as a 'new tool of great promise.' Nevertheless, the Regional Office proceeded 'very slowly and cautiously' with the new technique on the national forests. Some experimental sales were issued for uneven-aged stands where foresters hoped removal of decadent timber and snags would improve growing conditions. One tractor sale on the Mt. Baker National Forest that stipulated removal of over-mature timber left the area 'park-like in appearance' but involved high slash disposal costs. Some sales were vetoed out of fear that removal of the fir would allow hemlock to dominate.[54]

Leo Isaac, the silviculturalist responsible for discrediting the theory that supported extensive clearcutting, initiated research on the silvicultural impact of selective logging. He established plots on partially cut areas to test the suitability of various stand structures for selection, and analyze the physical and biological effects of the technique on residual timber. Tom Murray's West Fork Logging Company operation at Mineral, Washington, served as a particularly valuable laboratory for foresters. In 1936 Murray began using tractors to remove the large Douglas fir and cedar from his mixed stands there, reserving the hemlock for a future cut in expectation of increased value as the pulp and paper industry expanded. West Fork became the region's most prominent and controversial selective logging site. Murray hired forester Louis Schatz to supervise cutting, cooperated with the Pacific Northwest Forest Experiment Station in studies, and hosted numerous visits by foresters, opinion makers, and government officials.[55]

Lumbermen grew increasingly wary as the Murray operation and others attracted public support. Simpson Logging Company manager George Drake admitted to excessive 'sweeping, indiscriminate cutting,' but pointed out that industry had invested heavily in overhead logging equipment and any directive 'to junk these machines overnight would present a financial problem that many operators frankly could not meet.' Firms must retain the freedom to adapt technologies to changing topographical, stand, and market conditions, he argued, denying the feasibility of applying selection in an 'arbitrary fashion.'[56]

Roosevelt's re-election later in 1936 gave lumbermen further cause for concern. The Democratic victory affirmed public approval of a New Deal that, with passage of the Social Security, National Labor Relations, and Wealth Tax Acts the previous year, left business leaders grumbling over these encroachments on the free enterprise system.[57] Ferdinand Silcox and Assistant Chief Earle Clapp took the election result as a mandate to re-emphasize

Forest Service support for a program of federal regulation. Regional foresters and experiment station directors were expected to back policy statements from the chief forester's office. Historians offer conflicting evaluations of Silcox's commitment to government intervention in forestry. For David Clary, these instructions reflect Silcox's desire to maintain a united front within the agency as he 'prepared to do righteous battle' for social control, a cause having fewer supporters within the profession as members began securing corporate employment. Indeed, a Division of Private Forestry had been organized that spring to give industrial foresters an official voice within the SAF.[58]

William Robbins argues that the 'rhetorical haze' surrounding the chief forester's advocacy of regulation should not obscure his ongoing cooperation with trade association leaders in fire control, research, and forest survey work. One of Silcox's principal antagonists, William Greeley, himself wondered about the chief's devotion to the idea of government taking on the 'role of forest policeman.' Regulation, Greeley suggests, was a threat Silcox used to 'needle' lumbermen into improved forest practices.[59]

If Robbins is correct in describing Silcox's tactic as a 'carrot-and-stick' approach to achieving improved silvicultural performance on private lands, fragmentary and at times contradictory data leaves the impression that progress in the Douglas fir region was marginal, and probably due largely to market forces that discouraged wholesale clearcutting. In October 1936 the Forest Service national office requested reports on the status of management among operators in Region Six. Forester H.E. Haefner found no operations being conducted on a sustained-yield basis, although Weyerhaeuser was considering such a plan for its giant Longview property. In addition to that operation, three other Weyerhaeuser units, Crown Zellerbach, and the Simpson Logging Company left cutover lands in 'good producing condition.' No definitive survey had been conducted, but Regional Forester Buck reported a 'material and widespread improvement' in the protection, slash disposal, and seed tree reservation procedures of firms since the inception of the Lumber Code. He cited depressed markets, the introduction of selective logging, and the influence of Article X as factors encouraging operators to 'leave standing more trees of marginal commercial size.'[60]

Buck, in all likelihood, relied mainly on the impressions of W.B. Osborne, who had been appointed to the agency's new Division of State and Private Forestry and whose role was to cooperate with the region's trade association foresters in the administration of the forest practice rules after the code's collapse. Osborne's close relationship with industry's representatives contributed, it seems, to a rose-coloured perception of corporate progress in forest management. Results obtained under the Lumber Code had been 'extremely good,' Osborne declared, and the operators' voluntary observance of the rules 'even better.' Only in the case of the occasional 'shoestring operation' would compulsion be more effective than volunteerism. Most lumbermen happily provided seed sources if this could be accomplished in a 'practical manner and without much cost.' Industry had recorded an outstanding achievement in adopting the forest practice rules, he concluded, although admittedly provisions for natural reseeding were 'probably not wholly adequate for the total area involved,' in all cases.[61]

Assistant Regional Forester H.L. Plumb later examined Osborne's inspection record, coming away convinced that the latter had been spending too much time on a few large operations and devoting less attention to silviculture than fire protection. A subsequent report by Osborne was suppressed on the grounds that its glowing depiction of industrial forestry distorted reality. Certainly B.E. Hoffman detected no significant advance in cutting practice. New technologies together with the operators' inclination to 'go further in study and planning' provided a medium for improvement, he acknowledged, and at least a few attempted to reserve seed sources. But Hoffman concluded that there had been no 'great improvement in the matter of regeneration provisions under clearcutting.'[62]

Operators could not afford complete indifference to Silcox's regulation campaign. Reluctant to introduce sweeping reforms in cutting practice, the most astute corporate executives chose the less costly alternative of fostering the appearance of real progress. In 1937 the Weyerhaeuser Timber Company hired public relations expert Roderic Olzendam to spruce up the firm's image, and the firm began running full-page newspaper advertisements extolling its commitment to resource stewardship under the slogan 'Timber is a Crop.' Some senior Forest Service officials welcomed Weyerhaeuser's publicity venture. Assistant Chief E.W. Tinker was gratified to 'see the money being spent by private operators and timberland owners to show that timber is a crop and making suggestions as to how that crop should be handled.' Lumbermen proved much less receptive to advice from government representatives. Joint Committee Forester Warren Tilton conveyed his employers' objection to Forest Service men offering recommendations in the field, and the Regional Office cautioned supervisors to refrain from giving 'advice to operators on private lands which might be contrary to the ... [Joint] Committee's policies.'[63]

While industry remained adamantly opposed to any hint of federal interference with the conduct of enterprise, some evidence indicates that trade association leaders were awakening to the possible advantages of a carefully managed regulatory program. In July 1937, at Greeley's request, Tinker met with the Joint Committee on Forest Conservation to clarify the agency's position on the regulation issue. He first asked Region Six staff what they would require of operators if 'full regulatory authority existed.' They agreed on the need for improvement in five areas: protection of cutover lands and second-growth; restocking provisions; utilization; retention of logged-off lands; and amalgamation of holdings to permit sustained-yield management. Although the foresters in attendance agreed that selective logging should be used on timber sales where economically feasible, they also decided, with only Buck dissenting, that the method had no widespread value in the Douglas fir region.

The Joint Committee succeeded in convincing Tinker of progress in all these management categories. He also came away impressed with the owners' genuine acceptance of their obligations to the public. 'I was thoroughly impressed,' he informed Silcox, 'that an intimate working relationship between the Forest Service and the industry would mean steady progress toward the public objectives that are of such vital concern.' More significantly, Tinker sensed that the Committee saw something to be gained by regulating the laggards to raise their practices up to the standard of the most enlightened operators. For the recalcitrant, regulation 'would mean merely compulsory fair dealings with the public and with their associates.'[64]

Regional Forester Buck emphasized cooperation over confrontation in relations with industry for the remainder of 1937, reporting further progress on corporate lands and hiring of foresters by some of the larger concerns. 'Some may be fearful of public regulation,' he explained to Silcox, 'but in any case the changed attitude and improved practice is encouraging.' Hopeful that a program having 'mutual understanding and support' was attainable, he invited the Joint Committee's forestry staff to participate with government representatives on a Forest Practice Committee. Formation of cooperative sustained-yield units topped the agenda at the group's first meeting, reflecting awareness that some timber-dependent communities faced extinction unless dwindling private holdings were augmented with assured control over adjacent public reserves.[65]

Silcox's annual report for 1937 undermined the emerging spirit of harmony in the Pacific Northwest. Lumbermen had no quarrel with the chief forester's proposal for increased public acquisition of forestland and continued cooperation in research and fire protection, but he also reiterated his demand for government control of private cutting practices. Regulation, he argued, was necessary to protect both the public and owners who accepted their social obligations from those who 'might otherwise continue ruthless exploitation.' He offered few specifics, but Tinker suggested to the WFCA members that the agency sought state administration of controls to meet federal standards. Douglas fir operators castigated the chief for rekindling the regulation controversy. In characterizing owners as despoilers, the *West Coast Lumberman* complained, Silcox 'did great harm to the cause of real forestry in the west.'[66]

A January 1938 meeting of the Forest Practice Committee gave industrial foresters an opportunity to vent their displeasure to Forest Service representatives. Warren Tilton complained of Silcox's tendency to 'wave a big stick,' and, anticipating future developments, warned that unless the agency made the public aware that 'a little bit of forest devastation is a part of any industrial cutting,' it too would soon encounter criticism. He went on to ask the local federal men how regulation could improve on industry performance under the existing cooperative relationship. Associate Regional Forester F.H. Brundage acknowledged the progress made by operators, confessed that no specific requirements had been formulated, and assured his colleagues in industry that cooperation remained a fundamental element of Forest Service policy. Were it not for a small group of troublemakers in Washington, DC, the Western Pine Association's Clyde Martin said, matters could be resolved locally to the satisfaction of all. Forest Service officers in the region must follow the national office's lead, Brundage replied.[67]

Rather than respond officially to the chief forester's report, the Joint Committee on Forest Conservation directed Weyerhaeuser's C.S. Chapman to convey their opposition to federal regulation at forthcoming meetings in the nation's capitol. President Roosevelt's March 1938 request that Congress appoint a joint committee to study the forestry question prior to the introduction of legislation at the next session caused lumbermen to direct more of their attention to developments in Washington. Embedded in Roosevelt's directive was a specific request for legislators to consider the 'need for such regulatory controls as will adequately protect private as well as the broad public interests in all forest lands.'[68]

The Joint Congressional Committee on Forestry took shape in June, with Alabama Senator John Bankhead serving as chairman. The *West Coast Lumberman* welcomed the investigation, but cautioned against 'any attempt to inject ill-considered, impractical, untried, crackpot schemes which will tend to confuse and further demoralize the ... industry.' Trade association leaders chose to avoid a personal confrontation with Silcox and instead emphasized the need for additional federal cooperation to encourage investment in private forestry. David Mason, a member of the NLMA's Conservation Committee, indicated early on in the deliberations that lumbermen would accept regulation by the states if necessary to secure assistance and prevent imposition of federal control.[69]

On the west coast the Joint Committee on Forest Conservation met in July, with no Forest Service advisory members in attendance, to draft proposals for a Chicago meeting of the national association's Conservation Committee. The operators agreed that a 'strong statement' opposing Silcox's regulation scheme was necessary, but the most thoughtful suggestion came from the shrewd Greeley, who argued for a public relations campaign designed to play up the forestry accomplishments of western lumbermen within the context of state regulation. This approach, he explained, would buttress their position that the region's firms had long been 'building a regulatory control, using the police powers of the State, as measures are found practicable.' Over the next two years, trade association foresters penned numerous articles along these lines, defending timber capital's capacity for self-regulation through state legislatures.[70]

Forest Service preparations for the Congressional Committee's hearings began with a request for information on management practice from the various regions. Reports submitted by Region Six forest supervisors suggest that conservation by coastal operators was confined largely to the pages of newspapers and trade and forestry journals. Around the Willamette National Forest selective logging was the norm; timber that would not bear the cost of transportation to the mill thus remained to serve as an agent of reforestation. Seed sources were also 'automatically provided for' by operators in the vicinity of the Snoqualmie National Forest. The large clearcutting enterprises in that locale had already cut out the valley bottoms, leaving a fringe of timber on inaccessible upper elevations to distribute some seed over the logged-off lands below.[71]

E.J. Hanzlik was more critical of the major firms cutting near the Olympic National Forest. Like his colleagues, he reported general satisfaction with fire protection measures. Restocking provisions, however, were haphazard at best. 'Upon the whole,' he wrote, 'there is no conscious effort made by any of these operating companies to provide for a new crop during their logging operations.' Where topography prevented easy access or the timber was without value, patches remained, but he detected 'no such thing as a definite, conscious effort to leave seed strips or seed blocks.' All practised the usual clearcutting method, which saw the expanse of cutover land expanding yearly with no provision for natural reforestation. Barring fire, these lands would eventually take on a new growth, inevitably delayed because of the distance from seed sources. At one of the Simpson Timber Company's operations, always held up as a model by industry, average stocking was only 10-15 percent after a five- to ten-year period. 'The large operations on the Olympic Peninsula,' Hanzlik concluded, 'are making very little conscious effort to practice forestry.'[72]

Officials found it impossible to square Hanzlik's observations with those submitted by W.B. Osborne, who reported 'great progress' and claimed to be most impressed by the 'sincere interest and honest effort' operators displayed in leaving lands in productive condition. Logging methods had undergone 'rather radical changes' since the days of the Lumber Code, he declared, and thanks to the reservation of long corners, patches of second growth and the staggered setting pattern of cutting, 80-95 percent of the region's private cutover lands exhibited an adequate basis for reforestation. The Regional Office received Osborne's document with scepticism, withholding it from release because of the 'entirely too favourable picture' of regeneration provisions presented.[73]

Further evidence that even the most progressive operators on the American side of the Douglas fir region had not allowed conservation considerations to fundamentally influence the conduct of logging comes in the form of a British Columbia forester's impressions. Anxious to keep abreast of developments to the south, Forest Branch officials sent Gordon Godwin on an inspection tour of operations judged the most advanced in Washington state. A visit to the Simpson Timber Company left Godwin unimpressed. Although cutting plans prepared by an engineer featured temporary reservation of timber blocks to segregate areas of slash for burning, and the firm left unmerchantable trees, seed source provision was 'quite haphazard and usually inadequate.'[74]

Godwin also found the forest practices of the Weyerhaeuser Timber Company at Longview to fall short of expectations. Despite an abundance of expertise, the staff under C.S. Chapman had 'not yet succeeded in preparing a plan of operation designed to ensure restocking of their land.' Weyerhaeuser foresters had classified a good portion of that firm's holdings, giving them some indirect input into future cutting plans, but current operations remained the exclusive domain of the logging department. 'They muddle along the same way I do,' Godwin remarked, 'talk forestry to managers and superintendents, get close to their ears, but never in their hair.' Seed sources on clearcuts, many of which reached a size of 2,000 acres, were insufficient to ensure reforestation.[75]

Little distinguished Godwin's account of Weyerhaeuser's logging from that penned by an IWA member. Calling the slogan 'Timber is a Crop' a 'piece of fabrication,' Don Hammerquist wrote that one could travel for miles at that firm's Vail operation without seeing any greenery except for a few patches of spindly, valueless trees. These existed 'not because of the foresight of the operators, but because there was no excuse for destroying them.' After inspecting the cutover lands of the St. Paul and Tacoma Lumber Company, where industrial forester Norman Jacobson expressed satisfaction with a sparse showing of young growth, Godwin remarked that 'American foresters, from what I have seen, are either kidding themselves, or the public.'[76]

Rhetoric aside, the weight of evidence supports the conclusion that the clearcutting practices of American operators remained a process of liquidation, with only the slightest concession to encouragement of a second crop of commercial timber. Although some firms with substantial holdings had begun to plan operations with a concern for long-term economic viability, neither the prospect of forthcoming timber shortages nor Silcox's regulation campaign had yet exerted the pressure necessary to force a significant concern for silviculture into the day-to-day management of resource exploitation.

Meanwhile, the selective logging issue continued to bedevil foresters and pose a threat to operators. L.T. Murray's West Fork Logging Company operation became the focal point of controversy during the latter 1930s. The growing notoriety of this firm's procedure prompted Godwin to visit that site and describe it as a well-planned, profitable tractor operation. By 1939 Murray had also adapted traditional overhead technology to selectively harvest Douglas fir on difficult terrain. His 'low high-lead' method involved placement of a lead block at a height of 50-70 feet on a spar tree, running lines through a number of blocks around the setting, and yarding logs individually in order to minimize damage to residual timber. When Murray hosted a group of foresters in late 1937 to demonstrate the system most were sceptical but, the Forest Service's L.R. Olson remarked, at least the operator showed what was possible 'when he breaks away from the old school of logging thought.'[77]

Whatever the silvicultural validity of Murray's techniques, many of his fellow timbermen grew alarmed at the attention garnered by the operation, fearing that it increased the likelihood of the alternative to clearcutting becoming incorporated into the Forest Service's regulatory agenda. According to Olson's account of the West Fork meeting, a letter from the chief forester to Weyerhaeuser officials hinted at this conjunction. The firm's representatives took the opportunity to ask repeatedly 'if certain policies followed by the West Fork Logging Company were in line with Mr. Silcox's ideas on regulation.' Little wonder that Olson detected a 'certain undertone of hostility ... towards the Forest Service' at the event, which Murray only exacerbated by heaping praise on the agency at every opportunity.[78]

The politicization of Murray's operation continued in August 1938 when Secretary of Interior Harold L. Ickes visited with *Seattle Post-Intelligencer* editor John Boettinger, Roosevelt's son-in-law. Boettinger contrasted the appearance of the lands logged selectively with the devastated clearcuts the party encountered, and Ickes declared that the technique 'may well be the means of saving for all time the great timber resources of this region.' A subsequent Boettinger editorial critical of clearcutting drew a personal response from William Greeley. Anxious to dampen the newspaperman's conviction that the entire industry should follow the West Fork model, Greeley described conditions on Murray's property as exceptional. Selective logging had great possibilities, he advised, but required much study to solve the regeneration, protection, and blowdown problems posed by the method.[79]

After Silcox's inspection of the West Fork and several other selective operations during a western tour in September 1938, industry stepped up its defence of clearcutting. At that winter's Pacific Logging Congress several speakers noted the presence of 'splendid reproduction' on clearcut lands. Articles in industry and professional journals emphasized the alternative's shortcomings. 'Selective logging appeals to the forestry minded well-meaning public,' St. Paul and Tacoma Lumber Company forester Norman Jacobson wrote, but it was 'not a forestry procedure for general treatment of virgin timber.' No positive relationship existed between selection and sustained-yield, argued another industrial forester. None of this dissuaded Murray from spirited advocacy of his practices, fuelling a debate that dismayed St. Paul and Tacoma Lumber Company executive Corydon Wagner. 'Ordinarily discussions and arguments on such matters are stimulating and constructive,' he observed, but differences of opinion on this issue had 'been heard in high places, with apparent relish on the part of those advocating public ownership of natural resources.' Lumbermen should make common cause in defence of private enterprise 'rather than attacking one another's methods publicly.'[80]

Given the mounting opposition to selective logging within the ranks of western foresters, operators probably exaggerated the danger of the system figuring prominently in the Forest Service's regulatory plan for the Douglas fir region. Thornton Munger, now head of forest management research at the Pacific Northwest Forest and Range Experiment Station, expressed his resistance to the practice in an address to the SAF's Puget Sound Section in January 1939. Speaking from observation and personal opinion, he condemned use of the selective system in Douglas fir forests. Munger began by distancing himself from those who saw no necessity for change, noting that 'absolute clearcutting of large areas is incompatible with good silviculture.'[81] But, he argued, past abuses should not cause foresters to reject a system that, properly conducted, was superior to tree selection logging. Limiting cut-blocks to groups and 'reasonably sized areas' would produce optimum silvicultural results.[82]

By this time 'bad blood' had developed between Munger and Buck, who was still enthusiastic about the potential of selective logging. The regional forester apparently tried to block publication of Munger's critique, but Forest Service headquarters approved its appearance in the 1939 issue of the *University of Washington Forest Club Quarterly*.[83] Preliminary data gathered by Isaac tended to support Munger's pessimistic appraisal, and by decade's end all agreed that the Pacific Northwest Forest Experiment Station should make selective logging a top priority. Lyle Watts, who replaced Buck as regional forester in late 1939, called for large-scale experiments to accelerate the accumulation of scientific findings on its economic and silvicultural impact.[84]

Isaac's research on the subject did not produce results until the following decade, leaving the regulation debate in the Pacific Northwest with its most fundamental technical question unresolved as the 1930s drew to an end. Silcox, however, continued to insist on the need for a national scheme of silvicultural controls, combining exhortation and threat in his public statements. A February 1939 *Journal of Forestry* article admitted to some progress in the area of private forestry, but reiterated the need for regulation under federal guidelines. That summer Silcox returned to the coast and spoke to the Washington State Planning Council, taking industry to task for its policy of liquidation and reminding lumbermen of their obligation to protect timber-dependent communities. Pledging government support in fire protection, securing new markets, and low interest loans, he warned that if they failed to reciprocate with conservative practices, 'I would unhesitatingly move for public regulation and if that doesn't work I would move for public ownership.'[85]

Silcox's confrontational rhetoric does not tell the whole story of the Service's relationship with operators on the west coast during the late 1930s. Behind the scenes some officials worked to cultivate a more harmonious atmosphere. Shortly after the chief's speech to the Planning Council, Associate Regional Forester Brundage urged men in the Division of State and Private Forestry to 'be careful not to antagonize the lumber industry.' Constant reference to devastation and ghost towns bred resentment among operators. True, industry's commitments to provide a source of seed supply had 'not worked out too well' and protection of cutover lands was inadequate, but these facts should be presented in a more 'tactful manner.'[86]

Officially, the Forest Service held to its interventionist stance. The agency's draft report to the Joint Congressional Committee recommended that all cooperative services extended by government be contingent upon submission to federal controls. When trade association leaders in the west became aware of the document's contents they moved further along the path toward state regulation as a hedge against federal intervention. Meeting in August 1939, the Conservation Committee of the Douglas fir region resolved tentatively to support state legislation regulating restocking practices in Oregon and Washington if Clarke-McNary appropriations were raised to an acceptable level. Operators would submit reforestation plans for the approval of state foresters, with the proviso that their rulings could be appealed to 'nonpolitical' forestry boards.[87]

State-sanctioned self-regulation took on additional appeal in December, when A.W. Clapp became acting chief forester after Silcox's death. Whereas his predecessor had been somewhat equivocal and vague in his proposals, the new chief, Greeley recalls, was 'wholly sincere and forthright in wanting forest regulation and single-minded in pursuit of it.' Lyle Watts, the new regional forester in the Pacific Northwest, chose to address corporate capital's desire for overall control of the timber economy. Those firms with large timber reserves already practising a higher standard of forestry, he pointed out to the SAF's Puget Sound Section, would 'be protected from irresponsible operators who are dislocating markets and do not intend to stay in business.'[88]

Clapp presented the Forest Service's report to the Joint Congressional Committee during its final hearings early in 1940, making the anticipated case for government assistance to industry becoming conditional upon better private forestry. Although he preferred that the agency administer a program of direct federal regulation, he offered a compromise proposal that would see states have an opportunity to enact legislation satisfying minimum national standards. If a state failed to act, or enforcement fell short, the federal government would have authority to intervene.[89]

Concerned that Clapp's proposal might be incorporated in the Congressional Committee's report and subsequently appear in a legislative package, Greeley and Oregon Forest Fire Association manager John B. Woods advised the Joint Committee on Forest Conservation that lumbermen should develop a Congressional bill 'both for the good of forestry and for industry protection against less favorable proposals.' The industry committee decided to seek approval of the parent trade associations for amendments to the Clarke-McNary Act that would include federal cooperation through the states in the regulation of cutting practices. Greeley, E.T. Clark, and Warren Tilton were also appointed to draft a state forest practice act for submission to the trustees of the West Coast Lumbermen's and Pacific Northwest Loggers Associations and to arrange meetings with the region's governors and state foresters. As Greeley explained to his employers, 'sooner or later, the type of regulatory legislation advocated in the Committee hearings by the Forest Service and the Secretary of Agriculture is inevitable.' Countering with their own proposal would give lumbermen their 'best defence against the possibility of federal regulation of the kind that most of us heartily disbelieve in.'[90]

Elsewhere, lumbermen were coming to the same conclusion. After attending a Chicago meeting of the NLMA's Conservation Committee in May, Greeley and David Mason reported the presence of strong sentiment in Washington, DC, that 'public regulation of the forest industries will be demanded regardless of administrative changes or party lines.' Unable to reach a decision on whether to seek amendment of the Clarke-McNary Act or have operators work solely through their state legislatures, the national group referred the question back to the regional associations. Having already begun developing state programs, the Joint Committee on Forest Conservation decided in June to continue along this course and delay further action on the Clarke-McNary proposal.[91]

By this time Greeley had developed a tentative plan involving the inclusion of cutting plans on operating permits, and subcommittees for each state had begun working with Western Pine Association representatives on drafting forest codes. Later in June operators received further incentive to press for state legislation. Tilton returned from a Washington, DC, conference where Clapp outlined a proposed federal regulation bill to inform Conservation Committee members that the acting chief intended to 'avoid widespread clearcutting' and 'limit the area to which clearcutting could be applied in any one year.'[92]

Presented with evidence that federal regulation constituted a serious threat to their practices, coastal lumbermen such as St. Paul and Tacoma's Corydon Wagner were confirmed in thinking that no issue 'has more far-reaching implications, or offers more complicated considerations than this one.' Now more than ever, industry sponsorship and control of legislation at the state level seemed the appropriate defence against a possible federal attack on the productive efficiencies of the factory regime. Much remained to be accomplished, but by the end of the decade, with war in Europe and Asia threatening to engulf the world, operators had determined that Greeley's strategy offered the best chance for victory in the domestic regulation battle.[93]

Although the federal regulation debate continued throughout the war, conditions had begun to shift in favour of industry. With the revival of the timber economy under the stimulus of defence demands, and possible military involvement looming, conservation became a less important objective than full production during a time of national emergency. The emergence of a powerful conservative coalition in Congress and the mounting opposition to Roosevelt within state governments conspired to block further expansion of federal power along New Deal lines.[94] Foresters in the west, troubled by the selective logging controversy that undermined their claim to public confidence, were closing ranks in support of clearcutting. Most important, corporate leaders in the Douglas fir region had begun to cut the ground from beneath their opponents by staging a pre-emptive strike in local legislatures.

5

Forest Practice Regulation and the British Columbia State in the 1930s: A Missed Opportunity for Reform

The 1930s were pivotal years in British Columbia's forest history, exhibiting much the same pattern of development as has been charted for the southern part of the Pacific rain forest. Concern over the pace of deforestation, failure of a new crop of timber to follow cutting of the old, and the presence of an alternative – selective logging – coincided to produce a vigorous critique of unrestrained clearcutting. But unlike the American context, where a federal agency provided leadership for conservationists, in British Columbia the provincial Forest Branch took on this role during Ernest C. Manning's tenure as chief forester after 1935. A 'liberal interventionist' like his American counterparts Silcox and Clapp, Manning considered regulation necessary to curb destructive logging, and until his death in 1941 he exerted pressure on Duff Pattullo's Liberal government to introduce a provincial system of silvicultural controls.[1]

Other factors both within and beyond provincial boundaries encouraged the emergence of a conservation movement in British Columbia during the 1930s. The catastrophic impact of the Great Depression itself generated sentiment favourable to stronger state intervention in social and economic affairs. To the south, Roosevelt's New Deal provided an example of moderate reform, and in 1933 Pattullo came to power similarly committed to the preservation of capitalism through use of state power to balance private and public interests.[2] The Cooperative Commonwealth Federation (CCF) contributed to the pressure for reform of the exploitation practices of British Columbia operators. Founded in 1932, the party became the legislature's official opposition the next year, lending a significant socialist perspective to political discourse on resource issues.

Manning, the CCF, and a variety of business, civic, and religious groups focused much of their attention on the deforestation of Vancouver Island's E & N Railway Belt, site of the heaviest concentration of mass production logging in the province. Since acquiring the two million-acre grant in 1905, the Canadian Pacific Railroad had sold huge parcels of rich forestland to timber companies that operated with no infringement on their property rights. During the decade, residents of timber-dependent communities and foresters became concerned that resource exhaustion would inevitably bring dislocation as these firms cut out their holdings. Thus, logging on private land, not the public forest, provided the focal point for British Columbia's regulation debate.

The selective logging and regulation issues were, it appears, more closely associated in British Columbia than in the American context. Many conservationists called for an outright ban on overhead systems, perceiving the greater precision offered by the caterpillar tractor as a superior alternative to the rapidly expanding clearcuts that exhibited marginal reproduction. Government foresters investigated the few selective operations on their coast, monitored US Forest Service studies, but concluded that the technique did not merit regulatory action.

Manning advocated a reform of the traditional harvesting technique, proposing regulations that would compel private operators to burn slash in accordance with Forest Branch instructions and to reserve seed trees on clearcuts. With legislation in place governing the practices of dominant firms within the E & N belt, it would be a simple matter to enforce the same standards on the province's public lands. The chief forester achieved partial success in 1937 with an amendment to the Forest Act giving his department authority over slash burning activities. The measure also empowered the Branch to introduce 'seed tree' regulations after research had determined a proper balance between silvicultural and economic considerations. Unfortunately, no such restrictions on the clearcutting practices of operators were adopted. The outbreak of war in 1939 diverted attention from conservation issues, and Manning's death two years later deprived the movement for logging regulation of its leader within government circles. But for a time during the 1930s, public and professional concern produced a serious challenge to the factory regime of British Columbia operators. That the Pattullo administration proved unwilling or unable to take advantage of this opportunity reveals how deeply entrenched were the obstacles to reform in the resource-dependent client state.

Selective Logging vs. Clearcutting in British Columbia, 1930-35

British Columbia felt the impact of the October 1929 stock market crash almost immediately. Overwhelmingly dependent upon exporting primary products, the provincial economy reeled under the collapse of international commodity markets. Demand in Europe, the United States, and Asia evaporated as trading partners erected tariff barriers to protect domestic industry. Enactment of the American Smoot-Hawley tariff contributed to the drop in lumber exports to that market from a high of 306 million feet during the late 1920s to 12 million feet in 1934.[3]

Many camps and mills sat idle until 1932 when the signing of the Imperial Preferential Agreement permitted Canadian lumber to enter Commonwealth ports free of duty while imposing a 10 percent tariff on forest products
from other countries. British Columbia lumbermen quickly captured these
markets from competitors in Washington and Oregon, increasing their exports from 70 million feet in 1929 to 666 million by 1936. Shipments to the
United States also increased as the Americans lowered tariffs later in the
decade.[4]

One consequence of the decline in government revenues during the early
1930s was a smaller allotment for the Forest Branch. A cut in funds for the
small Research Division forced layoffs in technical staff, prompting Percy
Barr's resignation to accept a teaching position at the University of California. Future chief forester C.D. Orchard took Barr's place as head of Research.[5]
Little thought was given to regulation in this context, owing, foresters
claimed, to the pressure of competition from operators cutting on private
lands in Washington and Oregon. Even on timber sales, contract terms went
largely unenforced. As Chief P.Z. Caverhill explained to his Manitoba counterpart, the Branch followed a policy of 'education and cooperation rather
than a blind and unyielding effort to enforce to the letter the rather wide
powers conferred by the Act.'[6]

Even a stronger commitment to enforcement would not have satisfied
those interests demanding no less than an end to overhead logging. Timber
cruiser John Piche expressed this point of view in a 1931 letter to an official
in Simon Fraser Tolmie's Conservative government, arguing that the
high-lead system 'should be outlawed for destruction of life and property.'
Anxious about the long-term prospects of their communities, the Associated Boards of Trade of Vancouver Island (ABTVI) asked Tolmie to appoint a
commission to inquire into the damage inflicted on young growth and consequent loss of provincial revenue caused by the high-lead.[7]

The Forest Branch was poorly stationed to make an authoritative response
to the first demands for a turn to selective logging. Although a few special
timber sales to encourage selective tractor logging had been issued in the
Vancouver Forest District in 1928 with the intention of avoiding 'damage
to timber and advance growth that would be caused by any kind of overhead system,' the Forest Branch had little knowledge of the alternative
technique. The memorandum Caverhill prepared for A. Wells Gray, Minister of Lands in Pattullo's new Liberal government, in response to the island group's resolution emphasized the experimental nature of selective
logging, advising against the premature drawing of conclusions. Clearly
relying upon reservations expressed by US Forest Service silviculturalists,
he advised his minister that the objective of selection was to 'cheapen the
process and return greater profits to the operator.' Until certain of the technique's practicality, individual areas should be given careful study before

recommending such operations, Caverhill concluded. Wells Gray assured the ABTVI that the Branch would monitor US Forest Service experimental work on selective logging.[8]

Inevitably, the attack on overhead logging took on political overtones. In March 1934 the CCF's Ernest Bakewell rose in the legislature to demand a government study of the selection system to 'allay the growing discontent among the public over the ruthless and unprofitable destruction of our forests.' Pattullo conceded that British Columbia timber was being 'mined,' blamed American competition, and announced an investigation of logging methods, slash burning, reforestation, and royalty rates. Wary of the growing enthusiasm for selective logging, the *British Columbia Lumberman* denied that tractors proved an effective alternative to high-lead equipment. Unmollified by either Pattullo's pledge to investigate or industry's defence of traditional technology, the ABTVI resolved in 1934 that 'the system known as High Lead Logging is not in the best interest of the Vancouver Island community at large.'[9]

Early the following year the province's operators faced exactly what their American counterparts feared – an explicit linkage of the demand for more conservative exploitation techniques with a campaign for government regulation of logging practices. Compulsory selective logging should be enforced on Vancouver Island and the lower coast, Bakewell argued in the legislature; Crown grant operators who refused should have their lands expropriated. Citing a small tractor operation near Nanaimo as an example of what could be gained from such a policy, the MLA foresaw permanent timber supplies, an improved capacity to meet market demands, safer working conditions for loggers, a lower fire hazard, and greater revenues for the Crown.[10]

Government foresters who examined this operation contradicted most of Bakewell's points. On the debit side of the ledger, E.W. Bassett's report to Caverhill pointed out that tractors functioned best on relatively gentle terrain, that the residual stand would consist of less valuable timber, and that severe slash disposal and windthrow problems could be expected. Moving on to more basic financial considerations, Bassett anticipated that enforced selective logging would mean hardship for operators with capital tied up in overhead systems, and a drop in immediate Crown revenues. On the other hand, clearcutting and broadcast burning, as presently conducted, provided inadequate regeneration, destroyed soil conditions, and created a need for extensive artificial reforestation. Selection cutting might offer a more rapid return to productivity of cutover areas, albeit of commercially inferior species, and involve additional expenditures for protection between cuttings.[11]

In a subsequent, slightly more supportive memorandum Bassett urged his superiors to keep an open mind on the new cutting method. No one, he asserted, knew the future market value of currently inferior species. Were foresters justified, then, in favouring clearcutting over selection 'merely to open up the area to reproduction of intolerant species which, as it happens, are now more valuable'? Even the slash disposal problem could be solved by analyzing the requirements of specific areas. Light accumulations of debris might be left to decompose naturally, and areas of higher hazard isolated by 'cat' roads to form temporary fire breaks, permitting spot burning. Given the many unknowns, Bassett suggested that foresters 'give selection cutting in the Fir Region the fair trial it deserves and a reasonable time to prove or disprove to the satisfaction of all, our many doubts and theories.'[12]

Gordon Godwin inspected the same operation, describing it as a silvicultural disaster area in a 1936 report. The scene on these selectively logged holdings, he wrote, 'is one of some twenty hemlock poles per acre ... many of them battered by the felling of their neighbours, struggling to keep their heads above a sea of slash. A few malformed cedar poles have also escaped the slaughter and remain to die slowly of exposure. For about every two acres a large defective fir is left with the impossible task of re-seeding the ground.' But Godwin, like Bassett, also saw the potential for a more rational use of forest resources. Certain that many coastal stands suited selective logging, he foresaw possible benefits for all: operators would receive higher profits; the Forest Branch would have a basis for the eventual introduction of sustained-yield plans; and citizens, 'becoming more than a little bit alarmed at the disappearance of their forests' would see more trees left standing.[13]

Operators, fearing the growing public support for selective logging, displayed no such tolerance. The *British Columbia Lumberman* heaped scorn on the 'impractical conservationist ... the armchair forester, the newspaper logger and the parliamentary amateur.' However, it was easier to dismiss a politician such as Bakewell than a trained forester, and another proponent of selective logging arrived on the scene around this time in the person of Max Paulik, formerly an advisor to the government of South Russia and chief forest inspector in the Ukraine. Soon associated with the CCF, Paulik appeared before the legislature's Forestry Committee in February 1935, predicting imminent exhaustion of the province's timber supply unless industry adopted new methods.[14]

At the same session R.Y. Stuart, secretary-manager of the BC Loggers Association, countered that the clearcuts produced by overhead systems encouraged abundant reforestation by virtue of the seed trees left standing after these operations. The chief forester also appeared, denying Paulik's forecast of impending doom. To Pattullo, he described Paulik's submissions as the product of European forestry concepts that did not apply to local conditions, resulting in 'many errors, inconsistencies and misrepresentations.'[15]

Caverhill heard directly from Stuart on the subject of harvesting practices, the latter citing competition with Oregon and Washington producers and difficult terrain as factors dictating the practice of overhead logging.

The alternative remained 'in the experimental stage,' Stuart argued, and to the extent selection proved feasible, operators would adopt the system of their own accord. Finally, government-mandated tractor logging 'would mean the scrapping of millions of dollars of equipment.' A memorandum from the chief forester to Wells Gray echoed many of Stuart's arguments. It would be the 'utmost folly' to force industry to scrap existing equipment in the midst of difficult economic conditions. If, as Bakewell suggested, selection yielded higher profits than overhead logging 'it would be adopted as a general practice ... without compulsion from this House.' At present the restriction of tractor logging to gentle ground, the fire protection and blowdown difficulties, and the lower quality of residual timber ruled against its general application. Continued cooperation with operators to bring about improved practices consistent with the goals of industrial expansion and increased employment constituted a wiser policy than compulsion.[16]

Bakewell renewed his attack on clearcutting in March 1935, prompting Wells Gray to announce that he and Caverhill would inspect the Crown Willamette Paper Company's selective operation in Oregon – an operation acknowledged by American foresters as one of the best examples on that side of the border. Operators were delighted when the two returned to declare that the method was still experimental, impractical on steep slopes, and therefore could not be 'applied generally to lumbering.' Where tractors proved superior, the method would 'be applied by the logging industry in its own interest.' The *British Columbia Lumberman* hoped that the government's official position on the selective logging issue would quiet those who believed that 'in its immediate adoption lies the solution of forest conservation on the Pacific Coast.'[17]

Caverhill's death late in 1935 ended one phase of British Columbia's Depression-era regulation debate with nothing resolved. Despite government's best efforts, considerable sentiment remained that the greatest obstacle to conservation lay in the extensive clearcuts produced as a consequence of the operators' use of overhead logging technology. Foresters such as Bassett and Godwin saw no reason to rejoice in the selective cutting they observed, but considered the method an option meriting further study and development. For Caverhill and Wells Gray, of course, there was never any question of using state authority to compel the practice. In this context, professional expertise served primarily in defusing enthusiasm for a technique posing a potential challenge to the accumulation of private profit and public revenue. As with all forestry issues in the province, the governing factors in the selective logging debate were economic rather than silvicultural.[18]

Even had the scientific evidence been conclusive, no measure that threatened the capital accumulation process in British Columbia's most vital industry would be countenanced. The regulation issue was far from dead, however. With the appointment of Ernest Manning to the position of chief forester, the reform movement gained a leader determined to effect a compromise between the principles of sound forest practice, the state's revenue needs, and industry's reluctance to accept restrictions on the factory regime.

E.C. Manning and the Fight for Regulation, 1936-40

Manning became British Columbia's chief forester with the support of at least one operator, A.P. Allison, but his progressive leanings also created considerable suspicion. Former chief Martin Grainger, now a prominent figure in industry, remarked in a letter of congratulations that some lumbermen perceived him as 'too much tinged with "New Deal" philosophy, which suggests to this sort of people ... pink and reddish feelings.' Manning's initial actions must have confirmed their fears. Shortly after taking office he opened discussions with the BC Loggers Association about steps required to leave cutover lands in better condition, and communicated to the legislature's Forestry Committee his wish for legislation to increase protection of forestland, provide additional control over slash burning, and compel the reservation of seed trees.[19]

But the new chief first sought to gain a better understanding of the persistent selective logging controversy. Although public agitation seemed to have abated somewhat, many of the province's large companies had purchased tractors, and he wanted to 'secure first-hand information through personal observation before I offer any opinions of my own.' So, that summer he repeated Caverhill's journey south to visit a number of American operations. Although intrigued by the theory, he too returned convinced that in its present state the system offered no solution to waste and regeneration problems.[20]

Having dispensed, to his satisfaction at least, with one troublesome issue Manning turned his attention to the creation of a regulatory framework more in keeping with traditional cutting practices. He targeted Vancouver Island's E & N Railway belt, where logging was most intense and carried out with absolute freedom by the province's largest firms. He conveyed both the need for immediate action and his awareness of political realities to MLA C.S. Leary after a 1936 inspection trip. 'The situation with regard to reproduction on the cut-over lands within the E & N belt ... is even worse than I anticipated and something must be done,' he advised. 'Otherwise, if we continue as we are doing now, we don't need to talk about the crop of the future. However, the whole subject may be gone into in a logical, reasonable way and an effort made to restrict the measures undertaken to those that will involve as little cost as possible and interfere as little as possible with the logging operations which are so essential in the economic life of the province.'[21]

Shortly thereafter Manning submitted his proposals for improved forest practice to Wells Gray. Since the government could not afford to plant barren lands, it should seek cooperation with industry to 'follow the cheaper method of securing natural regeneration and *protecting* it.' Operators were justifiably apprehensive of the critical public attitude, he noted, creating an opportune moment to press for their consent to slash burning, snag falling, and seed tree regulations. A demonstration of the proper cooperative spirit by government, through increased funding of forest protection and research, would place the Liberals in a favourable light and generate pressure for reciprocal action by industry. Otherwise, he warned, 'our efforts at creating public opinion favourable to further progress may be a little embarrassing to the Government.'[22]

Early in November Manning made his pitch to the Forestry Committee. Referring directly to Silcox's arguments, he urged that the government's contribution to the forest protection fund, slashed earlier in the decade, be returned to former levels, and amendments to the Forest Act empowering his foresters to regulate slash burning and cutting operations on Crown-grant lands. The BC Loggers Association responded with a brief denying any relationship between low restocking levels and poorly conducted slash burns or logging practices. The organization was careful to emphasize, however, that 'the character of logging and its relation to a satisfactory restocking of cut-over lands is secondary to proper slash disposal and improved forest protection.' Having made clear their reluctance to discuss logging regulations, the loggers expressed sincere interest in reforestation and a willingness to study the problem in cooperation with the Forest Branch, pointing out that 'any changes which might add to our operating costs must of necessity impair our competitive position.'[23]

Six of the largest E & N firms proposed a cooperative project after objecting to Manning's amendment as 'entirely too sweeping' and liable to 'seriously affect the titles held by us as well as the market value of the timber thereon.' If the amendment was withdrawn they pledged to burn slash during the coming year in accordance with Forest Branch instructions so that young growth received protection. Over that period they would work with government foresters in the formulation of mutually satisfactory procedures and obtain the participation of other Crown-grant operators. The Liberals accepted, promising the introduction of legislation the following year, but drew criticism from the CCF for their weak-kneed approach to reforestation.[24]

Manning expressed satisfaction with the 'very fine spirit of cooperation' shown by operators after a March 1937 meeting to discuss ways to improve restocking. 'The nature of the problems involved, including the question of costs, will make progress slow,' he admitted to the *Timberman's* George Cornwall, 'but I feel we have taken a real step in the right direction.' Forest survey work confirmed the need for closer attention to logging practices. Fully 65 percent of 243,000 acres studied on Vancouver Island and the lower coast were understocked or barren.[25]

Foresters recognized provision of a seed source as being of 'first importance,' but economic considerations dictated that action on this silvicultural problem be delayed. Prompt and proper slash burning, a far less contentious topic because it posed no direct threat to operators' control over production, was assigned priority. Of the 42,000 acres cut over in the coastal region during 1936, along with a huge accumulation of slash left over from previous years, less than 8,000 acres had been burned. Now certain that Douglas fir seed remained viable on the forest floor for just a single year, and that plentiful seed crops occurred at irregular intervals, the Branch hoped to have slash burned the first autumn after logging before seedlings became established. The E & N operators' agreement to consult with government staff in the disposal of current slash addressed an important, if less controversial, dimension of the reforestation problem.[26]

But by autumn's end it was apparent that the operators had failed to live up to their rhetoric of cooperation. The six E & N companies that signed the pledge displayed a fair measure of compliance but several others, Manning complained, 'made absolutely no attempt to prepare for burning and, in fact, ignored our requests.' This performance reinforced the chief forester's conviction that the amendment submitted the previous year should be approved. 'Does the title to E & N land convey to the owner the right to log in a way to leave it barren and a burden to the next generation'? he asked in renewing his request for regulations to control cutting and slash burning practices.[27]

Operators responded eagerly to Wells Gray's invitation to discuss Manning's amendment. Alberni-Pacific Lumber Company manager Ross Pendleton, chairman of the Loggers Association's Forestry Committee, declared that they had 'fully implemented' the slash burning agreement, protested the 'turning over to the Chief Forester of dictatorial powers,' and suggested the creation of an industry-dominated board to advise the Minister of Lands. Manning denied that the 'slash disposal phase of the problem is well in hand,' reaffirmed the need for a strengthened Forest Act, and characterized the proposed advisory board as an attempt by operators to usurp the authority of senior Forest Branch staff.[28]

By this time Manning possessed definitive data on the extent of British Columbia's reforestation problem. F.D. Mulholland's 1937 report *The Forest Resources of British Columbia* revealed that over 600,000 acres of cutover land in the Vancouver Forest District were barren of commercial forest growth, with a further 400,000 acres showing only minimal restocking. Just as alarming, these lands, 75 percent in private ownership, were being cut at a rate far beyond their sustained-yield capacity. On the E & N belt a companion survey found that only 25 percent of the logged and burned lands featured satisfactory regeneration. Excluding those areas cut during the previous few years, where some new growth would eventually appear, foresters found adequate stocking on 44 percent of the cutover land. But, they pointed out, this total included land logged under oxen and ground-lead methods that carried abundant timber. 'Restocking in the future will not be even as satisfactory as in the past, unless improved forest protection and forest practice takes place,' a forester concluded. Such reforms were necessary to correct the practices of operators who sought 'rapid liquidation of their timber assets.'[29]

Publication of these findings and Manning's many speaking engagements generated further public support for regulatory action. The *Cowichan Leader* demanded the immediate introduction of a 'constructive policy' of conservation. CCF MLA Colin Cameron supported the chief forester's proposals for government control over E & N land grant operators. Max Paulik, now chairman of that party's Forestry Planning Commission, advanced this same argument in a wide-ranging critique of Pattullo's forest policy. From the other end of the political spectrum came the ABTVI's call for passage of legislation in the coming session to 'enforce suitable regulations whereby future regeneration of our forests will be ensured and also given the necessary protection as to guarantee a continuous crop.'[30]

The Liberals acted in December 1937 with a legislative program giving Manning's Branch the power to compel annual slash burning on all tenures and fashion regulations requiring Crown-grant operators to leave seed trees. Once again slash burning was targeted for immediate attention, with the assignment of four foresters to supervise disposal on Vancouver Island and the lower coast. Opposition critics approved of the measures, but condemned the government for failing to authorize extensive planting of denuded lands or increase the Branch's allotment sufficiently to administer the new plan. Manning expressed his appreciation to Wells Gray for the legislation, while pointing out the necessity of additional funds. Pattullo insisted that the province could not afford an expensive artificial regeneration effort; more intensive forest protection and a commitment to 'help the natural reforestation along where possible' must suffice.[31]

Organizations such as the ABTVI and Ladysmith's Liberal Club hailed the amendment, but Manning's legislative achievement never made the anticipated transition from the statute book to the forest. Although firms that failed to follow Forest Branch slash burning directives might face financial penalties, no cutting regulations to achieve natural regeneration were developed. The chief forester himself now seemed quite reluctant to confront operators. When the ABTVI's president congratulated Manning and expressed his organization's hope that the Branch could now 'insist on logging operations within the E & N belt being carried on in such a manner that reforestation and conservation be given a chance,' the chief counselled patience. 'Much study will have to be given to this seed tree problem,' he wrote, 'progress will be slow and without question, we will be limited in what we can do by the ever-present problem of logging methods and logging costs.' He gave even less encouragement to another Vancouver Island resident, emphasizing that any regulations 'must be practical ones and not impose too great a handicap on the industry.' A real start would be made on the slash disposal issue, but the seeding problem required further study.[32]

With the exception of timber sales, then, where the Forest Branch placed new emphasis on seed tree reservation, logging continued with the usual disregard for silviculture after the 1937 amendments. The Branch did, however, move forward on the research front early the next year when Alberni Pacific Lumber Company manager Ross Pendleton agreed to have Gordon Godwin study that firm's cutting practices as a sort of unofficial consulting forester. The project's objective was to 'institute logging practices conducive to the greatest possible degree of natural regeneration possible under the economic limitations involved.'[33]

The Alberni-Pacific operation provided an ideal location for a study of this nature. Having recently purchased over a billion feet of Crown-grant timber in the Ash River valley from the Rockefeller interests, the firm was in the process of adapting railroad technology to a rough patch-logging system. Instead of the typical practice, which involved progressive clearcutting of valley bottoms in step with railroad construction, Pendleton and logging superintendent Don McColl planned to leave blocks of timber to serve as fire breaks during slash burns. This demanded a large initial financial outlay, since a greater portion of the primary rail system had to be constructed at the outset rather than 'gradually working your way into the timber from the water, clearcutting as you go,' McColl explained.[34]

McColl's public statements on the patch-logging system claimed a reseeding function for reserved timber blocks, but Godwin observed that their 'effectiveness as fire breaks' determined location. In any event, the firm's intention to log these areas the year following slash burning negated their usefulness as agents of reforestation because of the infrequency of heavy seed crops. Despite the abundant shortcomings, Godwin described the Alberni-Pacific method as 'a decided improvement on any yet attempted by the major logging companies.' Clearcuts had been reduced in size such that in a prolific seed year 'a greater percentage of satisfactorily restocked acreage may be expected than on other large operations.' Still, he hoped to achieve real progress by persuading the firm's management to further reduce clearcuts to the 30-60 acre range and preserve uncut blocks of timber until adjacent cutover areas had received an adequate distribution of seed.[35]

By the time of Godwin's resignation from the Forest Branch in December 1939 to accept a position with the Ontario Paper Company, the project had been underway for twenty-one months, with mixed results. He reported some unspecified success in having the company select reserve blocks in relation to their suitability as seed sources, and officials recognized the necessity of leaving this timber as long as possible to permit maximum seeding. On one setting, defective timber had been marked for reservation as seed trees, but in insufficient numbers to ensure satisfactory restocking. The company gave no thought to leaving sound timber because, as Godwin explained, the cost 'is sometimes as much as were the land to be planted, to say nothing of the profit that must be foregone.'[36]

Although the project continued, the outbreak of World War II led to a steel shortage that reduced Alberni-Pacific's commitment to patch-logging. After 1939 the firm lacked sufficient rail to allow the sort of area selection necessary for natural reforestation, since available track was moved to areas of virgin timber. 'Owing to a limited amount of steel being available,' Godwin's successor, D.L. McMullen, observed, 'it is often impossible to leave reserved settings long enough to obtain good restocking.' Moreover, clearcuts were 'usually larger than what would be desirable from a seeding in viewpoint.'[37]

The Alberni-Pacific trial, for all of its limitations, was a progressive endeavour for the time. More importantly, it represented an isolated case of industrial forest practice on the British Columbia coast. The failure of other firms to follow that example unleashed another wave of protest against unrestricted clearcutting as the decade waned. In what appears to have been a coordinated offensive, a variety of organizations declared their opposition to destructive forest exploitation. In October 1938 the Victoria Horticultural Society urged that 'other systems of logging be given an honest trial in the Province, free from all political and industrial influence and bias.' The Sapperton Young Peoples Association requested an investigation into the 'extravagant depletion of our forests,' and further concluded that 'the time is now ripe for legislation enforcing selective logging.' A Victoria church group, the South Saanich Farmers' Institute, and Imperial Order Daughters of the Empire all expressed similar convictions to the Liberal government.[38]

When the Synod of the Anglican Diocese went on record against 'wasteful methods of logging,' Pattullo chastised the group for its 'superficial knowledge of the whole situation,' and defended his record in resource conservation. The premier had also become unhappy with Manning, whose constant agitation cast the government in an unfavourable light. A flurry of letters and editorials supported the chief forester's request for increased funding for his agency. Even the Vancouver Young Liberal Association called for the Liberals to 'vote whatever funds may be necessary to more fully implement the report of the Chief Forester.' His reformist zeal now spent, Pattullo chastised Manning for using propaganda to secure larger appropriations.[39]

Despite his strained relationship with the premier, Manning continued pressing for stronger government controls, warning in his November 1939 address to the Forestry Committee that continued destructive overcutting on the coast was 'leaving an impoverished heritage to our children.' He followed up with a proposed forestry program designed to ensure industrial stability through provision of continuous timber supplies. This objective, he argued, could only be achieved by the 'growing of new crops and correlating the rate at which virgin stands are depleted with the rate at which second-growth becomes merchantable.' While working toward the long-term goal of sustained-yield, however, the province should immediately compel the planning of operations to increase natural restocking. To counter the 'determined opposition from industry' this policy would generate, he recommended that the public bear some of the cost in leaving seed trees. Manning also urged funding increases to permit planting of the millions of acres denuded on the lower coast, but maintained that the expense would not be justified unless accompanied by improved protection and cutting practices.[40]

By this time, of course, Canada had entered World War II alongside Britain, and in the context of war, conservation took second place to all-out production of natural resources for a range of military purposes. In mid-1940 Manning accepted the invitation of H.R. MacMillan, Canada's wartime Timber Controller, to become his assistant in British Columbia while remaining chief forester. Upon returning to Victoria from Ottawa in connection with his new duties, Manning died in a plane crash, eliminating his voice from the province's forest conservation debate.[41]

Manning's death brought a contentious period in British Columbia's forest history to an end with little tangible improvement in forest policy or practice. True, he had secured a degree of authority over slash burning, but his pleas for even moderate government control over logging to increase the rate of reforestation never mustered sufficient support among the province's Depression-era political elite. Given British Columbia's overwhelming dependence on forest revenues, the influence wielded by lumbermen, and lack of support from the federal government, he probably had even less chance of achieving significant reforms than his fellow reformers in the United States.

Only in retrospect is the magnitude of the opportunity that had been missed apparent. Never again would the provincial forest bureaucracy be led by a forester so willing to challenge corporate practices. Manning's immediate successor, C.D. Orchard, charted a more cooperative course for the state – a course that helped direct policy into avenues entirely consistent with industry's demand for harvesting rights unencumbered by meaningful public intervention. The sustained-yield model adopted by the provincial state during the late-1940s gave dominant firms exclusive control over huge parcels of the coast's public timber supply, but failed to deliver on the promise of regulatory control to ensure community stability.

6

State and Provincial Regulation: Industry Control and the Denial of Silviculture, 1940-65

Industry in the Pacific Northwest and British Columbia consolidated its control over the labour process and the forest during World War II and the immediate postwar decades. Against a backdrop of technological change that culminated in the extractive efficiencies of the grapple yarder, healthy demand for a wide range of wood products, increasing reliance upon public timber, and industrial concentration, trade association leaders successfully defended the foundations of the factory regime against government intervention. By the mid-1950s federal regulation no longer threatened American operators, and in British Columbia the provincial state and dominant firms had settled into a comfortable relationship based upon a monopolistic tenure system that imposed few meaningful restrictions on the method and rate of cutting.

Industry moulding and sponsorship of state forest codes thwarted the American regulationists. Although the process went more smoothly in Oregon than Washington, in both states government-sanctioned self-regulation did little more than legitimize the practices of firms possessing sufficient timber reserves and financial resources to have a concern for long-term operation. Neither the 1941 Oregon Forest Conservation Act nor the 1945 Washington Forest Practices Act posed a serious infringement upon the managerial prerogatives of operators, having more to do with preserving the sovereignty of timber capital against possible federal intervention than resource conservation. Each required operators to reserve a small percentage of timber to encourage natural reforestation of cutovers, or deposit a bond in the state treasury for regeneration by artificial means if the operator chose to cut clean. Neither code assured the rapid development of a second commercial crop, falling well short of the practices scientific research findings suggested were necessary to achieve abundant natural reforestation.

The British Columbia state adopted the sustained-yield model of forest management during the 1940s, but proved equally unwilling to impose meaningful controls on the conduct of corporate resource exploitation. Unlike the American context, where dominant firms were able to consolidate control over forestland through purchase, in that province public ownership of the resource limited the timber available for corporate acquisition. In late 1943, concerned that decades of logging activity on Vancouver Island and the lower coast threatened the survival of established lumbering centres, John Hart's Liberal-Conservative government called a royal commission to investigate the timber situation and make policy recommendations. Three years later that administration followed the example of the 1944 American Sustained-Yield Forest Management Act, amending the province's Forest Act to permit the amalgamation of private and public forestland into huge working circles to be operated by integrated firms. Forest Management Licences, later named Tree Farm Licences, were intended to attract investment capital, encourage the practice of forestry, and ensure the survival of timber-dependent communities. The first objective was met, but the recent de-industrialization of many of these communities suggests that the latter two fell victim to the subordination of forestry principles to short-term profit considerations.[1]

Foresters also resolved the debate over harvesting techniques in the Douglas Fir region on terms acceptable to timber capital. Government purchases of lumber for defence programs and postwar expansion of the pulp and paper industry removed much of the incentive for operators to harvest their holdings selectively. After a brief interlude when looming timber shortages and the increased flexibility afforded by truck logging prompted firms to restrict the scale of their clearcuts, out of protection and reforestation considerations, industry turned again to continuous clearcutting to intensify the rate of labour and resource exploitation. The conclusion of Leo Isaac's research on selective logging supported industry's claim that the method did not constitute an appropriate technique for most stand conditions in the mature Douglas fir forest. The US Forest Service discontinued the practice in favour of small patch or staggered setting clearcutting to ensure an abundant seed source and more certain fire control. But as resource agencies strove to foster an integration of engineering and silvicultural principles in logging, a mid-1950s recession narrowed corporate profit margins. Firms adopted continuous clearcutting in an effort to cut production costs, finding justification for the practice in the development of artificial reforestation techniques permitting immediate restocking of cutover lands with desired species. This style of plantation forestry offered the potential for maximum corporate efficiency in deforestation and renewal by separating the processes from one another. Critics assert a range of ecological costs associated with this model of intensive land management: soil erosion and nutrient loss, fish and wildlife habitat degradation, loss of species diversity, and increased risk of disease. Professional foresters have recently begun to defend their conception of the 'working forest' in an effort to regain public approval.[2]

State Regulation of Forest Practices in the American Pacific Northwest

The initiation of defence purchases by the American government in 1939 revived the market for wood products. As a consequence, many of those operators who logged selectively during the Depression again took up clearcutting. Most foresters applauded the return to traditional practice, but Acting Chief Forester E.H. Clapp became concerned that renewed demand induced more destructive cutting on private lands. Regional Forester Lyle Watts replied to his superior's request for information in December 1940, reporting that increased lumbering in the Douglas fir region merely aggravated the problem of overcutting. A supporter of federal intervention, Watts hoped for passage of a regulatory bill recently introduced by Oregon Congressman Walter M. Pierce on the grounds that 'national welfare and strength come through wise use and conservation of our natural resources.'[3]

America's participation as a combatant in World War II eventually elevated timber production over conservation concerns in policy-making circles, and the Pierce bill never came to a vote. But the existence of this and subsequent legislative proposals kept the regulation issue very much alive in the minds of Oregon's trade association leaders who pushed ahead with preparations for a state forest code. By August 1940 the Joint Committee on Forest Conservation's draft bill was ready for submission to the legislature. Oregon's Forest Conservation Act became law without change the next year, making it mandatory for operators to 'leave reserve trees of commercial species deemed adequate under normal conditions to maintain continuous forest growth and/or provide satisfactory restocking to ensure future forest growth.' The law defined 300 live seedlings per acre as adequate restocking, but held operators responsible only for seed tree reservation, not the extent of reforestation accomplished.[4]

The rules accompanying the act drew on Article X, the original example of industrial self-regulation, and provided for a cutting standard 'only slightly more drastic' than that measure. West of the Cascades, the reforestation provision required the reservation of not less than 5 percent of the seed-bearing trees on each quarter-section in the form of marginal long corners, strips of timber along ridges or creeks, natural fire breaks, or staggered settings. Alternatively, operators might leave two seed trees per acre, 'well scattered over the entire cut area.' Finally, they were permitted to submit individual management plans for the state forester's approval or cut clean and deposit a $2.50 per acre bond in the state treasury to cover the expense of planting denuded land. This amount also stood as the maximum fine for violation of the act, too little to meet the cost of artificial reforestation or compel compliance.[5]

The Conservation Act's fundamental weakness lay not in inadequate enforcement or insufficient penalties, but in trade association control over its silvicultural content. US Forest Service officials who participated in drafting the measure concluded that the bill would accomplish little more than a legalization of clearcutting practices already common among its sponsors. Given the large proportion of defective timber in Oregon's forests that operators normally left solely because it did not repay the cost of removal, one forester observed, 'the practices in the proposed bill are not any better than we could expect without regulation.' He found fault with a number of the bill's features, but particularly the two seed tree per acre requirement because of the likelihood both would be lost to blowdown or fire.[6]

Lyle Watts expressed 'considerable disappointment' when the industry-dominated Oregon State Board of Forestry met in November 1940. The legislation, he stated, would 'place the stamp of approval on poorer practices than many operators are now using.' Watts presented a more thorough critique in response to board member George Gerlinger's request. In setting out specific rules for a region where conditions varied so widely, he argued, the bill merely codified practices followed in the 'poorest type of operation.' Requiring operators to reserve 5 percent of the timber on each section was a step forward, but the two seed tree per acre minimum fell short of that standard. Moreover, Forest Service researchers had already concluded that seed trees in this amount were 'by no means a satisfactory source of seed,' even in the unlikely event they survived wind and slash fires.[7]

As an advisory member of the Joint Committee on Forest Conservation, Watts continued to press for more rigorous restocking provisions, but without success. Primarily interested in a state code for its value as a symbol of forest conservation in the fight against federal intervention, Oregon's lumbermen were not interested in a meaningful integration of science and public policy. After listening politely to the regional forester, the Joint Committee voted on 11 December 1940 to recommend that the trustees of the parent trade associations approve the bill as drafted for submission to the state legislatures of Oregon and Washington.[8]

When the Oregon Bill became law in April 1941, State Forester Nelson Rogers lavished praise on industrial organizations for initiating the legislation. A government publication characterized the Conservation Act as 'an honest effort to keep forest lands restocked at a cost which the industry could afford to pay,' but it had little influence on the operation of firms not cutting on a strict liquidation basis. A year after its approval, forester Charles Marston remarked that the law required only an occasional change in operating plans, posed no restriction on logging, and had no adverse effect on profits. Rogers took a conciliatory approach to those who ignored the act, reminding them that its purpose was to 'protect the industry from adverse public opinion resulting from the actions of an irresponsible minority.' When he learned that a Forest Service official in Washington, DC, described the legislation as 'lousy,' Rogers fumed at the 'insidious propaganda' circulating in the nation's capital.[9]

In contrast to Oregon, where operators engaged the legislative process without hesitation, in the neighbouring state of Washington conflicting opinion among lumbermen and suspicion of Governor Arthur Langlie's administration delayed enactment of a forest practice code until 1945. St. Paul and Tacoma Lumber Company executive Corydon Wagner hoped that more stringent industrial self-regulation under the Joint Committee's guidance would produce results equal to some form of government control. Only if this program failed should the West Coast Lumbermen's Association initiate state legislation to bring the recalcitrant minority up to industry standards. In the interim, Wagner was confident that this sort of initiative would dilute the threat of harmful state or federal regulation and provide a 'solid foundation in forestry on which to base a public relations program.'[10]

Simpson Logging Company vice-president C.H. Kreienbaum saw merit in the proposal, but doubted industry's willingness to pay the cost of effective self-regulation or to enforce compliance. Work along the lines suggested by Wagner might counter critics 'during the period of time which we feel it unsafe to propose regulation by our state government,' but Kreienbaum felt strongly that they would be in error not to 'accept the first opportune moment to go along with the Governor and support a reasonable state regulatory bill.' Facing a steady expansion of federal authority in social and economic affairs, it seemed to the Simpson executive that 'the only bulwark we have left to safeguard some of our personal liberties is through cooperation with our state government.'[11]

Anxious to see the Joint Committee's bill become law in Washington in spite of its shortcomings, Watts evaluated the measure at Langlie's request, approving its confirmation of the public's right to a voice in the management of private forestland. Although the draft's silvicultural content was 'admittedly weak,' it provided a basis for education and future amendments to strengthen forest practice rules. 'I personally would vote for your bill because of its strong points rather than vote against it because it lacks a good deal from being fully adequate,' he asserted.[12]

But among lumbermen opposition mounted as modifications to the legislation increased the severity of penalties. Winkenwerder cautioned Langlie that the code represented a significant departure from existing forest law, and the government should not exert 'too great a pressure right at the start.' More rapid and lasting progress would be achieved by 'beginning with doses that are not too bitter.' Evidently, Winkenwerder's analysis of sentiment among Washington operators hit the mark. The bill failed to pass in the spring of 1941.[13]

As Pacific coast lumbermen worked with mixed results to counter the federal regulation threat, the Joint Congressional Committee on Forestry submitted its report in March 1941. The document pleased neither industry nor interventionists. Most of the recommendations were in the cooperative tradition, calling for an extension of government aid in the usual areas along with a proposal for creation of cooperative sustained-yield units. The report's sole reference to regulation suggested an increase in Clarke-McNary funds to $10 million 'provided the respective states pass legislation providing for proper ... fire protection and regulations governing minimum forestry practices to be administered as approved by the Secretary of Agriculture.' Secretary of Agriculture Claude Rickard and Acting Chief Clapp criticized the Congressional Committee for not endorsing direct federal control by the Forest Service.[14]

Clapp continued to maintain that the accelerated pace of logging under the stimulus of national defence demands heightened the need for intervention. Eager for data to support this argument, in April he again asked regional foresters and experiment station directors if government purchases were 'leading to especially destructive forest practices which would warrant emergency control measures.' Pacific Northwest Forest Experiment Station Director Stephen Wycoff noted the impact of federal defence activities and stronger civilian demand on production levels in Oregon and Washington, but detected no deterioration in practices. Utilization had improved because of a healthier market for pulp and all grades of lumber, but this constituted a mixed blessing as clearcutting of second-growth Douglas fir to supply big mills, now running double shifts, was on the rise.[15]

Dissatisfied with the 'intangible' quality of these accounts, Clapp requested more specific information. M.L. Merritt described logging in Region Six as unchanged with the exception of second-growth cutting and a 'speeding up of the liquidation process [by] perhaps as much as 40 per cent.' Of course, he pointed out, practices before the war were 'not in all cases desirable, particularly from the standpoint of leaving and properly protecting seed sources and advanced reproduction.' The Experiment Station's Robert Cowlin supported this summary, but found an improvement in woods practice by some of the larger clearcutting operations.[16]

Late that year, only weeks before the Japanese attack on Pearl Harbour, Alabama senator John Bankhead introduced a Cooperative Forest Restoration Bill to implement the Congressional Committee's report. It proposed that state legislation for the 'conservation and proper use of privately owned forest lands' be submitted to the secretary of Agriculture, who was authorized to extend financial cooperation for the administration of those acts meeting his approval. Unlike the Pierce bill, Bankhead's measure did not provide for direct federal control in the event of state inaction, but permitted withdrawal of Clarke-McNary funds.[17]

Relatively moderate when placed alongside more ominous proposals, operators such as Corydon Wagner foresaw inevitable federal domination if the Bankhead bill became law. Weyerhaeuser's head forester Clyde Martin had confidence in industry's ability to exert the necessary influence on Congressional delegations when it came to a vote, but William Greeley predicted correctly in February 1942 that no decision would be made on the regulation issue for the war's duration. He warned the Joint Committee on Forest Conservation, however, that it was 'only a question of time before it must be fought to a finish over either the Bankhead bill or some other form of legislation.' According to Greeley, American entry into the war provided a valuable 'breathing spell' that lumbermen must utilize by 'perfecting and extending our own private enterprise forestry.'[18]

The Tree Farm program represented a carefully orchestrated initiative to cultivate public approval of industry's management practice. The concept originated in the Weyerhaeuser Timber Company's desire to safeguard future timber supplies by improving fire protection on productive cutover lands at Montesano, in Grays Harbour county, Washington. Company officials approved an increase in the protection budget, and in June 1941 the

Tree farming exhibit by American Forest Products Industries at a US Chamber of Commerce meeting.

Clemons Tree Farm was dedicated at a much publicized ceremony attended by Governor Langlie.[19]

The 'tree farm' label had such enormous appeal that image-conscious trade association leaders quickly decided to launch a national campaign. In October the Joint Committee on Forest Conservation proposed the creation of a National Tree Farm League, and two months later began certifying tree farms in the Douglas fir region. The movement soon went nationwide under the sponsorship of American Forest Products Industries, a public relations body founded in 1941 by the lumber, pulp and paper, and plywood sectors.[20]

Within a year, twenty Certified West Coast Tree Farms existed, comprising over 1.5 million acres of industrial forestland. Most of this acreage belonged to Weyerhaeuser, Crown Zellerbach, Simpson, and the St. Paul and Tacoma Lumber Company, each pledging to 'maintain a specified area of land for growing crops' by providing fire protection and utilizing proper cutting methods 'so as to maintain continuous forest growth.' Signs placed wherever boundaries crossed main roads informed the public that such projects were initiated by private industry. 'Many of us out here,' Corydon Wagner explained to an Alabama lumberman, 'feel the development of the Tree Farm idea ... is the most constructive thing we can do to demonstrate industry's sincerity in carrying out policies which it has announced on frequent occasions, and to off-set the aggressive efforts of the Forest Service to secure federal regulation.'[21]

Sign alerting motorists to the Weyerhaeuser Timber Company's White River Tree Farm.

The same considerations prompted the public relations committee of the West Coast Lumbermen's Association to recommend in May 1941 the establishment of an industry nursery to provide growing stock for interested firms. That fall the organization's trustees approved the idea, voting to finance, develop, and manage a facility. The above firms contracted for 80 percent of the nursery's proposed annual output of five million seedlings. The Joint Committee chose a site at Nisqually, Washington, over an alternative because of its 'very decided advantage for public relations purposes.' When British Columbia forester Finlay McKinnon discovered that Association policy was to plant only 500 seedlings per acre, half the number planted by the Forest Branch, he concluded the American lumbermen were 'not sincere in their statements that they want to practice good forestry.'[22]

Although Greeley's prediction that Congressional preoccupation with war legislation would delay any resolution of the regulation question proved correct, the presence of the Pierce and Bankhead bills along with Clapp's constant agitation prevented operators from becoming complacent. The Tree Farm program and Oregon Forest Conservation Act provided the acting chief's opponents with evidence, so they claimed, of industry's willingness to embrace reform voluntarily. These same defenders of the status quo also argued that federal interference would detract from the war effort. Undeterred, Clapp kept pressing Roosevelt to use his emergency powers to control logging on private land. Even after the president indicated in May 1942

Foresters pose while inspecting Douglas Fir seedlings at the West Coast Lumbermen's Association nursery, Nisqually, Washington.

that he did not intend to support federal regulation while war raged, Clapp continued to request supporting data from the regions. Responding in September 1942, Watts estimated that 35-40 percent of logging in the Douglas Fir region could not be expected to produce adequate restocking.[23]

If ongoing pressure for introduction of silvicultural controls failed to produce significant improvement in woods practice, it did prompt further legislative action by western operators and state officials who considered it essential that eligibility for cooperative funds be maintained while discouraging federal intervention. In Washington state these considerations resulted in another unsuccessful attempt to enact a forest practice code. Although fragmentary, the evidence provides additional insight into the consequences of industrial influence in the policy-making process at the state level. Shortly after introduction of the Bankhead bill, Governor Langlie appointed a forest advisory committee to formulate a code enabling the state 'to operate under proposed federal regulations embraced in a bill now pending in Congress.' The body's main objective was to recommend legislation so that 'Federal Regulations will be administered by the State, and not taken over by the Federal Government.'[24]

Under the chairmanship of University of Washington professor Gordon Marckworth, the committee began work by assuming that the reforestation provisions of the bill introduced in the 1941 session of the Washington legislature, and now in effect in Oregon, would meet federal requirements. But committee member and Assistant Regional Forester Horace Andrews relayed Watts's opinion that the Oregon code was too weak for him to recommend a share of administrative funds for the state, should the Bankhead bill pass. In Andrews's view, that act exhibited two principal shortcomings: it failed to address destructive cutting of second-growth; and it required operators to reserve only two seed trees per acre, a provision that 'would not guarantee a good crop of second-growth in a reasonably short time.'[25]

Andrews's critique appeared to have an immediate impact. When the committee met with Langlie on 8 May, its members agreed to double the seed tree requirement. Andrews left the meeting sensing the group's willingness to recommend a more substantial law for Washington. In a significant departure from the Oregon Forest Conservation Act, the committee recommended that where reservation of 5 percent of the timber on each quarter-section was impractical, four seed trees per acre should remain after logging and slash fires. Compliance would be achieved by compelling operators to secure a release from the state forester, who was empowered to shut down logging until the offender made restitution.[26]

Although approved in July for preparation as a bill, progress on the report stalled at that point for reasons that are not entirely clear. Objections lodged by the Joint Committee's Washington Section appear to have played a significant part in obstructing enactment of the measure. In November that body appointed Corydon Wagner, E.T. Clark, Charles Cowan, Norman Jacobson, and Clyde Martin, also a member of Langlie's advisory committee, to study the proposal. Martin immediately conveyed their reservations about the 'extremely heavy penalty imposed for any violation of the cutting practices.' In theory, the destruction of one or two seed trees during a slash fire could result in a lengthy shutdown until the operator completed planting of the area. This conferred excessive power upon the state forester, he argued, going on to protest another feature requiring operators to obtain that official's authorization before cutting reserved seed sources.[27]

Langlie still intended to have the bill introduced in the January session of the Washington legislature when operators decided that compulsory reservation of four seed trees per acre was 'excessive' for the Douglas fir region. Perhaps a version of the code would have become law if lumbermen had succeeded in securing passage of a companion measure to gain industry representation on the State Forest Board. Since 1923 this body, consisting of the governor, commissioner of public lands, dean of the University of Washington College of Forestry, director of the Department of Conservation and Development, and the supervisor of Forestry, had been responsible for management of state timberlands, but now seemed destined to gain influence over the conduct of private logging through passage of the forest practices code. Trade association leaders wanted the bills consolidated to prevent a 'political coup' – they feared approval of the regulation bill but defeat of the reorganization proposal. Langlie assured Corydon Wagner that regulations 'would be administered by considerate officials who had demonstrated their cooperation,' but he failed to allay industry's wariness. Further research on this legislative proposal is required, but operators' objection to the reforestation and penalty provisions of the forest practice bill, coupled with their determination to gain control over future rule-making, appears to have ensured its demise.[28]

While political conflict prevented the enactment of a forest code in Washington until 1945, Oregon lumbermen collaborated with state officials to strengthen their Conservation Act without sacrificing authority over production. A 1942 survey suggested a need for amendments, which Nelson Rogers and Assistant State Forester W.F. McCulloch discussed with the Conservation Committee's Oregon section in December. McCulloch reported satisfactory compliance with the act's wording, but suggested that operators' performance in heeding its intent left much to be desired. The officials proposed giving the state forester authority to 'promulgate elastic rules and regulations' consistent with the act's objective. They also wanted landowners as well as operators made responsible for violations.

Rogers and McCulloch ventured onto more dangerous ground when they recommended several amendments to enhance the law's silvicultural effectiveness. The state forester was particularly anxious to gain the power to rule on the acceptability of species reserved as seed sources, and to approve their location prior to cutting. Other changes would require that seed sources remain viable after slash burning, double the number of seed trees to four per acre, and demand the presence of 500 established seedlings per acre from operators who chose to clearcut totally and plant. Finally, Rogers requested an increase in the maximum authorization for state rehabilitation of delinquent lands from $2.50 to $10.00 per acre, an amount slightly more reflective of artificial reforestation costs.[29]

Although the minutes indicate approval of the proposals, at least one operator balked at the prospect of the state forester possessing 'unlimited authority' to introduce regulations. McCulloch explained to William Greeley that the intent was merely to 'permit substitution of methods which might be more desirable on a specific operation than the inflexible provisions required by statute,' and suggested a change in wording prohibiting the official from exceeding the act's stated requirements. Still cautious, the trade association representatives who dominated the State Board of Forestry demanded further time for industry to consider the recommendations.[30]

Several of the more substantive proposals did not survive industry scrutiny, but Rogers later claimed that those that gained acceptance 'greatly enhanced' the Conservation Act's effectiveness. Landowners became jointly responsible with operators for violations, seed trees were given legal definition as a 'live windfirm tree of commercial species and of seed-bearing size possessing a relatively full crown,' and a third prohibited removal of seed sources until restocking had occurred. The allowable expenditure for planting of delinquent lands rose to $5, but Rogers was proudest of the amendments granting him the authority to promulgate, with Board of Forestry approval, rules equivalent to the act's requirements and seek court injunctions against violators.[31]

The modifications did more to strengthen the act's legitimacy than to boost its power as agent of forest renewal; those measures posing the greatest threat to profits or property rights were rejected by industry. Neither the proposal doubling the number of seed trees nor that extending control over seed source position to the state forester, either of which would have increased the speed and quantity of natural reforestation, became codified. Initially Rogers had also hoped to achieve some degree of authority over the cutting of immature timber, but he dropped this measure when preliminary discussion with operators revealed that its inclusion jeopardized his entire legislative agenda.[32]

Despite the 1943 changes to the Oregon Forest Conservation Act, the law remained a poor substitute for public control of the sort envisioned by advocates of federal intervention. For his part, Rogers pushed for improved regulation and enforcement, but not past the point where he might begin to lose the confidence of lumbermen. During testimony to British

Columbia's Royal Commission on Forestry in 1944, he declared that 'within a democratic form of government I think there is a limit beyond which we should not go to regulate the method by which the citizens make a living.' Indeed, the state forester's enforcement policy seems to have been guided by a desire to grant operators the widest possible latitude. He encouraged those cutting in uniformly sound timber, where the value of a single log exceeded the cost of artificial reforestation, to cut clean and make the required $5 per acre deposit even though this sum did not cover the state's planting costs.[33]

Industry influence rather than Rogers's personal convictions constituted the essential constraint on Oregon's Conservation Act, preventing a successful meeting of the scientific and legislative processes. The publication of Leo Isaac's definitive *Reproductive Habits of Douglas Fir* in 1943 provided an ideal opportunity to integrate the knowledge accumulated over decades of research with the silvicultural content of state forest law. Although both the Oregon and Washington sections of the Joint Committee on Forest Conservation expressed interest in underwriting the manuscript's publication, Isaac's findings were ignored during the revision of the Oregon code.[34]

The silviculturalist's discussion of natural seeding exposes the chasm separating contemporary research findings from forest law in the region. Isaac had determined that adequate restocking under average conditions required the dissemination of eight pounds of Douglas fir seed per acre over a six to eight-year period. Reservation of two seed trees per acre on the national forests had 'seldom been satisfactory,' and while four would produce the requisite quantity within eight years of logging, he recommended double this number to provide a margin of safety against losses to fire, wind, or disease. Taking Isaac's most conservative estimate as a minimum requirement, it is apparent that the Oregon law fell woefully short of the provisions necessary to ensure natural reforestation of private forestland.[35]

Given the weakness of this and other examples of state legislation, Clapp remained convinced of the need for federal standards. After hearing the acting chief speak to the American Forestry Association in late 1942, Greeley returned to inform the Joint Committee that the threat of emergency cutting control would be imminent throughout the war period. The appointment of Lyle Watts as chief forester in January 1943 brought another progressive forester to the leadership of the US Forest Service. Although somewhat less strident in public than Clapp, Watts shared his interventionist philosophy.[36]

A few months after arriving in Washington, DC, the new chief informed regional foresters and experiment station directors that he considered forest regulation 'involving large Federal participation and strong Federal leadership indispensable in an adequate forest policy for the nation.' He wanted further time to study the question before indicating the precise form of legislation the agency should advocate, but they should endorse state legislation only to the extent that it met minimum standards and they should be clear about the need for federal participation.[37]

Later in the year Watts made his position public, arguing that the economic importance of forests required attention to postwar planning based on the premise that 'nation-wide regulation of cutting practices on private forest land under strong federal leadership is absolutely essential.' Neither action by the states alone, nor the extension of federal financial aid to meet the costs of state administration would suffice. Federal legislation should prescribe standards, authorize the secretary of Agriculture to determine if state laws met minimum requirements, monitor enforcement, and 'take direct action' if either was inadequate.[38]

University of California professor Emanuel Fritz and Idaho lumberman George Jewett both associated Watts's ideas with totalitarianism, Jewett comparing the chief's political philosophy with that of Hitler's Nazi government. NLMA manager Wilson Compton held to a more sophisticated line, urging landowners to continue working with state governments to adopt timber cutting regulations. But by 1943 even moderate foresters were disappointed with the limited accomplishments of state regulation. In addition to Oregon only Idaho, New Mexico, and Virginia had enacted forest practice legislation, a meagre showing that Samuel T. Dana attributed to industry's confidence that the Roosevelt administration would not introduce federal controls during the war. 'The net result of the action by the various state legislatures is not particularly impressive,' Dana concluded.[39]

The Joint Committee on Forest Conservation met in January 1944 to formulate suggestions for a national policy on the regulation question. Adamant that Watts would continue to back federal regulation along the lines of the Bankhead bill, Greeley conveyed the NLMA's wish for further progress in state regulation. While trade association leaders pondered what form their relationship to governments should take, they also had cause to rejoice when Congress passed the Sustained-Yield Forest Management Act in March. Based largely upon the ideas of David Mason, the legislation authorized the formation of two kinds of sustained-yield arrangements. Cooperative units would amalgamate national forest timber and adjacent private land into working circles to be operated by individual firms under cutting plans developed jointly by representatives of the Forest Service and the company. Federal units reserved national forest timber in specific areas for cutting by local companies.[40]

Watts saw the cooperative sustained-yield unit as a means to ensure survival for established timber-dependent communities, in contrast to industry executives who welcomed an opportunity to achieve a concentration of corporate control over public timber. In the end, conflict over the intent of the cooperative variety was overshadowed by opposition from small operators and firms fearing reduced access to much of the west coast's remaining old-growth timber. Although several federal units were established around the country, the 1946 agreement between the Simpson Logging Company and US Forest Service creating the Shelton Cooperative Sustained-Yield Unit was the sole contract signed in the United States.[41]

As World War II entered its final stages, Douglas fir lumbermen had achieved some measure of success in using the window of opportunity provided by the conflict to generate public confidence in their resource stewardship. Oregon had its amended Conservation Act, and throughout the region the Tree Farm program flourished among the largest firms. But they remained vulnerable to a revived postwar regulation crusade under Watts, particularly in Washington where operators had yet to emulate the legislative success of their Oregon counterparts.

The termination of World War II in allied victory freed Watts and other high-ranking Forest Service officials from the defence considerations that had constrained their public advocacy of federal regulation. Anticipating events, western lumbermen recognized the need to mount a stronger rebuttal to the arguments of interventionists. Dwindling timber supplies complemented the public relations imperative, giving lumber executives – those whose firms had sufficient timber to contemplate long-term operation – a material basis for larger forest management investments. Improved Tree Farm administration, the passing of the 1945 Washington Forest Practices Act, and further modification of the Oregon legislation reflected industry's intent to defeat the regulation threat while attaining some increase in the productivity of timberland.

After the first flush of enthusiasm over their Tree Farm program, trade association leaders discovered that certifying units that failed to exhibit a minimal standard of forestry invited public criticism. Crown Zellerbach's Don Denman advised Corydon Wagner in August 1944 of 'the very haphazard manner in which this ... certification of tree farms is being handled.' More careful attention was required or the project would 'boomerang and ... prove a liability to the industry.' A continuation of the present approval procedure would create 'all kinds of "cat and dog" tree farms that aren't any more tree farms than my backyard.' The Joint Committee moved to tighten up administration later that year, initiating an annual inspection of all Tree Farms and requiring submission of a five-year management plan.[42]

Separating the rhetoric from the reality of Tree Farm administration is a difficult task. After visiting Weyerhaeuser Tree Farms in November 1943, a Forest Service representative concluded that progress had been made, but the firm's foresters 'had a real problem to work out ... arrangements with the logging engineers and the loggers for getting satisfactory forestry practices into the woods.' A November 1945 report on Region Six Tree Farms found improved cutting practices, planting, and high-order protection on some properties, but little change on others since dedication. Still, the writer characterized the Tree Farm program as 'a very meritorious undertaking' that might yet become a vehicle for private forestry.[43]

Charges that the actual conduct of forest practices on Tree Farms did not measure up to the boasts found in industry press releases continued to threaten industry's claims of responsible stewardship. Ellery Foster, a professional forester who served as the IWA's Director of Research and Education, was a particularly persistent critic. In 1945 Foster scorned the Tree Farm program as little more than a 'publicity stunt to convince the indignant public that the lumber barons have finally got religion.' A resolution adopted at the union's 1948 convention warned the public not to be duped by misleading publicity. Even William Greeley later admitted that some Tree Farms were 'declared superficially with a public relations ... motive,' but described the great majority as 'serious undertakings in timber cropping.' By 1948 total Tree Farm acreage in the Douglas fir region reached over 3 million, about 14 percent of the timberland in private ownership. Four years later Crown Zellerbach's E.P. Stamm gave the program substantial credit for having 'helped change radically the public sentiment toward our industry in the last decade.'[44]

Important as the Tree Farm symbol was in their effort to demonstrate the folly of federal control, operators continued to view the legitimacy accorded by state regulation as an essential weapon in the defence of free enterprise. Finally, in 1945, Washington lumbermen and the Langlie administration agreed on a forest practices act for that state. A majority of Puget Sound foresters endorsed the adoption of a code similar to that of Oregon, no doubt confirming, in Ellery Foster's mind, the profession's subordination to corporate interests. 'The big boys are powerful in forestry circles,' he observed in describing industry's manipulation of the 1945 WFCA conference. 'A consulting forester has to keep on the good side of his clients. The professor in a forestry school has to be careful to keep in the good graces of reactionary forces who still have too much power in state politics and boards of regents, through which the state colleges and universities are controlled. State and federal foresters also have to be careful.' Oregon State University educator William F. McCulloch objected to Foster's characterization of his colleagues as 'mouthpieces for the industry,' but the IWA official remained adamant that foresters had permitted operators to use the conference as a 'sound-board for their own propaganda line.'[45]

The Washington Forest Practices Act was passed in 1945 after a series of meetings held in logging centres around the state to acquaint operators with its provisions. Industry accepted the measure despite apprehension that it might be abused by public officials, given the absence of accompanying legislation making the state forester responsible to a forestry board dominated by operators. Scheduled to go into effect on 1 January 1946, the Act required firms to obtain a permit from the state's Division of Forestry prior to logging and to 'reserve trees of commercial species deemed adequate under normal conditions to maintain continuous forest growth.'[46]

Like Oregon's Conservation Act, the Washington code directed Douglas fir operators to leave at least 5 percent of each quarter-section 'well stocked with commercial coniferous trees' until the area had adequately restocked, restocking being defined as 300 live seedlings per acre. Alternative plans could also be submitted for the state forester's approval, preserving the flexibility considered essential by operators. Section 8 of the act authorized the state forester to employ foresters and to shut down violators until receipt of a cash bond or deposit not to exceed $8 per acre for reforestation of land that lacked sufficient source of seed to restock the area.[47]

Modelled on the Oregon Forest Conservation Act, which itself originated in Article X of the New Deal experiment in industrial self-government, the Washington legislation posed little challenge to conventional clearcutting practices. Leo Isaac described the code as a 'tiny step in the right direction,' but an insight into just how infinitesimal is revealed by an exchange of correspondence between British Columbia industrial forester John Mottishaw and Gordon Marckworth. After receiving a copy of the Washington code, Mottishaw wrote to the University of Washington professor, pointing out that the BC Forest Service's standard of satisfactory reforestation was 1,000 seedlings per acre. 'It occurs to me,' he wrote, 'that the minimum for adequate restocking of 300 trees per acre adopted by the State government of Washington might be a compromise between the people affected rather than a measure of satisfactory restocking.' Marckworth agreed the requirement was a product of negotiation and, 'would not, in the true sense, be adequate restocking.'[48]

Neither was the act's $8 per acre penalty sufficient, either to cover the costs of artificial restocking or to deter potential violators. Given the rising price of logs and high planting costs, one Washington lumberman speculated that many operators logging on a liquidation basis would cut clean, pay the bond, and 'walk off, leaving the [state forester] holding the sack.' State Forester T.S. Goodyear admitted in early 1946 that the $8 per acre provision would be difficult to enforce, but defended the clearcutting operations of leading firms.[49]

Passage of the Washington Forest Practices Act placed the entire American Douglas fir industry under a similar blanket of state legislation. But some expressed dissatisfaction with the flimsy protection these codes afforded the public interest. A December 1945 article in the IWA's *International Woodworker*, probably written by Foster, described the Oregon law as 'little more than a feeble beginning at the kind of regulations which are needed.' Even trade association foresters expressed private reservations about the standard of forest practice. Austin McReynolds, a member of the

Conservation Committee's staff, reported that on 90 percent of western Oregon operations the 'observance of conservation practices is left to chance.' The vast majority of foremen received no instruction on the act's requirements or the necessity of advance planning for seed source reservation.[50]

Given the ease with which operators met the requirements of these laws, it should come as no surprise that government officials reported a high rate of compliance. After all, as Rogers told a group of Willamette Valley loggers, the Conservation Act contained 'nothing more drastic than rules of good practice long followed by prudent operators.' Of the 186,000 acres logged in Oregon's Douglas fir region in 1944, only about 18,700 were left in violation. By October 1946 the amount of delinquent land stood at approximately 60,000 acres, and it was expected some 20,000 acres of this total would eventually require planting. One hopeful estimate put the future annual acreage needing artificial reforestation at 10,000, well beyond the capacity of the state's nursery. The low bond required of violators or of those firms choosing to remove all the timber from high-quality stands compounded this problem. Lacking the finances to plant all the lands requiring artificial reforestation, the state opted to either spot-plant or 'do a complete job on as much of the area as funds will permit.'[51]

State Forester Rogers met with the Joint Committee's Oregon section late in 1946 to set out proposed amendments to the Oregon Conservation Act, and in December presented his recommendations to the annual WFCA conference. He expressed dissatisfaction with the 90 percent compliance rate in western Oregon where requirements could be met, with very few exceptions, 'at no appreciable cost.' Rogers attributed non-compliance to misunderstanding of the law, poor cutting methods, destruction of seed sources through careless slash burning, and his inability to 'prevent conscious and wilfull violations of the Act.' To correct this situation he proposed a state-wide cutting permit system and a raise in the rehabilitation fee from $5 to $8, now the Washington standard, to discourage violators and provide additional funds for artificial reforestation. Aware of the line separating administrative from fundamental criticism, Rogers expressed confidence in the act's seed source requirements to provide adequate reforestation within a relatively short time.[52]

The act was amended in 1947 to conform with Rogers's recommendations, and new regulations were issued after input from the Joint Committee on Forest Conservation. But a 1947 US Forest Service evaluation of practices on private land in the region hinted at the ineffectiveness of state legislation in improving the standard of corporate resource exploitation. The agency found no evidence of 'high order' cutting, classifying 6 percent as good, 38 percent as fair, 40 percent as poor, and 16 percent as destructive. The disparity between state Department of Forestry press releases touting the act's achievements and the Forest Service appraisal raised embarrassing questions. 'Does this mean that the state conservation laws of Oregon and Washington are not adequate, or are not being enforced'? asked the editor of the Portland *Oregonian*.[53]

Regional Forester H.J. Andrews explained to another editor that the survey revealed certain trends toward improved practices on private timberlands, and when challenged by Crown Zellerbach's Don Denman he conceded that the rating used data from the 1941-44 period. 'If cutting practices were to be judged at the present time many owners are now doing a better job and their rating in 1946-47 would be of a better order of cutting than in 1944,' he admitted. Denman argued that faster progress would result from 'cooperation and tolerance than by continual criticism and scrapping,' and claimed the forestry practised by his firm equalled the Forest Service's in the region. The Oregon State Board of Forestry immediately appointed a committee to determine if agencies could establish a closer correlation of standards in future.[54]

Firms such as Crown Zellerbach and Weyerhaeuser represented one side of the coin as the Douglas fir industry entered the postwar era – they were representative of the dwindling number of large concerns 'for whom a considerable length of life is still in prospect.' These were the integrated enterprises consolidating timber supplies, hiring foresters to gather data as a basis for management planning, practising a high standard of fire protection, and devoting at least some attention to restocking their holdings. The other camp consisted of operations facing the inevitable exhaustion of their holdings, which 'had little or nothing to gain from such activities and are proceeding with their liquidation in much the same manner as before.'[55]

The improvements recorded by some timber-rich firms did not sway Watts and some national political figures from their commitment to federal regulation. Douglas fir trade associations were not overly concerned about the 1946 Hook Bill, a proposal for direct federal control supported by the Congress of Industrial Organizations, but in his annual report for 1946 the chief forester again expressed his desire for state administration of federal standards. The Joint Committee held little hope for a more cooperative relationship with the Forest Service but decided against attacking the agency. Instead, it invited Regional Forester Horace Andrews to develop a basis for cooperation on all matters of common interest.[56]

The reluctance of western trade association leaders to launch an all-out offensive against the Forest Service lay in industry's mounting reliance upon national forest timber. Accordingly, when aggressive elements within the NLMA urged that organization's leadership to threaten the agency by pushing for a reduction in its appropriation, Simpson Logging Company executive C.H. Kreienbaum gave warning that the West Coast Lumbermen's Association would not tolerate this course of action. A reduction in funding, he explained, might threaten the Forest Service's plan to increase timber sales in the Douglas fir region 'where our operators will be so soon dependent upon Government timber.' Corydon Wagner maintained that industry should counter Forest Service propaganda but avoid the 'bar-room' tactics favoured by some impetuous lumbermen, which might disrupt 'the many activities on which there should be the closest sort of cooperation.'[57]

Despite public assurances by state forestry officials that the Oregon and Washington laws imposed the nation's most severe harvesting restrictions, in 1948 the Forest Service's Division of State and Private Forestry called for strengthening of both codes. Joint Conservation Committee forester William Hagenstein expressed a basic truth when he observed that the attainment of natural reforestation was primarily a matter not of law but 'enlightened self-interest on the part of timber landowners and operators who want a permanent timber supply.'[58]

But some of the Pacific Northwest's small landowners who lacked the sophistication and horizon of trade association leaders considered even the most minor infringement upon their freedoms unacceptable. One operator declared that the Washington Forest Practices Act created a 'one man dicta-tor over the harvesting of the crop on privately owned lands,' an unconsti-tutional abridgement of property rights. Sharing this sentiment, Avery Dexter challenged the constitutionality of the Washington Act in 1947. The owner of 320 acres of timber at Pend Oreille, Dexter began logging his tract in 1945 without first obtaining a permit from the state forester's office. When that official ordered the operation shut down Dexter refused, prompting the state to launch proceedings against him.[59]

Dexter won round one of the legal engagement, the Pend Oreille county court finding the act unconstitutional. Regional trade associations and sev-eral large firms supported the state's appeal to the Washington Supreme Court, which ruled in February 1949 that 'the challenged legislation is for the general and public welfare and is a proper exercise of the police powers of the State.' Undeterred, Dexter appealed to the United States Supreme Court, threatening the legality of the forest laws of seventeen states. On 9 November 1949, the high court upheld the Washington Supreme Court's decision, confirming the constitutionality of state forest practice legislation.[60]

Having turned back one attack on their regulatory order, corporate heads faced another from a more traditional source in 1949 when Arizona Senator and former Secretary of Agriculture Clinton P. Anderson submitted a bill proposing a program of federal forest practice guidelines for state adminis-tration. The 1949 Anderson bill drew an aggressive response from industry. Pressure was exerted on Congressional representatives while American For-est Products Industries upheld the effectiveness of state laws and corporate stewardship.[61]

In the west, the *Timberman* called for industry to continue the practice of 'economic statesmanship and self-regulatory control' to defeat Anderson's measure. Greeley touted the Washington and Oregon laws as 'the most drastic use of state police power yet attempted in this country,' defended the rigorous certification and inspection of West Coast Tree Farms, and assured *Journal of Forestry* readers that the prevailing method of block clearcutting in the Douglas fir region would produce adequate natural restocking on 85 to 95 percent of large properties. It is true that Weyerhaeuser, St. Paul and Tacoma, and other large firms placed more emphasis on selection of seed areas by the early 1950s. But within these same enterprises, engineering efficiency remained the primary determinant of logging practices. William Hagenstein's opinion, expressed in 1949 to the Joint Committee, now reorganized as the Forest Conservation Committee of the Pacific Northwest Forest Industries, that industry was 'dragging its feet some on cutting practices' was absent when he and other industry figures wrote for public consumption.[62]

The Anderson bill gave foresters an opportunity to demonstrate clearly that the principle of federal regulation had no place in the profession's vision of postwar America. Yale University's H.H. Chapman declared that the time for a 'showdown' on the SAF's stance had arrived, and a referendum on the question was organized. In the campaign preceding the vote, Watts depicted the few state forest practice laws as weak, more responsive to 'local needs and political pressures' than a genuine commitment to ending forest devastation. Most, he noted, had been enacted between 1941 and 1945 when the Bankhead bill had threatened to implement the Joint Congressional Committee's recommendations. The real issue was not federal versus state regulation, Watts emphasized, but whether there should be federal participation in a national program administered by the states.[63]

Industrial foresters challenged the chief's interpretation. Weyerhaeuser's Clyde Martin, just selected president of American Forest Products Industries after serving a term as SAF president, depicted a vote for the Anderson bill as a threat to state regulation and warned that its enactment would stifle initiative in private forest management. WFCA forest counsel Stuart Moir presented the conflict in similar terms, and most of the 60 percent of SAF members who participated in the May 1950 referendum apparently agreed. Only 1,107 of the 3,652 ballots cast expressed support for federal regulation. Chapman interpreted the result as a rejection of the policy forced upon the Forest Service by Clapp and Watts, and a vindication of industry's record.[64]

The Anderson bill died in committee, and the election of Dwight D. Eisenhower in 1952 brought a Republican to the White House for the first time since 1933. Eisenhower opposed federal regulation of natural resources, effectively ending the regulation debate that had animated foresters since the early twentieth century. In March 1952 Forest Conservation Committee chair E.P. Stamm reported with satisfaction that industry's public relations and lobbying efforts, in conjunction with better performance in the woods, had 'convinced the public that there is no need for the Great White Father from the shores of the Potomac to take his taxpaying country cousins by the hand and lead them down the avenue of forest management.' Lumbermen stood ready to 'stem the incoming tide of federal regulation when it again surges forward,' but the retirement of Watts in July confirmed that federal regulation no longer threatened. New Chief Forester Richard E. McArdle, a man of 'compromising ability,' opted for a policy of cooperation with industry.[65]

The end of the American regulation debate coincided with private expressions of concern by western forestry officials over both the content and administration of state laws. In a 1950 appearance before the operators' Conservation Committee, Washington's State Forester Bernard Orell described compliance with the Forest Practices Act as 'generally good,' but went on to point out the need for a larger inspection staff to control those 'recalcitrant operators' who neglected its provisions. Orell also wanted an amendment giving the state authority to determine placement of seed sources, or at least to require consultation between the Division of Forestry and landowners. Oregon experienced an even more pronounced shortage of enforcement personnel as it surpassed Washington as a centre of wood production. In neither state were rehabilitation fees sufficient to deter violators or provide funding equal to artificial reforestation needs.[66]

Another shortcoming of these state laws was their failure to address the cutting of young timber, a problem that grew in severity with expansion of the pulp economy. The Pacific Northwest Forest and Range Experiment Station's annual report for 1950 urged the incorporation of measures to preserve growing stock. Orell conceded to station director Robert Cowlin that operators cut second-growth prematurely and current logging practices destroyed young trees. But adding more stringent regulations to the Forest Practices Act, which admittedly required 'but a minimum of good forest management,' would increase the burden on his field force and raise the cost of enforcement.[67]

Cowlin doubted the sincerity of Orell's request for suggested improvements to the Washington legislation, but assigned one of his foresters to prepare a list of proposals. The resulting report recommended a redefinition of 'adequate stocking' to 500 live seedlings per acre, limitation of clearcut openings to 40 acres, an increase in the rehabilitation fee from $8 to $15 or $20 per acre, and a number of provisions to control cutting in young stands. Publicly, state forestry agencies continued to assert the adequacy of seed source requirements, but in 1952 Leo Isaac informed a WFCA committee that he could not recall a single area where the reservation of two seed trees per acre had produced satisfactory new growth. By 1953 the area of commercial forestland in Oregon requiring artificial regeneration had reached 1,538,000 acres. Although many large owners surpassed the minimum standards, Oregon Conservation Act supervisor Lee Harter argued in 1956 that his over-burdened staff was incapable of 'performing the enforcement job called for by statute,' or even of analyzing the effectiveness of seed source provisions.[68]

Throughout this period the forest laws of Oregon and Washington had marginal influence on the practices of large, stable corporations. The legislation, after all, had been drawn and amended to defeat federal regulation by bringing industry-wide standards up to, but not beyond, those of firms dominant in the regional trade associations. Moreover, depletion of old-growth reserves and an increasing commitment to restocking cutover lands prompted greater interest in artificial regeneration techniques during the 1950s, making seed source requirements even less relevant to the clearcutting operations of major corporations. Indeed, as this chapter's concluding section will show, developments in planting and seeding helped to eliminate whatever incentive had existed for Douglas fir operators to achieve natural restocking. Before proceeding to this subject, however, the study will analyze how adoption of the sustained-yield model in British Columbia encountered equally significant obstacles to meaningful regulation in the woods.

Sustained-Yield Policy in British Columbia

With the outbreak of war in 1939 the pace of activity in the British Columbia forest industry picked up. Although a shortage of shipping hindered access to the important British market, North American demand quickly took up the slack. As in the Pacific Northwest, defence demands provided a stimulus to the lumber business. Airports, for example, were constructed for training pilots in Canada under the British Commonwealth Air Training Plan. When the federal government took over control of natural resources from the provinces, H.R. MacMillan served as Timber Controller under Minister of Munitions and Supply C.D. Howe on the War Industries Control Board.[69]

British Columbia foresters continued to debate the proper relationship between government and industry during the early war years. Earnest Manning and F.D. Mulholland dominated professional discourse on the issue prior to the former's death. Mulholland, who left the Forest Branch in 1939, used his position as president of the Canadian Society of Forest Engineers (CSFE) to speak out for a laissez-faire policy. So effectively did he present the case that the *British Columbia Lumberman* termed his address to that organization's 1939 annual meeting 'an admirable brief for democratic principles in forest administration.' On another occasion he described the predominance of Crown-owned forestland in British Columbia as satisfactory only to those with Communist leanings.[70]

Manning and Mulholland locked horns at a December 1939 meeting of the CSFE's Victoria section. First citing European forest law in support of his call for a decentralized, cooperative policy, Mulholland introduced a resolution stating that greater private ownership, reduced taxation and royalties, and provision of technical advice by government would facilitate sustained-yield forestry. What arguments, Manning asked, could foresters make to encourage the practice of forestry by companies? Mulholland replied that when approached, operators usually argued that forestry was out of the question until their mills were written off, and none had 'sufficiently large limits to operate over a full rotation period at their present mill capacity.'[71]

The resolution, shorn of its reference to private ownership, passed at the section's next meeting. Manning and Mulholland continued their forest policy debate, but by late 1940 the latter was embroiled in a public controversy with the CCF's Ernest Winch over that party's intent to nationalize the industry. 'Surely,' the forester wrote, 'the world has had enough of coercive governments with their inevitable animosities, suppressions and injustices, preventing the fullest use of human intelligence and energy.' Winch, questioning Mulholland's professional ethics, quoted passages from his 1937 *Forest Resources of British Columbia,* which referred to the need for regulation to reconcile the conflict between public and private interest. The cooperative commonwealth was a worthy ideal, Mulholland responded, but it would not be attained by 'state administration on a totalitarian model.'[72]

With Manning's death early in 1941, leadership of the Forest Branch passed to C.D. Orchard, whose philosophy on business-government relations had more in common with that of Mulholland than either Manning or Winch. Pattullo's Liberal party triumphed again in the provincial election held late that year, but without a majority. The CCF emerged as the official opposition thanks in part to strong support in resource communities. Finance Minister John Hart and other cabinet members favoured the creation of a coalition government with the Conservatives to keep the socialists from power. Pattullo opposed the idea and resigned when the Provincial Liberal Association endorsed it. Hart became leader of the party, and premier, taking the Liberals into the promised coalition government with the Conservatives.[73]

British Columbia's chief forester set out his thoughts on forest policy to colleagues in February 1942, when the CSFE's Victoria section debated a resolution calling for the government to provide free technical advice to operators in tandem with the introduction of silvicultural regulations. Such advice was freely available, Orchard maintained, but never requested. The high cost of carrying lands forced firms into a policy of liquidating cutting rights. Historically, the provincial state had employed coercion to secure slash disposal, snag falling, and protection, but with limited success. Government would do better, he suggested, by replacing all land taxes with a severance tax on timber when cut, giving operators an incentive to seek and act on professional counsel.[74]

A few months later Orchard submitted a lengthy, detailed policy proposal to Minister of Lands Wells Gray. Because his plea for the formation of forest working circles bears a close similarity to Gordon Sloan's royal commission report and the subsequent 1947 Tree Farm Licence legislation, the memorandum merits scrutiny. Its ideological underpinning was Orchard's belief that 'private interests can be made to coincide with public interest, and that private interest can be substituted for penalties and coercion.' He began by outlining the severity of the situation on the south coast where the pace of logging was double the region's sustained-yield capacity, and industry added 30,000 to 40,000 acres each year to the million acres currently requiring planting. Forest revenues would inevitably decline if deterioration of the resource base continued.[75]

Orchard attributed this predicament to the government's outmoded forest policy. Although the 1912 Forest Act was 'admirably adapted to the needs of its day,' on timber sales and other temporary tenures operators were denied a personal interest beyond quick removal of values, resulting in a system of timber mining 'deliberately imposed by strictly enforced law.' Government penalties and coercion ran counter to immediate business interests, and must therefore fail except under a 'type of policing and surveillance which would be almost impossible in the woods and ... most undesirable and distasteful to all concerned.' The solution, according to Orchard, was to 'give the operator, wherever possible, an interest in the area he is working that will permit him to make long-term plans in co-operation with the Government, and permit him to see the possibility at some later date of retrieving capital invested and profits delayed in the immediate interest of forest conservation and perpetuation.'[76]

Public and private interests would be aligned by pooling private and Crown lands in working circles of sufficient size to support operations in perpetuity. Yield capacity and annual harvest levels on these units were to be determined jointly by company and government foresters, and cutting conducted in accordance with working plans subject to Forest Branch approval and inspection. Finally, the government should revoke all taxes, royalty, and stumpage payments on the tenures, replacing these charges with a nominal annual rental on the land plus a share of income on a scale to be determined. If introduced, Orchard concluded, his policy would provide a sustained yield of wood products, stabilize existing operations considered crucial to the provincial economy, and encourage the establishment of new enterprises on a perpetual rather than short-term basis.[77]

Orchard later claimed responsibility for the coalition's sustained-yield policy, delayed only because of Hart's reluctance to introduce such a radical change without first staging a royal commission to prepare the public. The close correspondence between his recommendation and the 1947 amendments to the Forest Act lends credence to Orchard's recollection, but prodding from the British Columbia Natural Resources Conservation League (BCNRCL) also appears to have played a part in Hart's decision to establish a public forum for discussion of forestry issues. On 19 January 1943, BCNRCL president H.H. Stevens, supported by a diverse group of patrons including future Social Credit Premier W.A.C. Bennett and the CCF's Ernest Winch and Colin Cameron, asked Hart for an appointment to present a brief before the next session of the legislature.[78]

A week later a BCNRCL delegation submitted a document asserting that the province's forest policies reflected 'an absence of early planning, resulting in a condition at the present time which demands careful scientific study of the fundamental principles involved.' Urging the premier to act before the problems of demobilization occupied the government, the brief called for the establishment of a board of inquiry to examine reforestation, protection, private land regulation, logging controls, and recreation as a basis for legislation. Hart immediately asked Orchard for his thoughts on the proposal. The chief forester bristled at the criticism but conceded that an investigation might 'serve a very valuable purpose in public education.'[79]

Although the precise nature of the factors entering into the government's decision is not clear, on 23 June 1943 Hart announced that an 'exhaustive inquiry into all phases of British Columbia's logging and lumber industry' would be undertaken in the near future. It is almost certain that the CCF's ongoing critique of government forest policy figured in the appointment of a commission, but powerful lumbermen were also receptive to the idea because of resource depletion caused by decades of reckless overcutting on Vancouver Island and the lower coast. Enjoying booming wartime markets, anxious to extract greater value from their logs by establishing pulp mills, but needing assured access to new timber supplies to attract investment capital, dominant operators supported an inquiry so long as it did not interfere with their personal affairs and presented an opportunity to gain monopolistic control over public timber.[80] Thus, by 1943, government officials, foresters, and lumbermen agreed that timberlands tributary to existing operations should be made available for their exclusive use, requiring only a commission of inquiry to legitimize the introduction of a tenure system along the lines suggested by Orchard.[81] Several town councils and civic groups hailed the announcement, but with no progress apparent by October, Stevens expressed the BCNRCL's impatience. Finally, on 31 December 1943, Chief Justice Gordon Sloan was appointed to head a royal commission on forestry.[82]

Sloan began his inquiry by questioning government forestry officials. Concerned with the issue of forest practice control, he expressed some consternation at the absence of seed tree regulations in cutting contracts during Orchard's appearances. The chief forester replied that foresters had only begun to contemplate timber scarcity in the last decade. Changes in procedure were now under consideration, he explained, but 'they cost so much money, they have so many aspects, and so many attendant circumstances, that we do not think we dare do it until we make a complete study of it.' When pressed further, Orchard expressed his reluctance to require operators to 'undertake this, that and the other obligation that is not based on good sound reasons.' Lack of opportunity, funds, and staff had prevented the Forest Branch from performing the sort of site-specific studies necessary to balance silvicultural and economic objectives.[83]

There is no doubt that the agency lacked the resources to subject each logging site in the province to intensive, on-site inspection and prescription. But the factors influencing Douglas fir seedfall, germination, and seedling survival were well known to government silviculturalists. The problem, as George Allen observed in a 1942 research note on the life history of the species, was that silvicultural recommendations, in most cases, must be subordinated to traditional logging practices. The next year the agency, now known as the BC Forest Service, published Finlay McKinnon's report on minimum requirements for Douglas fir management. McKinnon denied the practicality of adopting an 'all-inclusive formula for the management of these forests,' emphasized the need to treat stands in accordance with their characteristics, but asserted that enough common features existed to justify his statement of basic cutting and slash burning standards. He recommended that large firms and truck operations adopt the patch-logging system, and the reservation of seed trees individually or in groups for smaller operators. McKinnon told a colleague in 1944 that the agency had 'quite a complete understanding of the relationships involved in Douglas fir management.'[84]

Along with Isaac's *Reproductive Habits of Douglas Fir*, then, the BC Forest Service possessed a considerable body of scientific data accumulated by its own researchers when the Sloan Commission began hearing evidence. Orchard had also obtained and circulated copies of the Oregon Forest Conservation Act, 'embodying some of the most advanced forest legislation in either Canada or the United States.' Oregon and British Columbia differed in many respects, he remarked, but 'their problem as a whole is identical to ours.' These regulations, coupled with his agency's knowledge of local conditions, enabled Orchard to recommend to Sloan that he cooperate with industry in drawing up a set of forest practice guidelines for timber sales and private lands.[85]

Orchard also proposed that owners of land denuded prior to the time new legislation came into effect be compelled to plant or otherwise rehabilitate these areas at an annual rate of 1,000 acres, and ensure that lands cut after that date be fully stocked within eight years. In their testimony operators claimed a rapid rate of reforestation on private holdings. 'We have found that a satisfactory proportion of our logged lands will reproduce a forest naturally under our system of logging,' asserted Bloedel, Stewart, and

Welch manager Sid Smith. Powell River Company vice-president George O'Brien took pains to dispel the notion that selective logging was superior to clearcutting, and advocated 'friendly cooperation' between government foresters and company representatives rather than rigid cutting regulations.[86]

Vancouver Island's major landowners had newly employed foresters appear before the Commission, lending professional backing to industry's assertion of abundant restocking. Hired earlier in 1944 by H.R. MacMillan, prominent Canadian forester John D. Gilmour described natural reforestation on the Island as 'very encouraging.' A reproduction survey submitted by Bloedel, Stewart, and Welch's John Mottishaw on that firm's Franklin River property determined that restocking increased beyond one-quarter mile from adjacent timber. This curious finding enabled the company to conclude that in its region 'proximity to seed source is not a critical factor in the regeneration of forests.'[87]

Different sectors of the industry forged a united front in opposition to proposals for the introduction of meaningful silvicultural controls. A June 1945 brief submitted by the Coast Forest Operators, comprising the BC Loggers Association, Truck Loggers Association, and pulp and paper interests, expressed support for the adoption of 'practical means to secure regeneration on cut-over forest lands,' then went on to deny the existence of any relationship between logging practice and reforestation. Clearcutting of even-aged coastal forests, the timbermen maintained, had 'almost invariably been followed by satisfactory restocking if subsequently protected from fire.' Citing the US Forest Service's dissatisfaction with the reservation of seed trees individually or in small groups, in an effort to discourage consideration of these regulatory options, the operators urged the government to double seedling production to facilitate more planting.[88]

A subsequent submission to Premier Hart reinforced industry's position that new tenure arrangements should not be accompanied by restraints on the factory regime. The document described clearcutting as 'more conducive to proper regeneration than ... selective logging,' deemed patch-logging to have merit for those firms with sufficient timber and financial resources to adopt the practice, and called for more research on seeding of cutover lands to cheapen regeneration costs. The operators agreed to keep lands placed in any future sustained-yield units adequately stocked, but declared that cheap towing of logs to mills from the entire coastal region made cut curtailment unnecessary. They also recommended expansion of the Forest Service, so long as it was not permitted to assume 'greater powers than are consistent with a democratic form of government.'[89]

Anxious to secure an official role in the policy-making process, individual operators and industry's collaborative submissions proposed the establishment of a forest advisory board along the lines of the Oregon model. Having questioned Nelson Rogers and William Greeley on its composition and function, Sloan initially seemed cool to the idea. Greeley had denied that industry interests controlled the Oregon Forestry Board, but when the commissioner suggested it would not adopt a policy 'in direct opposition to the wishes of the representatives of the industry' the American forester acknowledged that such an outcome was unlikely. The province's foresters also promoted the formation of an industry-government advisory board in a joint brief submitted by the CSFE's Victoria and Vancouver sections. Sloan, however, understood Greeley to mean that Oregon's board would 'never attempt to promulgate or impose any order which was objected to by the industry.'[90]

The CSFE's policy recommendations to the royal commission were tailored in most respects to meet the economic needs of corporations and foster development of forestry in the private sector. Seizing the opportunity to cultivate corporate trust, foresters came out in favour of clearcutting 'in blocks large enough to make the use of heavy machinery profitable.' The organization did condemn the clearcutting of extensive, contiguous areas and support the formulation of silvicultural regulations, but when questioned by H.R. MacMillan, representative F.D. Mulholland assured him that the profession did not advocate 'any extreme form of silviculture.' The proposed seed source requirements were 'just preliminary suggestions' that loggers could accomplish under present conditions.[91]

The foresters' desire to create an affinity between the professional and corporate interest also showed in the CSFE's tenure recommendations, which proposed placing the entire coastal region on a sustained-yield footing through a series of small working circles. Advising against any immediate restriction of production by established companies, they claimed that converting the holdings of major operators to a sustained-yield 'cannot be achieved by arbitrary legislation.' The foresters defined the fundamental principle of sustained-yield as maintenance of continuous forest growth rather than limitation of cutting, and threw in a strong statement opposing regulations that might reduce returns on investment in the wood products sector. 'Forestry in British Columbia should be not only self-supporting but profitable,' they concluded.[92]

In the aftermath of the Commission's proceedings, Orchard congratulated Comox Logging and Railway Company vice-president R.J. Filberg on his appointment of F.D. Mulholland as the firm's forester. He also took the opportunity to express concern that the eighteen-month discussion had 'created an impression that forestry is primarily a matter of legislation and coercion.' Nothing, of course, could be further from the truth, and Mulholland's hiring provided a welcome example of private initiative. Speaking to the CSFE's annual meeting later that year, Orchard acknowledged the necessity of regulation, applied gradually and only in the minimum degree necessary to meet objectives. British Columbia should take a lesson from the Pacific Northwest, Orchard suggested, where Oregon and Washington operators had imposed basic silvicultural standards upon themselves and federal law sanctioned the creation of cooperative sustained-yield units.[93]

Sloan himself was well aware of recent developments in American forest law, and his January 1946 report owed something to those models as well as to the views expressed by Orchard and prominent lumbermen. Although he rejected the CCF's proposal for nationalization of the industry, Sloan did hope to achieve some measure of government control over logging practices on private land. He recommended that operators who did not intend to retain their holdings for sustained-yield production, defined as a 'perpetual yield of wood of commercially usable quality ... in yearly or periodic quantities of equal or increasing value,' be given two options. The logger would either submit a cutting plan for Forest Service approval if natural regeneration was the goal, or deposit funds in the amount required to plant the acreage. Approval of the cutting plan would release the operator from any further obligations, but in the second case the deposit would be held for eight years and used to reforest areas of incomplete stocking.

Sloan recognized that Crown-grant operators were 'likely to resent any interference with what they consider to be their property rights,' but in his view the time had arrived when 'the public welfare must take precedence.' Owners of denuded lands classified as 'forest lands' should be directed to plant those areas, with the Crown having power to expropriate the holdings of operators who refused to comply. 'To permit the owners of Crown grant lands to log them off and leave them without taking any steps to secure the growth of a new crop,' he asserted, 'is to jeopardize seriously the future development of our logging industry. This, in turn, will lead to unemployment and to the decline of communities to ghost towns.'[94]

Turning to the tenure issue, Sloan elaborated on Orchard's 1942 memorandum, proposing that operators be permitted to hold lands that were now under temporary tenures in perpetuity, provided that they maintain their productivity and 'regulate the cut therefrom on a sustained-yield basis.' Because no operator possessed sufficient timber to achieve a sustained-yield at present production levels, he advised the allocation of Crown timber to permit a continuation of logging while private lands and temporary tenures restocked and the second-growth grew to commercial dimension. On the second rotation, the combination of Crown and private forest would 'produce enough timber on a sustained-yield basis to maintain production of the unit in perpetuity – perhaps not at the peak of capacity, but sufficient to ensure a profitable operation with consequent benefit to the communities dependent upon the permanence of the industry.'[95]

Response to Sloan's tenure proposal was mixed. The CCF denounced the recommendation that the people 'turn over to the thieves the remainder of the treasure we still have in the safe with a plea that they be a little less extravagant than they have been in the past.' Orchard, on the other hand, was satisfied that the report embodied the 'essential features' of his 1942 memorandum and hoped for an amended Forest Act to 'enable the practice of forestry along rational lines by private industry.' The CSFE's Vancouver Island section endorsed the report. Anticipating that his agency would shortly be in a position to make similar arrangements with operators, Finlay McKinnon obtained copies of the contract between the US Forest Service and Simpson Logging Company governing procedures on the sole American cooperative sustained-yield unit.[96]

Unfortunately, when the coalition government amended the Forest Act in 1947 it ignored Sloan's wish for regulation of cutting on private land. Not until 1953 did a new Social Credit government give the minister of Forests the power to compel owners to reforest unsatisfactorily stocked lands at their expense. By this time the issue was much less contentious; the value of productive forestland and stumpage had risen to the point that many dominant firms recognized the wisdom of regenerating denuded lands.[97]

Action on Sloan's tenure proposal came much more quickly. The 1947 amendments created two types of sustained-yield units, both based loosely on American precedent. Forest Management Licences, later named Tree Farm Licences (TFL), authorized the consolidation of private land and temporary tenures with Crown timber into individual working circles to be operated by firms in accordance with Forest Service-approved management plans. To quell the fears of small operators that these tenures would result in timber monopolization, the government promised to establish Public Sustained Yield Units, originally called Public Working Circles, to be managed by the Forest Service and logged on a timber sale basis by local companies. These operators surmised correctly that large firms would seize control of huge reserves of choice public timber under the TFL program, but unlike their American counterparts were unable to prevent widespread implementation of sustained-yield tenures.[98]

Although the province's small group of industrial foresters were disappointed that the new act provided no encouragement of private ownership, those in public service on both sides of the border praised the measure. A national forest supervisor congratulated Orchard, noting 'the stress given in both your organization and ours on the stabilization of local industry.' The TFL, wrote the BC Forest Service's R.C. Telford, maintained the principle of government ownership and responsibility while providing long-term tenure and relief from heavy carrying charges, making possible 'industry's interest in the production of forest crops.' Minister of Lands and Forests E.T. Kenney explained in a 1948 radio address that the holder of a licence must practice forestry 'because it is financially advantageous to himself to do so, because he holds the land only by virtue of a plan of development approved by the Government, and because if he does not practice forestry he loses his licence.' According to Kenney regulation was necessary, but the

TFL arrangement would 'transfer the regulation to the individual, as opposed to the police state, subject to strict regulation by the Government itself.'[99]

Listeners who had difficulty comprehending Kenney's explanation of the relationship between state and industry on the new licences need only have referred to C.D. Orchard's less convoluted statements, expressing his conviction that the TFL effectively merged the private and public interest, making iron-fisted regulation unnecessary. Early in 1948 the chief forester informed the Truck Loggers Association of his intention to 'get away from government regulation, penalties and policing.' Late that year, addressing the WFCA's annual meeting, he declared that the TFL would 'enable the practice of forestry by private industry with the least possible fuss and bother, and with an absolute minimum of hampering legislation.' Early in 1951 he conveyed to a correspondent his hope that 'government interference and possible penalties will sink into the misty background,' but the most precise distillation of Orchard's thinking came during testimony to the second Sloan commission in 1955, when he described licencees as 'managers on behalf of the Government.'[100]

Evidence that the corporate and public interest did not mesh perfectly appeared with the first flood of applications for the bounty of public timber offered under the TFL plan. By the end of 1947 the Forest Service already had about 150 on hand, and even though application was a 'comparatively inexpensive' procedure requiring 'little more than a man's time for a couple of days plus a few inexpensive maps,' most failed to impress Orchard. In a good many cases, he informed consulting forester C.L. Lyford, 'it would appear that applicants have the impression that the Management Licence is nothing more than a variation on the timber sale, designed to give them a long-term supply of timber at very favourable holding rates and embodying little or no responsibility on their part other than to cut and pay stumpage as in past practice.'[101]

The new legislation gave the minister of forests the authority to award licences, and outside American capital quickly established position at the head of the line with promises to improve utilization through the establishment of pulp plants. The New York based Celanese Corporation received the first in 1948, agreeing to build a pulp plant at Prince Rupert in exchange for 2 million acres of Crown timber. The second went to Crown Zellerbach in 1949. The American giant absorbed the Canadian Western Lumber Company, contributed 193,000 acres of that firm's land, and committed to erecting a pulp mill at Duncan Bay, receiving 297,000 acres of choice Vancouver Island forestland in return. 'What are you trying to do,' a Pender Harbour tractor logger asked new Premier Byron Johnson, 'starve us small independent logging operators'?[102]

Companies set out long-term operating policy for these and subsequent licences in the Working Plan, and gained immediate harvesting rights through the Cutting Permit. Both documents required Forest Service approval to ensure the adoption of proper management principles. The most important feature of the Working Plan was the allowable annual cut (AAC) calculation. Foresters arrived at the AAC by applying the Hanzlik formula, dividing the volume of mature timber on a unit by the number of years in the rotation period, adding the mean annual increment of forest growth. Ken Drushka argues that the sustained-yield project was doomed from the outset because the lack of accurate data on growth rates and rotation periods made determining appropriate cut levels impossible. The introduction of sustained-yield became 'a matter of political and economic controversy,' dominated by industry demands for higher AACs. Patricia Marchak has also expressed doubt about the scientific validity of harvest rate calculations. Logging levels on TFLs, she maintains, have been 'determined as much by reference to the crown's social policies and the needs of existing mills as to any biological criteria.'[103]

Although neither authority provides supporting evidence, the record of early TFL administration appears to substantiate these assertions. Finlay McKinnon acknowledged early on that the Forest Service's original Working Plan expectations were 'too idealistic;' the agency would have to 'accept a rather general plan at first and gradually improve it as more information becomes available over the years.' He and his colleagues, McKinnon admitted to a New Brunswick forester, were 'not sure what we want in a practical working plan.'[104]

On many licence areas the BC Forest Service lacked even the most rudimentary inventory data, leaving it up to licencees to initiate surveys and growth studies considered essential in the formulation of cutting restrictions. In the interim, the absence of knowledge was not permitted to delay exploitation of the tenures. As Assistant Chief Forester R.C. St. Clair explained to Western Plywood Company forester E.E. Gregg shortly after that firm received the province's fifth TFL in 1951, Working Plans were open to periodic alteration 'in the light of experience gained and research findings.' Concerned about the 'approximate nature' of allowable cuts, in 1953 the Forest Service's Alan Fraser drew up a set of minimum requirements for the accumulation of growth data. Plans would necessarily be imprecise in the initial period of sustained-yield management, Fraser admitted, but accurate information must be obtained without delay to meet that goal. He recommended the establishment of 160-200 permanent growth plots within five to ten years of a unit's creation. On TFL tenures, where government and industry engaged in 'cooperative management,' company foresters should have to justify any departure from the minimum standard.[105]

Fraser's colleagues in industry greeted his proposal with disapproval. R.C. Telford, now woods manager for the Columbia Cellulose Company, conveyed his firm's 'keen interest' in obtaining this data but doubted directors would approve such a large expenditure. Elk Falls Company forester F.D. Mulholland advanced a more fundamental rebuttal, taking issue with Fraser's reference to cooperative management. American law provided for joint company and US Forest Service administration of the Shelton Cooperative Sustained Unit, he pointed out, but on British Columbia's TFLs the Forest Act authorized *'management by the licencee.'* Forest Service responsibility was confined to Working Plan approval and inspection. Implicit in Fraser's formula for standardized data gathering was a desire to guide provincial forest policy 'along the primrose path of uniformity by law, about the worst thing that could happen to it.' Mulholland also took pains to dispel the 'creeping' notion of cooperative TFL management in his published work.[106]

Even some in government service felt that too much emphasis should not be placed on growth information in setting cutting levels. Foresters needed such studies to calculate allowable cuts, D.M. Trew conceded, but in his experience current data on the province's unmanaged forests were of such limited use that 'you finally end up "guesstimating" to the best of your knowledge.' Trew meant not that government allow reckless overcutting, but given their ignorance of future product needs or utilization standards, foresters should concentrate on reducing waste and damage to young growth 'rather than be too strict about limiting the allowable cut.'[107]

If the rate of cut on TFL No. 22, awarded to BC Forest Products in 1955, is reflective of a general tendency, the sustained-yield concept was indeed applied with considerable elasticity in British Columbia. C.D. Schultz and Company prepared the initial Working Plan for the licence, consisting of blocks at Cowichan Lake, Port Renfrew, and Tofino on Vancouver Island. Lacking precise growth and yield data, the firm estimated a ninety-year rotation period, permitting determination of an annual cut 'sufficiently close to the sustained-yield capacity to permit rational management of the area.' Original calculations set the AAC at 16.1 million feet but Charles Sommers, minister of forests in W.A.C. Bennett's Social Credit government, authorized an annual harvest of 20 million feet for fifteen years so the company could adjust mill requirements gradually with minimum disturbance to dependent communities. After this grace period the AAC was to be reduced to compensate for the initial overcut, but BC Forest Products succeeded in negotiating higher harvest levels in subsequent Working Plans.[108]

Like all licencees, BC Forest Products had an obligation to reforest its TFL lands. Areas denuded prior to the award of the tenure were to be restocked at a rate of 1,000 acres per year. High-quality lands cut after that date and that failed to regenerate naturally were to be planted or seeded within five years. TFL foresters, like BC Forest Products' Gerry Burch, were 'very much aware of the importance of allowable cuts,' viewing improved utilization standards and rapid conversion of idle sites to productivity as a means to 'automatically increase' harvest levels. Accordingly, the Forest Service approved the 1961 Working Plan with an AAC of 24 million feet on the basis of the firm's commitment to restock soon after logging, an inventory revealing more timber than originally estimated, and data from growth plots showing a higher than anticipated mean annual increment. Then in 1968, despite some evidence that the old-growth timber would be depleted before young stands grew to merchantable quality, BC Forest Products received yet another increase to 30 million cubic feet on the condition that cutting met new 'close utilization' standards.[109]

In administering cutting practices on the tenures, the BC Forest Service struggled to balance a desire to hold firms to Working Plan and Cutting Permit commitments against their wish for freedom to alter plans as conditions warranted. In 1951 Finlay McKinnon acknowledged that licensees should have the flexibility to select species or quality in accordance with changing market demands, but advised adopting strict limits on the extent of acreage approved in Cutting Permits. Otherwise, the agency would find it impossible to 'make a satisfactory check on operations until it is too late to halt any malpractice.' W.G. Hughes, who became head of the new Working Plans Division in 1952, preferred these documents to contain specific logging plans, but recognized that changing weather and market conditions required flexibility.[110]

In his public statements Orchard emphasized the harmonization of public and private interests achieved by the licence plan. True, TFL management was not all that could be desired, but by 1953 the Forest Service had eliminated the traditional liquidation philosophy from thirteen operations and established them on a 'sound long-term basis.' Privately, the chief forester expressed concern about loose administration. In August 1952 he alerted district foresters to the importance of regular, close inspection of cutting during this 'formative stage' of the TFL program, observing that 'the necessary degree of attention is not being paid in the Districts to this important phase of management.' To correct this situation Orchard ordered the assignment of one forester in each district to oversee logging on licences.[111]

Vancouver District Forester D.B. Taylor was also 'greatly concerned in the knowledge that we are not giving the necessary degree of attention to the administration of Management Licences.' Taylor appointed F.S. Williams to supervise TFL operations on Vancouver Island and the lower mainland, and the latter concluded very quickly that Working Plans were 'of a very general nature,' containing specific information only on the annual volumes to be removed. Companies submitted applications for Cutting Permits on a 'make-shift basis, without too much regard being given to the direct over-all planning which ultimately forms the basis of good forest management.'

Williams was particularly disturbed by Forest Service approval of vague references to patch-logging and of plans to secure natural regeneration – generalizations that 'would not appear to convey to Company owners or directors the necessity of extra expenditures in connection with the planning and development involved when logging under a sustained yield program, nor convey to the logging superintendents much hint of the usual drastic changes when logging under License procedure rather than on a timber sale or liquidation basis.' The appointment of a single forester to TFL administration in the Vancouver Forest District hardly corrected the problem. In 1955, finding it impossible to devote sufficient attention to the nine licences, encompassing over 2 million acres, Williams pleaded for an assistant.[112]

Despite the agency's effort to tighten up controls by requiring more detailed mapping on Cutting Permit applications, abundant evidence exists to suggest that procedures on some of these tenures did not measure up to those on Forest Service-managed timber sales. After 1957 inspections revealed several instances of shoddy logging on TFLs, district foresters were reminded that poor utilization and removal or damage to timber not designated for cutting constituted violations subject to stumpage penalties. 'We have the necessary clauses to require as good or better logging than on timber sales,' Management Division forester J.S. Stokes advised, 'and we should so insist.'[113]

British Columbians would no doubt have been shocked to learn that the Forest Service considered it necessary to bring TFL practices up to the level of timber sales, which according to agency philosophy would be taken up by small operators requiring rigid supervision. Orchard remained convinced that the tenure system was 'an admirable approach to the sustained-yield objective' that would 'effectively attract the interested cooperation of industry,' but not all foresters shared his faith. In September 1957 the Management Division asked Orchard to authorize more rigorous logging inspection by District staff who ought to bear in mind that the standard of operation on TFLs 'should be as high as, if not higher than the best conducted timber sale operations in the District.' Unnecessary waste or damage to reproduction must not be permitted and penalties for such conduct should be imposed 'without hesitation.'[114]

Forest Service dissatisfaction with TFL management contributed to the decision to form a Tree Farm Forestry Committee in 1959. Intended to provide a forum for discussion, by government and industrial foresters, about ways to improve the program, consensus proved difficult to achieve when Working Plans were the topic. Forest Service representatives wanted these documents to reflect a definite, long-term plan for rational development of the licence area. 'When we recommend your Working Plan for approval it is understood you really intend to carry out the provisions of the plan,' Ian

Cameron informed TFL foresters in October 1960. Accusations that the Forest Service was 'high handed and dogmatic' lacked foundation, Cameron argued. Provided that licencees submitted an authentic Working Plan, they possessed considerable freedom, but once approved, 'there should be no argument that this new logging boss won't or can't abide by the Working Plan.' Company foresters replied that plans of more than one or two years duration were rendered useless 'because of the need for flexibility in operations to harvest desired products.'[115]

The discussion followed similar lines when the committee met again the following March, with no progress toward a resolution. At a subsequent May gathering, a BC Forest Products representative observed that public and private foresters 'did not seem to talk the same language.' Disappointed with the Forest Service's 'unyielding position,' the committee's corporate members declared they deserved greater trust, and licencees ought to be left to carry out their sustained-yield responsibilities 'without hindrance.' Those in government employ held that a properly conceived Working Plan must set out firm intentions regarding maximum distance of cutovers from seed source, artificial regeneration provisions, position and width of firebreaks, and any changes that might be required during the period.[116]

The Tree Farm Forestry Committee apparently failed as an instrument of reform. In May 1963 W.G. Hughes again advised district foresters not to accept performance on TFL Cutting Permits inferior to that of 'the average efficient timber sale operator in the district.' Later in the year Vancouver District Forester Ian Cameron refused an application for a Cutting Permit amendment representative of requests received from two or three licencees in his district. In this particular instance, he explained to Chief Forester Finlay McKinnon, the company forester 'was not familiar with the area or even the exact location of the trees being applied for,' providing no assurance of good forest management. Cases of this nature defeated one of the main purposes of the TFL, to lighten the Forest Service's administrative burden.[117]

By 1964 the agency was responsible for administration of thirty-nine licences, the oldest of which had entered their third or fourth Working Plan period. Little evidence existed to suggest that security of tenure had rendered regulation superfluous. Some licencees showed an appreciation of Forest Service objectives but the majority submitted 'vague plans which outline some history, list a few projects, but generally indicate little regarding the licencee's policy and long-term outlook for the licence.' Many company foresters were preoccupied with production, R. Tannhaeuser observed, and devoted insufficient time to Working Plan preparation.[118]

Again, in the mid-1960s, the BC Forest Service subjected its handling of TFL procedures to self-examination. 'Tree Farm Licence administration is and always has been permissive,' Management Division forester D.R. Glew wrote. Standards varied from licence to licence, and the organization had 'changed, modified or abandoned most our cherished precepts following representation by company foresters.' No progress would result until the agency issued more definite guidelines and assigned additional inspection personnel, placing its administration of TFLs on the same footing as timber sales.[119]

The frequency with which members of the BC Forest Service asserted the need for more rigorous TFL regulation points to the system's fundamental flaw: the assumption that security of tenure at low holding rates and favourable stumpage charge would provide sufficient incentive for firms to adopt standards of forestry practice that upheld the public interest. By the 1960s the naivety of Orchard's original faith in private enterprise was increasingly evident. As managers on behalf of the government, corporations had failed to satisfy BC Forest Service expectations in regard to operational planning.

On neither side of the border dividing the Douglas fir region, then, did the forestry legislation of the 1940s accomplish more than a legitimation of existing cutting practice. Operating under the protection afforded by state and provincial forest laws that placed more importance on capital accumulation than conservation, corporations continued to treat the old-growth forest as a source of profit to be swept from the land as cleanly and quickly as modern technologies would permit. This approach was particularly pronounced during the latter part of the period under study, when an economic downturn in conjunction with new efficiencies in artificial reforestation led operators to intensify resource and labour exploitation by returning to the continuous clearcutting practices prevalent during the heyday of overhead steam logging.

The Consolidation of Clearcutting and the Plantation Model
Although the US Forest Service continued to wrestle with the cutting practice question throughout World War II, the cost efficiencies of clearcutting in boom times gave the traditional technique a decisive advantage over its alternative. When representatives of the Region Six office and coastal national forests met in February 1944, the question of whether to clearcut or log selectively figured prominently in their discussion of timber sale procedures. At that point Chief Forester Clapp's policy seemed to dictate selective cutting wherever practical, but the foresters in attendance also recognized that operators' wishes carried more weight in wartime. Regional Forester Horace Andrews acknowledged the controversial nature of the issue, but saw no objection to clearcutting in the absence of aesthetic or recreational values requiring protection. Even where circumstances indicated that the selective method was appropriate, if operators objected or

lacked the necessary technology, the wartime imperative of maximum production should override silvicultural considerations.[120]

The Pacific Northwest Forest and Range Experiment Station oriented its work to the demands of the war economy, but preliminary results of ongoing studies generated increasing scepticism about tree selection. By 1945, progress reports indicated that 'caution should be observed in the use of partial cutting,' supporting the agency's return to clearcutting in the Douglas fir region. Damage inflicted on timber during logging concerned Leo Isaac, who informed the SAF's Puget Sound Section in March that entry of rot into root systems lowered the quality of reserve stands.[121]

Although foresters recognized the suitability of selective logging under certain conditions, most defined these much more narrowly than Burt Kirkland. As hemlock increased in value with the postwar expansion of the pulp and paper industry on the west coast, less emphasis was placed on maintaining pure stands of Douglas fir. Summarizing the Experiment Station position in March 1947, director J.A. Hall cited accelerated reserve stand mortality, difficulties in slash disposal, regeneration, and 'economic problems involved in opening such a large area through road construction' as the most serious shortcomings associated with the selective approach to harvesting.[122]

Patch-logging, featuring 40- to 80-acre clearcuts, in the Gifford Pinchot National Forest, Washington, 1949.

Reflecting this comprehensive critique, Lyle Watts's annual report for 1947 described his agency's experiments in selective logging as discouraging. Clearcutting in strips or patches appeared to provide a more promising method of converting static old-growth to growing forests. The US Forest Service continued to make some selective sales in stands comprising a mixture of mature and young trees, but increasingly clearcutting in staggered settings, or patch-logging, became standard practice in the national forests of the Douglas fir region.[123]

The concern with restricting the size of clearcuts was apparent on the Olympic National Forest by 1945. The Regional Office's O.F. Ericson approved of the attempt during an October inspection, considering cut-blocks from 30 to 60 acres appropriate. This was perhaps too ambitious for the forest's staff, who aimed to hold clearcuts down to between 60 and 80 acres. Selective logging had been discarded almost completely on the Willamette National Forest by 1947, where the preferred size of openings approximated 60 acres.[124]

Companies cutting US Forest Service-managed timber pressed for larger clearcuts. Willamette officials were 'inclined to resist operator pressures to make major adjustments' once cutting boundaries had been laid out, but the agency also proved willing to negotiate. On the Shelton Cooperative Sustained-Yield Unit, where Olympic National Forest timber sale officers and Simpson Logging Company managers developed logging plans jointly, there was frequent difference of opinion over the layout of openings. Government foresters strove to confine patches to a 60-acre maximum but recognized, Walter Lund reported in July 1948, that it was 'not always possible to restrict ... areas to not more than 60 acres, and that our cutting policy permits areas of larger size when circumstances and good cutting practice demand it.'[125]

As one of the Region's most vocal critics of the selective method, Lund took the opportunity of his Shelton inspection to question whether 'the selection system constitutes good forest management.' Trees had been logged individually from level ground adjacent to a river, but Lund argued that greater yields would be attained by clearcutting this sensitive area in 5- to 10-acre patches. Ericson, agreeing that 'the results of partial cutting have been poor from a silvicultural standpoint,' approved the recommendation, but cautioned Olympic personnel to give each stand careful analysis.[126]

The completion of Isaac's research on the silvicultural impact of selective logging signalled the end of US Forest Service interest in the technique except in uneven-aged stands or where recreational and aesthetic values dictated its application. Windfall losses, the introduction of rot because of scarring, slash burning considerations, and the failure of many partially cut stands to make significant growth terminated what Thornton Munger called the agency's fifteen-year 'silvicultural detour' into the 'labyrinth of partial cutting.' Foresters in British Columbia were as relieved as their American colleagues to have a scientific justification to end the debate that undermined public confidence in the profession.[127]

As foresters closed ranks in defence of clearcutting, only Ellery Foster stood forth as a public advocate of selective logging. In a 1948 Vancouver radio address, the IWA official called for the abolition of high-lead technology, and when a 1951 *Journal of Forestry* issue featured a cover photograph of patch-logging on the Olympic National Forest he berated the SAF for sanctioning this 'shameful destruction.' Several foresters responded by denouncing his 'sentimental' attachment to the old-growth forest.[128]

Leo Isaac, the acknowledged authority in Douglas fir silviculture, summarized his research findings and depicted clearcutting as the technological equivalent of nature's way of replacing these forests, an argument that gained in popularity among foresters in coming decades as environmentalists attacked the practice. 'When nature takes out a large old Douglas fir, she replaces it with a scrubby hemlock, cedar or true fir,' Isaac replied. 'But when she wants to reproduce a Douglas fir forest, she wipes the slate clean by fire, insects, or disease. And that is exactly what is being done by a patch-wise system of clearcutting in over-mature Douglas fir stands.' Yale University professor David Smith characterized partial cutting in Douglas fir as 'one of the great fiascos yet indulged in by American foresters,' and considered it fortuitous indeed that 'an ecologically sound method of regeneration happens to coincide with a means of logging feasible from the engineering standpoint.'[129]

Having resolved the cutting practice debate within its own ranks, the US Forest Service placed new emphasis on determining the optimum dimension of clearcuts in the staggered setting system, establishing the Blue River Experimental Forest in Oregon as a laboratory for intensive research on the region's shrinking supply of mature Douglas fir. Pacific Northwest Forest and Range Experiment Station publications advised operators that restriction of clearcut size to 80 acres would minimize the danger of uncontrollable fires and improve opportunities for natural restocking on private lands. The BC Forest Service conducted similar, if less comprehensive research in an effort to encourage operators to locate reserve timber blocks with reference to their reforestation potential.[130]

The gradual replacement of railways by trucks lowered transportation costs and facilitated adoption of the patch-logging system throughout the Douglas fir region during the immediate postwar period, when skyrocketing demand for wood products increased profit margins. Although industrial foresters had to defend the reservation of timber against the production concerns of logging managers, anecdotal evidence suggests that firms that were prepared to invest in the protection and productivity of private lands made varying commitments to the practice. St. Paul and Tacoma Lumber

Patch-logging layout at Crown Zellerbach's Nanaimo Lakes operation on Vancouver Island, 1962.

Company president E.G. Griggs sided with forester Norman Jacobson during the early 1950s when manager Frank Hobi argued that recovery of timber blown down along the edges of leave settings increased logging costs to the extent that patch-logging should be abandoned in favour of complete clearcutting and planting to comply with state law.[131]

Industry made much of its adoption of patch-logging. Corporate submissions to British Columbia's second Sloan Commission in 1954-55 placed considerable emphasis on the rigorous reservation of seed blocks, and foresters placed their stamp of approval on the technique without hesitation. After a 1954 tour of Vancouver Island operations, a Canadian Institute of Forestry delegation resolved that clearcutting in patches achieved 'all conditions essential to natural regeneration of Douglas fir.' In testimony before Sloan, the BC Forest Service's H.G. McWilliams observed that the recent introduction of patch-logging had increased the restocking of logged lands. Industry never reduced openings to the scale recommended by resource agencies, but for a short time, at least, forestry considerations made some inroads into the conduct of clearcutting operations.[132]

As the decade drew on, however, progress in artificial reforestation prompted operators and foresters to question the higher logging costs associated with natural methods. When their contemplation of this question coincided with a slump in the timber economy after 1956, they agreed to sever any relationship between exploitation and forest renewal. The US

BC Forest Service nursery at Duncan, BC, 1959.

Forest Service had begun planting nursery stock early in the century but British Columbia's first production facility did not open until 1930. Two years later, seedlings from the new Green Timbers nursery were shipped to West Thurlow Island. The first glimmer of corporate interest in reforestation came in 1938, when Bloedel, Stewart, and Welch accepted 60,000 seedlings for planting at Great Central Lake.[133]

In 1939 the disturbing expanse of barren lands in British Columbia led Minister of Lands Wells Gray to introduce a reforestation program for the coast region. The appropriation for this work more than doubled, to $43,000, allowing an increase in the annual capacity of the Green Timbers nursery to 6 million trees and construction of a second unit at Campbell River that went into production in 1941. That same year American operators established the Nisqually nursery in conjunction with their Tree Farm initiative. By this time foresters were confident in their ability to raise and plant nursery-grown seedlings successfully, and in 1943 the capacity of British Columbia's two facilities reached 10 million, sufficient to restock 10,000 to 15,000 acres. Three years later a Reforestation Division became part of the BC Forest Service, and a third nursery at Duncan began shipments to points on southern Vancouver Island. Orders from the West Coast Lumbermen's Association Nisqually nursery reached 6 million seedlings in 1946.[134]

By the mid-1950s, total annual seedling production at two US Forest Service facilities, an equal number operated by the states of Oregon and

Washington, and the Nisqually nursery reached 25 million. In British Columbia approximately 136,000 acres had been planted, companies contributing 33,000 acres to this total. Resource agencies and corporations recorded slower progress in developing the less expensive alternative of seeding cutover lands to achieve a new crop. In 1947 Isaac and Roy Silen were assigned to step up the Pacific Northwest Forest and Range Experiment Station's research on direct seeding. The Simpson Logging Company also began a trial of this method using hand-operated spreaders, while Weyerhaeuser, Crown Zellerbach, MacMillan Bloedel, and the Oregon State Department of Forestry initiated tests involving the use of airplanes and helicopters to dispense seed. Seeding techniques were also a 'very live problem' within the BC Forest Service, which kept track of developments throughout the Douglas fir region.[135]

Consumption of seed by rodents made early seeding attempts ineffectual. The treatment of seed with tetramine, a combined rodenticide and repellant developed by the US Fish and Wildlife Service, promised to eradicate this problem. Field tests showed a much higher rate of restocking on plots sown with treated seed than control areas. At the same time, herbicides came into use to inhibit brush encroachment on cutover lands.[136]

Foresters were excited by the increasingly sophisticated approaches to land management, but during the early 1950s most continued to consider natural restocking a more cost-effective method than either artificial technique. 'It is cheaper to let nature do the job,' MacMillan Bloedel's Angus MacBean wrote, 'and seed seems to do better on the site where it originated.' University of British Columbia professor George Allen, a consultant on aerial seeding for that firm, felt operators should resort to artificial methods only when natural stocking failed. In 1952 American trade association forester William Hagenstein told his employers that 'the cheapest, best and most effective way of getting a new crop of trees is to assist Nature in doing her stuff.' In resorting to planting or seeding, industrial foresters admitted that 'their judgment in the selection of cutting practices was not too skookum.'[137]

But by the end of the decade foresters in management positions had lost much of their enthusiasm for cutting practices that fostered forest renewal. Several factors were cited in the profession's acceptance of continuous clearcutting and artificial reforestation: the delays and uncertainty of natural seeding, blowdown along the exposed edge of reserve timber, the prospect of returning cutover land to productivity immediately by planting or seeding, and the opportunities for enhanced species control provided by these techniques.

The BC Forest Service's H.G. McWilliams outlined the new orientation in a 1955 address to the WFCA, declaring that resource agencies and companies 'must no longer be satisfied ... that an area is restocking unless it has the type of wood that is going to be required by the manufacturing plant.' The irregularity of seed crops resulted in too many years of lost forest growth, allowing brush and alder to take over high-quality sites. Although no cost analysis was available, McWilliams thought that in many cases it would be cheaper to simply clearcut completely and plant, particularly if there was no assurance Douglas fir would dominate new stands.[138]

Industrial foresters advanced similar views during the mid-1950s. In a discussion of his firm's cutting programs, a Crown Zellerbach representative stressed the need for more planting of Douglas fir to maintain its representation. Reliance on natural seeding sacrificed too much growth, stated a Weyerhaeuser forester; large-scale application of artificial techniques was 'fast becoming an economic necessity.' Tom Wright of Canadian Forest Products argued that the nominal cost of planting would be more than balanced by higher future yields resulting from complete, immediate planting of logged lands. But Wright also emphasized the short-term economic benefits of clearcutting with regard only for engineering efficiency. Because reforestation did not depend on reservation of seed blocks, managers would enjoy greater flexibility in the planning of current logging operations.[139]

Wright's association of larger clearcuts with financial gain took on increasing weight after 1956, when a slump in the construction market caused severe problems in the west coast timber industry. Patch-logging came under attack as economizing corporate directors reevaluated forestry investments. Crown Zellerbach prepared to revert to continuous clearcutting by engaging C.D. Orchard, now a consultant to industry, to conduct a special study of its Vancouver Island operations early in 1959. 'We have been greatly concerned with our patch logging programme we have been following,' Hugh Hodgins explained, 'and feel that our whole policy should be reviewed.'[140]

Orchard began by attending a Canadian Institute of Forestry discussion on the subject. Prominent British Columbia industrial foresters Tom Wright, Bill McGee, and Gerry Burch comprised a panel that concluded current patch-logging practices were uneconomical. They referred to regeneration failures, blowdown, and the cost of extensive road systems as the principal shortcomings. According to Wright, an expansion in the size of clearcuts would produce a 30 percent saving in road construction expenses – more than enough to cover the $10 per acre cost of planting. MacMillan Bloedel's Ian Mahood complained of the hours management staff spent in their trucks travelling between scattered production sites, detracting from their supervisory function. The practice should be continued, the foresters decided, but with a substantial increase in clearcut size to a 400 acre maximum.[141]

This critical perspective on patch-logging by some of British Columbia's 'smartest and brightest young foresters and engineers' caused Orchard to wonder if 'we hadn't swung a bit too far from the scandalous high-ball clear cut of steam days.' He went on to conduct interviews with several of his colleagues in corporate employ. Angus MacBean described patch-logging as more costly in terms of vehicles and roads, and agreed the savings produced by larger openings would easily pay for planting logged lands. The high elevation timber being logged by MacMillan Bloedel dominated Mahood's comments. Cone crops occurred with less frequency the higher one went into the mountains, and the cost of road construction had doubled to $25,000 per mile with the move from gentle lowland terrain to the high country. By the time Orchard completed an inspection of Crown Zellerbach's Nanaimo Lakes operation, his thesis was determined. 'I can't see anything to be gained leaving settings,' he concluded.[142]

Orchard's July 1959 report fulfilled the expectations of Crown Zellerbach officials in every respect, making a comprehensive case for the return to extensive clearcutting. 'The 40-acre patch has been outmoded by economic and technological evolution during the past few years,' he argued, 'and the concept should be modified to fit 1959 conditions.' Logging had advanced into the mountains since the practice became popular, and at these elevations weather and topographic conditions inevitably dictated logging plans 'no matter what we might like to do.' Downplaying the protection advantage inherent in isolating areas of slash, Orchard maintained that much less acreage was required to safeguard properties now than when timber had been easier to access. Fire breaks should be retained, but 'not necessarily in the form of a wide, continuous, and inviolate strip withdrawing extravagant thousands of acres from the logging scheme.'[143]

Having questioned the rationale for patch-logging from the fire protection standpoint, Orchard went on to express doubts about the technique's reforestation potential by dismissing the work of researchers who could not explain examples of young growth long distances from timber or complete restocking failures immediately adjacent to seed sources. 'Any certainty of regeneration is going to depend on planting, or seeding, no matter what the opening may be in terms of acres,' he asserted.[144]

Small clearcuts, then, guaranteed neither satisfactory regeneration nor protection commensurate with the associated costs. Getting to the heart of the matter, Orchard described patch-logging as a 'nice tidy concept,' but 'not an objective in itself.' Crown Zellerbach was in business to make profits and could not afford 'landscaping methods.' He proposed that the firm proceed on the basis of larger, concentrated clearcuts, resulting in lower road-building expenditures, more frequent contact with logging sites by supervisors, and less travel time for crews. Exhibiting his basic faith in corporate enterprise, Orchard recommended that Crown Zellerbach abandon any reliance upon natural reforestation, plant all cutover lands within a year of logging, and plow the savings accrued from lower logging costs into a program of intensive forestry.[145]

Crown Zellerbach, by all accounts a leader in corporate forestry circles, was not alone in its intention to reduce operating budgets by enlarging the scale of clearcuts. To the extent that reforestation had influenced harvesting plans during the previous two decades, a practice that no doubt varied widely throughout the Douglas fir industry, there is clear evidence of a pervasive shift back to clearcutting with primary reference to engineering considerations by the mid-1950s. When the Pacific Northwest Forest and Range Experiment Station reconstituted an advisory committee in 1954, several members took the opportunity to point out 'the fallacy of adding to logging costs in the effort to obtain natural regeneration.' A session on 'Economic Logging Layout' at the 1959 Pacific Logging Congress gave executives and foresters a larger forum to articulate the wisdom of divorcing silvicultural principles from the conduct of old-growth exploitation.[146]

'We've all seen the transition from complete clear-cut to small staggered settings with total disregard, apparently, to the increased costs of logging and the added road construction costs involved in the initial cut,' observed one operator in introducing the subject. 'Are we sacrificing too much logging economy in order to obtain good forestry on our lands'? he asked. The question was rhetorical. His engineer's paper on that topic began with the claim that the preceding years had seen basic economic principles of logging 'become somewhat obscured with questionable forest management practices.' The firm's current policy, predicated on the belief that natural regeneration provided insignificant benefits compared to the increased logging costs, was to clearcut progressively as operations proceeded into the timber. Machine capabilities, topography, and the sequence of logging determined cutting plans.[147]

A Weyerhaeuser Timber Company study concluded that 'the excellent seed source coverage provided in our logging operations was not giving the desired results.' According to Assistant Managing Forester Royce Cornelius, future cutting plans would place more emphasis on the 'convenience of efficient logging,' favourable distribution of production units, and fire protection, rather than provision for natural seedfall. Increasingly, Washington and Oregon firms chose to comply with state forest practice laws by committing to artificial reforestation. By 1963, over one-third of the privately owned forestland in Oregon came under state-approved harvesting plans providing for planting or seeding in the event of inadequate seed source reservation.[148]

The corporate embrace of continuous clearcutting was, if anything, even more pronounced in British Columbia where the Forest Service provided seedlings free of charge to firms. Late in 1959 the district forester in Prince Rupert conveyed to Chief Finlay McKinnon the importance of the agency coming to a quick decision on whether firebreaks and seed sources constituted good forestry practice, 'and if so to enforce them uniformly throughout the coastal TFLs.' District staff felt these were essential to protection and reforestation, an opinion 'unequivocally opposed' by Columbia Cellulose Company, and Alaska Pine and Cellulose foresters who 'would appear to be quite happy to have literally thousands of acres of continuous slash.' Assistant Chief J.S. Stokes agreed that promises to plant were unacceptable without a supporting plan providing a specific commitment to proceed soon after logging.[149]

Despite its concern, the BC Forest Service permitted a gradual enlargement of clearcuts by Tree Farm Licencees during the early 1960s as opinion swung to favour planting, a reforestation technique allowing 'for the use of the most convenient method of logging.' On BC Forest Products' TFL No. 22, for example, original Cutting Permit applications were based on 100-acre openings. But complaints of blowdown and a commitment to plant cutovers soon after logging resulted in the introduction of 300-acre cut-blocks by 1963, and subsequent discussions with Forest Service officials for 1,000-acre 'patches.'[150]

Government foresters in the Prince Rupert Forest District challenged MacMillan Bloedel for contravening Cutting Permit clauses restricting openings to a 200-acre maximum on TFL No. 39. A 1964 field inspection revealed a clearcut 'well in excess of 200 acres,' drawing a warning from Ian Cameron that cutting on adjacent areas would not be permitted until slash had been burned. The following year, however, Cameron granted the company permission to 'extend the size of openings of contiguous areas of unabated slash to a maximum of 400 acres.'[151]

Progressive Clearcutting and Plantation Forestry

After a tentative and limited experience with balancing silvicultural and engineering principles in the form of patch-logging, by the mid-1960s Douglas fir operators were well on their way back to continuous clearcutting, a practice that offered more intensive exploitation of workers and the resource. By coupling this turnabout with highly publicized artificial reforestation initiatives, corporations such as MacMillan Bloedel and Crown Zellerbach advertised their operating policies as sophisticated ventures in intensive forest management.

Foresters supported the reversion to continuous clearcutting in part because they perceived a positive relationship between profitable corporate eradication of the old-growth forest and enhancement of professional authority. 'The old-growth forest is just there,' Ian Cameron explained to a group of Crown Zellerbach employees around 1961, 'foresters cannot do anything about it. About all we can do is vary the method of harvesting the ready-made crop. The forester will not come into his own until we are getting a large part of our requirements from the second crop.'[152]

This view of the mature forest as so much stagnant wood standing in the way of both sustained-yield production and the realization of professional aspirations was complemented by a realization that employment in the private sector depended upon profits, a point driven home during the late 1950s when many foresters were laid off.[153] The expectation that a portion of the profits derived from progressive clearcutting would find their way into forestry budgets proved particularly influential when the environmentalist critique of the method began to draw attention early the following decade. As Oregon State University Forestry School Dean W.F. McCulloch put it in a 1963 endorsement of clearcutting for American Forest Products Industries, lower harvesting costs enabled operators to 'better afford practices which enhance sustained maximum production of forest products.'[154]

Young foresters like Jerry Franklin, who received his Master's degree in forest management from Oregon State University in 1961, inherited the traditional view that 'there was value only in wood,' and the old-growth forest should be converted as quickly as possible into young, growing stands. Franklin went on to become the leading exponent of the 'new forestry,' an ecosystem approach to the forest that tries to integrate ecological and environmental values with commodity production. But in the early 1960s he was beginning his career with the US Forest Service, studying the impact of modified clearcutting techniques on the H.J. Andrews Experimental Forest, research prompted by the suspicion that high surface soil temperatures and infrequent Douglas fir seed crops retarded natural regeneration.[155]

A decade earlier Norman Worthington had concluded a study of small group cutting on the Olympic National Forest, attaining much better natural regeneration on a series of openings 1.2 to 4 acres in size than on an adjacent 130-acre clearcut. Worthington's work was concerned largely with seed dissemination, but Eric Garman had concluded that some shade was important in seedling survival. Franklin's study area had been logged in 1954-55, with openings laid out in very small patches from one-quarter to 4 acres in size, narrow strips, and scattered seed tree cuttings, all designed to reduce soil temperatures by providing a measure of shade while improving seedfall distribution. He found a 'highly significant correlation' between hours of shade and number of established seedlings, and recommended the use of these cutting methods to improve natural stocking on severe sites.[156]

These findings called into question foresters' traditional faith in large openings as a prerequisite for the natural regeneration of Douglas fir, and posed an implicit critique of the continuous clearcutting taking place on industrial forestlands throughout the region. The corporate model of intensive forest management was increasingly hostile to the incorporation of silvicultural principles in logging plans. On many sites clearcutting followed by artificial reforestation provided for maximum efficiency in both exploitation and forest renewal, but the system failed to produce a healthy new crop in all conditions. Survival rates on some plantations were low, particularly on severe sites at high elevations where temperature extremes hindered seedling establishment.[157]

Even in British Columbia's moderate climate, planting did not guarantee success, as revealed by a 1967 discussion by the Tree Farm Forestry Committee's Reforestation Board. On south-facing slopes, 50 percent of MacMillan Bloedel's planting failed. Survival on Rayonier's Douglas fir plantations was also unsatisfactory, and Crown Zellerbach achieved only a 30 percent success rate on areas above 2,000 feet planted the previous year near Ladysmith. Then a 1971 meeting of private and government foresters generated a call for research to 'help prevent very costly breakdowns in the artificial regeneration programme of the BC Forest Service and industry.'[158]

Plantation forestry represented the logical extension of the factory regime from the realm of resource exploitation to a comprehensive system of forest management. Indeed, the human-engineered forest was almost universally hailed as a technocratic triumph, the culmination of progress in the manipulation of natural processes. Although the US Forest Service restricted clearcut size on the national forest timber sales, on corporate holdings in the Pacific Northwest and on British Columbia's mix of private and public lands, aggressive clearcutting regardless of site condition was the rule, a practice sanctioned by state and provincial forest laws that encouraged development of the plantation model. Given the demonstrated reluctance of policy makers in these jurisdictions to challenge the corporate concept of efficiency through regulation of cutting practices, it is difficult to imagine a different outcome.

In order to do so, it is necessary to recall the demands for government regulation of logging issued earlier in the century by Pinchot and foresters such as Clapp and Manning who shared his interventionist leanings. But when state and provincial governments enacted forestry legislation in the 1940s, the facilitation of corporate capital accumulation under existing structures of labour and resource exploitation took precedence over the introduction of meaningful silvicultural controls. The ineffectual seed tree regulations of the Oregon and Washington forest practice acts and the reforestation obligations of TFL contracts in British Columbia were intended to sanction rather than restructure industrial clearcutting practices.

The image of wise stewardship held until the environmental movement's ecological perspective cast the plantation model of forest management in an unflattering light, and the emergence of timber shortages threatened the existence of timber towns such as Coos Bay, Grays Harbor, and Cowichan Lake. These developments and the ensuing policy crisis that has recently gripped the western timber industry lie outside the boundaries of this study, but attest to the historic failure of the region's governments to regulate corporations in the manner necessary to achieve socially and ecologically sustainable forest practice.

Conclusion

During the late nineteenth and early twentieth centuries, west coast logging underwent its industrial revolution, involving an expansion in scale, the arrival of steam technology, and development of a more complex division of labour. Closer integration of the region with North American and international economies provided a wide if volatile market for wood products from the coastal forests of British Columbia, Washington, and Oregon. At the same time, timber depletion in the east and midwest prompted the Weyerhaeusers, Merrills, and other resource capitalists to move their operations west to take control over vast stretches of timberland. But instability plagued the new economic order. Slack state, federal, and provincial laws provided easy access for producers, creating an intensely competitive example of industrial capitalism.

The introduction of steam power contributed to the timber industry's chronic overproduction problem. Logging railways facilitated mass transportation of logs from woods to sawmill, but it was in negotiating their passage to track-side that machines had their greatest impact. Steam donkeys, first used as an energy source in ground-lead logging, then were integrated with overhead systems creating a rudimentary factory regime that boosted productivity while placing loggers under new forms of workplace discipline. Although the complex, ever-changing forest environment continued to dictate reliance upon workers' physical and conceptual skills, by 1930 operators had made considerable headway in forging a labour process embodying the essential features of mass production factory settings.

The industrial revolution in west coast logging advanced a concept of efficiency that eroded the autonomy of loggers, but also generated an early-twentieth-century managerial crisis. Technological sophistication, in association with an expanded scale of operation, exceeded the organizational capacities of the existing management structure. Concerned about restricted professional opportunities for graduates in the public sector, forestry school administrators complied happily with operators' requests for the establishment of programs in logging engineering. After completion of a curriculum blending a smattering of forestry education with training in the principles of civil engineering and logging, the new breed of technical experts entered corporate employment to gather data on the topographic and timber characteristics of private holdings. In so doing, engineers acted in the spirit of the early twentieth century scientific management and conservation movements, bringing rational planning to large-scale resource exploitation.

Their silvicultural knowledge went unutilized, as operators were not yet prepared to broaden their notion of efficiency to encompass a concern for forest renewal. Companies applied the first generation of overhead logging technology with catastrophic ecological results, typically pushing railroads up valley bottoms, clearcutting as they went. This practice denuded huge contiguous areas of seed sources and young growth, at best leaving a few marginal patches of unmerchantable trees with the impossible task of reseeding cutovers. Early state and provincial conservation laws afforded a measure of protection to mature timber against the threat of fire, but gave no encouragement to a more sustainable style of corporate forest practice.

The US Forest Service accepted the technological necessity of clearcutting on the national forests, finding a fortuitous correspondence between large openings and the silvical character of the region's dominant commercial species. But the agency hedged its bets on the veracity of H.V. Hoffman's seed storage theory of Douglas fir regeneration, which suggested that an abundant supply of seed lay on the forest floor awaiting removal of the canopy to germinate after exposure to sunlight. Hoffman's flawed research proved useful to Gifford Pinchot's opponents, however, when the ex-chief initiated a campaign for federal regulation of logging on America's private timberlands.

Chief Forester William Greeley cited Hoffman's findings, already the subject of considerable scepticism among silviculturalists, when attempting to obtain western operators' agreement to his less threatening proposal of state regulation in return for federal funding of forest protection programs. Despite this cynical use of science, industry's willingness to consider any regulatory plan waned as Pinchot's measure lost favour among legislators. Left with only the fire control element of his plan intact, Greeley settled for a purely cooperative policy in the 1924 Clarke-McNary Act.

Government supervision of logging on British Columbia's public and private lands was no less permissive, the professionals who administered the 1912 Forest Act sharing none of Pinchot's interventionist zeal. But during the 1930s, awareness of the social and ecological costs of continuous clearcutting on both sides of the international border generated public and professional demands for regulation. The availability of an alternative to overhead technology, in the caterpillar tractor, provided an opportunity for a selective approach to harvesting that captured the imagination of many conservationists. The collapse of an already unstable lumber market with the onset of the Great Depression made the tractor an attractive tool for firms anxious to reduce labour costs and confine operations to choice timber. A few forest economists perceived the machine, if introduced in connection with a systematic selective timber management program, as a solution to overproduction and regeneration problems.

American President Franklin D. Roosevelt's response to the Depression – industrial self-regulation under the National Recovery Administration – posed no challenge to the corporate factory regime. Although the Lumber Code's Article X committed operators to work with federal and state agencies in developing less destructive practices, trade association control over its content and administration ensured that New Deal logging proceeded without a heightened devotion to silviculture on commercial timberlands. After the Supreme Court found Roosevelt's industrial strategy unconstitutional, US Forest Service chiefs Silcox and Clapp backed proposals for state administration of national forest practice standards, but never mustered sufficient legislative support to add a regulatory component to federal forest policy.

British Columbia also experienced a period of reform enthusiasm during the Depression, with equally disappointing results in the woods. After rejecting selective logging as a remedy for the ills of clearcutting, Chief Forester Ernest Manning directed popular criticism of corporate practices toward a modest improvement of the traditional method. Focusing his attack on the major operations within Vancouver Island's E & N belt, he succeeded in gaining the authority to introduce silvicultural regulations, but government's commitment to economic growth and property rights prevented their implementation.

Determined as they were to resist any infringement on their managerial prerogatives, coastal firms could not ignore the dwindling supply of timber on the lands under their control. Concern over resource depletion developed during the 1930s, became more pronounced when World War II boosted production, and continued as executives anticipated the emergence of a booming postwar wood-products economy. The ensuing scramble for timberlands, along with the growing importance of fibre production, generated a demand among corporations for more exact data on the composition of industrial holdings. The region's forestry schools, troubled by diminishing demand for engineers as truck roads replaced more exacting rail systems, welcomed the long-awaited opportunity to establish a stronger professional presence within industry.

The new discipline of industrial forestry, devoted to the accumulation of technical information on the productive capacity of private holdings, saw graduate foresters enter corporate employ alongside their colleagues in the engineering field. In augmenting timber capital's formally educated stratum of employees, they extended the practice of scientific management from the traditional sphere of work organization into a new preoccupation with the understanding and manipulation of stand structure and growth.

While the first industrial foresters set about satisfying their superiors' need for facts concerning the profit potential of virgin and immature timberlands, Canadian and American involvement in World War II created a more prominent role for governments in a range of social and economic affairs. Although the war elevated production far above conservation as an objective of public policy, trade association leaders in the western states responded to the continued threat of federal regulation by pushing forest practice acts through local legislatures.

Inspired by industry's desire to protect the factory regime rather than commit to resource stewardship, the Oregon Forest Conservation Act and Washington Forest Practices Act placed a stamp of approval on existing corporate procedures. Viewing these measures in their scientific context exposes the irrelevance of technical knowledge to forest law, provides insight into the capacity of economic interests to dominate policy-making at the state level in America, and explains the slow rate of restocking achieved under their influence.

The path to sustained operation in the southern portion of the Douglas fir region lay in consolidated control of the resource base by firms possessing the inclination and financial strength to engage in acquisition programs, not silvicultural regulation. British Columbia's policy of Crown ownership limited the land available for corporate purchase, providing government and industry with a powerful motive to adopt a sustained-yield policy that granted major companies access to huge parcels of public forest at low holding rates. Chief Forester C.D. Orchard's assumption that the new TFLs would merge the private and public interest proved fanciful. Successful applicants operated their holdings under the banner of sustained-yield management, but with insufficient regard for its principles. The BC Forest Service, lacking the personnel to enforce control over the pace of cutting or quality of forest practice, presided over a tenure system that gave free rein to the corporate profit imperative.

Just as science was disregarded in the policy-making process, the regulatory apparatus itself had but a marginal influence on the business of forest exploitation in the Douglas fir region. There is some evidence, however, of a tentative postwar move to smaller clearcuts by the most forestry-conscious firms hoping to improve fire protection and achieve some natural restocking. The agility of the logging truck and mobile yarding equipment facilitated industry's half-hearted embrace of patch-logging, which came to an abrupt end with the onset of a mid-1950s market downturn. Recent improvements in artificial regeneration techniques and facilities provided further justification for managers to exclude silvicultural principles from the conduct of logging.

The return to continuous clearcutting occurred as the introduction of the portable steel-spar – a technology allowing operators to dispense with the services of high riggers, accelerate the yarding procedure, and reduce unproductive time consumed in accessing timber – enhanced the engineering efficiency of the factory regime. With the subsequent adoption of the automatic grapple for loading and yarding, mechanization penetrated to the heart of the logging labour process. Under favourable topographic conditions grapple technology reduced the coastal rigging crew to a skeleton group of machine operators and spotters, eliminating reliance upon traditional skills while concentrating control in the hands of those few who manipulated its functions. As the latest generation of logging machinery redefined the industry's occupational structure, forest managers and engineers began applying computer technology to a wide range of managerial problems.

After almost a century of innovation, corporate timber capital had achieved a significant measure of success, imposing a factory-like production process on the coastal forest environment and the workers who toiled amidst its rapidly shrinking grandeur. Mobile logging equipment shifted quickly from site to site in accordance with harvest plans devised to satisfy the requirements of the wood products economy, and many firms practised a system of plantation forestry that seemed to promise perpetual productivity. One could look anywhere in British Columbia, MacMillan Bloedel explained to readers of a 1967 company publication, and see 'static and wasting wilderness being replaced by ordered ranks of flourishing young trees, the first of a succession of cultivated forest crops more abundant and gainful than Nature could ever produce unaided.'[1]

Evaluation of the modern plantation model must await future research. In analyzing the emergence and consolidation of industrial capitalism in the Douglas fir region between 1880 and 1965, this study began with a focus on the technological and managerial structures of forest and worker exploitation. A few concluding remarks on the labour process are appropriate at this point. Although the diversity of workplaces poses difficulties for the construction of a satisfactory theory of the labour process, capitalists share a common goal in their relations with employees – to maximize profits by intensifying the transformation of labour power into work. As Graeme Salaman argues, 'the organization and design of work in capitalism represents its twin and inter-related needs: profit and control.'[2]

The conclusions reached here support some of the points raised by Braverman's critics. It is indeed vital to view the labour process within its social and economic context. Product markets played a part in the coastal logging industry's record of technological change, particularly evident during the 1930s when the moribund timber economy encouraged operators to adopt the caterpillar tractor. Less clear, but worthy of consideration, were labour market factors. The reluctance of young workers to take up falling contributed in some measure to the attractiveness of the power saw, and the introduction of grapple yarding came at a time when fewer men were attracted to the industry.

Historians of work are also justified in calling for attention to the role of class struggle in structuring the labour process. West coast loggers expressed their individual resistance to oppressive and dangerous technologies by quitting, protests that undoubtedly caused temporary difficulties for some operators without manifesting sufficient solidarity to exert a significant influence on the spread of new technologies. This is not to suggest that the workplace under capitalist relations of production is anything other than a contested terrain, but the evidence accumulated thus far suggests that corporations played their technological hand with relative freedom.

Recognizing that labour process change is not simply the outcome of a 'straight managerial conspiracy' devoted to stripping workers of autonomy, historians should not be too hasty to reject the notion of a class consciousness among owners that manifests itself in technologies. One of the major objectives of the Pacific Logging Congress was to foster 'a thorough and comprehensive knowledge of the most modern appliances and most scientific methods' of logging. Conducting their enterprises in a variable environmental setting, which endowed loggers with a high degree of control over production, operators sought to emulate the factory model of work organization. Moreover, the continuum of innovation culminating in the grapple yarder followed a single-minded logic of efficiency that overrode the changing conditions of timber and terrain, or product and labour markets, for that matter.[3]

As important as it is to guard against a 'sentimentalism of the left' that places too much emphasis on the success of worker resistance, we should be equally careful not to underestimate the extent of deskilling accomplished in the course of western timber capital's efficiency drive.[4] Falling and bucking occupations remain largely unchanged in spite of mechanization, and those who operate modern multi-function equipment do so with a high degree of skill and responsibility. But close analysis of the historical relationship between workers and machines in west coast logging confirms the 'long-run tendency' toward skill dilution identified by Braverman as a central feature of industrial capitalism.[5]

Perceptive readers might question if the knowledge and expertise possessed by the logging engineers and foresters undermines this argument. Although only a small proportion of these educated employees rose to the sort of executive authority warranting inclusion in the capitalist class, a powerful case can be made for their exclusion from the working class. As beneficiaries of the separation of conception and execution fundamental to Taylorist methods of management, engineers have a dominant relationship to loggers. They share with foresters a formal education, hopes for career advancement, claims to professional privilege, salaried status, and intellectual function in the division of labour.

According to a persuasive school of class analysis these characteristics merit their inclusion in the new middle class, consisting of professionals and managers who lack ownership of the means of production but carry out many of the control and surveillance duties performed by capitalists prior to the industrial revolution. Although largely ahistorical, these theoretical forays provide a reasoned basis for considering professionals in corporate employ to be members of a new class occupying a middle ground between capital and labour.[6]

One of this study's major objectives has been to integrate class and environmental analysis by discussing the factory regime in terms of its relationship to both workers and the Douglas fir forest. Corporate timber capital's pursuit of efficiency in west coast logging produced one of the worlds' most hazardous industries, made less so only by the progressive elimination of occupations, and an aggressive style of clearcutting that denied the technique's potential for forest renewal. In the final analysis, as IWA President Harold Pritchett pointed out in testimony to the first Sloan commission, workers 'pay the price for unlimited, unrestricted, destructive lumbering practices.' The social and economic problems confronted by residents of timber towns throughout the coastal region today bear grim witness to the consequences of resource exploitation conducted with primary regard for corporate profit.[7]

This account provides further evidence that North American resource industries require effective planning and regulation of production to achieve social and ecological sustainability.[8] At no time during the 1880-1965 period did provincial and state governments in the Douglas fir region demonstrate a capacity to balance the objectives of conservation and capital accumulation. Evidence of industry influence over the policy-making and administrative process is much clearer in the American setting, where trade associations exercised firm control over legislation, but British Columbia's sustained-yield program proved equally responsive to corporate needs. In neither context did the accord between government officials and executives provide for a rational integration of science and public policy. Refinement of the factory regime proceeded in conformity with engineering objectives, without the adjustments to clearcutting practices that research suggested were required to conform with the ecology of Douglas fir.

Finally, this study brings into plain view the role of technology in the related processes of natural resource and worker exploitation. Forests and labour power share a status as commodities in the calculus of industrial capitalism. The primary appeal of the factory regime lay in its capacity to extract the maximum immediate value from both, regardless of the cost in human and ecological terms. A stronger grasp of this reality on the part of woodworkers and environmentalists would serve to focus attention on their common concern with sustainable forest practice. The forging of an alliance between these interests will require a resolution of traditional rural vs. urban, working-class vs. middle-class tensions, but viewing forest history through the prism of the factory regime provides an intellectual basis for such a program.[9] So long as conflicts over the old-growth issue divide environmentalists and resource workers, governments will have greater freedom to respond to corporate imperatives.

Notes

Introduction
1 Thomas R. Cox, *Mills and Markets: A History of the Pacific Coast Lumber Industry to 1900* (Seattle: University of Washington Press 1974); Edwin T. Coman Jr. and Helen M. Gibbs, *Time, Tide and Timber: A Century of Pope and Talbot* (Stanford: Stanford University Press 1949), 50-9; Robert E. Ficken, *The Forested Land: A History of Lumbering in Western Washington* (Seattle: University of Washington Press 1987), 27-39; Donald MacKay, *Empire of Wood: The MacMillan Bloedel Story* (Vancouver: Douglas & McIntyre 1982), 1-12.
2 My use of gendered language in the case of the term 'lumbermen' conforms with historical usage, as the titles of relevant trade journals suggest.
3 Ficken, *The Forested Land*, 40-53; Carlos A. Schwantes, *The Pacific Northwest: An Interpretive History* (Lincoln: University of Nebraska Press 1989), 201; Archie Binns, *The Roaring Land* (New York: Robert M. McBride 1942), 61; C.J. Taylor, *The Heritage of the British Columbia Forest Industry: A Guide for Planning, Selection and Interpretation of Sites* (Ottawa: Environment Canada 1987), 75; R. Peter Gillis and Thomas R. Roach, *Lost Initiatives: Canada's Forest Industries, Forest Policy and Forest Conservation* (New York: Greenwood Press 1986), 131.
4 Thomas R. Cox, Robert S. Maxwell, Phillip Drennon Thomas, and Joseph J. Malone, *This Well-Wooded Land: Americans and Their Forests from Colonial Times to the Present* (Lincoln: University of Nebraska Press 1985), 167-8; Robert E. Ficken, 'Weyerhaeuser and the Pacific Northwest Timber Industry, 1899-1903,' *Pacific Northwest Quarterly* 70 (Oct. 1979): 146-54.
5 G.W. Taylor, *Timber: History of the Forest Industry in B.C.* (Vancouver: J.J. Douglas 1975), 49-74; Stephen Gray, 'The Government's Timber Business: Forest Policy and Administration in British Columbia, 1912-1928,' *BC Studies* 81 (Spring 1989): 25-6; Jean Barman, *The West Beyond the West: A History of British Columbia* (Toronto: University of Toronto Press 1991), 182-3.
6 Robert E. Ficken, *Lumber and Politics: The Career of Mark E. Reed* (Seattle: University of Washington Press 1979), 15; W.A. Carrothers, 'Forest Industries of British Columbia,' in *The North American Assault on Canadian Forest*, ed. Arthur M. Lower (Toronto: Ryerson Press 1938), 308.
7 William G. Robbins, 'The Social Context of Forestry: The Pacific Northwest in the Twentieth Century,' *Western Historical Quarterly* 16 (Oct. 1985): 416-9; see also Thomas R. Cox, 'Trade, Development, and Environmental Change: The Utilization of North America's Pacific Coast Forests to 1914 and Its Consequences,' in *Global Deforestation in the Nineteenth Century World Economy*, eds. Richard P. Tucker and J.F. Richards (Durham: Duke University Press 1983), 14-29.
8 Robert E. Ficken, 'Pulp and Timber: Rayonier's Timber Acquisition Program on the Olympic Penninsula, 1937-1952,' *Journal of Forest History* 27 (Jan. 1983): 4-14.
9 See Patricia Marchak, 'A Global Contest for British Columbia,' in *Touch Wood: B.C. Forests at the Crossroads*, eds. Ken Drushka, Bob Nixon, and Ray Travers (Madeira Park: Harbour Publishing 1993), 67-84; M. Patricia Marchak, *Logging the Globe* (Montreal: McGill-Queen's University Press 1995).

10   Richard White, *Land Use, Environment, and Social Change: The Shaping of Island County, Washington* (Seattle: University of Washington Press 1992); William G. Robbins, *Lumberjacks and Legislators: Political Economy of the U.S. Lumber Industry, 1890-1941* (College Station: Texas A & M University Press 1982); Ficken, *The Forested Land*; Harold K. Steen, *The U.S. Forest Service: A History* (Seattle: University of Washington Press 1976); David A. Clary, *Timber and the Forest Service* (Lawrence: University Press of Kansas 1986); Samuel Trask Dana, *Forest and Range Policy: Its Development in the United States* (New York: McGraw-Hill 1956); Paul W. Hirt, *A Conspiracy of Optimism: Management of the National Forests Since World War Two* (Lincoln: University of Nebraska Press 1994); Robert Bunting, *The Pacific Raincoast: Environment and Culture in an American Eden, 1778-1900* (Lawrence: University Press of Kansas 1997); Nancy Langston, *Forest Dreams, Forest Nightmares: The Paradox of Old Growth in the Inland West* (Seattle: University of Washington Press 1995).
11   Patricia Marchak, *Green Gold: The Forest Industry in British Columbia* (Vancouver: University of British Columbia Press 1983); Ken Drushka, *Stumped: The Forest Industry in Transition* (Vancouver: Douglas & McIntyre 1985); Ken Drushka, *HR: A Biography of H.R. MacMillan* (Madeira Park: Harbour Publishing 1995); Gray, 'The Government's Timber Business'; Gillis and Roach, *Lost Initiatives*; Mary McRoberts, 'When Good Intentions Fail: A Case of Forest Policy in the British Columbia Interior, 1945-1956,' *Journal of Forest History* 32 (July 1988): 138-49; Jeremy Wilson, 'Forest Conservation in British Columbia, 1935-1985: Reflections on a Barren Political Debate,' *BC Studies* 76 (Winter 1987-8): 3-32.
12   Ted Benton, 'Marxism and Natural Limits: An Ecological Critique and Reconstruction,' *New Left Review* 178 (1989): 51-86; see also Michael Clow, 'Alienation From Nature: Marx and Environmental Politics,' *Alternatives* 10 (Summer 1982): 36-40; James O'Connor, 'Socialism and Ecology,' *Our Generation* 22 (Fall 1990/Spring 1991): 75-87.
13   R.J. Johnson, *Environmental Problems: Nature, Economy and the State* (New York: Belhaven Press 1989), 50,75; see also K.J. Walker, 'Ecological Limits and Marxian Thought,' *Politics* 14 (May 1979): 41; H.M. Enzenberger, 'A Critique of Political Ecology,'*New Left Review* 84 (Mar./Apr. 1974): 3-31; Karl W. Kapp, 'Environmental Disruption and Protection,' in *Socialism and the Environment*, ed. Ken Coates (Nottingham: Spokesman Books 1972), 13-24; Donald Worster, 'Transformations of the Earth: Toward an Agroecological Perspective in History,' *Journal of American History* 76 (March 1990): 1090.
14   One important subject not dealt with here is the impact of logging practices on fish habitats. Relevant works include Joseph E. Taylor, III, 'Making Salmon: Economy, Culture, and Science in the Oregon Fisheries, Precontact to 1960,' (Ph.D. thesis, University of Washington 1996); Joseph Cone and Sandy Riddlington, eds, *The Northwest Salmon Crisis: A Documentary History* (Corvallis: Oregon State University Press 1996); Richard A. Rajala, 'Timber and Fish: Resource Agencies, Forest Practices, and Salmon Habitat in British Columbia, 1900-1965' (paper presented to the BC Studies Conference, Nanaimo, 1997).
15   For the importance of understanding science in environmental history see Elizabeth Ann Bird, 'The Social Construction of Nature: Theoretical Approaches to the History of Environmental Problems,' *Environmental Review* 11 (Winter 1987): 225-64; Robert C. Paehlke, *Environmentalism and the Future of Progressive Politics* (New Haven: Yale University Press 1989), 25.
16   See Samuel P. Hays, *Beauty, Health and Permanence: Environmental Politics in the United States, 1955-1985* (New York: Cambridge University Press 1987); Duncan Taylor and Jeremy Wilson, 'Environmental Health – Democratic Health: An Examination of Proposals for Decentralization of Forest Management in British Columbia,' *Forest Planning Canada* 9 (Mar./Apr. 1993): 34-45.

Part 1: Introduction

1   Jeremy Rifkin, *The End of Work: The Decline of the Global Labour Force and the Dawn of the Post-Market Era* (New York: G.P. Putnam's Sons 1996); David F. Noble, *Progress Without People: New Technology, Unemployment, and the Message of Resistance* (Toronto: Between the Lines 1995); Lars Osberg, Fred Wien, and Jan Grude, *Vanishing Jobs: Canada's Changing Workplaces* (Toronto: James Lorimer and Company 1995).
2   Harry Braverman, *Labor and Monopoly Capital: The Degradation of Work in the Twentieth Century* (New York: Monthly Review Press 1974), 54.

3   Ibid., 193, 186.
4   Chris DeBresson, *Understanding Technological Change* (Montreal: Blackrose Books 1987), 50; see also Ken C. Kusterer, *Know How on the Job: The Important Working Knowledge of 'Unskilled' Workers* (Boulder: Westview Press 1978); Bruno Latour, 'The *Prince* for Machines as well as for Machinations,' in *Technology and Social Process*, ed. Brian Elliot (Edinburgh: Edinburgh University Press 1988), 20-43; Paul Attewell, 'The Deskilling Controversy,' *Work and Occupations* 14 (Aug. 1987): 323-46; Bill Schwarz, 'Re-Assessing Braverman: Socialization and Dispossession in the History of Technology,' in *Science, Technology and the Labour Process*, vol. 2, ed. Les Levidow and Bob Young (London: Free Association Books 1985), 189-205; for a more fundamental critique of Braverman's reading of Marx see Paul S. Adler, 'Marx, Machines, and Skill,' *Technology and Culture* 31 (Oct. 1990): 780-812.
5   Craig Heron and Robert Storey, 'On the Job in Canada,' in *On the Job: Confronting the Labour Process in Canada*, ed. Heron and Storey (Montreal: McGill-Queen's University Press 1986), 28; see also Andrew Friedman, *Industry and Labour: Class Struggle at Work and Monopoly Capitalism* (London: MacMillan Press 1977); David Stark, 'Class Struggle and the Transformation of the Labour Process,' *Theory and Society* 9 (Jan. 1980): 89-130; Richard Edwards, *Contested Terrain: The Transformation of the Workplace in the Twentieth Century* (New York: Basic Books 1979); Michael Burawoy, *The Politics of Production: Factory Regimes Under Capitalism and Socialism* (London: Verso 1985).
6   Sheila Cohen, 'A Labour Process to Nowhere?,' *New Left Review* 165 (1987): 36.
7   Michael Reed, 'The Labour Process Perspective on Management Organization: A Critique and Reformulation,' in *The Theory and Philosophy of Organizations: Critical Issues and New Perspectives*, ed. John Hassard and Denis Dym (New York: Routledge 1990), 63-82; John Storey, 'The Means of Management Control,' *Sociology* 19 (1985): 193-211; Andrew Friedman, 'The Means of Management Control and Labour Process Theory: A Critical Note on Storey,' *Sociology* 21 (1987): 287-94.
8   Wallace Clement, *Hardrock Mining: Industrial Relations and Technological Change at Inco* (Toronto: McLelland and Stewart 1981), 62; Douglas M. Eichar, *Occupation and Class Consciousness in America* (New York: Greenwood Press 1989), 105.
9   Richard A. Rajala, 'Bill and the Boss: Labor Protest, Technological Change, and the Transformation of the West Coast Logging Camp, 1890-1930,' *Journal of Forest History* 33 (Oct. 1989): 168-79.
10 'Automation,' *BC Lumber Worker*, Second Issue (Oct. 1955): 4; see also 'Machines and Men,' *Timber Worker*, 23 Sept. 1939, p 2; 'Technological Advance,' *Timber Worker*, 6 Apr. 1940, 2.
11 Howell John Harris, *The Right to Manage: Industrial Relations Policies of American Business in the 1940s* (Madison: University of Wisconsin Press 1982), 4.

Chapter 1: The Forest as Factory

1   On hand logging see D.O.L. Schon, 'Unique British Columbia Pioneer,' *Forest History* 14 (Jan. 1971): 18-22.
2   See 'Logging on Puget Sound,' *Washington Standard*, 5 Nov. 1986, 1; Robert E. Swanson, 'A History of Railroad Logging,' *British Columbia Railway Department, Annual Report, 1954* (Victoria: Queen's Printer 1955), p 7; 'Logging Railway,'*Lumberman and Contractor* 2 (Oct. 1905): 17; Robert D. Turner, *Logging by Rail: The British Columbia Story* (Victoria: Sono Nis Press 1990), 48.
3   William H. Friedland, Amy E. Barton, and Robert J. Thomas, *Manufacturing Green Gold: Capital, Labor, and Technology in the Lettuce Industry* (New York: Cambridge University Press 1981), 1.
4   Ian Radforth, *Bushworkers and Bosses: Logging in Northern Ontario, 1900-1980* (Toronto: University of Toronto Press 1987); see also Camille Georges Legendre, 'Organizational Technology, Structure and Environment: The Pulp and Paper Industry of Quebec,' (Ph.D. thesis, Michigan State University 1977); Alfred J. Van Tassel, *Mechanization in the Lumber Industry: A Study of Technology in Relation to Resources and Employment Opportunity* (Philadelphia: Works Projects Administration 1940); Ken Drushka, *Working in the Woods: A History of Logging on the West Coast* (Madeira Park: Harbour Publishing 1992).
5   Van Tassel, *Mechanization*, 29; see also Erik Klepp, *Occupational Changes in Logging Occupations* (Olympia: State of Washington Employment Security Department 1968), 1.

6 David Dickson, 'Technology and the Construction of Social Reality,' in *Radical Science Essays*, ed. Les Levidow (London: Free Association Books 1986), 20; Friedland, Barton, and Thomas, *Manufacturing Green Gold*, 4; Paul Thompson, *The Nature of Work: An Introduction to Debates on the Labour Process* (London: MacMillan Press 1983), 46.

7 Jim Trebett, 'Logging Trends: New Equipment Necessary to Meet Government Policy of Close Utilization,' *British Columbia Lumberman* 54 (Jan. 1970): 29 (hereafter *BCL*).

8 J.J. Donovan to N.L. Wright, 27 May 1913, Box 1, University of Washington College of Forest Resources Records, Acc. 70-1, University of Washington Libraries (hereafter UWCFRR); see also Clarence Ross Garvey, 'Overhead Systems of Logging in the Northwest,' (M.Sc. in Forestry thesis, University of Washington 1914), 1.

9 Frank H. Lamb, 'Logging Engineering Requires Skill and Experience for Success,' *Timberman* 10 (Aug. 1909): 32 (hereafter *TMN*).

10 Minot Davis, 'Just What Do We Mean By A Logging Engineer,' *West Coast Lumberman* 42 (1 Apr. 1922): 36 (hereafter *WCL*).

11 William Leiss, 'Utopia and Technology: Reflections on the Conquest of Nature,' *International Science Journal* 22 (1970): 583; *WCL* 29 (15 Dec. 1915): 32; A.C. Dixon to Oregon-American Lumber Company, 2 July 1923, Box 2, Oregon-American Lumber Company Records, University of Oregon Archives (hereafter OAR, UOA).

12 Emil Engstrom, *The Vanishing Logger* (New York: Vantage Press 1956), 23.

13 Alfred W. Moltke, *Memoirs of a Logger* (College Place: College Press 1955), 61-2.

14 Elijah M. Meece, interview by Michael A. Runestrand, 16 June 1976, Washington State Oral/Aural History Project, 3; R.D. Merrill to C.L. Ring, 24 Aug. 1917, Box 26, Merrill and Ring Lumber Company Records, Acc. 726, University of Washington Libraries (hereafter MRR, UWL).

15 For an excellent description of bucking techniques see Bus Griffiths, *Now You're Logging* (Madeira Park: Harbour Publishing 1978).

16 'Gigantic Operation,' *Washington Standard*, Oct. 1901, 1; Edwin Van Sickle, *They Tried to Cut it All* (Seattle: Pacific Search Press 1980), 87; see also John Gilbert, 'Logging and Railroad Building on Puget Sound, Olympia, Washington Territory, 1878,' University of Washington Libraries; C.M. Scammon, 'Lumbering in Washington Territory,' *Overland Monthly* 5 (1870): 55; Drushka, *Working in the Woods*, 36.

17 Louise H. Wall, 'Hauling Logs in Washington,' *Northwest Magazine* (Apr. 1893): 21.

18 Wall, 'Hauling Logs,' 20; Lloyd C. Rogers, interview by C.D. Orchard, 1956, C.D. Orchard Collection, British Columbia Archives (hereafter BCA); see also Wallace Baikie, 'Early Logging Days on Denman Island,' *British Columbia Forest History Newsletter* 5 (Apr. 1983): 3.

19 George P. Abdill, 'Bull Team Logger,' *True West* 21 (1974): 28.

20 Tony Alexander, 'Early Day Logging,' in *The Willapa County History Report*, ed. Mrs. Nels Olsen (Raymond: Raymond Herald and Advertiser 1965), 28; John Reavis, 'Logging on Puget Sound,' *Washington Magazine* (Sept. 1899): 16; George H. Emerson, 'Lumbering on Grays Harbor,' *The Coast* 14 (July 1907): 3; Albert Drinkwater, interview by Imbert Orchard, 1964, BCA; see also W. Baikie, 'Logging with Bulls,' *British Columbia Forest History Newsletter* 8 (Apr. 1984): 3.

21 D. Varney to Port Blakely Mill Company, 1 Jan. 1878, Box 71, Port Blakely Mill Company Records, UWL; Emerson, 'Lumbering on Grays Harbor,' 3.

22 'Pacific Coast Logging Methods,' *Pacific Lumber Trade Journal* 5 (Aug. 1899): 10 (hereafter *PLTJ*); Donald McKay, *Empire of Wood*, 16; W.H. Corbett, 'Development of the Logging Engine,' *Columbia River and Oregon Timberman* 3 (Jan. 1903): 66; Peter J. Rutledge, 'Genesis of the Steam Logging Donkey,' *TMN* 35 (Mar. 1933): 10; Peter J. Rutledge and Richard H. Tooker, 'Steam Power for Loggers: Two Views of the Dolbeer Donkey,' *Journal of Forest History* 14 (1970): 27; 'Dolbeer's Logging Engine,' *WCL* 3 (May 1892): 6; Emerson, 'Lumbering on Grays Harbor,' 3.

23 Van Tassel, *Mechanization*, 31; Ficken, *The Forested Land*, 70; see also Michael Williams, *Americans and Their Forests: A Historical Geography* (New York: Cambridge University Press 1989), 301; Sol G. Simpson to Port Blakely Mill Company, 18 Aug. 1888, Box 68, Port Blakely Mill Company Records, UWL.

24 Edward Miller to Port Blakely Mill Company, 20 Feb. 1885, Box 48, Port Blakely Mill Company Records, UWL; Robert Brian Griffin, 'The Shawnigan Lake Lumber Company, 1899-1943' (M.A. thesis, University of Victoria 1979), 37; Ray Raphael, *Tree Talk: The People and Politics of Timber* (Covelo: Island Press 1981), 13; E.T. Clark, 'Pacific Coast Logging,' *WCL* 38 (1 May 1920): 81-2.

25 D. Varney to Port Blakely Mill Company, 17 Feb. 1878, Box 71; Blackman Brothers to Port Blakely Mill Company, 10 Jan. 1878, Box 36; Edward P. Miller to Port Blakely Mill Company, 20 Feb. 1885, Box 36, all in Port Blakely Mill Company Records, UWL; Alex Polson to R.D. Merrill, 28 Sept. 1905, MRR, Acc. 726-4, UWL.

26 S.G. Simpson to Port Blakely Mill Company, 8 May 1889, Box 68, Port Blakely Mill Company Records, UWL; Stewart Holbrook, *Green Commonwealth* (Simpson Logging Company 1945), 34-5; H.W. McDonald to Alexander Barnet, 4 Dec. 1896, Reel 8, Barnet Family Papers, Public Archives of Ontario.

27 Emerson, 'Lumbering on Grays Harbor,' 3.

28 L.T. Murray, interview by Elwood R. Maunder, 1957, Forest History Foundation, 23, UWL.

29 'Logging Methods in British Columbia,' *Canada Lumberman* (Nov. 1902): 8; 'The Development of the Logging Engine,' *West Coast and Puget Sound Lumberman* 13 (Jan. 1906): 167; G.A. Walkem, 'Evolution of the British Columbia Logging Industry,' *BCL* 10 (Aug. 1926): 97; H.R. Christie, 'Logging Methods on Vancouver Island,' *Canada Lumberman and Woodworker* 36 (1 Sept. 1916): 78-80; 'Recent Progress in Power Logging Equipment,' *Western Lumberman* 8 (Aug. 1921): 76 (hereafter *WL*).

30 Rutledge and Tooker, 'Steam Power for Loggers,' 27; William H. Gibbons, *Logging in the Douglas Fir Region* (Washington, DC: United States Department of Agriculture, Bulletin No. 711 1918), 72; Richard H. Kennedy, 'Logging Our Great Forests,' *Pacific Monthly* 13 (Jan. 1905): 28.

31 Curt Beckham, *Gyppo Logging Days* (Myrtle Point: Hillside Book Company 1978), 7; John Van Orsdel, 'Machine Yarding and Loading,' *Proceedings of the Pacific Logging Congress* (Bellingham 1914), 44 (hereafter *PPLC*); D.H. Grigg, *From One to Seventy* (Vancouver: Mitchell Printing and Publishing Company 1953), 53.

32 R.V. Stuart, interview by C.D. Orchard, 1960, C.D. Orchard Collection, BCA.

33 See Paul A. Baran and Paul M. Sweezy, *Monopoly Capital: An Essay on the American Economic and Social Order* (New York: Monthly Review Press 1966), 70-2.

34 Francis Frink, interview by Elwood R. Maunder, 1958, Forest History Foundation, 8-10, UWL.

35 L.T. Murray, 'Changes in Type of Donkey Engine,' *WL* 11 (Nov. 1922): 56; W.H. Corbett, 'The Larger Yarding Engine,' *TMN* 7 (Apr. 1906): 33; W.H. Corbett, 'The Era of the Big Drum Yarder,' *TMN* 6 (Apr. 1905): 320.

36 James O'Hearne, 'How Shall We Teach Logging Engineering,' *PPLC* (Spokane 1913), 21.

37 D. Varney to Port Blakely Mill Company, 6 Mar. 1878, Box 71, Port Blakely Mill Company Records, UWL; *Labour Gazette* 8 (Sept. 1908): 308; 'Coast Logging Conditions,' *PLTJ* 10 (Aug. 1904): 11.

38 Van Orsdel 'Machine Yarding and Loading,' 45; Charles S.L. Koelsche, 'Yarding and Loading Logs,' *PPLC* (Bellingham 1914), 42.

39 Andrew Mason Prouty, *More Deadly Than War: Pacific Coast Logging, 1827-1981* (New York: Garland Publishing 1985), 62; Frink, interview by Maunder, 3; E.S. Grammer, 'Evolution of the Logging Donkey,' *PPLC* (San Francisco 1921), 32; *BCL* 26 (Dec. 1942): 44.

40 W.S. Taylor, 'Different stages in the Evolution of Overhead Systems of Logging,' *TMN* 15 (Jan. 1914): 30; 'Hauling Logs Through Mid-Air,' *PLTJ* (May 1901): 11; 'The Lamb Cableway System,' *Columbia River and Oregon Timberman* 3 (Jan. 1903): 21-3; 'The Evolution of Coast Logging,' *Columbia River and Oregon Timberman* 4 (August 1904): 21-33.

41 'Aerial Skidding Not an Experiment, Lidgerwood Invention Twenty-Seven Years Old,' *WCL* 25 (1 Nov. 1913): 27; R.W. Vinnedge, 'Overhead Logging Systems,' *PPLC* (Tacoma 1922), 14; 'Yarding Logs With Empire Cableway Skidder,' *WL* 13 (Sept. 1916): 31.

42 *WCL* 29 (1916): 34; for description of the many different overhead systems see K. Berger, 'Skyline Methods Used for Logging,' *BCL* 10 (Sept. 1926): 82-3.

43 James O'Hearne, 'Description and Value of High Leads,' *PPLC* (Portland-Grays Harbor 1916), 16; Josiah T. Shull, 'Overhead Logging on the Pacific Coast,' (M.Sc. in Forestry thesis, University of Washington 1926), 19; George Cornwall, 'Secretary's Report,' *PPLC* (San Francisco 1915), 5.

44 Shull, 'Overhead Logging on the Pacific Coast,' 11-12; Griffin, 'The Shawnigan Lake Lumber Company,'45; Williams, *Americans and Their Forests*, 316-7; Dorothy O. Johansen, *Empire of the Columbia: A History of the Pacific Northwest* (New York: Harper and Row 1967), 403.

45 T. Jerome to R.D. Merrill, 9 Oct. 1908; Jerome to T.D. Merrill, 16 Nov. 1908, Box 2; Jerome to Salsich Lumber Company, 1 Feb. 1910, Box 3, MRR, Acc. 726-4, UWL.

46 R.D. Merrill, 'Utilization of the Lidgerwood System of Logging,' *PPLC* (Vancouver 1911), 58; T. Jerome to C & C Lumber Company, 15 Feb. 1916, Box 6, MRR, Acc. 726-4, UWL.

47 Charles Stimson, 'Adoption of the Lidgerwood Skidder System in Fir Logging,' *TMN* 10 (Aug. 1909): 57; H.B. Gardner, 'Ground Skidder or High Lead,' *PPLC* (Portland-Grays Harbour 1916), 13; R.W. Vinnedge, 'A Composite Flying Machine,' *PPLC* (Spokane 1913), 10; E.G. English, 'Cableway Yarding System, Its Efficiency in Difficult Logging Operations,' *PPLC* (Portland 1910), 28.

48 F.C. Riley, 'The High Lead,' *PPLC* (Portland-Grays Harbor 1916), 11; O'Hearne, 'Description and Value of High Leads,' 12; see also W.D. Anderson, 'The Story of Log Transportation,' *BCL* 8 (Aug. 1924): 91.

49 Merrill, 'Utilization of the Lidgerwood System,' 58; Ronald MacDonald, 'High Lead and Ground Yarding Compared,' *PPLC* (Portland-Grays Harbor 1916), 11; Robert Waddell, 'Ground Works vs High Lead Logging Systems,' *WL* 13 (July 1916): 41-3.

50 'The Evolution of Coast Logging,' 23; Merrill, 'Utilization of the Lidgerwood System,' 55; 'The Lamb Cableway System,' 47.

51 'The Lamb Cableway System,' 47; Vinnedge, 'A Composite Flying Machine,' 9; see also Victor Stevens, *The Powers Story* (North Bend: Wegford Publications 1979), 69; R.J. O'Farrell, 'The Evolution of Logging – Some Personal Glimpses,' *University of Washington Forest Club Quarterly* 8 (Autumn 1929): 15.

52 'The Lamb Cableway System,' 47; 'The Evolution of Coast Logging,' 22; S.G. Smith, interviewed by C.D. Orchard, 1960, Orchard Collection, BCA.

53 *Willamette Logging Machinery* (Portland 1925), 30; 'New Two-Speed Yarder Developed by Willamette Iron and Steel Works,' *WCL* 35 (Oct. 1918): 22.

54 E.R. Orr, Vancouver Machinery Depot to G.P. Melrose, 7 Dec. 1922, Roll B-3229, File 040071, British Columbia Department of Lands Records, BCA (hereafter GR 1441); A.G. Labbe, Willamette Iron and Steel Works to Central Coal and Coke Co., 16 Dec. 1921, Box 2, OAR, UOA; 'Progress in Popularizing the Two-Speed Yarder,' *WL* (Aug. 1921): 80; James T. Larkin, Western Loggers Machinery Company, to C.E. Davidson, 27 Aug. 1926, Box 1, OAR, UOA; H.H. Baxter, General Report on Britannia Mining and Smelting Company Ltd., Logging Operations, 22 Apr. 1924, Box 15, Britannia Mining and Smelting Company Records, BCA.

55 W.H. McGregor to F. Schopflin, 28 Nov. 1923; C.E. Davidson to Schopflin, 22 Aug. 1924, Box 2, OAR, UOA.

56 C.E. Davidson to J. Greenman, 22 Sept. 1927; Davidson to Greenman, 28 June 1928; Greenman to C.S. Keith, 30 June 1928, Box 1, OAR, UOA.

57 See Spencer Miller, 'The Overhead Cableway Method of Logging,' *WCL* 48 (1 Aug. 1925): 41-4, 48-9.

58 W.H. McGregor to Frank Schopflin, 1 Mar. 1926, Box 1, OAR, UOA; R.D. Merrill to R. Polson, 6 Nov. 1913, Box 35, MRR, UWL.

59 W.F. MacPherson to T. Jerome, 3 Apr. 1917, Box 216, MRR, UWL.

60 'The Steel Spar Log Skidder,' *WCL* 26 (15 Sept. 1914): 32; 'The Steel Spar Skidder,' *PPLC* (Seattle 1925), 33-5; Paul Freydig, 'Why We Bought Four Steel Spar Skidders,' *PPLC* (Vancouver 1926), 11-12; Van Tassel, *Mechanization*, 125.

61 T. Jerome to T.D. Merrill, 4 Aug. 1909, Box 3; Jerome to T.D. Merrill, 5 Oct. 1909, Box 3, MRR, Acc. 726-4, UWL.

62 E.G. English, 'Cableway Yarding System,' 28; W. Ellison to Comox Logging and Railway Co., 4 Oct. 1911, Envelope 1, Comox Logging and Railway Company Records, Courtenay

and District Museum and Archives; Alden Jones, *From Jamestown to Coffin Rock: A History of Weyerhaeuser Operations in Southwestern Washington* (Weyerhaeuser Company 1974), 12.

63 *Industrial Worker*, 11 June 1910, 1; *Industrial Worker*, 25 June 1910, 1; *Industrial Worker*, 15 Feb. 1912, 1; for a preliminary discussion see Richard A. Rajala, 'A Dandy Bunch of Wobblies: Pacific Coast Loggers and the Industrial Workers of the World, 1900-1930,' *Labor History* 37 (Spring 1996): 205-34.

64 Vinnedge, 'Overhead Logging Systems,' 14; see also A.P. Hennegan, 'Fighting "Hang-Ups" in High Lead Yarding,' *BCL* 15 (Apr. 1931): 19-20; Frank H. Lamb, 'The Principles of Labor Maintenance,' *PPLC* (Seattle 1917), 31; R.D. Merrill to J.R. Benjamin, 12 June 1918, Box 28, MRR, Acc. 726, UWL.

65 Stewart H. Holbrook, *Holy Old Mackinaw: A Natural History of the American Lumberjack* (New York: Macmillan 1945), 184.

66 J.A. Cross, 'Productivity in British Columbia,' *BCL* 46 (Sept. 1962): 21.

67 *WL* 14 (June 1917): 20; 'Use of Compressed Air For Tree Felling,' *PPLC* (Portland 1919), 12-13; 'The Wolfe Gasoline Tree Felling Machine,' ibid., 12; 'Secretary's Report,' *PPLC* (Tacoma 1922), 2.

68 T.D. Merrill to E.P. Arseneau, 6 Mar. 1924, Box 44, MRR, Acc. 726-4, UWL; John N. Burke, 'British Columbia Loggers' Interest in Power Saws,' *Logger's Handbook* 9 (1949), 70 (hereafter *LH*); C.E. Davidson to W.H. McGregor, 3 Dec. 1926, Box 1, OAR, Oregon State Archives (hereafter OSA).

69 'Believers in Power Saws,' *TMN* 35 (Nov. 1934): 99; 'Mechanical Falling and Bucking,' *TMN* 37 (July 1936): 80; 'Power Saw Studies,' *TMN* 37 (Oct. 1936): 80; 'German Chain Power Saw,' *TMN* 38 (Dec. 1936): 92.

70 'Power Saw Experiences in British Columbia,' *TMN* 38 (1937): 95-6; J.W. Challenger, 'Felling Timber with Power Saws,' *TMN* 38 (Sept. 1937): 56; 'Power Saw Developments,' *TMN* 39 (Mar. 1938): 64; 'The Stihl Power Saw,' *BCL* 22 (June 1938): 81; J.W. Challenger, 'Power Saws – An Analysis of Four Year's Operation,' *PPLC* (Vancouver 1940), 27; 'Power Saws,' *LH* 1 (1941), 114; John Ulinder, 'The Mechanics of Falling and Bucking Timber,' *BCL* 32 (Feb. 1948): 58.

71 J.W. Challenger, 'Five Years of Power Sawing,' *TMN* 41 (Nov. 1942): 10; 'One-Man Buckers,' *TMN* 44 (Aug. 1943): 46; 'The Falling Contractor in British Columbia,' *Truck Logger* 24 (July 1968): 28-9 (hereafter *TL*).

72 A.L. Raught to J. Greenman, 5 Feb. 1940, Box 23, OAR, OSA; 'Average Age of Long-Bell Lumber Company at Ryderwood as of 1 June 1940,' ibid.; 'Oregon-American Lumber Corporation, Average Age of Various Classifications in the Logging Crew,' 27 May 1940, ibid.; Radforth, *Bushworkers and Bosses*, 159-68.

73 'Power Operated Saws,' *TMN* 38 (May 1937): 88; A.L. Mercer, 'Power Saws Reduce Falling Costs,' *WCL* 68 (June 1941): 12; 'Mechanical Saw May Throw Many Men Out of Work,' *B.C. Lumber Worker*, 21 Oct. 1936, 1; 'Power Saw,' *Timber Worker*, 16 Sept. 1939, 1; Julia Bertram, 'Power Saw Introduction Raises New Problem for IWA,' *Timber Worker*, 16 Sept. 1939, 1; 'B & K Lock Gates,' *B.C. Lumber Worker*, 25 Apr. 1939, 2; 'More Power Saws Would Help Production,' *WCL* 70 (Mar. 1943): 30.

74 J.W. Challenger, 'Progress in Power Timber Felling,' *TMN* 40 (Nov. 1938): 54; Challenger, 'Power Saws – An Analysis,' 28; 'Opening of Power Saw School Important Step in Veteran's Rehabilitation Program for British Columbia,' *BCL* 29 (Nov. 1945): 36; Norman Harris, 'Training and Placement of Workers by Cooperation in the Logging Industry,' *PPLC* (Vancouver 1960), 60.

75 James Freeman, 'Discusses Effect of Power Saws on Cutting Crews,' *B.C. Lumber Worker*, 1 May 1940, 3; 'Power Saws,' *B.C. Lumber Worker*, Dec. 1945, 2; 'Meet the IWA,' *B.C. Lumber Worker*, 20 Sept. 1941, 4.

76 'Tractor Logging Discussion,' *TMN* 33 (Nov. 1931): 75; G.L. Drake, 'Developments in Tractor Logging,' *TMN* 35 (Nov. 1933): 18; 'Tractor Logging Growth in B.C.,' *WCL* 64 (Jan. 1937): 40.

77 R. Mills to G. Cornwall, 20 Jan. 1932, Box 1, UWCFRR, Acc. 70-1; 'Logging Big Timber with Tractors and Donkeys,' *WCL* 62 (Oct. 1935): 13.

78 'Integrating Tractor and Skidder,' *WCL* 62 (July 1935): 40.

79 'Tractors Work With Skidders,' *WCL* 66 (May 1939): 56.
80 'Logging with Tractors,' *WCL* 61 (Nov. 1934): 25-6.
81 J. Kenneth Pearce to G. Cornwall, 10 Nov. 1935, Box 1, J. Kenneth Pearce Papers, UWL; E.W. Allison to E.G. Griggs, 27 Oct. 1941, Box 131, Corydon Wagner Papers, UWL.
82 For discussion of oil-fired steam donkeys see Richard A. Rajala, 'The Forest As Factory: Technological Change and Worker Control in the West Coast Logging Industry, 1880-1930,' *Labour/Le Travail* 32 (Fall 1993): 97-8; J. Greenman to F.R. Olin, 18 Apr. 1939, Box 22, OAR, UOA.
83 T.D. Merrill to R.D. Merrill, 6 Oct. 1928, Box 64, MRR, UWL; see also E.W. Allison to E.G. Griggs, 25 Jan. 1934, Box 179, St. Paul and Tacoma Lumber Company Records, University of Washington Libraries (hereafter STPTR, UWL).
84 Gerald Frink, 'The Donkey Engine of the Future,' *WCL* 71 (Feb. 1944): 35; R.M. Schaefer, 'Hydraulic Torque Converters,' *WCL* 67 (May 1940): 28; 'New Yarder Simplifies Operations,' *Forest Industries* 93 (Mar. 1966): 71 (hereafter *FI*); W.B. Osborne and E.H. MacDaniels, 'Logging Douglas Fir in 1941 Style,' *WCL* 68 (Aug. 1941): 40.
85 Donald MacKay, *The Lumberjacks* (Toronto: McGraw-Hill 1978), 193.
86 'Trucking at Ryderwood,' *TMN* 40 (Mar. 1939): 14-5; 'Locomotives Cross Line,' *TMN* 48 (Dec. 1946): 132; 'Railroad Used in Conjunction with Truck-Feeder Operation,' *TL* 20 (July 1964): 26-8.
87 R.J. Filberg, 'In My Time,' *TL* 24 (Jan. 1968): 48; E.F. Rapraeger, 'How Motor Trucks are Used in Douglas Fir Logging,' *Journal of Forestry* 32 (Jan. 1934): 28 (hereafter *JF*); F.C. Baker, 'Cold Decking,' *TMN* 34 (Nov. 1932): 33-4.
88 R.J. Filberg, 'Truck Logging on Vancouver Island,' *TMN* 39 (Oct. 1938): 36.
89 W. Tilton to E.G. Griggs, 20 June 1947, Box 85, STPTR, UWL.
90 Frank Hobi, 'St. Paul and Tacoma Lumber Company, Conversion – Railroad to Truck Road, 1947,' ibid.; see also 'Transition From Rails to Trucks Begins,' *TMN* 49 (Dec. 1947): 155.
91 J. Kenneth Pearce, 'Report on Comparative Costs of Railroad and Truck Logging, Wakewasis Creek – Indian Creek Drainages, Kosmos Timber Company,' Box 2, Pearce Papers, UWL.
92 'Low Cost Logging,' *WCL* 65 (Sept. 1938): 30; C.C. Jacoby, 'New vs. Old Type Logging Machinery,' *WCL* 68 (July 1941): 40.
93 'A Challenge That Grows More Urgent,' *BCL* 48 (July 1964): 11.
94 'Sled Mounted Log Loader,' *TMN* 36 (Mar. 1935): 58; 'Logging Methods and Equipment Developments During the Year,' *WCL* 62 (Oct. 1935): 8-9.
95 J.W. Baikie, 'Portable Equipment,' *LH* 16 (1956), 19; R.F. Dwyer, 'Log Loading Equipment,' *LH* 8 (1948), 86; Edward Baker, 'Loading Motor Trucks,' *WCL* 64 (Apr. 1937): 19.
96 Don Smith, 'A Logger Appraises Preloaders,' *BCL* 41 (June 1957): 36.
97 Dwyer, 'Log Loading Equipment,' 17; James Harper, 'Economics of Contract Logging,' *LH* 27 (1967), 20; A. Zoffel to E.G. Griggs, 5 May 1950, Box 150, STPTR, UWL.
98 'Grabinski's Slackline Skidder,' *WCL* 71 (Jan. 1944): 14.
99 Gerald Frink, 'Mobile Loading Machine and Improved Skidder,' *LH* 5 (1946), 17; 'New Combination Yarder-Loader,' *TMN* 52 (June 1951): 64; 'The Skagit Logger,' *LH* 11 (1951), 90.
100 Keith Gibson, 'Imagination Plus Adaptation Fosters Innovation,' *BCL* 44 (Apr. 1960): 10-1.
101 J.K. Pearce to G.S. Barrett, 23 Apr. 1945, Box 1, Pearce Papers, UWL; E.G. Griggs to N. Jacobson, 2 Nov. 1945, Box 84, Wagner Papers, UWL; 'Re-Logging Machines and Developments,' *TMN* 48 (Sept. 1947): 46-8; 'Portable Spar Tree Built From the Scrap Pile,' *BCL* 36 (Jan. 1952): 116.
102 'Mobility in the Woods Gained with a Portable Logging Tower,' *TMN* 54 (Oct. 1953): 17; 'Olympic Logger Designs New Type of Portable Skidder,' *LH* 14 (1954), 81; 'Berger Porta-Tower,' *LH* 19 (1959), 49-50; Joe Garner, *Never Chop Your Rope* (Nanaimo: Cinnibar Press 1988), 158.
103 Ian Mahood, 'Contracting,' *BCL* 54 (Feb. 1970): 35; 'Towers Replacing Spar Tree System,' *FI* 91 (May 1964): 83; 'Spar Trees Yield to Portable Towers,' *FI* 93 (Sept. 1966): 54-5; 'Nineteen Camps Geared for High Production,' *TL* 21 (Jan. 1965): 34.
104 H.J. Ness, 'Present Logging Compared With That Prior to 1936,' *WCL* 70 (Aug. 1943): 48; T.W. Ilstad, 'New Ideas in Practice,' *LH* 17 (1957), 13; Charles Dunham, 'Windrowing With Portable Spars,' *LH* 18 (1958), 22-3.

105 Wallace Baikie, 'Portable Equipment,' *LH* 16 (1956), 20; Wallace Baikie, 'Mobile Spar Tree,' *LH* 17 (1957), 63.
106 'Howe Sound Timber Goes Mobile and Ups Log Production,' *BCL* 43 (June 1959): 28; 'Spars Bring in 90mm Feet,' *FI* 90 (Nov. 1963): 60.
107 'Machinery for Replacement,' *BCL* 46 (Jan. 1962): 19; 'Vanishing Breed,' *BCL* 50 (Aug. 1966): 52; 'Narrow Road Only Landing Necessary With New Swinging Boom Yarder,' *FI* 101 (Oct. 1974): 54.
108 James Harper, 'Economics of Contract Logging,' *LH* 27 (1967), 20.
109 Alden Jones, 'Logging With Steel Spars,' *PPLC* (Vancouver 1965), 27; 'Mr. Priest's Paper,' *PPLC* (Portland 1966), 56; Bill Moore, 'Walking Loggers Becoming Rare,' *BCL* 58 (Nov. 1974): 74.
110 Nils Hult, 'President's Address,' *LH* 19 (1959), 12; Herman Sommer, 'Cutting Costs by Snorkel Loading Road Strips and Cable Grapple Yarding,' *PPLC* (San Francisco 1966), 51.
111 Coulson Prescott, 'How Good Practices Save $,' *BCL* 50 (Dec. 1966): 10; Steve Conway, 'Rigging Reduces Delays, Expenses,' *FI* 96 (Feb. 1969): 58; Bill Moore, 'On Monsters and Malfunctions,' *BCL* 55 (Mar. 1971): 8.
112 Sommer, 'Cutting Costs,' 51; J. Kenneth Pearce, 'A Visitor's Guide to Logging in the Douglas fir Region,' 3, Box 2, Pearce Papers, UWL.
113 Earl Ritzheiner, 'Log Grapple Gives Flexibility in the Woods,' *LH* 18 (1958), 17; 'Skagit Machines Pace Logging Industry,' *Western Conservation Journal* 32 (Aug./Sept. 1972): 46; 'Skagit Offers New Yarding Method,' *BCL* 51 (Apr. 1967): 66; 'Grapple Yarders Gaining in Number,' *FI* 96 (May 1969): 62-3; 'Nitinat 'Talks' Logs to Road With Grapple Yarding System,' *Crown Zellerbach News* 10 (Mar. 1967): 7.
114 Jim Trebett, 'Logging Trends: New Equipment Necessary to Meet Government Policy of Close Utilization,' *BCL* 54 (1970): 30.
115 Bob Kennedy, 'President's Address,' *PPLC* (Portland 1965), 13; Howard Baker, 'Entry Level Training Opportunities,' *PPLC* (Vancouver 1964), 118; Norman Harris, 'Trained Manpower Needed in Logging Industry: Loggers' School Advocated,' *TL* 21 (Jan. 1965): 80-3.
116 Jerry Tessier, 'Progress Report on Cable Grapple Yarding,' *PPLC* (Portland 1968), 85; Sommer, 'Cutting Costs,' 54-5; Donald Stainsby, 'What's With Grapple Yarding,' *BCL* 52 (Apr. 1968): 30; Bill Wainwright, 'Grapple Yarding,' *TL* 25 (Feb. 1969): 21; Don Landon, 'Madill Yarding Crane,' *Proceedings of the Oregon Logging Conference* (Eugene 1970), 43.
117 'Fewer Produce More,' *BCL* 53 (Oct. 1979): 34.
118 Edmond Preus, 'Application of Equipment,' *PPLC* (Vancouver 1978), 131; Tom Murray, 'Keynote Address,' *PPLC* (Portland 1979), 11; E.A. Saunder, 'Grapple Yarding Today and in the Future,' *Proceedings of the Fifth Skyline Symposium*, eds. Doyle C. Burke, C. Mann, and P. Schiess (Seattle: University of Washington College of Forest Resources 1982), 92.
119 Terry Johnson, 'Work and Power,' in *The Politics of Work and Occupations*, ed. Geoff Esland and Graeme Salaman (Milton Keynes: Open University Press 1980), 355-71.
120 David Noble, *Forces of Production: A Social History of Industrial Automation* (New York: Alfred A. Knopf 1984), 36.
121 For a general discussion of this theme see James P. Hull, 'A Common Effort to Determine the Facts: The Sharing of Technical Knowledge in Canadian Industry, 1900-1939,' *Journal of Canadian Studies* 25 (Winter 1990-91): 50-63.
122 Thomas G. Wright, 'Is the Loggers' Role in Forest Management Fully Recognized,' *BCL* 50 (Nov. 1966): 18; R.M. Newham, 'Process Control in Forest Harvesting,' *Forest Chronicle* 49 (Feb. 1973): 35 (hereafter *FC*).
123 On this conceptualization of skill see Alan Fox, *Beyond Contract: Work, Power and Trust Relations* (London: Faber and Faber 1974), 19.
124 Phillip L. Cottell, 'Human Factors in Logging Productivity,' in *Manpower – Forest Industry's Key Resource*, ed. Lloyd C. Irving (New Haven: Yale University 1975), 70; 'What Have You Found to be a Major Contributing Factor to Successful Logging?' *TL* 20 (Jan. 1964): 37; David C. Verchere, 'The Log Grapple on a Mobile Loader,' *BCL* 42 (Dec. 1958): 13; Pat Carney, 'Moore's Logging Operation,' *TL* 19 (Sept. 1963): 11; Steve Conway, 'Log Loading Procedure Serves as Example for Stopwatch Study,' *FI* 95 (Oct. 1968): 39.
125 Thompson, *The Nature of Work*, 49.

Chapter 2: Managing the Factory Regime

1 For one example see Ronald L. Delorme, 'Rational Management Takes to the Woods: Frederick Weyerhaeuser and the Pacific Northwest Wood Products Industry,' *Journal of the West* 25 (Jan. 1986): 39-43.

2 See Louis Galambos, 'The Emerging Organizational Synthesis in Modern American History,' *Business History Review* 44 (Autumn 1970): 279-90; Robert D. Cuff, 'American Historians and the Organizational Factor,' *Canadian Review of American Studies* 4 (Spring 1973): 19-31; Samuel P. Hays, 'The New Organizational Society,' in *American Political History as Social Analysis: Essays by Samuel P. Hays* (Knoxville: University of Tennessee Press 1980), 244-63.

3 Alfred D. Chandler, Jr., *The Visible Hand: The Managerial Revolution in American Business* (Cambridge: Harvard University Press 1977); Alfred D. Chandler, Jr., 'The Emergence of Managerial Capitalism,' *Business History Review* 58 (Winter 1984): 473-503; For insightful critiques of Chandler's work see Richard B. Du Boff and Edward S. Herman, 'Alfred Chandler's New Business History: A Review,' *Politics and Society* 10 (1980): 87-110; Thomas K. McCraw, 'The Challenge of Alfred D. Chandler, Jr.: Retrospect and Prospect,' *Reviews in American History* 15 (Mar. 1987): 160-78.

4 Al Szymanski, 'Braverman as a Neo-Luddite,' *Insurgent Sociologist* 8 (Winter 1978): 48; see also Thompson, *The Nature of Work*, 91.

5 For discussion of this theme see William H. Lazonick, 'Technical Change and the Control of Work: The Development of Capital-Labour Relations in U.S. Mass Production Industries,' in *Managerial Strategies and Industrial Relations: An Historical and Comparative Study*, ed. Howard F. Gospel and Craig R. Littler (London: Heinemann Books 1983), 111; Peter Meiskins, 'Science in the Labor Process: Engineers as Workers,' in *Professionals as Workers: Mental Labor in Advanced Capitalism*, ed. Charles Derber (Boston: G.K. Hall 1982), 123-7; Paul Goldman and Donald R. Van Houten, 'Managerial Strategies and the Worker: A Marxist Analysis,' *Sociological Quarterly* 18 (Winter 1977): 118-20; Edwin T. Layton, *The Revolt of the Engineers: Social Responsibility and the American Engineering Profession* (Cleveland: Case Western Reserve University Press 1971), xiii; Megali Sarfatti Larson, 'The Production of Expertise and the Constitution of Expert Power,' in *The Authority of Experts*, ed. Thomas L. Haskell (Bloomington: Indiana University Press 1984), 38-9.

6 Il Manifesto, 'Challenging the Role of Technical Experts,' in *The Division of Labour: The Labour Process and Class Struggle in Modern Capitalism*, ed. Andre Gorz (Sussex: Harvester Press 1976), 128.

7 See Kenneth A. Dahlberg, 'The Changing Nature of Natural Resources,' in *Natural Resources and People: Conceptual Issues in Interdisciplinary Research*, ed. Kenneth A. Dahlberg and John W. Bennett (Boulder: Westview Press 1986), 12-3.

8 Cox, *This Well-Wooded Land*, 180-1.

9 Steen, *The U.S. Forest Service*, 36; see also Harold T. Pinkett, 'Western Perception of Forest Conservation,' *Journal of the West* 18 (1977): 72-3.

10 Samuel P. Hays, *Conservation and the Gospel of Efficiency: The Progressive Conservation Movement, 1880-1920* (Cambridge: Harvard University Press 1959), 36; William G. Robbins, 'Federal Forestry Cooperation: The Fernow-Pinchot Years,' *Journal of Forest History* 28 (Oct. 1984): 168.

11 Andrew Denny Rogers, *Bernard Edward Fernow: A Story of American Forestry* (Princeton: Princeton University Press 1951), 230; Steen, *The U.S. Forest Service*, 74; Harold T. Pinkett, *Gifford Pinchot: Private and Public Forester* (Chicago: University of Chicago Press 1970), 58-9.

12 Ralph S. Hosmer, 'The Society of American Foresters: An Historical Summary,' *JF* 48 (Nov. 1950): 756-7; Henry Clepper, *Professional Forestry in the United States* (Baltimore: The Johns Hopkins Press 1971), 124-7.

13 Frances Wetton, 'Evolution of Forest Policies in Canada,' *JF* 76 (Sept. 1978): 563; Rogers, *Bernard Edward Fernow*, 381.

14 See Thomas R. Roach, 'Stewards of the People's Wealth: The Founding of British Columbia's Forest Branch,' *Journal of Forest History* 28 (Jan. 1984): 14-23; 'British Columbia Forest Branch,' *Canadian Forestry Journal* 9 (June 1913): 86.

15 R. Peter Gillis and Thomas R. Roach, 'The American Influence on Conservation in Canada, 1899-1911,' *Journal of Forest History* 30 (Oct. 1986): 160-74.

16   George A. Garratt, *Forestry Education in Canada* (Vancouver: Evergreen Press 1971), 17, 21-2; Rogers, *Bernard Edward Fernow*, 430-3.

17   G. Peavy to W.J. Kerr, 14 Apr. 1910, Reel 14, Oregon State University School of Forestry Records, Oregon State University Archives (hereafter OSUSFR). See also Henry Schmitz, *The Long Road Travelled: An Account of Forestry at the University of Washington* (Seattle: Arboretum Foundation 1973), 9-16; Axel F.J. Brandstrom, *Development of Industrial Forestry in the Pacific Northwest* (Seattle: University of Washington College of Forestry 1957), 8; W.F. McCulloch, *Forest Management Education in Oregon* (Corvallis: Oregon State College 1949), 12-6.

18   F.H. Lamb, 'Logging Engineering Requires Skill and Experience for Success,' *TMN* 10 (Aug. 1909): 32; Donald H. Clark, *Eighteen Men and a Horse* (Seattle: Metropolitan Press 1949), 25.

19   Robert E. Ficken, *Lumber and Politics: The Career of Mark E. Reed* (Seattle: University of Washington Press 1985), 15; E.T. Clark, 'Pacific Coast Logging,' *WCL* (May 1920): 82; W.W. Peed, 'Necessity for the Logging Engineer in Modern Logging Operations,' *PPLC* (Portland 1910), 28; E.T. Clark, 'The Logging Engineer,' *University of Washington Forest Club Quarterly* 3 (1915), 56.

20   J.P. Van Orsdel, 'Topographic Survey and its Economic Value in Logging Operations,' *PPLC* (Portland 1910), 44; Joseph Morgan, 'The Logging Engineer's Place in Logging,' *University of Washington Forest Club Annual* 3 (1921), 57; C.S. Roray to Britannia Mining Company, 3 July 1928, Box 28, Britannia Mining and Smelting Company Records, BCA; J. Greenman to C.S. Keith, 29 May 1935, Box 13, OAR, UOA.

21   Clark, 'The Logging Engineer,' 57; see also J.J. Donovan, 'The Functions of Steam Railroads in Modern Logging Operations,' *PPLC* (Portland 1910), 35.

22   Daniel Nelson, *Managers and Workers: Origins of the New Factory System in the United States, 1880-1920* (Madison: University of Wisconsin Press 1975), 35; Andrew Friedman, *Industry and Labour: Class Struggle at Work and Monopoly Capitalism* (London: MacMillan Press 1979), 72.

23   David Noble, *America by Design: Science, Technology and the Rise of Corporate Capitalism* (New York: Alfred A. Knopf 1977), 131; see also Raymond E. Callahan, *Education and the Cult of Efficiency* (Chicago: University of Chicago Press 1962), 6-8; Harvey Kantor, 'Vocationalism in American Education: The Economic and Political Context,' in *Work, Youth and Schooling: Historical Perspectives on Vocationalism in American Education*, ed. Harvey Kantor and David B. Tyack (Stanford: Stanford University Press 1982), 14; Jurgen Kocka, *White Collar Workers in America, 1890-1940* (Beverly Hills: Sage Publications 1980), 103; J. Rodney Millard, *The Master Spirit of the Age: Canadian Engineers and the Politics of Professionalism, 1872-1922* (Toronto: University of Toronto Press 1988), 7.

24   'The Pacific Logging Congress,' *TMN* 10 (Aug. 1909): 19; G.M. Cornwall, 'Secretary's Report,' *PPLC* (Bellingham 1914), 2; Lamb, 'Logging Engineering Requires Skill and Experience,' 32; J.J. Donovan, 'Topographic Surveys Must Not Be Carried Beyond the Economic Point,' *PPLC* (Tacoma 1912), 49; Harold K. Steen, 'Forestry in Washington to 1925' (Ph.D. thesis, University of Washington 1969), 226.

25   Schmitz, *The Long Road Travelled*, 133; W.T. Andrews, 'Introduction of the Practical Teaching of Logging Engineering and Lumber Manufacture at the University of Washington,' *University of Washington Forest Club Annual* 4 (1925), 34.

26   E.T. Clark, 'The Development of Logging Engineering at the University of Washington,' *University of Washington Forest Club Annual* 4 (1925), 43-4.

27   H. Winkenwerder to G.M. Cornwall, 17 Oct. 1912, Box 2, UWCFRR, Acc. 70-1; *WCL* 30 (15 June 1916): 42; Winkenwerder to J. O'Hearne, 6 June 1919, Box 64, UWCFRR, Acc. 70-1; *WCL* 30 (1 Aug. 1916): 19, 30; Winkenwerder to A.E. Welch, 26 Feb. 1918, Box 14, UWCFRR, Acc. 70-1. For discussion of conflict over curriculum see Richard A. Rajala, 'Managerial Crisis: The Emergence and Role of the West Coast Logging Engineer, 1900-1930,' in *Canadian Papers in Business History* 1 (1989), ed. Peter Baskerville, 111-4.

28   Winkenwerder to J.P. Weyerhaeuser, 14 Mar. 1919, Box 3; Winkenwerder to R. Zon, 23 Aug. 1920, Box 53, UWCFRR, Acc. 70-1.

29   G. Peavy to Winkenwerder, 27 Sept. 1912, Box 1, UWCFRR, Acc. 70-1; Peavy to the President, Oregon State College, 27 May 1913, Reel 14, OSUSFR; W.H. Davies, 'Western Logging Engineering Schools: Oregon Agricultural College,' *LH* 9 (1951), 87; 'Uniform Logging Engineering Courses,' *PPLC* (Spokane 1914), 49.

30 George Peavy, 'School of Forestry,' 4 Sept. 1914, Reel 14, OSUSFR; *WCL* 30 (15 May 1919): 42; G. Cornwall, 'Secretary's Report,' *PPLC* (Portland-Grays Harbor 1916), 5.

31 'The Science of Logging,' *WL* 9 (June 1912): 28; 'Fourteenth Annual Meeting of the Canadian Forestry Association,' *PLTJ* 18 (Sept. 1912): 27; 'Hint to University Authorities,' *WL* 9 (Feb. 1912): 25; H.N. Whitford and R.D. Craig, *The Forests of British Columbia* (Ottawa: Commission on Conservation 1918), 163; G. Cornwall to F.F. Westbrook, 12 Nov. 1917, Box 10, President's Papers, University of British Columbia Libraries, Special Collections Branch (hereafter UBC-SC); A.B. Buckworth to Westbrook, 19 Mar. 1917, ibid.; 'B.C. Forest Club Makes Progressive Moves,' *WL* 14 (Apr. 1917): 31.

32 H.R. Christie, 'Forestry at the University, B.C.,' *Pacific Coast Lumberman* 5 (Feb. 1921): 27; Lowell Besley, 'Western Logging Engineering Schools: University of British Columbia,' *LH* 9 (1951), 80; F.M. Knapp to Winkenwerder, 8 Dec. 1922, Box 4, UWCFRR, Acc. 70-1; J. Harry G. Smith, *UBC Forestry, 1921-1990: An Informal History* (Vancouver: Faculty of Forestry, University of British Columbia 1990), 6.

33 H.R. Christie to R.C. St. Clair, 15 Jan. 1924, British Columbia, Department of Lands Correspondence Files, GR 1441, Roll B-3532, File 051597, BCA (hereafter GR 1441); F.M. Knapp to Winkenwerder, 12 Feb. 1929, Box 4, F. Malcolm Knapp Papers, UBC-SC; S.G. Smith to Winkenwerder, 10 Oct. 1923, Box 26, UWCFRR; R.L. Cobb to E.T. Clark, 7 Nov. 1926; J.H. MacDonald to Winkenwerder, 16 Sept. 1928, ibid.

34 Myron Krueger, 'Trends in Forestry Education in North America,' *JF* 51 (June 1953): 404.

35 Winkenwerder to A.N. Pack, 29 Dec. 1922, Box 4, UWCFRR, Acc. 70-1; Hays, *Conservation and the Gospel of Efficiency*, 2.

36 Carroll Pursell, 'Conservation, Environmentalism, and the Engineers: The Progressive Era and the Recent Past,' in *Environmental History: Critical Issues in Comparative Perspective*, ed. Kendall E. Bailes (Lanham: University Press of America 1985), 176.

37 S.A. Stamm to H.C. Hornby, 19 Sept. 1916, Box 4, UWCFRR, Acc. 70-1; Clark, 'The Logging Engineer,' 57.

38 J. Greenman to F. Schopflin, 17 May 1926, Box 1, OAR, UOA; see Murray's comments in the discussion of E.J. Brigham's, 'Cruising and Mapping Timber Lands,' *PPLC* (Vancouver 1926), 7.

39 R.D. Merrill to J.P. Van Orsdel, 29 June 1911, Box 4, MRR, Acc. 726, UWL; E.T. Clark to Winkenwerder, 2 June 1918, Box 45, UWCFRR, Acc. 70-1; 'Late Southwest Washington News,' *WCL* 40 (15 May 1921): 50; Jones, *From Jamestown to Coffin Rock*, 84; 'Logging With Weyerhaeuser at Longview,' *WCL* 61 (May 1934): 8.

40 W.H. Thomas to Oregon-American Lumber Company, 6 Jan. 1922, Box 3, OAR, UOA; Greenman to C.S. Keith, 12 Sept. 1929, Box 1, ibid.

41 'Topographical Maps of Timber Limits,' *WL* 9 (Dec. 1912): 37; *WL* 16 (Mar. 1917): 38; 'Coast Personals,' *BCL* 5 (Feb. 1921): 82; F.W. Kirkland to F. Malcolm Knapp, 21 Feb. 1928, Box 1, Knapp Papers, UBC-SC; E. Dougan to Knapp, 27 July 1930, ibid.; A.P. Browning to Mr. Gardner, 8 Apr. 1924, Box 15, Britannia Mining and Smelting Company Records, BCA; *UBO Bulletin* 5 (Jan. 1949): 2; A.E. Pickford to P.Z. Caverhill, 2 Aug. 1925, File 077546, British Columbia, Ministry of Forests, O Series Correspondence Files, Ministry of Forests Office (hereafter BCMFR).

42 C.V. Wilson, 'Logging Engineering,' *WCL* 31 (15 Mar. 1917): 112; 'Logging Railroad Construction,' *PPLC* (Spokane 1923), 21; E.P. Stamm, 'All Aboard for Cathlamet,' *TMN* 35 (Nov. 1933): 15; W.K. Meredith, 'Locating Spar Trees,' *WCL* 62 (Feb. 1935): 12-3; J. Kenneth Pearce to R.W. Clark, 17 Dec. 1946, Box 1, Pearce Papers, UWL; D. Hanna to Pearce, 22 June 1949, ibid.

43 A.B. Wood, 'Accurate Topographical Map a Good Investment in Logging Operations,' *PPLC* (Tacoma 1912), 47; Morgan, 'The Logging Engineer's Place,' 35.

44 See Rajala, 'Managerial Crisis,' 114-21.

45 Harold Goodrich, 'Logging On A Sustained Operation,' *Proceedings of the Western Forestry and Conservation Association* (1944), 14 (hereafter *PWFCA*).

46 T.T. Munger to Winkenwerder, 3 Oct. 1919, Box 53, UWCFRR, Acc. 70-1; E.T. Clark to Winkenwerder, 4 Jan. 1922, Box 45, ibid.; see also Thomas R. Cox, 'The Stewardship of Private Forests: Evolution of a Concept in the United States, 1864-1950,' *Journal of Forest*

History 25 (Oct. 1981): 192; William B. Greeley, *Forests and Men* (Garden City: Doubleday 1951): 49.

47 John B. Woods, 'What is Private Forestry in the Pacific Northwest' (paper presented to the North Pacific Section, Society of American Foresters, Portland), Box 53, UWCFRR, Acc. 70-1; see also J.B. Woods, 'Reforestation,' *TMN* 27 (Aug. 1926): 190; Hugo Winkenwerder, *Forestry in the Pacific Northwest* (Washington, DC: American Tree Association 1928), 36; C.S. Chapman, 'Industrial Problems of Forest Practice in the North West,' *JF* 36 (July 1938): 188-93.

48 J.A. Black to C.E. Davidson, 19 Dec. 1929, Box 1, OAR, UOA; Winkenwerder to C.S. Chapman, 31 Mar. 1931, Box 71, UWCFRR, Acc. 70-1; J.W. Ferguson, 'How Oregon's Reforestation Law is Working,' *WCL* 66 (July 1939): 46; W.B. Greeley, 'The Outlook for Timber Management by Private Owners,' *JF* 31 (Feb. 1933): 209; Murray Morgan, *The Mill on the Boot: The Story of the St. Paul and Tacoma Lumber Company* (Seattle: University of Washington Press 1982), 247; Henry Widner, ed., *Forests and Forestry in the American States* (Washington, DC: National Association of State Foresters 1968), 273, 282.

49 Emanuel Fritz, 'A Good Time for the Forestry Schools to Take Stock,' *JF* 30 (May 1932): 631-2.

50 E. Fritz to Winkenwerder, 18 July 1932, Box 7, UWCFRR, Acc. 70-1.

51 Emanuel Fritz, 'Forest Education: The Anxious 4,000,' *JF* 32 (May 1934): 563; H. Stratton to D.S. Jeffers, 22 Apr. 1934, Box 8, UWCFRR, Acc. 70-1.

52 Clepper, *Professional Forestry,* 130; Winkenwerder to R. Dao, 13 Mar. 1935, Box 8, UWCFRR, Acc. 70-1; Winkenwerder to H.D. Tiemann, 14 Oct. 1935, ibid.; Joint Committee on Forest Conservation, Minutes of Meeting, 12 May 1938, Vol. 160, West Coast Lumbermen's Association Records, Oregon State Historical Society Archives (hereafter WCLAR, OHSA); H.S. Graves, 'Looking Forward in Forest Education,' *JF* 36 (Feb. 1938): 229-34; J.K. Pearce, 'Training Foresters for Industry,' *JF* 29 (Feb. 1941): 250.

53 McCulloch, *Forest Management Education in Oregon,* 17; N.G. Jacobson to Dean H.H. Preston, 12 Mar. 1940, Box 7, UWCFRR, Acc. 70-1; W. Mumford to G. Marckworth, 10 Apr. 1947, Box 10, ibid.

54 Society of American Foresters, Puget Sound Section Records, Minutes of Meeting, 1 Apr. 1944, Box 2, University of Washington Libraries (hereafter SAF-PSSR, UWL); W.G. Tilton to E. Fritz, 12 Aug. 1941, Box 10, UWCFRR.

55 Pearce, 'Training Foresters for Industry,' 251.

56 McCulloch, *Forest Management Education in Oregon,* 100, 111-2; McCulloch to N.S. Rogers, 8 Nov. 1946, Box 2, Oregon State Department of Forestry Records, Oregon State Archives (hereafter OSDFR, OSA); W.F. McCulloch, 'Foresters for Private Industry,' *TMN* 48 (Mar. 1947): 60; 'Data for Administrative Task Force,' Oregon State College, Forestry Alumni Association, Apr. 1957, Reel 13, OSUSFR.

57 'Academic Achievement Report, School of Forestry, Oregon State College, 1946-49,' Reel 7, OSUSFR; see also W.A. Davies, 'History of Forest Engineering at Oregon State College,' ibid.; W.F. McCulloch to A.L. Strand, 6 Sept. 1952, Reel 6, ibid.

58 W.F. McCulloch, 'The Work and Education of Industrial Foresters in the Pacific Northwest,' *JF* 45 (Nov. 1947): 784; N.S. Rogers to Chief Forester, 24 Aug. 1946, Box 8, OSDFR, OSA; 'Forestry Conference Sets New Mark,' *TMN* 49 (Jan. 1948): 196; 'Forestry Senior Statistics,' *TMN* 50 (June 1949): 148.

59 W.D. Hagenstein to C. Wagner, 13 Sept. 1956, Box 34, Wagner Papers, UWL; Paul M. Dunn to C. Crow, 8 Mar. 1950, Reel 6, OSUSFR; 'University of Washington Graduates Employed by Weyerhaeuser,' n.d., Box 4, UWCFRR, Acc. 77-12; E. McPheeters to G. Marckworth, 6 Dec. 1963, ibid.; W. Burch to McCulloch, 19 Feb. 1962, Reel 10, OSUSFR; E.S. Sedlacek to McCulloch, 21 Apr. 1967; J.O. Rogers to McCulloch, 10 Jan. 1963, ibid.

60 F.D. Mulholland to A.C. Thrupp, 12 July 1935, Box 1, Empire Forestry Association Records, BCA; C.D. Schultz, 'The Future of the Forestry Undergraduate of Today,' *BCL* 32 (Feb. 1948): 61; Smith, *UBC Forestry,* 41.

61 Association of Professional Engineers in British Columbia, Minutes of the Ninth Meeting of the Council, 9 Nov. 1937, Reel A-1451, Association of Professional Engineers of British Columbia Records, BCA; 'Report of the Sub-Committee on Education,' *FC* 14 (June 1938):

44; 'Notes on the Annual Dinner Held at the Pacific Club,' 19 Apr. 1937, Box 1, Canadian Institute of Forestry, Vancouver Island Section Records, BCA (hereafter CIF-VISR); J.E. Liersch, 'Forestry Education in British Columbia,' *FC* 22 (Dec. 1946): 253.

62　C.D. Orchard to G.H. Prince, 4 Mar. 1947, Box 1, Chauncey D. Orchard Papers, BCA; F.D. Mulholland to E.G. Touzeau, 28 Apr. 1945, Box 1, F.D. Mulholland Papers, BCA; Orchard to D. Mansfield, 25 June 1947, Box 1, Orchard Papers; T.G. Wright to R. St. Clair, 18 June 1947, BCMFR, File 0154987-1; F.J.G. Johnson, 'Registered Foresters in British Columbia,' n.d., Box 8, Association of British Columbia Professional Foresters Records, BCA (hereafter ABCPFR).

63　Orchard to G.H. Barnes, 7 Oct. 1946, Box 2, Orchard Papers, BCA; 'University Expansion Plans Outlined,' *TMN* 46 (Nov. 1944): 16; H.J. Hodgins, 'A Professional Forester Looks at Forest Management Licences,' *BCL* 32 (Mar. 1948): 59; Gordon Sloan, *Report of the Commissioner Relating to the Forest Resources of British Columbia* (Victoria: King's Printer 1945), 155-6.

64　Liersch, 'Forestry Education in British Columbia,' 253-60; see also D.G. Griffith, 'Panel Discussion on Forest Education,' 15 Jan. 1963, Box 2, CIF-VISR, BCA; 'Forestry at U.B.C.,' *Blueprint* 4 (Mar. 1946): 42.

65　'Forestry Raised to Full Faculty at University of British Columbia,' *BCL* 34 (July 1950): 89; Smith, *UBC Forestry*, 19-20, 37, 47; G.S. Allen, 'Report to the Royal Commission on Forests and Forestry, 1955,' Box 9, British Columbia, Commission on Forest Resources Records, 1955, BCA (hereafter GR668); Lowell Besley, 'A Dean's Opinion After Five Years,' *BCL* 37 (Apr. 1953): 78; J.P. Tessier, 'Forestry Courses,'*TL* 19 (May 1963): 39-40.

66　See Sheldon Krimsky, 'The New Corporate Identity of the American University,' *Alternatives* 14 (May/June 1987): 20-9.

67　Roland D. Craig, 'Forest Surveys in Canada,' *FC* 11 (Sept. 1935): 27; see also L.D. Lloyd and S.J. Mammano, 'A Review of Advancements Made in Forest Mapping and Cruising,' *WCL* 69 (Aug. 1942): 34-6; C.D. Schultz, 'The Forester in Private Practice in British Columbia,' *FC* 24 (Sept. 1948): 222-5.

68　Arnold W. Petzold, 'Intensive Management of Established Second Growth,' *PWFCA* (1956), 37; Fred J. Sandoz, 'An Analysis of Industrial Forestry,' *JF* 44 (Aug. 1946): 546; W.B. Greeley, 'Forestry Background of the Pacific Northwest,' *JF* 48 (Mar. 1950): 163.

69　Charles E. Twinning, 'Weyerhaeuser and the Clemons Tree Farm: Experimenting with a Theory,' in *History of Sustained-Yield Forestry: A Symposium*, ed. Harold K. Steen (Durham: Forest History Society 1984), 37-9; Gordon Godwin, 'Inspection of Forest Practices in the State of Washington,' 1939, 4-7, BCMFR, File 037941; Charles E. Twinning, *Phil Weyerhaeuser: Lumberman* (Seattle: University of Washington Press 1985), 88-9; Ralph W. Hidy, Frank Ernest Hill, and Allan Nevins, *Timber and Men: The Weyerhaeuser Story* (New York: Macmillan 1963), 493; D.S. Jeffers to T.T. Munger, 4 Apr. 1933, Box 14, UWCFRR, Acc. 70-1; Winkenwerder to J. Kittredge, 16 Nov. 1935, Box 8, ibid.; George L. Drake, 'Machinery and Methods,' *TMN* 39 (Oct. 1938): 329.

70　'Commercial Logging Companies of Western Washington and Oregon Forced to Liquidate or Sell Out to Manufacturers, 1943-1945,' Box 2, Pacific Northwest Loggers Association Records, University of Washington Libraries (hereafter PNWLAR, UWL); Robert Spector, *Family Trees: Simpson's Centennial Story* (Bellevue: Documentary Book Publishers Corporation 1990), 69-70, 83; George Drake to Winkenwerder, 9 Oct. 1941, Box 12, UWCFRR, Acc. 70-1; Drake to Winkenwerder, 21 Dec. 1944, Box 31, ibid.

71　Godwin, 'Inspection of Forest Practices,' 8; C. Wagner to E.G. Griggs II, 1 Nov. 1950, Box 86, Wagner Papers, UWL; Wagner to Griggs, 23 Nov. 1953, Box 88, ibid.

72　O. Harry Schrader, 'New Developments in the Forest Products Industries,' *JF* 48 (June 1950): 425-8; MacKay, *Empire of Wood*, 174; 'CZ Records Progress in Integration,' *BCL* 41 (Apr. 1957): 74; Don McColl, 'Fact Finding and Analysis in the Development of Timber Management Plans,' *FC* 25 (Sept. 1949): 196.

73　T. Wright to E.H. Garman, 25 Aug. 1951, BCMFR, File 0190786.

74　Percy M. Barr, 'Management of Western Forest Lands as a Permanent Business,' *TMN* 47 (Sept. 1946): 39.

75　Stuart Moir, 'Aerial Forest Mapping,' *JF* 30 (Mar. 1932): 336-9; T.D. Merrill to R.D. Merrill, 27 Jan. 1928, Box 64, MRR, Acc. 726, UWL; F.D. Mulholland, 'British Columbia's Forest

Resources and State Forests,' *FC* 11 (Dec. 1935): 312; Robert W. Cowlin, 'Federal Forest Research in the Pacific Northwest: The Pacific Northwest Research Station,' (unpublished manuscript, copy in the possession of the author), 38. In 1938 this research facility was renamed the Pacific Northwest Forest and Range Experiment Station. Henceforth I will refer to the station by its correct title at any given time.

76 'Praise for Aerial Forest Maps,' *WCL* 68 (Dec. 1941): 45; Kendall B. Wood, 'Practical Aerial Logging Engineering,' *LH* 10 (1950), 55; C.L. Tebbe to N.S. Rogers, 27 Jan. 1945, Box 8, OSDFR, OSA; F.S. McKinnon to K. Shaw, 18 Sept. 1942, GR 1441, Reel B3230, File 04170, BCA; W. Hall to F.S. McKinnon, 17 June 1947, ibid.; Stuart Moir, 'Air Surveys in Logging and Forestry,' *LH* 6 (1946), 89.

77 'Precision Aerial Mapping,' *TMN* 48 (Aug. 1947): 78, 80; 'Cruising and Mapping by Plane Back,' *TMN* 49 (Aug. 1948): 55-7; K.B. Wood to J.K. Pearce, 5 May 1949, Box 1, Pearce Papers, UWL; 'Surveys,' *FC* 23 (June 1947): 179-82; 'New Air Survey Firm Established in City,' *BCL* 23 (June 1949): 49; 'A Tree in 3-D,' *Weyerhaeuser Magazine* 5 (May 1953): 10-1.

78 G. Marckworth to Arthur B. Langlie, 25 Apr. 1949, Box 2, UWCFRR, Acc. 77-12; 'Submission to the Royal Commission on Forestry, British Columbia, by Columbia Cellulose Ltd,' Feb. 1956, Box 13, GR 668, BCA; British Columbia Forest Products, Ltd., 'Working Plan No. 2 of Maquinna Tree Farm Licence No. 22,' 3 Oct. 1961, 17, 22, Box 1, BC Forest Service, Lake Cowichan Ranger District Records, GR 1062, BCA; 'Forestry Department Meeting, St. Paul and Tacoma Lumber Co.,' 7 Apr. 1955, Box 89, Wagner Papers, UWL; J.K. Pearce to J.D. Jenkins, 19 Mar. 1952, Box 1, Pearce Papers, UWL; I. Liimatta to Pearce, 13 June 1952, ibid.

79 Lyle C. Trorey, 'Commercial Air Survey,' *Blueprint* 7 (Feb. 1949): 30; see R.W. Wilson, 'Controlled Forest Inventory by Aerial Photography,' *TMN* 51 (Feb. 1950): 42-3, 98; Floyd A. Johnson, 'Estimating Forest Areas for Large Tracts,' *JF* 48 (Aug. 1950): 341; W.L. Johnson, 'Comparative Accuracy and Cost of Topographic Mapping by Ground and Air Survey Methods,' *BCL* 35 (May 1951): 114, 147; McColl, 'Fact Finding,' 197-8; K. Meredith to J.K. Pearce, 1951, Box 1, Pearce Papers, UWL.

80 G. Marckworth to R.C. Cowlin, 27 Nov. 1946, Box 14, UWCFRR, Acc. 70-1; Marckworth to S. Spurr, 18 Sept. 1947, Box 10, ibid.; 'Aerial Survey Course Being Offered,' *TMN* 50 (Feb. 1949): 116; 'Foresters Attend OSC Short Course,' *BCL* 34 (May 1950): 116; S.G. Ready to W.F. McCulloch, 28 Dec. 1962, Reel 15, OSUSFR; 'Students Attending Short Course in Photogrammetry,' 24 Mar. 1952, Box 6, UWCFRR, Acc. 77-12.

81 A.M. Nelson, 'The Towill Photo-Contour Map,' *FC* 34 (Sept. 1958): 319; Herb Lambert, 'Session Accents "How and Why" Plus "Do's and Don'ts" in Skyline Operations,' *Forest Log* 101 (Mar. 1974): 58 (hereafter *FL*); see also H.E. Stevens, 'Locating and Surveying,' *BCL* 47 (Oct. 1963): 35; W.S. Latta, 'Field Layout for Skyline Logging,' *Proceedings of the Skyline Logging Symposium* (Vancouver 1976), 133-4.

82 'This Firm Chose the Service Type of Organization,' *TMN* 58 (13 Dec. 1957): 38-40; C. Joergensen to F.M. Knapp, 4 Feb. 1959, Box 17, ABCPFR, BCA.

83 'Simpson Maintains Many Inventories,' *TMN* 58 (13 Dec. 1957): 57; 'Computers, Helicopters in CZ's Future,' *FL* 92 (Feb. 1965): 114; Grant Ainscough, 'New Developments in Working Plans in British Columbia,' *PWFCA* (Vancouver 1965), 110; 'Stock Taking Set for Tree Farm,' *Crown Zellerbach News* 8 (Sept. 1964): 1-2; 'How Computers Work in Timber-Based Companies,' *FL* 94 (Oct. 1967): 34-5; Cowlin, 'Federal Forest Research,' 157; Spector, *Family Trees*, 117.

84 Paul F. Ehringer, 'Markets and Management,' *Western Forester* 13 (Nov. 1967): 1-2; W.F. McCulloch to J.B. Craig, 19 July 1965, Reel 5, OSUSFR; see also Boyd Rasmussen, 'Computerized Forestry – The Incipient Necessity,' *Western Forester* 12 (June 1967): 1, 3; 'News Release,' 7 Dec. 1960, Reel 12, OSUSFR; 'Timber Yields Estimated From Math Models and a Computer,' *FL* 93 (Feb. 1966): 58-9; Rosemary Neering, 'Make-Believe Forests,' *BCL* 52 (Jan. 1968): 74-5; Harry E. Morgan, 'On Management and Utilization: The Age of System Forestry,' *PWFCA* (Portland 1971), 37.

85 'Computer Figures Coordinates,' *FL* 35 (Nov. 1965): 4; *BCL* 52 (Jan. 1968): 21; *FL* 97 (Oct. 1970): 64-5; Doyle Burke, 'Running Skylines Reduce Access Road Needs, Minimize Harvest Site Impact,' *FL* 102 (May 1975): 46; see also Hilton H. Lyons, 'Skyline Design Problems to be Computerized,' *Western Forester* 16 (Apr. 1971): 14.

86 G. Glen Young and Daniel Z. Lemkow, 'Digital Terrain Simulators and their Application to Forest Development Planning,' *Proceedings of the Skyline Logging Symposium* (Vancouver 1976), 81-99.

87 John Sessions, 'Training the Logging Specialist,' in *Proceedings of the Skyline Logging Symposium* (Vancouver 1976), 144; Brian W. Kramer, 'High Technology: The Logging Industry's Future,' in *Proceedings of the Fifth Northwest Skyline Symposium*, ed. Doyle Burke, C. Mann, and P. Schiess (Seattle: University of Washington College of Forest Resources 1982), 1-3; Young and Lemkow, 'Digital Terrain Simulators,' 98; F.P. Garrison, 'Data Required for Planning Skyline Shows,' *Proceedings of the Skyline Logging Symposium*, 139.

88 George W. Brown, 'Forest Engineering Education: Where the Action Is,' *JF* 75 (Feb. 1977): 74.

89 C.D. Orchard, 'The Function of the State in the Management of Crown and Private Forests for the Production of an Assured Supply of Wood for Industry,' *FC* 22 (June 1946): 102.

90 See Robert Zussman, 'The Middle Levels: Engineers and the "Working Middle Class,"' *Politics and Society* 13 (1984): 217-52.

91 Judson Clark, 'The Place of Logging Engineering in Logging,' *WL* 12 (Nov. 1915): 15; Minot Davis, 'Just What Do We Mean By A Logging Engineer,' *WCL* 42 (1 Apr. 1972): 36.

92 Daniel Nelson, *Frederick W. Taylor and the Rise of Scientific Management* (Madison: University of Wisconsin Press 1980), 137; Paul Thompson and David McHugh, *Work Organizations: A Critical Introduction* (London: MacMillan 1990), 64-5; Judith Merkle, *Management and Ideology: The Legacy of the International Scientific Management Movement* (Berkeley: University of California Press 1980), 67.

Part 2: Introduction

1 Robbins, *Lumberjacks and Legislators*; H.V. Nelles, *The Politics of Development: Forests, Mines and Hydro-Electric Power in Ontario, 1891-1941* (Toronto: Macmillan 1974); Gray, 'The Government's Timber Business'; Hirt, *A Conspiracy of Optimism*; Langston, *Forest Dreams, Forest Nightmares*; Graeme Wynn, *Timber Colony: A Historical Geography of Early Nineteenth Century New Brunswick* (Toronto: University of Toronto Press 1981); William M. Parenteau, 'Forest and Society in New Brunswick: The Political Economy of the Forest Industries' (Ph.D. thesis, University of New Brunswick 1994).

2 See James Weinstein, *The Corporate Ideal in the Liberal State, 1900-1918* (Boston: Beacon Press 1968); Gabriel Kolko, *The Triumph of Conservatism: A Reinterpretation of American History, 1900-1916* (New York: Free Press 1963).

3 For discussion of this approach see David A. Gold, Clarence Y.H. Lo, and Eric Olin Wright, 'Recent Developments in Marxist Theories of the Capitalist State,' *Monthly Review* 27, 5 (1975): 29-43; 6 (1975): 36-51; Theda Skocpol, 'Bringing the State Back In: Strategies of Analysis in Current Research,' in *Bringing the State Back In*, ed. Peter B. Evans, Dietrich Rueschmeyer, and Theda Skocpol (Cambridge: Cambridge University Press 1985), 3-37; Gregory Albo and Jane Jensen, 'A Contested Concept: The Relative Autonomy of the State,' in *The New Canadian Political Economy*, ed. Wallace Clement and Glen Williams (Montreal: McGill-Queen's University Press 1989), 180-211.

4 Fred Block, 'The Ruling Class Does Not Rule: Notes on the Marxist Theory of the State,' *Socialist Revolution* 33 (1977): 6-28; Leo Panitch, 'The Role and Nature of the Canadian State,' in *The Canadian State*, ed. Leo Panitch (Toronto: University of Toronto Press 1977), 4-27; Claus Offe, 'The Theory of the Capitalist State and the Problem of Policy Formation,' in *Stress and Contradiction in Modern Capitalism: Public Policy and the Theory of the State*, eds. Leon N. Lindberg, Robert Alford, Colin Crouch, and Claus Offe (Toronto: D.C. Heath 1975), 125-44.

5 Ted Schrecker, 'Resisting Environmental Regulation: The Cryptic Pattern of Business-Government Relations,' in *Managing Leviathan: Environmental Politics and the Administrative State*, ed. Robert Paehlke and Douglas Torgerson (Peterborough: Broadview Press 1990), 165-99; Joel Nokev and Karen Kampen, 'Sustainable or Unsustainable Development? An Analysis of an Environmental Controversy,' *Canadian Journal of Sociology* 17 (1992): 249-73.

6 See, for example, Patrick McGuire, 'Instrumental Class Power and the Origin of Class-Based State Regulation in the U.S. Electric Utility Industry,' *Critical Sociology* 16 (Summer/Fall 1989): 181-203.

7 See L. Anders Sandberg, 'Introduction,' in *Trouble in the Woods: Forest Policy and Social Conflict in Nova Scotia and New Brunswick,* ed. L. Anders Sandberg (Fredericton: Acadiensis Press 1992), 2.
8 R.L. Johnson, 'Management License Practice,' *BCL* 37 (May 1953): 87.
9 Stanley Aronowitz, *Science as Power: Discourse and Ideology in Modern Society* (Minneapolis: University of Minnesota Press 1988), 293; see also David Dickson, *The New Politics of Science* (New York: Pantheon Books 1984), 314.

Chapter 3: Clearcutting, Forest Science, and Regulation
1 Hays, *Conservation and the Gospel of Efficiency,* 2.
2 Ibid., 363; for an example of Pinchot's rhetoric see Gifford Pinchot, *The Fight For Conservation* (Seattle: University of Washington Press 1967).
3 Nelles, *The Politics of Development,* 2-44; R. Brian Woodrow, 'Resources and Policy-Making at the National Level: The Search for Focus,' in *Resources and the Environment: Policy Perspectives for Canada,* ed. O.P. Dwivedi (Toronto: McClelland and Stewart 1980), 27-9.
4 Nelles, *The Politics of Development,* 491-2; L. Anders Sandberg, ed., *Trouble in the Woods: Forest Policy and Social Conflict in Nova Scotia and New Brunswick* (Fredericton: Acadiensis Press 1992); Richard A. Rajala, 'The Receding Timber Line: Forest Practice, State Regulation, and the Decline of the Cowichan Lake Timber Industry,' in Peter Baskerville ed., *Canadian Papers in Business History* 2 (1993), 179-210.
5 Rogers, *Bernard Edward Fernow,* 127-8; A.P. Pross, 'The Development of Professions in the Public Service: The Foresters in Ontario,' *Canadian Public Administration* 10 (Sept. 1967): 379.
6 Earle H. Clapp, 'The Interdependence of Utilization and Silviculture,' *JF* 24 (Mar. 1926): 230.
7 I am indebted to William Robbins for this point.
8 I.W. Bailey and H.A. Spoehr, *The Role of Research in the Development of Forestry in North America* (New York: Macmillan 1929), 32.
9 Axel J.F. Brandstrom, *Analysis of Logging Costs and Operating Methods in the Douglas Fir Region* (Seattle: Charles Lathrop Pack Forestry Foundation 1933), 7; White, *Land Use, Environment, and Social Change,* 88-91; Leo A. Isaac, *Reproductive Habits of Douglas Fir* (Washington, DC: Charles Lathrop Pack Forestry Foundation 1943), 10; William G. Robbins, 'The "Luxuriant Landscape": The Great Douglas Fir Bioregon,' *Oregon Humanities* (Winter 1990): 4; Robert Bunting, 'Abundance and the Forests of the Douglas-Fir Bioregion, 1840-1920,' *Environmental History Review* 18 (Winter 1994): 44-6; Bunting, *The Pacific Raincoast,* 144-5; Langston, *Forest Dreams,* 82.
10 E.H. Garman and P.M. Barr, 'A History Map Study in British Columbia,' *FC* 6 (Dec. 1930): 14-5.
11 Clary, *Timber and the Forest Service,* 190.
12 Burt P. Kirkland, 'The Need of a Vigorous Policy of Encouraging Cutting on the National Forests of the Pacific Coast,' *Forestry Quarterly* 9 (Sept. 1911): 376; Thornton T. Munger, 'Lectures Delivered at the University of Washington on Silvics, Planting and Reconnaissance' (13-20 Feb. 1911, University of Washington College of Forest Resources Library), 22.
13 G. Pinchot to District Forester, 2 Mar. 1909, Box 14, RG 95, US Forest Service, District Historical Files (hereafter RG 95, DHF), US National Archives and Records Service, Pacific Northwest Region (hereafter NARS-PNW).
14 E.E. Carter to E.T. Allen, 18 Apr. 1909, Box 14, RG 95, DHF, NARS-PNW; Allen to The Forester, 20 Apr. 1909, ibid.; Carter to Allen, 10 May 1909, ibid.
15 E.T. Allen, 'A Study of the Red Fir,' 1903, 77, US Forest Service, Timber Management Files, RG 095 -54A-0111, Box 59862, NARS-PNW.
16 Ibid., 21-3.
17 'Reports of Offices in District Office, District 6, Fiscal Year 1911,' 29, RG 95, Box 1, Regional Office, Portland Inspections, NARS-PNW; Clary, *Timber and the Forest Service,* 34-6; Langston, *Forest Dreams,* 98-113.
18 Associate Forester to G.A. Coleman, 2 Jan. 1908, RG 095-54A-0111, Box 59854, NARS-PNW; B.P. Kirkland, 'Silvical Report, Washington National Forest,' Apr. 1908, Box 59861, ibid.; W.H. Gibbons, 'Olympic National Forest Silvical Report,' 8 Dec. 1910, ibid.

19   Robert W. Cowlin, 'Federal Forest Research in the Pacific Northwest: The Pacific Northwest Research Station,' (unpublished manuscript), 10-1; Samuel T. Dana, 'Experiment Stations on the National Forests,' *Proceedings of the Society of American Foresters* 4 (1909): 23.
20   Arthur R. Wilcox, 'Forest Reproduction in Wind River Valley,' 1908, 11-2, RG 095-54A-0111, Box 59858, NARS-PNW.
21   Kirkland, 'Silvical Report,' 5-6.
22   E.T. Clark, 'Snoqualmie National Forest,' Technical Report for the Quarter ending Dec. 31, 1908, 'Management of Douglas Fir in the Northwest,' RG 095-54A-0111, Box 59862, NARS-PNW; see also Burt P. Kirkland, 'Working Plans for National Forests of the Pacific Northwest,' *Proceedings of the Society of American Foresters* 6 (1911): 16-35.
23   H.S. Graves to G.P. McCabe, 3 Nov. 1911, Box 14, RG 95, DHF, NARS-PNW.
24   G.P. McCabe to H.S. Graves, 20 Nov. 1911, ibid.; G.H. Cecil to The Forester, 29 Feb. 1912, ibid.
25   W.B. Greeley to G.H. Cecil, 14 Mar. 1912, ibid.
26   W.B. Greeley, 'National Forest Sales on the Pacific Coast,' *Proceedings of the Society of American Foresters* 7 (1912): 48-9; W.B. Greeley, 'Reforestation on the National Forests,' *Proceedings of the Society of American Foresters* 8 (Oct. 1912): 264-71; David A. Cameron, 'The Silverton Nursery: An Early Experiment in Pacific Northwest Reforestation,' *Journal of Forest History* 23 (July 1979): 122-9.
27   T.T. Munger, 'Silvical Problems of the Northwest, Address at the Supervisor's Meeting, Portland, Oregon,' 21-26 Mar. 1910, Box 8, RG 95, DHF, NARS-PNW; Munger, 'Lectures Delivered at the University of Washington,' 12; 'Report of Offices,' 37; Ivan Doig, *Early Forestry Research: A History of the Pacific Northwest Forest and Range Experiment Station* (US Department of Agriculture 1977), 4.
28   George T. Morgan, Jr., 'Conflagration as Catalyst: Western Lumbermen and American Forest Policy,' *Pacific Historical Review* 47 (1978): 169-74; Robert E. Ficken, 'Gifford Pinchot Men: Pacific Northwest Lumbermen and the Conservation Movement, 1902-1910,' *Western Historical Quarterly* 13 (Apr. 1982): 165-74; Widner, *Forests and Forestry*, 173-4; Charles S. Cowan, *The Enemy is Fire!* (Seattle: Superior Publishing Company 1961), 38.
29   Morgan, 'Conflagration as Catalyst,' 174-80; Ficken, 'Gifford Pinchot Men,' 173-5; Widner, *Forests and Forestry*, 165-9; Harold K. Steen, 'Forestry in Washington to 1925' (Ph.D. thesis, University of Washington 1969), 171.
30   Dana, *Forest and Range Policy*, 182-4; William G. Robbins, *American Forestry: A History of National, State, and Private Cooperation* (Lincoln: University of Nebraska Press 1985), 53-5; Cowan, *The Enemy is Fire!*, 42.
31   E.H. MacDaniels, *A Decade of Progress in Douglas Fir Forestry* (Seattle: Joint Committee on Forest Conservation 1943), 48; Ficken, 'Gifford Pinchot Men,' 177-8.
32   E.T. Allen, *Practical Forestry in the Pacific Northwest* (Portland: Western Forestry and Conservation Association 1911), 46.
33   Munger, 'Lectures Delivered at the University of Washington,' 21-3; Amelia R. Fry, *Thornton T. Munger: Forest Research in the Pacific Northwest, An Interview Conducted by Amelia R. Fry* (Berkeley: University of California Regional Oral History Office 1967), 66.
34   Gray, 'The Government's Timber Business,' 25; Taylor, *Timber*, 50.
35   Jamie Swift, *Cut and Run: The Assault on Canada's Forests* (Toronto: Between the Lines 1983), 58-9; Taylor, *The Heritage*, 100.
36   A. Haslam to F.J. Fulton, 31 July 1909, Box 1, BC, Records of the Royal Commission on Timber and Forestry, 1909-1910, GR 271, BCA; N. Humphreys to R.E. Gosnell, 27 Sept. 1909, ibid.; R.J. Skinner to Fulton, 31 Aug. 1909, ibid.
37   W.I. Patterson to P. Ellison, 7 Jan. 1910, ibid.; *Final Report of the Royal Commission of Inquiry on Timber and Forestry* (Victoria 1910), 58-65; Gray, 'The Government's Timber Business,' 27-8; MacKay, *Empire of Wood*, 33-5; R. Peter Gillis and Thomas R. Roach, *Lost Initiatives*, 146-50. For discussion of the McBride administration see Barman, *The West Beyond the West*, 177-81; Martin Robin, *The Rush for Spoils: The Company Province, 1871-1933* (Toronto: McClelland and Stewart 1972), 87-98.
38   H.R. MacMillan, 'Present Condition of Applied Forestry in Canada,' *Proceedings of the Society of American Foresters* 10 (Apr. 1915): 126-8; Overton W. Price, 'Progress in British Columbia,' *American Forestry* 20 (1914): 273.

39 Thornton T. Munger, 'Minimum Requirements Report: Provisional Draft Submitted for Criticism of Cooperators,' 5 Dec. 1922, 16, University of Washington College of Forest Resources Library.
40 R.Y. Stuart, 'Memorandum for the Chief Forester,' 12 Aug. 1916, Box 14, RG 95, DHF, NARS-PNW.
41 David M. Smith, 'Even-Age Management: Concept and Historical Development,' in *Even-Age Management, Proceedings of a Symposium Held August 1, 1922,* ed. Richard K. Hermann and Denis P. Lavender (Corvalis: Oregon State University, School of Forestry 1973), 9.
42 Western white pine was known to have the capacity for delayed germination at this time; see Isaac, *Reproductive Habits of Douglas Fir,* 25.
43 C.D. Howe, *The Reproduction of Commercial Species in the Southern Coastal Forests of British Columbia* (Ottawa: Commission on Conservation 1915), 117; C.D. Howe, 'Address Delivered Before B.C. Forest Club,' *Proceedings of the British Columbia Forest Club* 2 (1916): 86; 'Summary of Report of C.D. Howe on the Condition of Reproduction of Commercial Species in the Coastal Region of British Columbia,' BC Ministry of Lands and Parks Records, Reel 442, File 065342, Ministry of Lands and Parks, Lands Management Branch (hereafter BCMLPR).
44 Amelia R. Fry, *Leo A. Isaac: Douglas Fir Research in the Pacific Northwest, 1920-1956* (Berkeley: University of California Regional Oral History Office 1967), 65-6.
45 J.V. Hoffman, 'The Establishment of a Douglas Fir Forest,' *Ecology* 1 (1920): 51; see also J.V. Hoffman, 'How to Obtain a Second Crop of Douglas Fir,' *TMN* 23 (Mar. 1921): 90-1; J.V. Hoffman, *Natural Regeneration of Douglas Fir in the Pacific Northwest* (Washington, DC: US Department of Agriculture 1924).
46 F.E. Ames to G. Quayle, 11 Dec. 1920, Box 11, UWCFRR, Acc. 70-1; Munger, 'Minimum Requirements Report,' 8.
47 Henry S. Graves, 'Private Forestry,' *JF* 17 (Feb. 1919): 113-21.
48 See Henry S. Graves, 'A National Lumber and Forest Policy,' *JF* 17 (Apr. 1919): 351-60; Henry S. Graves, 'A National Forest Policy: The Proposed Legislation,' *American Forestry* 25 (Aug. 1919): 1281-2; H.S. Graves to R.S. Kellogg, 29 May 1919, Box 11, UWCFRR, Acc. 70-1.
49 Robbins, *Lumberjacks and Legislators,* 93; H. Winkenwerder to H.S. Graves, 2 Apr. 1919, Box 11, UWCFRR, Acc. 70-1; Everett G. Griggs, 'A Lumberman's Viewpoint,' *American Forestry* 25 (Sept. 1919): 1340-1.
50 R.S. Kellogg to H.S. Graves, 21 June 1919, Box 11, UWCFRR, Acc. 70-1; R.S. Kellogg, 'A Discussion of Methods,' *American Forestry* 25 (Aug. 1919): 1282; Robbins, *Lumberjacks and Legislators,* 93-4.
51 George T. Morgan, *William B. Greeley: A Practical Forester* (St. Paul: Forest History Society 1961), 39-40; Clepper, *Professional Forestry,* 138.
52 'Forest Devastation: A National Danger and a Plan to Meet It,' *JF* 17 (Dec. 1919): 923; Gifford Pinchot, 'The Lines Are Drawn,' *JF* 17 (Dec. 1919): 899-900.
53 Ralph S. Hosmer, 'The Society of American Foresters: An Historical Summary,' *JF* 38 (Nov. 1940): 844-5.
54 See William G. Robbins, 'Lumber Production and Community Stability: A View From the Pacific Northwest,' *Journal of Forest History* 31 (Oct. 1987): 189.
55 W.B. Greeley, 'Self-Government in Forestry,' *JF* 18 (May 1920): 103-5.
56 Gifford Pinchot, 'National or State Control of Forest Devastation,' *JF* 18 (Feb. 1920): 106-9; Burt P. Kirkland, 'The Democracy of National Control,' *JF* 18 (May 1920): 449-50.
57 Gifford Pinchot, 'Where We Stand,' *JF* 18 (May 1920): 442.
58 Robbins, *Lumberjacks and Legislators,* 98; Morgan, *William B. Greeley,* 41-3; W.B. Greeley to District Foresters, 18 June 1920, RG 095-54A-0111, Box 59854, NARS-PNW.
59 W.B. Greeley, 'How Shall We Secure Reforestation,' 1920, RG 095-54A-0111, Box 59854, NARS-PNW.
60 'Keeping Our Tree Lands at Work,' *TMN* 21 (Aug. 1920): 29; Greeley, *Forests and Men,* 105; W.B. Greeley to L.C. Boyle, 8 Jan. 1921, Box 1, RG 95, US Forest Service, State and Private Forestry Division Records, NARS-PNW (hereafter RG 95, SPFDR).
61 Dana, *Forest and Range Policy,* 214-5; Robbins, *Lumberjacks and Legislators,* 99; Ficken, *The Forested Land,* 165; W.B. Greeley, 'Message From the Chief Forester,' *TMN* 22 (Dec. 1920): 113; Greeley, *Forests and Men,* 103; E.T. Allen, 'Federal Legislation,' *TMN* 22 (Dec. 1922): 113.

62   Robbins, *Lumberjacks and Legislators*, 101-3; Morgan, *William B. Greeley*, 46-50.
63   'The Capper Forestry Bill,' *TMN* 22 (May 1921): 29; Steen, *The U.S. Forest Service*, 185; Greeley, *Forests and Men*, 104-5.
64   W.B. Greeley, 'What National Forest Policy Asks of States and Industry,' *PWFCA* (1922), 10.
65   Ibid., 11.
66   Munger, 'Minimum Requirements Report,' 13-8, 31.
67   H. Winkenwerder to W.B. Greeley, 1 Dec. 1922, Box 11, UWCFRR, Acc. 70-1; see also Winkenwerder to E.T. Clark, 11 Jan. 1923, Box 45, ibid.
68   W.B. Greeley to H. Winkenwerder, 11 Jan. 1923, Box 12, UWCFRR, Acc. 70-1; Winkenwerder to Greeley, 9 Feb. 1923, ibid.
69   Robbins, *American Forestry*, 92-3; Steen, *The U.S. Forest Service*, 185.
70   Greeley, *Forests and Men*, 107; Morgan, *William B. Greeley*, 55.
71   'Forest Figures for the Pacific Coast States, Jointly Compiled and Endorsed by the State, Private and Federal Agencies in California, Oregon, Washington, Idaho and Montana for the Senate Select Committee on Reforestation,' (Unpublished Report 1923), 1-2.
72   George W. Peavy, *Oregon's Commercial Forests: Their Importance to the State* (Salem: State Printing Department 1922), 23; H. Winkenwerder, 'Forestry Materials for Howard A. Hanson,' 1922, Box 52, UWCFRR, Acc. 70-1.
73   W.B. Greeley to District Forester, 20 Oct. 1924, Box 29, RG 95, SPFDR, NARS-PNW; G.H. Cecil to The Forester, 21 Feb. 1924, ibid.
74   Julius Kummel, 'Devastated Forest Lands in the Douglas Fir Region,' 15 Feb. 1924, RG 095-54A-0111, Box 59858, NARS-PNW; Dana, *Forest and Range Policy*, 221-4.
75   C.M. Grainger, 'The Business Man's Part in Forest Conservation,' *TMN* 26 (Oct. 1925): 200.
76   Greeley, *Forests and Men*, 110; Morgan, *William B. Greeley*, 45-58; Cox, *This Well-Wooded Land*, 212; Robbins, *Lumberjacks and Legislators*, 109-11.
77   H.R. MacMillan, 'Present Condition of Applied Forestry in Canada,' *Proceedings of the Society of American Foresters* 10 (Apr. 1915): 128; M.A. Grainger to E.H. Clapp, 16 May 1919, BCMLPR, Reel 1213, File 09579; G.M. McVickar, 'Memorandum to the Chief Forester,' 10 Apr. 1919, BC Department of Lands and Forestry Records, Reel B3230, File 04170, BCA (hereafter GR 1441); P.M. Barr, 'Summary of Forest Research in British Columbia, 1921-1927,' Sept. 1927, ibid.
78   'Reforestation in British Columbia,' *TMN* 23 (Jan. 1922): 53; P.Z. Caverhill, 'Forestry Problems in British Columbia,' *JF* 20 (Jan. 1922): 50; B.C., *Report of the Forest Branch of the Department of Lands* (Victoria 1923), 16; R.C. St. Clair to F. Ames, 18 Oct. 1923, GR 1441, Reel B3531, File 051596, BCA.
79   T.T. Munger, 'Memo for Mr. Ames, Silvicultural Condition of Cut-Over Areas,' 19 Sept. 1972, Box 15, RG 95, DHF, NARS-PNW; P.Z. Caverhill to C.D. Howe, 26 Mar. 1923, GR 1441, Reel B3230, File 04170, BCA; see also BC, *Report of the Forest Branch of the Department of Lands* (Victoria 1924), 10.
80   BC, *Report of the Forest Branch of the Department of Lands* (Victoria 1924), 10; Chief Forester, 'Memorandum to the Minister of Lands,' 12 Nov. 1924, BCMLPR, Reel 442, File 065342; J.L. Alexander, 'Government Forest Research in British Columbia,' 1924, GR 1441, Reel 3531, File 051596, BCA; G.E. Stoodley to Chief Forester, 26 Oct. 1925, ibid.; P.Z. Caverhill to E.H. Finlayson, 21 Apr. 1925, ibid.; P.Z. Caverhill, 'B.C. Forest Administration,' *TMN* 28 (Feb. 1927): 161.
81   E.C. Manning to P.Z. Caverhill, 13 Mar. 1924, GR 1441, Reel B3532, File 051597; Chief Forester to the Minister of Lands, 8 Oct. 1923, ibid., Reel B3531, File 051596; P.M. Barr to A.H. Richardson, 1 Sept. 1927, ibid., Reel B3230, File 04170, BCA.
82   Doig, *Early Forestry Research*, 4-5; Robert W. Cowlin, 'Federal Forest Research in the Pacific Northwest: The Pacific Northwest Research Station,' (unpublished manuscript), 20-1; Amelia R. Fry, *Thornton T. Munger: Forest Research in the Pacific Northwest, An Interview Conducted by Amelia R. Fry* (Berkeley: University of California Regional Oral History Office 1967), 173-4; 'Minutes of the First Meeting of the Advisory Council of the Pacific Northwest Forest Experiment Station,' 12 Feb. 1926, Box 13, UWCFRR, Acc. 70-1.
83   T.T. Munger, 'Outline of the Subject of Natural Reproduction of Douglas Fir,' 15 May 1926, GR 1441, Reel B3531, File 051596, BCA; T.T. Munger to Forest Supervisor, 22 May 1926, Box 13, UWCFRR, Acc. 70-1.

84 E.T. Allen, 'Pacific Coast Forestry Research,' GR 1441, Reel B3531, File 051596, BCA; E.T. Allen, 'New Theory on Fir Reproduction,' *TMN* 26 (May 1925): 212; 'Forest Management Conference, Research Sessions,' *PWFCA* (1925), 10.
85 'T.T. Munger Gives Official Views,' *PWFCA* (1925), 10; T.T. Munger, 'Recent Evidence Affecting Reforestation Theories: Paper for Annual Meeting of the West Coast Forestry Association at Victoria, B.C., Dec. 10, 1925,' 2, GR 1441, Reel B3531, File 051596, BCA; P.Z. Caverhill to G.M. Cornwall, 29 Apr. 1925, ibid.; J.L. Alexander to E.T. Allen, 27 Oct. 1925, ibid. Sociologists have noted that internal controversy over scientific findings is often masked when presented to the public. See Andrew Webster, *Science, Technology and Society: New Directions* (New Brunswick: Rutgers University Press 1991), 25.
86 Leo A. Isaac, 'Life of Douglas Fir Seed in the Forest Floor,' *JF* 33 (1935), 62.
87 J.L. Alexander, 'Silvicultural Investigation in B.C., Paper Read at the Meeting of the Canadian Society of Forest Engineers, Vancouver, 27 Oct. 1926,' 4, BC Ministry of Forests Library; C.K. Flemming to J.K. Alexander, 28 Feb. 1927, GR 1441, Reel B3531, File 051596, BCA; Alexander to Flemming, 8 Mar. 1927, ibid.
88 Amelia R. Fry, *Leo A. Isaac: Douglas Fir Research in the Pacific Northwest, 1920-1956* (Berkeley: University of California Regional Oral History Office 1967), 66-7; L.A. Isaac, 'Destiny of Douglas Fir Seeds That Fail in the Virgin Forests,' *Forest Research Notes* (Pacific Northwest Forest Experiment Station, 3 Jan. 1931), 4-5; Isaac, 'Life of Douglas Fir Seed,' 61-6. On the resistance to 'intellectual deviation' within the scientific community see M.J. Mulkay, 'Sociology of the Scientific Research Community,' in *Science, Technology and Society: A Cross Disciplinary Perspective,* ed. Ina Spiegel-Rosing and Derek de Solla Price (Beverly Hills: Sage Publications 1977), 104-8.
89 Fry, *Leo A. Isaac,* 64-5; Doig, *Early Forestry Research,* 9; T.T. Munger, 'Restocking Habits: Fir Types,' *PWFCA* (1926), 6; T.T. Munger to J.L. Alexander, 8 Jan. 1927, GR 1441, Reel B3531, File 051596, BCA; Leo A. Isaac, 'Seed Flight in the Douglas Fir Region,' *JF* 28 (1930), 492-9.
90 T.T. Munger, 'Statement for Advisory Council of the Pacific Northwest Forest Experiment Station,' 6 Feb. 1928, GR 1441, Reel B3531, File 048525; A.E. Pickford to P.M. Barr, 3 Nov. 1927, ibid., Reel B3230, File 04170, BCA; A.E. Pickford, 'Studies of Seed Dissemination in British Columbia,' *FC* 5 (1929), 8-16; Fry, *Leo A. Isaac,* 69.
91 Leo Isaac, 'The Survival of Douglas Fir Seed Trees,' *Forest Research Notes* (Pacific Northwest Forest Experiment Station 27 June 1930), 1-2.
92 Leo A. Isaac and Howard G. Hopkins, 'The Forest Soil of the Douglas Fir Region, and Changes Wrought Upon it By Logging and Slash Burning,' *Ecology* 18 (1937): 264-79.
93 'Survival of One-Year Old Douglas Fir Seedlings,' *Forest Research Notes* (Pacific Northwest Forest Experiment Station 1 Nov. 1928), 3; see also Alexander, 'Silvicultural Investigation,' 3-4.
94 Thornton T. Munger, 'A Brief Summary of Timber Growing and Logging Practice in the Douglas Fir Region,' 1927, 2, File 0103410, BCMFR; John B. Woods, 'What is Private Forestry in the Pacific Northwest,' 2 (paper presented to the North Pacific Section, Society of American Foresters, Portland), Box 53, UWCFRR, Acc. 70-1.
95 G.P. Melrose to Lands Department, Esquimalt and Nanaimo Railway Co., 22 May 1924, GR 1441, Reel B3531, File 051596; P.M. Barr to P.Z. Caverhill, 26 Feb. 1928, ibid., Reel B3230, File 04170, BCA; P.M. Barr, 'An Outline of the Work of the Research Division of the British Columbia Forest Service During 1928,' ibid.; BC, *Report of the Forest Branch of the Department of Lands* (Victoria 1929), 12; P.Z. Caverhill to C.M. Grainger, 19 Sept. 1927, GR1441, Reel B3515, File 048525, BCA.
96 K. Carlisle, 'Report on Early Timber Sales in Vancouver District,' 17 Sept. 1928, BCMFR, File 077546; P.M. Barr to R.C. St. Clair, 24 Oct. 1928, BCMLPR, Reel 442, File 065342.
97 E.H. Garman and P.M. Barr, 'A History Map Study in British Columbia,' *FC* 6 (Dec. 1930): 14-22; see also P.M. Barr, 'Forest Research in British Columbia,' *BCL* 14 (Feb. 1930): 72.
98 F.S. McKinnon and T. Wells, *The Green Timbers Forestry Station and Forest Tree Nursery: A Brief Review of its Purpose and Development* (Victoria: King's Printer 1943), 4; P.M. Barr to J.M. Gibson, 10 Jan. 1930, GR 1441, Reel B3230, File, 04170, BCA; C.J. Buck to F.H. Lamb, 27 May 1930, Box 33, RG 95, SPFDR, NARS-PNW.

99 Cowlin, 'Federal Forest Research,' 29; E.N. Munns to P.M. Barr, 5 Dec. 1928, GR 1441, Reel B3230, File 04170; P.M. Barr to P.Z. Caverhill, 19 Mar. 1929, ibid., BCA; Ralph Schmidt, *The History of Cowichan Lake Research Station* (Victoria: BC Ministry of Forests 1992), 4-5.
100 Gray, 'The Government's Timber Business,' 24.
101 William G. Robbins, *Hard Times in Paradise: Coos Bay, Oregon, 1850-1986* (Seattle: University of Washington Press 1988), 53; Williams, *Americans and Their Forests*, 325; Richard Rajala, *The Legacy and the Challenge: A Century of the Forest Industry at Cowichan Lake* (Victoria: Lake Cowichan Heritage Advisory Committee 1993), 49.
102 P.Z. Caverhill to J.R. Dickson, 17 Oct. 1929, File 306313-2, BCMFR.
103 C.M. Grainger to The Forester, 14 Jan. 1925, Box 1, RG 95, SPFDR, NARS-PNW; Steen, *The U.S. Forest Service*, 195.
104 C.M. Grainger to R.Y. Stuart, 24 Jan. 1929, Box 1, RG 95, SPFDR, NARS-PNW.
105 On the American context see Ellis Hawley, 'Herbert Hoover, the Commerce Secretariat, and the Vision of an Associative State,' *Journal of American History* 61 (June 1974): 116-40; Ellis Hawley, 'Three Facets of Hooverian Associationalism: Lumber, Aviation, and Movies, 1921-1930,' in *Regulation in Perspective: Historical Essays*, ed. Thomas K. McCraw, (Cambridge: Harvard University Press 1981), 95-123; Grant McConnell, *Private Power and American Democracy* (New York: Alfred A. Knopf 1966), 64-9. On the Canadian pattern of business-government relations during the 1920s see John Herd Thompson and Allen Seager, *Canada, 1922-1939: Decades of Discord* (Toronto: University of Toronto Press 1985), 76-103; Tom Traves, *The State and Enterprise: Canadian Manufacturers and the Federal Government, 1917-1931* (Toronto: McClelland and Stewart 1979).

Chapter 4: Depression-Era Forestry

1 Ficken, *The Forested Land*, 177-80.
2 Ficken, *The Forested Land*, 183-5; Richard Lowitt, *The New Deal and the West* (Bloomington: Indiana University Press 1984), 73-4.
3 Robbins, *Lumberjacks and Legislators*, 155-7; Ficken, *The Forested Land*, 185-6.
4 Axel J.F. Brandstrom, 'An Estimate of the Economic Effect of Selective Logging in the Douglas Fir Region,' 10 Nov. 1931, RG 095-54A-0111, Box 59858, NARS-PNW; J. Greenman to C.S. Keith, 4 Dec. 1931, Box 9, OAR, UOA.
5 Axel J.F. Brandstrom, 'Relief of Financial Stress in Pacific Northwest Logging Operations,' *University of Washington Forest Club Quarterly* 6 (1927): 5-29.
6 Axel J.F. Brandstrom, 'Case Study Demonstrating the Industrial Opportunity for Private Forestry in the Pacific Northwest,' n.d., RG 095-54A-0111, Box 59858, NARS-PNW; Brandstrom, 'Relief of Financial Distress,' 16-7.
7 Burt P. Kirkland, 'Nation-Wide Solution of Forest Production Problems of the United States,' *JF* 28 (Apr. 1930): 430-5; David T. Mason, 'The Redwoods: What Factors Have Favored or Retarded the Private Practice of Forestry in the Douglas Fir and White Pine Regions by Comparison with the Redwood Region,' *JF* 26 (Mar. 1928): 347-51; David T. Mason, 'Selective Logging and its Application in the Douglas Fir Region,' *TMN* 30 (Oct. 1929): 38-42. See also C.A. Lyford, 'Memorandum Re Application of Economic Selection to the Conversion of Standing Timber in the Douglas Fir Region,' 27 Aug. 1930, Box 17, RG 95, DHF, NARS-PNW.
8 W.B. Greeley, 'The Outlook for Timber Management by Private Owners,' *JF* 31 (Feb. 1933): 212.
9 Fred Ames, 'Selective Logging on the National Forests of the Douglas Fir Region,' *JF* 29 (May 1931): 768.
10 Ames, 'Selective Logging,' 769-74.
11 'Kirkland and Brandstrom Leave University of Washington to Study Selective Logging,' *JF* 29 (May 1931): 826-7; T.T. Munger to H. Winkenwerder, 24 Mar. 1931, Box 12, UWCFRR, Acc. 70-1; 'Minutes of the Seventh Annual Meeting of the Forest Research Council of the Pacific Northwest,' 9 Mar. 1935, Box 54, ibid.
12 'Committee Reports, Region 6, Approved by the Portland Meeting of Forest Supervisors and Comments by the Regional Forester,' 30 Nov.-12 Dec. 1931, Box 8, RG 95, DHF, NARS-PNW; Cowlin, 'Federal Forest Research,' 36-9; George L. Drake, 'Tractor Logging Costs in the Douglas Fir Region,' *TMN* 33 (Nov. 1931): 92.

13 A.J.F. Brandstrom, 'Flexibility in Logging Makes Economic Selection Practical and Profit-able,' *WCL* 60 (Mar. 1933): 13-4; R.Y Stuart to C.J. Buck, 5 Aug. 1932, Box 17, RG 95, DHF, NARS-PNW; R.Y. Stuart, 'National Forest Timber and the West Coast Lumber Industry,' *JF* 31 (Jan. 1933): 49.
14 'Future Douglas Fir Logging: A Review of the Brandstrom Report, A Document Well Worth Study by the Fir Logger,' *WCL* 60 (Nov. 1933): 22.
15 O.F. Ericson, 'Memorandum for FM,' 16 Jan. 1933, Box 17, RG 95, DHF, NARS-PNW; C.J. Buck to The Forester, 18 Oct. 1932, RG 095-54A-0111, Box 59858, NARS-PNW.
16 'A Letter to Foresters,' *JF* 28 (Apr. 1930): 456-8; Clepper, *Professional Forestry*, 142.
17 Robert Marshall, *The Social Management of American Forests* (New York: League for Industrial Democracy 1930), 10, 26.
18 Ibid., 28-35.
19 R.S. Kellogg, 'As I See It,' *JF* 28 (Apr. 1930): 461-2; F.W. Reed, 'Is Forestry a Religion,' ibid., 462-4; Clepper, *Professional Forestry*, 145.
20 'Contributed by Pacific Northwest Forest Experiment Station, – Special – Copeland Resolu-tion,' 5-6, 26 Sept. 1932, RG 095-54A-0111, Box 59858, NARS-PNW.
21 Ibid., 9.
22 Ward Shepard, 'Forestry Leadership,' *JF* 31 (Oct. 1933): 631-3; Robbins, *Lumberjacks and Legislators*, 169-70; Dana, *Forest and Range Policy*, 244-5.
23 William G. Robbins, 'The Great Experiment in Industrial Self-Government: The Lumber Industry and the National Recovery Administration,' *Journal of Forest History* 25 (July 1981): 130-1.
24 Kim McQuaid, *Big Business and Presidential Power: From FDR to Reagan* (New York: William Morrow 1982), 26-7.
25 McQuaid, *Big Business*, 27-9; see also Ellis Hawley, *The New Deal and the Problem of Monopoly* (Princeton: Princeton University Press 1968); Nicolas Spulber, *Managing the American Economy from Roosevelt to Reagan* (Bloomington: Indiana University Press 1989), 13.
26 Ficken, *The Forested Land*, 196; Robbins, 'The Great Experiment,' 134; Greeley, *Forests and Men*, 134.
27 Robbins, 'The Great Experiment,' 135; Clary, *Timber and the Forest Service*, 97; Dana, *Forest and Range Policy*, 225.
28 Robbins, 'The Great Experiment,' 137; Steen, *The U.S. Forest Service*, 199; Greeley, *Forests and Men*, 210.
29 Dana, *Forest and Range Policy*, 256; 'Article 10 Conferences,' *WCL* 61 (Feb. 1934): 11.
30 'West Coast Lumber Bulletin,' 20 Mar. 1934, Box 13, PNWLAR, UWL; 'Code Enthusiasti-cally Endorsed,' *WCL* 61 (Mar. 1934): 16.
31 'New Reforestation, Sustained Yield and Conservation Ideas Commencing to Take Definite Form,' *WCL* 61 (Apr. 1934): 20-4.
32 'Comments on the Brandstrom Report,' *WCL* 60 (Dec. 1933): 20-2; J. Greenman to C.S. Keith, 4 Dec. 1933, Box 13, OAR, UOA.
33 'Progress on Article X,' *TMN* 35 (Apr. 1934): 9; 'Recommendations of General Meeting to Discuss Rules of Forest Practice,' 19 Apr. 1934, vol. 160, WCLAR, OHSA.
34 C.S. Chapman to C.J. Buck, 10 Apr. 1934, Box 13, PNWLAR, UWL.
35 J.D. Tenant to A.L. Collins, 3 Mar. 1934, Box 1, Pearce Papers, UWL; E.T. Clark to H. Winkenwerder, 6 Apr. 1934, Box 13, PNWLAR, UWL; 'Article Ten Personnel,' *WCL* 61 (May 1934): 11; Joint Committee on Forest Conservation, Minutes of Meeting, 28 May 1934, vol. 160, WCLAR, OHSA; Greeley, *Forests and Men*, 135.
36 R. Mills, 'Report of Divisional Forester, Joint Committee on Forest Conservation,' 30 July 1934, vol. 160, WCLAR, OHSA; 'Logging with Weyerhaeuser at Longview,' *WCL* 61 (May 1934): 6; Twinning, *Phil Weyerhaeuser*, 117-8.
37 John B. Woods, 'Forest Rules in the Douglas Fir Region,' *TMN* 36 (Nov. 1934): 42; Joint Committee on Forest Conservation, Minutes of Meeting, 23 Oct. 1935, vol. 160, WCLAR, OHSA; R. Mills, 'Progress in the West Coast Division Under the Conservation Section of the Lumber Code,' 9 Mar. 1935, ibid.
38 Ficken, *The Forested Land*, 206.

39 Clary, *Timber and the Forest Service*, 97-8; Dana, *Forest and Range Policy*, 97-8; R. Mills, 'Report of Divisional Forester, Joint Committee on Forest Conservation,' 22 Mar. 1935, vol. 160, WCLAR, OHSA.

40 F.A. Silcox, 'Foresters Must Choose,' *JF* 33 (Mar. 1935): 198-204.

41 Elwood Wilson, 'Report of the Meeting of the Society of American Foresters, Washington, D.C., Jan. 28, 29, 30, 1935,' *FC* 11 (Feb. 1935): 40-2; F.A. Silcox, 'Forestry – A Public and Private Responsibility,' *JF* 33 (May 1935): 461.

42 A Statement of Objectives and a Program of Activities of the Joint Conservation Committee, West Coast Lumbermen's Association and Pacific Northwest Loggers Association, 1935, vol. 160, WCLAR, OHSA.

43 J.B. Woods and W.G. Tilton, 'Program of Work Under Direction of the Joint Committee on Forest Conservation,' 30 June 1936, vol. 160, WCLAR, OHSA; Robbins, *Lumberjacks and Legislators*, 206; 'Western Forestry and Conservation Association Annual Meeting,' *JF* 34 (Feb. 1936): 107-10.

44 C.J. Buck to The Forester, 4 Oct. 1934, Box 17, RG 95, DHF, NARS-PNW; Buck to Forest Supervisors, 16 Oct. 1934, Box 19, ibid.

45 E.E. Carter to Buck, 20 Oct. 1934, Box 17; Carter to Buck, 29 Oct. 1934, Box 15; Buck to The Forester, 22 Nov. 1934, ibid.

46 Carter to Buck, 6 Dec. 1934, Box 17; Buck to The Forester, 10 Dec. 1934, Box 19, ibid.

47 Burt P. Kirkland and Axel J.F. Brandstrom, *Selective Timber Management in the Douglas Fir Region* (Seattle: Charles Lathrop Pack Forestry Foundation 1936), 115-6.

48 Amelia R. Fry, *Leo A. Isaac: Douglas Fir Research in the Pacific Northwest, 1920-1956* (Berkeley: University of California Regional Oral History Office 1967), 90; Amelia R. Fry, *Thornton T. Munger: Forest Research in the Pacific Northwest, An Interview Conducted by Amelia R. Fry* (Berkeley: University of California Regional Oral History Office 1967), 123-5; Doig, *Early Forestry Research*, 13.

49 Fred Ames, 'Comments on Brandstrom's Bulletin,' 29 Jan. 1935, Box 17, RG 95, DHF, NARS-PNW; B.E. Hoffman, 'Comments on Brandstrom's Bulletin,' 30 Jan. 1935, ibid.

50 Buck to The Forester, 9 Feb. 1935, ibid.

51 Buck to The Forester, 5 Apr. 1935, ibid.

52 Cowlin, 'Federal Forest Research,' 58; Kirkland and Brandstrom, *Selective Timber Management*, i-ii.

53 C.S. Cowan to P.Z. Caverhill, 3 Apr. 1935, File 0103410, BCMFR; T.T. Munger to E.C. Manning, 5 Aug. 1936, ibid.; see also Ralph C. Hawley, 'Professional Honesty as Regards Selective Logging,' *JF* 34 (Feb. 1936): 136-8; Joint Committee on Forest Conservation, Minutes of Meeting, 9 Oct. 1935, vol. 160, WCLAR, OHSA; F.D. Mulholland, 'Notes From Meeting of Forest Research Council, Portland,' 4 Mar. 1936, GR 1441, Reel B3515, File 048525, BCA.

54 N.L. Wright, 'Memorandum Regarding Progress of Selective Logging in Region Six,' 13 May 1936, Box 17, RG 95, DHF, NARS-PNW; 'Digest Report,' Region 6 Supervisors' Conference, 11-19 Mar. 1937, Box 8, ibid.; E.J. Hanzlik, 'Memorandum for Forest Supervisor,' 21 June 1937, RG 095-54A-0111, Box 59854, NARS-PNW.

55 Thornton T. Munger, 'Statement for Advisory Council, Forest Management Research,' 21 June 1939, Box 13, UWCFRR, Acc. 70-1; 'Tree Selection Logging,' *WCL* 64 (Mar. 1937): 34-5; 'Minutes of the Joint All-Day Meeting of the Columbia River and Puget Sound Sections, Society of American Foresters,' 7 May 1938, Box 2, SAF-PSSR, UWL.

56 George L. Drake, 'The Douglas Fir Logger Looks at Selective Logging,' *JF* 34 (July 1936): 705-7.

57 Paul K. Conklin, *The New Deal* (Arlington Heights: AHM Publishing 1975), 69-71.

58 Clary, *Timber and the Forest Service*, 103-6.

59 Robbins, *American Forestry*, 131-3; Greeley, *Forests and Men*, 212.

60 G.D. Cook to Regional Forester, 6 Oct. 1936, Box 29, RG 95, SPFDR, NARS-PNW; H.A. Haefner, 'Report Showing the Character of Management of Private Cut-Over Lands as Requested by the Forester's Letter of Oct. 6, 1936,' 5 Nov. 1936, ibid.; C.J. Buck to Chief, Forest Service, 9 Nov. 1936, ibid.

61 W.B. Osborne, 'Memorandum, Forest Practice Rules,' 27 Nov. 1936, ibid.

62 H.L. Plumb, 'Memorandum for Files,' 5 Feb. 1927, ibid.; B.E. Hoffman, 'Memorandum for SP,' 4 Dec. 1936, ibid.

63 E.W. Tinker to Regional Forester, 16 Sept. 1937, ibid.; W.S. Tilton to C.J. Buck, 6 May 1937, ibid.; F.H. Brundage to Forest Supervisor, 15 July 1937, ibid.

64 E.W. Tinker, 'Memorandum for The Chief,' 16 Sept. 1937, ibid.

65 C.J. Buck to Chief, Forest Service, 23 Oct. 1937, ibid.; Buck to C. Martin, 26 Oct. 1937, ibid.; C.O. Lindh, 'Brief of Meeting of Forest Practice Committees,' 5-6 Nov. 1937, ibid.; see also William G. Robbins, 'The Social Context of Forestry: The Pacific Northwest in the Twentieth Century,' *Western Historical Quarterly* 16 (1985): 45.

66 Dana, *Forest and Range Policy*, 276; 'Forest Policies and Practices Aired,' *WCL* 65 (Jan. 1938): 38; John B. Woods, 'The Chief Forester's Report,' *JF* 36 (Mar. 1938): 335-7; 'U.S. Forester Says Public Regulation of Private Forests is Essential,' *WCL* 65 (Mar. 1938): 9.

67 C.O. Lindh, 'Report on Cooperative Forest Practice Meeting,' 27 Jan. 1938, Box 8, OSDFR, OSA.

68 Joint Committee on Forest Conservation, Minutes of Meeting, 16 Feb. 1938, vol. 160, WCLAR, OHSA; Dana, *Forest and Range Policy*, 276.

69 'West Has Splendid Record of Forestry Achievement,' *WCL* 65 (Aug. 1938): 21; 'Be Careful,' *WCL* 65 (Sept. 1938): 7; Robbins, *Lumberjacks and Legislators*, 225.

70 Joint Committee on Forest Conservation, Minutes of Meeting, 15 July 1938, vol. 160, WCLAR, OHSA; Roderic Olzendam, 'Freedom and Unity: A Philosophy of Action for Private and Public Forest Enterprise,' *WCL* 65 (Oct. 1938): 8-10, 50-5; Clyde S. Martin, 'What Woods Practices are Necessary for the Development of Private Forestry,' *JF* 37 (June 1939): 465-70; W.S. Tilton, 'Progress of Private Forestry in the Douglas Fir Region,' *JF* 38 (Feb. 1940): 136-7; William B. Greeley, 'Forty Years of Forest Conservation,' *JF* 38 (May 1940): 386-9.

71 C.J. Buck to Forest Supervisors, 24 June 1938, Box 29, RG 95, SPFDR; J.P. Hough, 'Report on Forest Practice on Private Lands Within Protective Boundary,' 28 July 1938, ibid.; Paul H. Logan, 'Memorandum for Regional Forester,' 4 Oct. 1938, ibid.

72 E.J. Hanzlik, 'Report on Forestry Practices of Private Operators Adjacent to the Olympic National Forest,' 2 Sept. 1938, ibid.

73 W.B. Osborne, 'Report Regarding Lumber Companys' Compliance with Forest Practice Rules,' 31 Aug. 1938, ibid.; F.H. Brundage, 'Memorandum for DP,' 6 Dec. 1938, ibid.

74 G. Godwin, 'Inspection of Forest Practices in the State of Washington,' 1, BCMFR, File 037941.

75 Ibid., 4-5.

76 Ibid., 8; Don Hammerquist, 'Timber is a Crop?' *Timber Worker*, 16 Apr. 1938, 6.

77 Godwin, 'Inspection of Forest Practices,' 7; 'The Low Highlead,' *WCL* 64 (Dec. 1937): 16-7; L.R. Olson, 'Memo for Files,' 20 Nov. 1937, Box 29, RG 95, SPFDR, NARS-PNW.

78 Olson, 'Memo for Files.'

79 John Boettinger, 'Ickes Praises N.W. Selective Logging Work,' *Seattle Post-Intelligencer*, 26 Aug. 1938; 'Clearcutting and Forest Regeneration,' ibid., 10 Oct. 1938; W.B. Greeley to J. Boettinger, 12 Oct. 1938, Box 13, PNWLAR, UWL.

80 'Western Loggers Discuss Problems,' *WCL* 65 (Nov. 1938): 8; Norman G. Jacobson, 'Cutting Practices in the Mixed Douglas Fir, Hemlock and Cedar Forests of the Pacific Northwest,' *JF* 38 (Sept. 1940): 690; Charles O. Marston, 'Are Loggers Foresters?' *WCL* 66 (Mar. 1939): 21; C. Wagner to Minot Davis, 4 Oct. 1940, Box 4, Wagner Papers, UWL.

81 Thornton T. Munger, 'The Silviculture of Tree Selection Cutting in the Douglas Fir Region,' *University of Washington Forest Club Quarterly* 12 (1938-1939): 6.

82 Ibid., 12-3.

83 Fry, *Leo A. Isaac*, 88; Fry, *Thornton T. Munger*, 126-7; Cowlin, 'Federal Forest Research,' 82-4.

84 Leo A. Isaac, 'Progress Report on Silvicultural Condition of West Fork Logging Company, Permanent Sample Plot,' 26 May 1939, Box 22, RG 95, SPFDR, NARS-PNW; 'Minutes of Meeting of the Forest Research Council,' 19 Sept. 1939, GR 1441, Reel B3515, File 048525, BCA; 'Minutes of Superintendent's Meeting, Experimental Station,' 9 Nov. 1939, Box 8, RG 95, DHF, NARS-PNW.

85 F.A. Silcox, 'A Federal Plan for Forest Regulation Within the Democratic Pattern,' *JF* 37 (Feb. 1939): 116-20; 'Silcox Meets Northwest Lumbermen,' *WCL* 66 (Aug. 1939): 15.

86 'Minutes of Supervisors' Meeting, State and Private Forestry,' 7 Nov. 1939, Box 2, RG 95, SPFDR, NARS-PNW.

87 Joint Committee on Forest Conservation, Minutes of Meeting, 4 Aug. 1939, vol. 160, WCLAR, OHSA.
88 Greeley, *Forests and Men*, 212; Society of American Foresters, Puget Sound Section, Minutes of Meeting, 2 Feb. 1940, Box 2, SAF-PSSR, UWL.
89 Robbins, *Lumberjacks and Legislators*, 228; Dana, *Forest and Range Policy*, 277.
90 Joint Committee on Forest Conservation, Minutes of Meeting, 20 Mar. 1940, vol. 160, WCLAR, OHSA; W.B. Greeley to the Board of Trustees, West Coast Lumbermen's Association, 15 Apr. 1940, Box 34, Wagner Papers, UWL.
91 Joint Committee on Forest Conservation, Minutes of Meeting, 10 June 1940, vol. 160, WCLAR, OHSA.
92 Ibid.; W.H. Tilton, 'Notes on the Proposed Forest Regulation Bill Submitted and Discussed by Mr. Earle Clapp, Acting Chief Forester at the Meeting of the Forest Industries Conference,' 27 June 1940, Box 34, Wagner Papers, UWL.
93 C. Wagner to F. Reed, Box 34, ibid.
94 See James T. Patterson, *Congressional Conservatives and the New Deal* (Lexington: University of Kentucky Press 1967); James T. Patterson, *The New Deal and the States* (Princeton: Princeton University Press 1969).

Chapter 5: Forest Practice Regulation

1 Jeremy Wilson, 'Forest Conservation in British Columbia, 1935-1985: Reflections on a Barren Political Debate,' *BC Studies* 76 (Winter 1987-8): 10.
2 Robin Fisher, *Duff Pattullo of British Columbia* (Toronto: University of Toronto Press 1991), 215.
3 Mackay, *Empire of Wood*, 110-2; Joseph C. Lawrence, 'Markets and Capital: A History of the Lumber Industry of British Columbia, 1778-1952' (M.A. thesis, University of British Columbia 1957), 136-8.
4 Taylor, *The Heritage*, 180-6; McKay, *Empire of Wood*, 113-8.
5 P.M. Barr to J.D. Curtis, 2 Apr. 1932, GR 1441, Reel B3230, File 04170, BCA; C.D. Orchard to J.H. White, 8 Oct. 1932, ibid.; P.M. Barr to F.D. Mulholland, 17 Oct. 1932, ibid.
6 J.R. Dickson, 'Summary of Timber Disposal Regulations and Cutting Conditions on Crown Lands in Canada, Showing Changes During 1930,' *FC* 7 (June 1931): 132; P.Z. Caverhill to H.I. Stevenson, 27 Jan. 1934, BCMFR, File 06313-2.
7 J. Piche to Minister of Works, 8 Oct. 1931, BCMFR, File 0103410; M.C. Ironside to S.F. Tolmie, 15 July 1933, ibid.
8 A.E. Parlow to Rangers and Supervisors, Vancouver Forest District, 13 June 1928, Box 1, Vancouver Forest District Records, BCA (hereafter GR 955); P.Z. Caverhill, 'Memorandum to the Honourable the Minister of Lands,' 31 Jan. 1934, BCMFR, File 0103410; A. Wells Gray to M.C. Ironside, 16 Feb. 1934, ibid.
9 'Logging Plan is Advocated,' *Victoria Daily Times*, 16 Mar. 1934, 5; 'B.C. Logging To Be Investigated,' ibid., 26 Mar. 1934, 15; 'High Lights and High Lead,' *BCL* 18 (May 1934): 11; M.C. Ironside to A. Wells Gray, 21 July 1934, BCMFR, File 0103410.
10 'Argues for New Logging Plan,' *Victoria Daily Times*, 19 Feb. 1935, 5.
11 E.W. Bassett, 'Brief Report on Selective Logging With Caterpillar Equipment in Vancouver Forest District and Some General Observations on Possible Future Policy,' Sept. 1934, BCMFR, File 0103410.
12 E.W. Bassett, 'Some General Observations on Present Selective Cutting on the Pacific Coast,' Nov. 1934, ibid.
13 G. Godwin to F.D. Mulholland, 17 May 1936, ibid.
14 'The Evolution of the Logging Tractor,' *BCL* 18 (Dec. 1934): 8-9; 'Says Huge Forest Revenue Available,' *Victoria Daily Times*, 20 Feb. 1935, 13. For a brief discussion of Paulik's association with the CCF see Irene Howard, *The Struggle For Social Justice in British Columbia: Helena Gutteridge, the Unknown Reformer* (Vancouver: UBC Press 1992), 177-80.
15 'Opinions Given on Selective Logging,' *Victoria Daily Times*, 28 Feb. 1935, 13; 'Doubts Value of Selective Logging,' *TMN* 36 (Mar. 1935): 56; 'Chief Forester Refutes Sensational Statements,' *BCL* 19 (Mar. 1935): 11; P.Z. Caverhill, 'Memorandum Re Suggestions of Mr. Paulik,' 25 Aug. 1934, Box 3, Premiers' Papers, BCA (hereafter GR 1222).

16 R.S. Stuart to Caverhill, 27 Feb. 1935, BCMFR, File 0103410; Caverhill to Minister, Feb. 1935, ibid.
17 'Selective Log Method Urged,' *Victoria Daily Times*, 8 Mar. 1935, 9; 'Selective Log Plan Studied,' ibid., 3 Apr. 1935, 15; Caverhill to C.S. Cowan, 29 Mar. 1935, BCMFR, File 0103410; 'Not Ready Yet For Selective Logging,' *Victoria Daily Times*, 13 Apr. 1935, 9; 'Log Methods Studied,' ibid., 7 June 1935, 18; 'The Chief Forester and Selective Logging,' *BCL* 19 (May 1935): 8.
18 R.A. Brown, 'The Forester's Viewpoint of Selective Logging,' *FC* 12 (Feb. 1936): 47.
19 A.P. Allison to T.D. Pattullo, 17 Dec. 1935, Box 10, GR 1222, BCA; Helen Akrigg Manning, 'Ernest C. Manning,' in *Manning Park Memories: Reflections of the Past* (Victoria: British Columbia Ministry of Lands and Parks 1991), 8; R.V. Stuart to E.C. Manning, 22 Jan. 1936, BCMFR, File 085886; 'Protect Seed Trees is Plan,' *Victoria Daily Times*, 5 Mar. 1936, 13.
20 E.C. Manning to E. Stamm, 17 July 1936, BCMFR, File 0103410; Manning to R.V. Stuart, 1 Oct. 1936, ibid.; 'Tractor Logging Growth in B.C.,' *WCL* 64 (Jan. 1937): 40.
21 E.C. Manning to C.S. Leary, 12 Sept. 1936, BCMFR, File 0103410.
22 E.C. Manning to the Minister of Lands, 5 Oct. 1936, BCMFR, File 053442-1.
23 'Copy of Evidence Given by the Chief Forester Before Forestry Legislative Committee,' 3 Nov. 1936, Box 19, British Columbia Records of the Commission on Forest Resources, 1943-1945, BCA (hereafter GR 520); 'Observations on Forestry Matters by F.B. Brown, Chairman, Board of Directors, B.C. Loggers Association, Before the Legislative Committee on Forestry,' 14 Nov. 1936, BCMFR, File 085886.
24 'Submitted on Behalf of Alberni Pacific Lumber Co., Elk River Timber Co., Canadian Western Lumber Co., Victoria Lumber and Manufacturing Co., Thomsen Clarke Timber Co., Malahat Logging Co., to Hon. T.D. Pattullo,' Nov. 1936, BCMLPR, File 0126878; 'New Timber Plan Made,' *Victoria Daily Times*, 20 Nov. 1936, 7.
25 E.C. Manning to G. Cornwall, 12 Mar. 1937, BCMLPR, Reel 1420, File 0126878; 'Report on Forestry Conference,' Mar. 1937, ibid.; BC, *Report of the Forest Branch for the Year Ending December 31, 1936* (Victoria 1937), L16.
26 R.C. St. Clair to Supervisors and Rangers, Vancouver Forest District, 23 Mar. 1937, Box 1, GR 955, BCA.
27 E.C. Manning, 'Memorandum to the Forestry Committee,' 28 Oct. 1937, BCMLPR, Reel 1420, File 0126878; see also 'Address by the Chief Forester to the Forestry Committee of the B.C. Legislature,' 2 Nov. 1937, Box 19, GR 520, BCA.
28 R. Pendleton to A. Wells Gray, 3 Nov. 1937, BCMLPR, Reel 1420, File 0126878; E.C. Manning, 'Memorandum to the Minister,' 5 Nov. 1937, ibid.
29 F.D. Mulholland, *The Forest Resources of British Columbia* (Victoria: King's Printer 1937), 75-7; D.L. McMullen, 'Esquimalt and Nanaimo Railway Land Grant: Survey and Recommendations for Improved Forest Practice' (BC Forest Branch, unpublished report, 1937), 1, 34.
30 E.C. Manning, 'Is B.C. to be Sea of Barren Hillsides,' *Victoria Daily Times*, 5 Nov. 1936, 1, Magazine Section; 'The Forest Situation,' *Cowichan Leader*, 30 Sept. 1937, 4; 'Land Grant on Island Scored,' *Victoria Daily Times*, 19 Nov. 1937, 16; Max Paulik, *The Truth About Our Forests* (Vancouver: Foresta Publishers 1937); 'Expert Throws Light on B.C.'s Forest Situation,' *Federationist*, 6 May 1937, 4; 'Delegation Asks Action on Forests,' *Cowichan Leader*, 18 Nov. 1937, 8.
31 C.D. Orchard to J.R. Dickson, 13 Dec. 1937, BCMFR, File 06313: 2; 'New Forest Legislation,' *BCL* 21 (Dec. 1937): 20; Colin Cameron, 'Forest Depletion is a Grave Problem,' *Federationist*, 16 Dec. 1937, 5; E.C. Manning, 'Memorandum to the Honourable the Minister of Lands,' 6 Dec. 1937, BCMLPR, Reel 1420, File 0126878; 'Forestry Plan is Passed by House,' *Victoria Daily Times*, 7 Dec. 1937, 5.
32 E.A. Hayes to T.D. Pattullo, 16 Feb. 1938, Box 142, GR 1222, BCA; W.W.R. Mitchell to Manning, 9 Dec. 1937, BCMLPR, Reel 1420, File 0126898; Manning to Mitchell, 10 Dec. 1937, ibid.; G.D. Curtis to Chief Forester, 6 Dec. 1937, ibid.; Manning to Curtis, 10 Dec. 1937, ibid.; C.C. Ternan, 'Development of State Forest Practice Laws: British Columbia,' *PWFCA* (1946), 27.
33 E.C. Manning to District Forester, Vancouver, 11 June 1938, GR 1441, Reel B3229, File 04104, BCA; F.D. Mulholland to R. Pendleton, 1 Feb. 1938, ibid.; Gordon Godwin, 'Progress

Report on Co-operation in Forest Practice with the Alberni-Pacific Lumber Company, Report No. 5,' Dec. 1938, GR 1441, Reel 4069, File 0134225, BCA.
34 'Patch Logging,' *WCL* 65 (Nov. 1938): 30; 'Clear Cutting Helps Reforestation,' *WCL* 66 (July 1939): 28.
35 Gordon Godwin, 'Progress Report on Co-operation in Forest Practice with Alberni-Pacific Lumber Co.,' 10 May 1938, BCMLPR, Reel 1420, File 0126878.
36 Gordon Godwin, 'Progress Report on Co-operation in Forest Practice with Alberni-Pacific Lumber Company, Report No. 4,' 5 Dec. 1939, GR 1441, Reel 4069, File 0134225, BCA.
37 Ibid.; D.L. McMullen to D. McColl, 1 Dec. 1941, BCMFR, File 0134075.
38 R.D. McTavish to A. Wells Gray, 13 Oct. 1938, BCMFR, File 0103410; D. Bennett to Forestry Department, 1938, ibid.; P. Thompsett to Wells Gray, 19 Nov. 1938, ibid.; G. Spencer to Wells Gray, 22 Nov. 1938, ibid.; S.W. Muncey to T.D. Pattullo, 24 Nov. 1938, Box 19, GR 1222, BCA.
39 'Resolution of the Synod of the Anglican Diocese of British Columbia,' 16 Feb. 1939, Box 29, GR 1222, BCA; Pattullo to H.E. Sexton, 18 Feb. 1939, ibid.; A. Hall to Pattullo, 6 Dec. 1938, Box 19, ibid.; Akrigg Manning, 'Ernest C. Manning,' 11.
40 E.C. Manning, 'Memo Re a Proposed Forestry Programme,' 12 Jan. 1940, BCMLPR, Reel 1420, File 0126878.
41 Akrigg Manning, 'Ernest C. Manning,' 13.

Chapter 6: State and Provincial Regulation
1 For a discussion of one example see Rajala, *The Legacy and the Challenge*, 84-136.
2 See Gordon Robinson, *The Forest and the Trees: A Guide to Excellent Forestry* (Covelo: Island Press 1988); Herb Hammond, *Seeing the Forest Among the Trees: The Case For Wholistic Forest Use* (Vancouver: Polestar 1991); Peter A. Robson, *The Working Forest of British Columbia* (Madeira Park: Harbour Publishing 1995).
3 Robert P. Conklin, 'Trends Toward Improved Cutting Practices on Private Land in the Douglas Fir Region,' *JF* 39 (Nov. 1941): 955; E.J. Hanzlik, 'Cutting Practices in the Douglas Fir Type,' *JF* 38 (Sept. 1940): 686-91; E.H. Clapp to Regional Foresters and Directors, 16 Dec. 1940, Box 29, RG 95, SPFDR; L.F. Watts to Chief, Forest Service, 28 Dec. 1940, ibid.
4 Gordon B. Anderson, 'Oregon's Forest Conservation Laws,' Part I, *American Forests* 83 (Mar. 1977): 54; see also Debra Jennifer Salazar, 'Political Processes and Forest Practice Legislation' (Ph.D thesis, University of Washington 1985), 63-4; Thomas C. Stacer, 'The Oregon Conservation Act,' *Willamette Law Journal* 2 (1962-3), 268-84; W.G. Tilton to Joint Committee on Forest Conservation, 16 Sept. 1940, Box 34, Wagner Papers, UWL.
5 Nelson S. Rogers, 'Who Shall Regulate Our Forests?' *JF* 40 (May 1940): 384-7.
6 'Comments by Burgess,' 8 Nov. 1940, Box 9, RG 95, SPFDR, NARS-PNW.
7 Oregon State Board of Forestry, Minutes of Meeting, 9 Nov. 1940, ibid.; L.F. Watts to G.T. Gerlinger, 15 Nov. 1940, ibid.; 'Re-Seeding Cut Over Lands,' *WCL* 64 (May 1937): 23.
8 Joint Committee on Forest Conservation, Minutes of Meeting, 11 Dec. 1940, vol. 160, WCLAR, OHSA; 'Forest Bills in Oregon,' *WCL* 68 (Feb. 1941): 62.
9 'New Oregon Forestry Legislation,' *TMN* 42 (Apr. 1941): 47; N.S. Rogers to A.G.T. Moore, 26 June 1941, Box 1, OSDFR, OSA; N.S. Rogers to A.G. Lawrence, 21 Oct. 1943, Box 2, ibid.; W.F. McCulloch, *Forest Practice in Oregon* (Salem: Oregon State Board of Forestry 1943), 59; N.S. Rogers to W.H. Horning, 14 Apr. 1941, Box 1, OSDFR, OSA.
10 C. Wagner to W.R. Morley, 4 Feb. 1941, Box 84, Wagner Papers, UWL.
11 C.H. Kreienbaum to C. Wagner, 11 Feb. 1941, ibid.
12 L.F. Watts to A.B. Langlie, 17 Feb. 1941, Box 55, UWCFRR, Acc. 70-1.
13 H. Winkenwerder to A.B. Langlie, 17 Feb. 1941, Box 76, ibid.; Puget Sound Section, Society of American Foresters, Minutes of Meeting, 7 Mar. 1941, Box 2, SAF-PSSR, UWL.
14 Dana, *Forest and Range Policy*, 277-9; Clepper, *Professional Forestry*, 153.
15 E.H. Clapp to Regional Foresters and Directors, 1 Apr. 1941, Box 29, RG 95, SPFDR, NARS-PNW; S.N. Wycoff to Assistant Chief, 5 Apr. 1941, ibid.; E.H. Brundage to Chief, 5 Apr. 1941, ibid.
16 E.H. Clapp to Regional Foresters, 16 June 1941, ibid.; M.L. Merritt to Chief, 26 June 1941, ibid.; R.W. Cowlin to Chief, 11 July 1941, ibid.

17 Dana, *Forest and Range Policy*, 279-80.
18 'Industry's Interest and Responsibility,' *WCL* 69 (Jan. 1942): 13; C. Martin to G. Marckworth, 3 Feb. 1942, Box 55, UWCFRR, Acc. 70-1; W.B. Greeley to Joint Committee on Forest Conservation, 18 Feb. 1942, Box 34, Wagner Papers, UWL.
19 Brandstrom, *Development of Industrial Forestry*, 19-20; Twinning, 'Weyerhaeuser and the Clemons Tree Farm,' 33-41.
20 Greeley, *Forests and Men*, 159; Joint Committee on Forest Conservation, Minutes of Meeting, 22 Oct. 1943, vol. 160, WCLAR, OHSA; Hidy, Hill, and Nevins, *Timber and Men*, 505.
21 Brandstrom, *Development of Industrial Forestry*, 21; 'The Tree Farm Program in the Douglas Fir Region of Washington and Oregon,' 15 Mar. 1943, vol. 169, WCLAR, OHSA; Joint Committee on Forest Conservation, Minutes of Meeting, 22 Oct. 1943, ibid.; C. Wagner to E. McGowan, 2 Mar. 1943, Box 16, Wagner Papers, UWL.
22 Joint Committee on Forest Conservation, Minutes of Meeting, 1 May 1941, 4 Sept. 1941, vol. 160, WCLAR, OHSA; 'Industry to Establish Huge Tree Nursery,' *WCL* 68 (Oct. 1941): 58; F.S. McKinnon to C.D. Orchard and G. Melrose, 17 Dec. 1943, GR 1441, Reel B3230, File 04170, BCA.
23 H.H. Chapman, 'Forest Regulation, as Treated in the Report of the Chief of the Forest Service, 1941,' *JF* 40 (June 1942): 421; W.B. Greeley to Newspaper Editors and Publishers, 23 July 1942, Box 2, OSDFR-OSA; Steen, *The U.S. Forest Service*, 235-6; Clepper, *Professional Forestry*, 156-7; E.H. Clapp to Regional Foresters and Directors, Forest Experiment Stations, 7 Aug. 1942, Box 29, RG 95, SPFDR, NARS-PNW; L.F. Watts to Chief, 30 Sept. 1942, ibid.
24 'Memorandum for Governor Langlie,' 20 Feb. 1942, Box 55, UWCFRR.
25 H.J. Andrews to G. Marckworth, 21 Apr. 1942, ibid.
26 'Minutes of the Meeting of the Forest Advisory Committee,' 8 May 1942, Box 66, Arthur B. Langlie Papers, University of Washington Libraries; H.J. Andrews to G. Marckworth, 15 May 1942, Box 55, UWCFRR, Acc. 70-1; 'Report on Forest Practices,' 27 May 1942, ibid.
27 Washington Section, Joint Committee on Forest Conservation, Minutes of Meeting, 5 Nov. 1942, vol. 160, WCLAR, OHSA; C. Martin to H. Jones, 9 Nov. 1942, Box 55, UWCFRR, Acc. 70-1.
28 A.B. Langlie to N.S. Rogers, 7 Dec. 1942, Box 2, OSDFR, OSA; Washington Section, Joint Committee on Forest Conservation, Minutes of Meeting, 16 Dec. 1942, vol. 160, WCLAR, OHSA; Wagner to M. Deggeller, 22 Dec. 1942, Box 34, Wagner Papers, UWL.
29 Oregon Section, Joint Committee on Forest Conservation, Minutes of Meeting, 8 Dec. 1942, vol. 160, WCLAR, OHSA; see also W.F. McCulloch, 'Forest Production Without Forest Destruction,' *WCL* 70 (Feb. 1943): 51-2.
30 W.F. McCulloch to W.B. Greeley, 15 Dec. 1942, Box 2, OSDFR, OSA; Oregon State Board of Forestry, Minutes of Meeting, 16 Jan. 1943, Box 9, RG 95, SPFDR, NARS-PNW.
31 'Oregon's New Forestry Laws Summarized,' *WCL* 70 (June 1943): 63; N.S. Rogers to C.F. Korstian, 17 Mar. 1943, Box 2, OSDFR, OSA; N.S. Rogers, 'Development of Forest Practice Laws in Oregon,' *PWFCA* (1946), 23.
32 N.S. Rogers to H.J. Andrews, 10 Mar. 1945, Box 9, RG 95, SPFDR, NARS-PNW.
33 British Columbia, Royal Commission on Forestry, 1944-1945, Transcripts, p. 1924; W.F. McCulloch to J. Greenman, 12 May 1943, Box 2, OSDFR, OSA; W.F. McCulloch to R.S. Taylor, 9 May 1944, ibid.
34 Washington Section, Joint Committee on Forest Conservation, Minutes of Meeting, 4 Mar. 1943; Oregon Section, Joint Committee on Forest Conservation, Minutes of Meeting, 12 Mar. 1943, WCLAR, OHSA.
35 Isaac, *Reproductive Habits of Douglas Fir*, 93-5.
36 Washington Section, Joint Committee on Forest Conservation, Minutes of Meeting, 16 Dec. 1942, vol. 160, WCLAR, OHSA.
37 L.F. Watts to Regional Foresters and Experiment Station Directors, 13 May 1943, Box 2, RG 95, SPFDR, NARS-PNW.
38 Lyle Watts, 'Comprehensive Forest Policy Indispensable,' *JF* 41 (Nov. 1943): 783-8.
39 Emanuel Fritz, 'Dangers in Federal Control,' *JF* 41 (Dec. 1943): 850-1; G.F. Jewett, 'Why I Oppose Federal Regulation,' *JF* 42 (Aug. 1944): 483-8; Wilson Compton, 'Private Enterprise Offers Better Opportunity for Progress in Forestry Than Nationalization,' *JF* 41 (Nov. 1943):

788-91; Samuel T. Dana, 'Forestry Legislation in the States in 1943,' *JF* 41 (Aug. 1943): 560; Samuel T. Dana, 'States' Rights or States' Responsibilities,' ibid., 548.

40 Joint Committee on Forest Conservation, Minutes of Meeting, 27 Jan. 1944, vol. 160, WCLAR, OHSA; Steen, *The U.S. Forest Service*, 251-2.

41 Robbins, 'Lumber Production and Community Stability,' 194-6; see also David A. Clary, 'What Price Sustained Yield? The Forest Service, Community Stability, and Timber Monopoly Under the 1944 Sustained-Yield Act,' *Journal of Forest History* 31 (Jan. 1987): 4-18.

42 D. Denman to C. Wagner, 7 Aug. 1944, Box 84, Wagner Papers, UWL; Wagner to Denman, 9 Aug. 1944, ibid.; Brandstrom, *Industrial Forestry*, 21.

43 M.S. Lowden to Files, 11 Nov. 1943, Box 30, RG 95, SPFDR, NARS-PNW; 'Notes to Accompany Status of Management Statistics,' 20 Nov. 1945, Box 22, ibid.

44 Ellery Foster, 'Lumber's Last Barbecue,' *International Woodworker*, 28 Nov. 1945, 4; W.D. Hagenstein to Members, Joint Committee on Forest Conservation, 25 Oct. 1948, Box 34, Wagner Papers, UWL; Greeley, *Forests and Men*, 162-3; 'Society Affairs,' *FC* 23 (Dec. 1947): 314; Joint Committee on Forest Conservation, Minutes of Meeting, 29 Nov. 1948, vol. 161, WCLAR, OHSA; 'Report of Chairman to Subscribers of Forest Conservation Committee of Pacific Northwest Forest Industries,' 26 Mar. 1952, vol. 161, WCLAR, OHSA.

45 Puget Sound Section, Society of American Foresters, Minutes of Meeting, Box 2, SAF-PSSR, UWL; Ellery Foster 'Lumber Barons Postwar Plans Bared at Confab,' *International Woodworker* 19 Dec. 1945, 8; 'Forestry Professor Critical of Report,' ibid., 4; 'Another Forester Replies,' ibid., 2 Jan. 1946, 4.

46 Puget Sound Section, Society of American Foresters, Minutes of Meeting, 1 Dec. 1944, Box 2, SAF-PSSR, UWL; Washington Section, Joint Committee on Forest Conservation, Minutes of Meeting, 4 Apr. 1945, vol. 160, WCLAR, OHSA; G. Marckworth to C.S. Harley, 6 Mar. 1945, Box 10, UWCFRR, Acc. 70-1.

47 Claudia Anderson Craig, 'Forest Practices, Legislation and Social Valuation of Forested Land in Three Western States' (M.Sc. thesis, University of Washington 1977), 53-4; *Washington Forest Practices Act, Chapter 193, Laws of 1945*, Box 9, RG 95, SPFDR, NARS-PNW; T.S. Goodyear, 'Development of State Practice Laws in Washington,' *PWFCA* (1946), 23-4.

48 Puget Sound Section, Society of American Foresters, Minutes of Meeting, 2 Mar. 1945, Box 2, SAF-PSSR, UWL; J.S. Mottishaw to G. Marckworth, 5 Apr. 1945, Box 10, UWCFRR, Acc. 70-1; Marckworth to Mottishaw, 13 Apr. 1945, ibid.

49 'Washington State Forestry Conference,' *TMN* 47 (Jan. 1946): 178-9; Goodyear, 'Development of State Forest Practice Laws,' 24.

50 'Sustained Yield Program Outlined in IWA-CIO Brief on Proposed Sivslaw Plan,' *International Woodworker*, 12 Dec. 1945, 1; Joint Committee on Forest Conservation, Minutes of Meeting, 16 Oct. 1945, vol. 160, WCLAR, OHSA.

51 'Willamette Valley Loggers Meet in Seventh Session,' *TMN* 47 (Dec. 1945): 49-50; T.H. Burgess, 'Review of Sept. 19 Meeting of the Oregon State Board of Forestry,' 4 Oct. 1946, Box 9, RG 95, SPFDR, NARS-PNW.

52 W. Tilton to Oregon Members, Joint Committee on Forest Conservation, 28 Oct. 1946, vol. 161, WCLAR, OHSA; Rogers, 'Development of Forest Practice Laws,' 23; 'Thirty-Seventh Annual Forestry Conference,' *TMN* 48 (Jan. 1947): 222.

53 N.S. Rogers to H.J. Andrews, 5 Jan. 1948, Box 8, OSDFR, OSA; Joint Committee on Forest Conservation, Minutes of Meeting, 27 Apr. 1948, vol. 161, WCLAR, OHSA; Rogers to W.D. Hagenstein, 14 Sept. 1948, Box 1, OSDFR, OSA; 'Is Forestry Metaphysics,' *Oregonian*, 29 Mar. 1947, Box 10, RG 95, SPFDR, NARS-PNW; Oregon State Board of Forestry, Minutes of Meeting, 17 Apr. 1947, ibid.

54 H.J. Andrews to M.N. Dana, 28 Feb. 1947, Box 25, RG 95, SPFDR, NARS-PNW; D.S. Denman to H.J. Andrews, 7 Feb. 1947, ibid.; Andrews to Denman, 24 Feb. 1947, ibid.; 'Oregon Forestry Board to Check Cutting Practices in Douglas Fir,' *BCL* 31 (June 1947): 148.

55 'Notes to Accompany Status of Management Statistics,' 20 Nov. 1945, Box 22, RG 95, SPFDR, NARS-PNW.

56 Joint Committee on Forest Conservation, Minutes of Meeting, 11 Mar. 1947, vol. 160; 20 May 1947, vol. 161, WCLAR, OHSA.

57 C.H. Kreienbaum to R.A. Colgan, 1 Dec. 1947, Box 16, Wagner Papers, UWL; Wagner to Kreienbaum, 4 Dec. 1947, ibid.

58 N.S. Rogers to D.P. Abbott, 29 Sept. 1947, Box 1, OSDFR, OSA; T.H. Burgess, 'Accomplishment Report, Division of State and Private Forestry, 1948,' 14 Dec. 1948, Box 2, RG 95, SPFDR, NARS-PNW; W.D. Hagenstein to G. Gerlinger, 22 June 1948, Box 16, OSDFR, OSA.
59 R. Woodruff to G. Marckworth, 24 Nov. 1947, Box 10, UWCFRR, Acc. 70-1; Anderson Craig, 'Forest Practices Legislation,' 12-3.
60 Joint Committee on Forest Conservation, Minutes of Meeting, 27 Apr. 1948, vol. 160, WCLAR, OHSA; W.D. Hagenstein to Members, Pacific Northwest Loggers Association and West Coast Lumbermen's Association, 22 Feb. 1949, Box 34, Wagner Papers, UWL; 'Supreme Court Upholds Forest Practice Act,' *JF* 48 (Feb. 1950): 131; Anderson Craig, 'Forest Practices Legislation,' 13.
61 Steen, *The U.S. Forest Service*, 267.
62 'Economic Statesmanship and Self Regulation,' *TMN* 50 (July 1949): 43; W.B. Greeley, 'Forestry Background of the Pacific Northwest,' *JF* 48 (Mar. 1950): 161-4; T.H. Burgess, 'Memo for File,' 18 Apr. 1950, Box 20, RG 95, SPFDR, NARS-PNW; 'Minutes of Subscribers' Meeting of the Forest Conservation Committee of the Pacific Northwest Forest Industries,' 28 July 1949, vol. 161, WCLAR, OHSA.
63 H.H. Chapman, 'A Showdown on Federal Forest Regulation,' *JF* 47 (Sept. 1949): 746-8; 'Watts Discusses Referendum on Federal Regulation,' *JF* 48 (Mar. 1950): 208-10.
64 Clyde Martin, 'Federal Participation Means Federal Regulation,' *JF* 48 (May 1950): 374; Stuart Moir, 'Dangers of Regulation,' *TMN* 51 (Feb. 1950): 4; 'Society Opposes Federal Regulation,' *JF* 48 (July 1950): 510; H.H. Chapman, 'Significance of the Recent Referendum on Federal Forest Regulation,' *JF* 48 (Aug. 1950): 6.
65 Clary, *Timber and the Forest Service*, 147-51; William E. Leuchtenburg, *A Troubled Feast: American Society Since 1945* (Boston: Little, Brown and Co. 1983), 88-9; Hirt, *A Conspiracy of Optimism*, 107; E.P. Stamm, 'Report of Chairman to Subscribers of Forest Conservation Committee of Pacific Northwest Forest Industries,' 26 Mar. 1952, vol. 161, WCLAR, OHSA; Henry Clepper, 'Chiefs of the Forest Service,' *JF* 59 (Nov. 1961): 800.
66 Forest Conservation Committee of Pacific Northwest Forest Industries, Minutes of Executive Board Meeting, 8 June 1950, Box 35, Wagner Papers, UWL; 'The Oregon Conservation Act,' 8 Dec. 1952, Box 16, OSDFR, OSA.
67 B.L. Orell to R.W. Cowlin, 18 Jan. 1952, Box 30, RG 95, SPFDR, NARS-PNW.
68 R.W. Cowlin to J.H. Stone, 13 Feb. 1952, ibid.; 'Division Work Copy by Syverson,' 16 May 1952, ibid.; West Coast Forestry Procedures Committee of the Western Forestry and Conservation Association, Minutes of Meeting, 9 Dec. 1952, Box 8, RG 95, SPFDR, NARS-PNW; Louis Hamill, 'A Preliminary Study of the Status and Use of the Forest Resources of Western Oregon in Relation to Some Objectives of Public Policy' (Ph.D. thesis, University of Washington 1963), 88; L. Harter to D.L. Phipps, 9 July 1956, Box 16, OSDFR, OSA.
69 MacKay, *Empire of Wood*, 138; Taylor, *Timber*, 154-5.
70 'Responsibilities and Leadership,' *BCL* 23 (Mar. 1939): 18-9; F.D. Mulholland, 'Forest Policy – Ownership and Administration,' *FC* 16 (Mar. 1940): 99-106.
71 Canadian Society of Forest Engineers, Victoria Section, Minutes of Meeting, 18 Dec. 1939, Box 1, CIF-VISR, BCA.
72 Canadian Society of Forest Engineers, Victoria Section, Minutes of Meeting, 8 Jan. 1940, 1 Apr. 1940, Box 1, CIF-VISR, BCA; 'Nationalization of Forests,' *Daily Colonist,* 15 Nov. 1940, 4; 'Forest Resources,' ibid., 17 Nov. 1940, 4; 'State and Forestry,' ibid., 19 Nov. 1940, 4.
73 Margaret Ormsby, *British Columbia: A History* (Toronto: Macmillan 1958), 473-7; Fisher, *Duff Pattullo*, 341-51.
74 Canadian Society of Forest Engineers, Victoria Section, Minutes of Meeting, 16 Feb. 1942, Box 1, CIF-VISR, BCA.
75 C.D. Orchard, 'Forest Working Circles: An Analysis of Forest Legislation in British Columbia as it Relates to Disposal of Crown Timber, and Proposed Legislation Designed to Institute Managed Harvesting on a Basis of Perpetual Yield,' Memorandum to the Honourable the Minister of Lands, 27 Aug. 1942, 3-4, Box 41, GR 1222, BCA.
76 Ibid., 15.
77 Ibid., 16, 23.
78 Wilson, 'Forest Conservation,' 11; H.H. Stevens to J. Hart, 19 Jan. 1943, Box 41, GR 1222, BCA.

79 'Brief Presented to the Honorable Premier of British Columbia, and Members of the Executive Council by the British Columbia Natural Resources Conservation League,' 26 Jan. 1943, ibid.; J. Hart to C.D. Orchard, 27 Jan. 1943, ibid.; C.D. Orchard, 'Review of Brief Presented by British Columbia Natural Resources Conservation League,' 26 Jan. 1943, ibid.

80 Keith Reid and Don Weaver, 'Aspects of the Political Economy of the B.C. Forest Industry,' in *Essays in B.C. Political Economy,* ed. Paul Knox and Philip Resnick (Vancouver: New Star Books 1974), 16-9; Swift, *Cut and Run*, 84; Gillis and Roach, *Lost Initiatives*, 157; 'Press Release, Office of the Premier,' 23 June 1943, Box 41, GR 1222, BCA.

81 See Adam Ashworth, 'Reckoning Schemes of Legitimation: On Commissions of Inquiry as Power/Knowledge Forms,' *Journal of Historical Sociology* 3 (Mar. 1990): 1-22; Timothy O'Riordan, 'Policy Making and Environmental Management: Some Thoughts on Processes and Research Issues,' in *Natural Resources for a Democratic Society: Public Participation in Decision-Making*, ed. Albert E. Utton, W.R. Sewell, and Timothy O'Riordan (Boulder: Westview Press 1976), 56.

82 E.C. MacKenzie to J. Hart, 25 June 1943, Box 41, GR 1222, BCA; F.W. Tull to Hart, 6 July 1943, ibid.; H.H. Stevens to Hart, 6 Oct. 1941, ibid.; Hart to Stevens, 14 Oct. 1943, ibid.; Ian Mahood and Ken Drushka, *Three Men and a Forester* (Madeira Park: Harbour Publishing 1990), 88.

83 British Columbia, Royal Commission on Forestry, 1944-1945, Transcripts, 3-30.

84 G.S. Allen, 'Douglas Fir: A Summary of its Life History,' British Columbia Forest Service, Research Notes, No. 9, 4 Sept. 1942, in BC Ministry of Forests Library; F.S. McKinnon, 'An Outline of the Minimum Requirements for Management of Douglas Fir,' British Columbia Forest Service, Research Division, Research Note, 19 Apr. 1943, ibid.; F.S. McKinnon to C.L. Arthur, 12 Apr. 1944, GR 1441, Reel B3230, File 04170, BCA.

85 L. Isaac to F.S. McKinnon, 11 Feb. 1944, GR 1441, Reel B3239, File 04170, BCA; C.D. Orchard, 'Circular Letter No. 1570,' 8 Feb. 1943, Box 2, OSDFR, OSA; C.D. Orchard to N.S. Rogers, 8 Feb. 1943, ibid.; C.D. Orchard, 'Forest Administration in British Columbia – A Brief for Presentation to the Royal Commission on Forestry,' Jan. 1945, Box 18, GR 520, BCA.

86 'Basis of a Perpetual Forest Program Outlined,' *WCL* 71 (Oct. 1944): 82; BC Royal Commission on Forestry, 1944-1945, Transcripts, 4197-9; see also Rajala, *The Legacy and the Challenge*, 93.

87 'Nature Reforesting Vancouver Island Enquiry Told,' *Victoria Daily Times*, 25 Aug. 1944, 2; 'Analysis of Reproduction Survey on West Coast Logged Lands,' Bloedel, Stewart and Welch Ltd., Aug. 1944, Box 19, GR 520, BCA.

88 'Brief for Presentation to the Commission of Inquiry on Forest Resources of British Columbia by the Forest Operators of the Coast Region,' 18 June 1945, Box 19, GR 520, BCA.

89 J.N. Burke to J. Hart, 22 June 1945, Box 174, GR 1222, BCA; J.N. Burke, 'Summary of Brief Presented by Coast Forest Operators to the Commission of Inquiry on the Forest Resources of British Columbia,' 25 July 1945, ibid.

90 'Permanent Forest Board Recommended,' *WCL* 71 (Nov. 1944): 42; BC, Royal Commission on Forestry, 1944-1945, Transcripts, 2191-2, 3125; 'A Statement Presented to the Royal Commission on Forestry,' *FC* 20 (Sept. 1944): 157.

91 'A Statement,' 171-2; BC, Royal Commission on Forestry, 1944-1945, Transcripts, 2677.

92 'A Statement,' 173-87; see also Peter G. Aylen, 'Sustained Yield Forestry Policy in B.C. to 1956: A Deterministic Analysis of Development' (M.A. thesis, University of Victoria 1979), 123.

93 C.D. Orchard to R.J. Filberg, 18 Aug. 1945, BCMFR, File 053442-1; C.D. Orchard, 'The Function of the State in the Management of Crown and Private Forests for the Production of an Assured Supply of Wood for Industry,' *FC* 22 (June 1946): 105.

94 Gordon Sloan, *Report of the Commissioner Relating to the Forest Resources of British Columbia* (Victoria: King's Printer 1945), 141-2.

95 Ibid., 143-4.

96 'Sloan Report,' *CCF News*, 17 Jan. 1946, 4; C.D. Orchard to G.H. Prince, 4 Mar. 1947, Box 1, Chauncey D. Orchard Papers, BCA; Canadian Society of Forest Engineers, Vancouver Island Section, Minutes of Meeting, 26 Apr. 1946, Box 1, CIF-VISR, BCA; F.S. McKinnon to H.J. Andrews, 17 Dec. 1946, BCMFR, File 0137941.

97 'B.C. Forestry Act Brings Criticism,' *TMN* 54 (Apr. 1953): 145; *BC, Report of the Forest Service, 1953* (Victoria 1954), 9.

98 A.B. Recknagel, 'An American Looks at Canadian Forestry,' *FC* 24 (June 1948): 133.

99 'Forest Engineers Urge Revision of Unreasonable Provisions in Forest Act Amendments Before House,' *BCL* 31 (Mar. 1947): 46, 56-9; W.H. Johnson to C.D. Orchard, 24 Feb. 1948, BCMFR, File 0154987-1; R.C. Telford, 'Sustained Production in British Columbia,' *FC* 24 (Mar. 1948): 22; E.T. Kenney, 'Forest Management Licences,' A Radio Address Given Over Station C.B.R. – Vancouver, 15 Mar. 1948, Box 70, GR 1222, BCA.

100 'Loggers Debate Licence Plan,' *TMN* 49 (Feb. 1948): 100; C.D. Orchard, 'British Columbia's Forest Management Licences,' *PWFCA* (1948), 21; C.D. Orchard to R.D. Roe, 14 Feb. 1951, BCMFR, File 0154987-2; BC, Proceedings of the Royal Commission on Forestry, 1955, 1191, vol. 19, GR 668, BCA.

101 E. Druce to H.W. Weatherby, 21 Jan. 1948, BCMFR, File 0154987-1; C.D. Orchard to P.L. Lyford, 17 Nov. 1947, ibid.

102 'First FML in B.C. Issued to Cellulose Firm,' *BCL* 32 (May 1948): 57; 'Timber Management Licence Awarded,' *TMN* 50 (Mar. 1949): 144; Drushka, *Stumped*, 71-3; Mahood, *Three Men*, 114-9; An Independent Cat Logger to B. Johnson, 15 June 1948, Box 70, GR 1222, BCA.

103 Drushka, *Stumped*, 46; Patricia Marchak, 'Public Policy, Capital and Labour in the Forest Industry,' in *Workers, Capital and the State in British Columbia*, ed. Rennie Warburton and David Coburn (Vancouver: UBC Press 1988), 192. Mounting postwar pressure on the American National Forests also led to higher allowable cuts on those tenures. See Hirt, *A Conspiracy of Optimism*, 44-57.

104 F.S. MacKinnon to J.M. Gibson, 17 July 1948, BCMFR, File 06313-1.

105 R.C. St. Clair to E.E. Gregg, 12 Oct. 1951, BCMFR, File 0154987-2; A.R. Fraser, 'On Minimum Requirements of Growth Information for Public Working Circles and Management Licences in British Columbia,' Nov. 1953, BCMFR, File 0201101.

106 R.C. Telford to W.G. Hughes, 2 Dec. 1954, BCMFR, File 0201101; F.D. Mulholland, 'Comment on Alan Fraser's Suggested Minimum Requirements of Growth Information for Public Working Circles and Management Licenses,' 1954, ibid.; F.D. Mulholland, 'Sustained Yield as a Business Enterprise,' *FC* 30 (Dec. 1954): 352-61.

107 D.M. Trew to A. Fraser, 20 July 1954, BCMFR, File 0201101.

108 'Working Plan of Maquinna Forest Management Licence,' May 1955, for British Columbia Forest Products Ltd., by C.D. Schultz & Company Ltd., 4-6, Box 1, GR 1062, BCA; see also Rajala, *The Legacy and the Challenge*, 108-12.

109 W.G. Burch, 'Managing a Tree Farm Licence,' *FC* 39 (Mar. 1963): 98; BCFP Ltd., 'Working Plan No. 2 of Maquinna Tree Farm Licence No. 22,' 30 Oct. 1961, 30-1, Box 1, GR 1062; L.F. Swannell to W.G. Burch, 9 July 1968, ibid.

110 F.S. McKinnon, 'Memorandum to the Chief Forester,' 23 Nov. 1951, BCMFR, File 0154987-2; 'New Working Plans Division to Handle License Applications,' *BCL* 36 (May 1952): 47; W.G. Hughes to F.S. Williams, 5 Feb. 1953, BCMFR, File 0154987-3.

111 C.D. Orchard, 'Sustained Yield Forest Management in British Columbia,' *FC* 29 (Mar. 1953): 50-1; C.D. Orchard to District Foresters, 30 Aug. 1952, BCMFR, File 0154987-3.

112 D.B. Taylor to C.D. Orchard, 9 Sept. 1952, BCMFR, File 0154987-3; F.S. Williams to J. Stokes, 13 Jan. 1953, ibid.; F.S. Williams to D.B. Taylor, BCMFR, File 0154987-5.

113 H.G. Bancroft to District Foresters, 29 Feb. 1956, BCMFR, File 0154987-5; J.S. Stokes to District Foresters, 3 July 1957, BCMFR, File 0193731-1.

114 C.D. Orchard to G. Godwin, 29 Apr. 1957, BCMFR, File 06313-3; L.W. Lehre to Chief Forester, 3 Sept. 1957, BCMFR, File 0193731-1.

115 Tree Farm License Study Group, Minutes of Meeting, 28 Jan. 1959, BCMFR, File 0224292-1; Tree Farm Forestry Committee, Minutes of Meeting, 7 Oct. 1960, ibid.

116 Report of Meeting of Mar. 23, 1961, Tree Farm Forestry Committee, Working Plans and Cutting Plans Sub-Committee, BCMFR, File 0224292-1; Tree Farm Forestry Committee, Minutes of the Meeting of May 5, 1961, ibid.

117 W.G. Hughes to All District Foresters, 17 May 1963, BCMFR, File 0154987-6; I.T. Cameron to F.S. McKinnon, 21 Nov. 1963, ibid.

118 R. Tannhauser to H.M. Pogue, 23 Oct. 1964, BCMFR, File 0276361.

119 D.R. Glew to W.G. Hughes, 7 Mar. 1966, BCMFR, File 0154987-7.

120 'Notes on Timber Management Meeting – Olympic Forest,' 24 Feb. 1944, Box 15, RG95, DHF, NARS-PNW.

121 'Forest Research Activities – 1941-1944 Inclusive, Pacific Northwest Forest and Range Experiment Station,' Reel 14, OSUSFR; Puget Sound Section, Society of American Foresters, Minutes of Meeting, 2 Mar. 1945, Box 2, SAF-PSSR, UWL.

122 J.A. Hall to R.E. Marsh, 1 June 1947, Box 25, RG 95, SPFDR, NARS-PNW.

123 'Chief Forester Reports,' *TMN* 49 (Feb. 1948): 43; Robert W. Cowlin, 'Federal Forest Research in the Pacific Northwest: The Pacific Northwest Research Station,' (unpublished manuscript), 110.

124 O.F. Ericson, 'Inspection, Olympic,' 29 Oct. 1945, RG 095-54A-0111, Box 59854, NARS-PNW; O.F. Ericson and K. Wolfe, 'Report on General Inspection, Olympia National Forest,' 16 Sept. 1946, ibid.; D.J. Kirkpatrick, 'Memorandum of Inspection,' 27 May 1947, ibid.; W.H. Lund, 'Memorandum of Inspection,' 7 July 1948, ibid.

125 Kirkpatrick, 'Memorandum;' W.H. Lund, 'Memorandum of Inspection,' 26 July 1948, ibid.; see also Delbert R. Taylor, 'Forestry in Old-Growth in the Douglas Fir Region,' *JF* 49 (Jan. 1951): 37.

126 Lund, 'Memorandum'; O.F. Ericson to Supervisor, 'Olympic National Forest,' 2 Aug. 1948, ibid.; see also Walter H. Lund, *Timber Management in the Pacific Northwest Region, 1927-1965, An Interview Conducted by Amelia R. Fry* (Berkeley: University of California Regional Oral History Office 1967), 49.

127 Thornton T. Munger, 'A Look at Selective Cutting in Douglas Fir,' *JF* 48 (Feb. 1950): 77-9; Leo A. Isaac, 'Recent Developments in Silvicultural Practices in the Douglas Fir Region,' *JF* 47 (Dec. 1949): 957-60; 'Developments in Methods and Equipment – 1941-1944,' 13 Mar. 1950, RG 095-54A-0111, Box 59853, NARS-PNW.

128 'Abolition of B.C. High Lead Logging Urged,' *Vancouver Sun*, 13 July 1948, 26; 'Approved (?) Logging Technique,' *JF* 50 (Feb. 1949): 136.

129 'Forest Practice Based on Facts, Not Fancy,' *JF* 52 (July 1952): 562-3.

130 Cowlin, 'Federal Forest Research,' 117; Robert Auferheide, 'Getting Forestry into the Logging Plan,' *TMN* 50 (Mar. 1949): 53-6, 96; Robert H. Ruth and Roy R. Silen, 'Suggestions for Getting More Forestry in the Logging Plan,' *Research Notes*, No. 72, (Portland: Pacific Northwest Forest and Range Experiment Station 1950); G.S. Allen to F.S. McKinnon, 6 May 1947, GR 1441, Reel B3230, File 04170, BCA; G.S. Allen, 'Seed Dissemination Project: Progress Report, 1947,' BCMFR, File 04170; George S. Allen, 'Applied Silviculture in the Coastal Region of British Columbia,' *FC* 26 (Sept. 1950): 221-5.

131 West Coast Forestry Procedures Committee, Minutes of Meeting, 19 May 1949, GR 1441, Reel B3231, File 04170, BCA; F.D. Hobi to E.G. Griggs II, 23 June 1952, Box 88, Wagner Papers, UWL; N.G. Jacobson to Griggs, 26 June 1952, ibid.; Griggs to Hobi, 15 July 1952, ibid.

132 'Submission to the Royal Commission on Forestry by Canadian Forest Products Ltd.,' Box 11, BC, GR 668, BCA; 'Brief Submitted to the Royal Commission of Enquiry into the Forest Resources of British Columbia, Presented by B.C. Forest Products,' Box 12, ibid.; 'Is the Fir Belt's Future in Patch Logging,' *TL* (Nov. 1954): 24; H.G. McWilliams, 'Report to the Royal Commission on Forests and Forestry,' Box 2, GR 668, BCA; A.P. MacBean to E. Garman, 11 Apr. 1949, BCMFR, File 0190786.

133 P.M. Barr to E. Wilson, 6 Dec. 1930, BCMFR, File 06313; C.D. Orchard, 'Memorandum to the Minister of Lands,' 8 Dec. 1938, GR 1222, Box 19, BCA.

134 'For Minister of Lands, Reforestation and Forest Nurseries,' 28 Nov. 1941, GR 1441, Reel B3230, File 04170, BCA; Jack Long, 'The Quinsam Nursery,' *British Columbia Forest History Newsletter* 38 (Dec. 1993), 1-3; A.P. MacBean, 'Silvicultural Studies on the Coast,' Dec. 1940, BCMFR, File 0134222; F.S. McKinnon to J.C. Veness, 22 Dec. 1942, BCMFR, File 06313-2; C.D. Orchard, 'Memorandum,' 22 May 1943, Box 41, GR 1222, BCA; 'Forestry Seed Beds Will Supply Big Area,' *Cowichan Leader*, 9 May 1946, 1; Joint Committee on Forest Conservation, Subcommittee, 30 Jan. 1946, vol. 161, WCLAR, OHSA.

135 'Needed State and Private Timberland Owner Assistance During the Next 5 Years for the Pacific Northwest,' 31 May 1955, Box 20, RG 95, SPFDR, NARS-PNW; H.G. McWilliams to Ginn & Company, 31 May 1956, BCMPLR, Reel 1546, File 0170724; Cowlin, 'Federal Forest

Research,' 118; William Loney, 'History of Fish-Wildlife Problems in the Pacific Northwest,' in *Wildlife and Reforestation in the Pacific Northwest,* ed. Hugh C. Black (Corvallis: Oregon State University School of Forestry 1969), 5; N.S. Rogers to W.E. McQuilkin, 2 Feb. 1948, Box 1, OSDFR, OSA; E.H. Garman to Director, Appalachian Forest Experiment Station, 26 Nov. 1946, GR 1441, Reel B3515, File 048525, BCA.

136 H.G. McWilliams to A.P. MacBean, 5 May 1951, BCMLPR, Reel 1546, File 0170724; R.M. Kallander to A.P. MacBean, 30 July 1951, Box 1, OSDFR, OSA; T. Wright to E.H. Garman, 25 Aug. 1951, BCMFR, File 0190786; Robert M. Malcolm, 'Report of the Vancouver Island Section, C.I.F. Silvicultural Committee, 1952-1953,' ibid.; Cowlin, 'Federal Forest Research,' 135, 141.

137 A.P. MacBean, 'Responsible Forest Management,' *BCL* 35 (Sept. 1951): 40; George Allen, 'Reforestation: Giving Meaning to an Overused Word,' *TL* (Nov. 1954): 28; W.D. Hagenstein, 'Forest Engineer's Report to Subscribers at Annual Meeting of the Forest Conservation Committee of the Pacific Northwest Forest Industries,' 26 Mar. 1952, vol. 160, WCLAR, OHSA.

138 H.G. McWilliams, 'Problems of Restocking in the West,' *PWFCA* (1955), 55.

139 George H. Schroeder, 'Restocking Problems of Western Washington and Oregon,' *PWFCA* (1955), 30; Vincent W. Bousquet, 'The Status of Management in the Old Growth Forests of the Northwestern United States,' *PWFCA* (1956), 30; T.G. Wright, 'Managing Our Old Growth Forests,' *FC* 33 (Dec. 1957): 315.

140 Cowlin, 'Federal Forest Research,' 183; Alex G. Rankin, 'Management of Capital in the Forest Industry of British Columbia,' *FC* 37 (Sept. 1961): 261-2; H. Hodgins to C.D. Orchard, 14 Jan. 1959, Box 7, Orchard Papers, BCA.

141 'Patch Logging – C.I.F. Panel,' 16 Jan. 1959, Box 7, Orchard Papers, BCA; 'Patch Not Up to Scratch,' *Forest and Mill* 13 (Mar. 1959): 2.

142 C.D. Orchard to C. Cowan, 17 Jan. 1959, ibid.; 'Crown Zellerbach-Consulting Files,' ibid.

143 C.D. Orchard, 'Patch Logging,' 31 July 1959, ibid., 4.

144 Ibid., 5.

145 Ibid., 6-7.

146 Pacific Northwest Forest and Range Experiment Station Advisory Committee, Report of First Meeting, 25 Feb. 1954, Box 14, UWCFRR, Acc. 77-12.

147 'Economic Logging Layout,' *LH* 19 (1959): 22; 'Mr. Pope's Paper,' *LH* 19 (1959): 30-1.

148 'Economic Logging Layout,' 23; 'Mr. Harter's Paper,' *LH* 19 (1959): 31-2; 'Oregon Conservation Act is Reviewed,' *Western Forester* 4 (Feb. 1959): 2; 'State Forestry Department: Functions and Responsibilities,' Presented to the Governor's Committee on Natural Resources, 24 Sept. 1963, Reel 12, OSUSFR.

149 Nelson Jeffers, 'Restocking Practices,' *PPLC* (Vancouver 1964), 110; J.R. Robinson to F.S. McKinnon, 17 Nov. 1959, BCMFR, File 0154986-7; J.S. Stokes to J.R. Robinson, 25 Nov. 1959, ibid.

150 S.R. Halton to J.A. Moyer, 13 Feb. 1964, BCMFR, File 060238-15; 'Definitions Cloud Multiple Use,' *FI* 90 (Jan. 1963): 63; T.G. Wright, 'Some Approaches to Regeneration From the Logging Standpoint,' *FC* 39 (June 1963): 145-8; W.G. Burch, 'Managing a Tree Farm Licence,' *FC* 39 (Mar. 1963): 98; BCFP Ltd.; 'Maquinna Tree Farm Licence No. 22, Annual Report, 1963,' 1, GR 1062, BCA; Daryl D. Paver, 'Basic Considerations of a Coast Logging Plan,' *BCL* 49 (Apr. 1965): 36-8.

151 I.T. Cameron to G.L. Ainscough, 23 Sept. 1964, Box 4, BC Forest Service, Powell River Forest District Records, GR 957, BCA; Cameron to Ainscough, 1 Mar. 1965, ibid.

152 Ian Cameron, 'Talk to Crown Zellerbach Employees About 1961,' Box 1, Ian T. Cameron Papers, BCA.

153 F.L. Harrison to J.K. Pearce, 19 Aug. 1957, Box 1, Pearce Papers, UWL; Pearce to J.W. Allen, 21 Jan. 1958, ibid.; W.F. McCulloch to F. Schultz, 15 Feb. 1961, Reel 8, OSUSFR.

154 W.F. McCulloch to F.W. Lara, 5 Nov. 1963, Reel 5, OSUSFR.

155 William Dietrich, *The Final Forest: The Battle for the Last Great Trees of the Pacific Northwest* (New York: Simon & Schuster 1992), 104; Gordon H. Orians, '"New Forestry" and the Old-Growth Forests of Northwestern North America: A Conversation with Jerry F. Franklin,' *Northwest Environmental Journal* 6 (1990), 446-61; Ken Drushka, 'The New Forestry: Middle Ground in the Debate Over the Region's Forests,' *The New Pacific* 4 (Fall 1990): 7-24.

156 Norman P. Worthington, 'Reproduction Following Small Group Cuttings in Virgin Doug-
     las Fir,' Research Note No. 84 (Portland: Pacific Northwest Forest and Range Experiment
     Station 1953); E.H. Garman, 'Regeneration Problems, and Their Silvicultural Significance
     in the Coastal Forests of British Columbia,' (BC Forest Service, unpublished report 1954),
     69; Jerry F. Franklin, 'Natural Regeneration of Douglas Fir and Associated Species Using
     Modified Clear-Cutting Systems in the Oregon Cascades,' US Forest Service Research Paper,
     PNW-3 (Portland: Pacific Northwest Forest and Range Experiment Station 1963).
157 Brian D. Cleary, Robert D. Greaves, and Richard K. Hermann, *Regenerating Oregon's Forests:
     A Guide for the Regeneration Forester* (Corvallis: Oregon State University School of Forestry
     1978), 29; Ivan Doig, 'The Murky Annals of Clearcutting: A 40 Year-Old Dispute,' *Pacific
     Search* 10 (Dec. 1975-Jan. 1976): 12-4.
158 'Minutes of the Meeting of the Reforestation Board of the Tree Farm Forestry Committee,'
     23 Nov. 1967, BCMFR, File 0226775-2; G.P. Thomas to Members, BC Regional Advisory
     Committee, Pacific Forest Research Centre, BCMFR, File 02009-8.

Conclusion

1 MacMillan Bloedel Ltd., *Building Better Forests in British Columbia* (Vancouver 1967), 11.
2 Graeme Salaman, *Class and the Corporation* (Glasgow: Fontana Paperbacks 1981), 168.
3 Stephen Wood, ed., *The Degradation of Work: Skill, Deskilling and the Labour Process* (London:
   Hutchinson & Co. 1982), 22; 'Address by E.P. Blake,' *TMN* 10 (Aug. 1909): 22.
4 Lawrence T. McDonnell, '"You Are Too Sentimental": Problems and Suggestions for a New
   Labor History,' *Journal of Social History* 17 (Summer 1984): 630.
5 Andrew Zimbalist, ed., *Case Studies on the Labor Process* (New York: Monthly Review Press
   1979), xv.
6 See Erik Olin Wright, 'Varieties of Marxist Conceptions of Class Structure,' *Politics and Soci-
   ety* 9 (1980): 323-70; Barbara and John Ehrenreich, 'The Professional-Managerial Class,' in
   Between Labor and Capital, ed. Pat Walker (Boston: South End Press 1979), 5-48; Nicos
   Poulantzas, *Classes in Contemporary Capitalism* (London: Verso 1978); G. Carchedi, 'On the
   Economic Identification of the New Middle Class,' *Economy and Society* 4 (1975), 1-85; Val
   Burris, 'Capital Accumulation and the Rise of the New Middle Class,' *Review of Radical
   Political Economics* 12 (Spring 1980): 17-34.
7 BC, Royal Commission on Forestry, 1944-1945, Transcripts, 7949.
8 Glen Williams, 'Greening the Canadian Political Economy,' *Studies in Political Economy* 37
   (Spring 1992): 8; 'Capitalism and the Environment,' *Monthly Review* 41 (June 1989): 7.
9 John Bellamy Foster, 'The Limits of Environmentalism Without Class: Lessons from the
   Ancient Forest Struggle in the Pacific Northwest,' *Capitalism, Nature, Socialism* 13 (Mar.
   1993): 12-3; Richard White, '"Are You An Environmentalist or Do You Work for a Living?":
   Work and Nature,' in *Uncommon Ground: Rethinking the Human Place in Nature*, ed. William
   Cronon (New York: W.W. Norton 1995), 171-85; Thomas Dunk, 'Talking About Trees: Environment and Society in Forest Workers' Culture,' *Canadian Review of Sociology and Anthropology* 31 (1994): 14-34.

Bibliography

Manuscript Collections

Association of British Columbia Professional Foresters Records. British Columbia Archives and Records Service

Association of Professional Engineers of British Columbia Records. British Columbia Archives and Records Service

Barnet Family Papers. Public Archives of Ontario

Britannia Mining and Smelting Company Records. British Columbia Archives and Records Service

British Columbia. Commission on Forest Resources Records, 1955, GR 668. British Columbia Archives and Records Service

British Columbia. Department of Lands Records, GR 1441. British Columbia Archives and Records Service

British Columbia Forest Service. Lake Cowichan Ranger District Records, GR 1062. British Columbia Archives and Records Service

British Columbia Forest Service. Powell River Forest District Records, GR 957. British Columbia Archives and Records Service

British Columbia Forest Service. Vancouver Forest District Records, GR 955. British Columbia Archives and Records Service

British Columbia Ministry of Forests. O Series Correspondence Files, Ministry of Forests Office, Victoria, BC

British Columbia. Ministry of Lands and Parks Records. Ministry of Lands and Parks Office, Victoria, BC

British Columbia. Premiers' Papers, GR 1222. British Columbia Archives and Records Service

British Columbia. Records of the Commission on Forest Resources, 1943-1945, GR 520. British Columbia Archives and Records Service

British Columbia. Records of the Royal Commission on Timber and Forestry, 1909-1910, GR 271. British Columbia Archives and Records Service

Ian T. Cameron Papers. British Columbia Archives and Records Service

Canadian Institute of Forestry, Vancouver Island Section Records. British Columbia Archives and Records Service

Comox Logging and Railway Company Records, Courtenay and District Museum and Archives

Empire Forestry Association Records. British Columbia Archives and Records Service

F. Malcolm Knapp Papers. University of British Columbia Library, Special Collections Branch

Arthur B. Langlie Papers. University of Washington Libraries

Merrill and Ring Lumber Company Records. University of Washington Libraries

F.D. Mulholland Papers. British Columbia Archives and Records Service

C.D. Orchard Collection. British Columbia Archives and Records Service

C.D. Orchard Papers. British Columbia Archives and Records Service
Oregon-American Lumber Company Records. University of Oregon Archives
Oregon State Department of Forestry Records. Oregon State Archives
Oregon State University School of Forestry Records. Oregon State University Archives
Pacific Northwest Loggers Association Records. University of Washington Libraries
J. Kenneth Pearce Papers. University of Washington Libraries
Port Blakely Mill Company Records. University of Washington Libraries
Presidents' Papers. University of British Columbia Library, Special Collections Branch
St Paul and Tacoma Lumber Company Records. University of Washington Libraries
Society of American Foresters, Puget Sound Section Records. University of Washington
     Libraries
United States Forest Service. District Historical Files, RG 95. National Archives and Records
     Service, Pacific Northwest Region
United States Forest Service. State and Private Forestry Division Records, RG 95. National
     Archives and Records Service, Pacific Northwest Region
United States Forest Service. Timber Management Files, RG 095-54A-0111. National Ar-
     chives and Records Service, Pacific Northwest Region
University of Washington College of Forest Resources Records. University of Washington
     Libraries
Corydon Wagner Papers. University of Washington Libraries
West Coast Lumbermen's Association Records. Oregon Historical Society Archives

Selected Periodicals
British Columbia Lumberman, 1930-75
Forest Chronicle, 1929-75
Forest Industries, 1963-75
Forest Log, 1960-70
Forest Quarterly, 1902-16
Journal of Forestry, 1918-75
Logger's Handbook, 1941-78
Proceedings of the Society of American Foresters, 1905-16
Proceedings of the Pacific Logging Congress, 1910-30
Proceedings of the Western Forestry and Conservation Association, 1947-75
Puget Sound and West Coast Lumberman, 1898-1904
Timberman, 1905-57
Truck Logger, 1963-70
West Coast Lumberman, 1892-1946
Western Forester, 1955-75
Western Lumberman, 1905-30

Books and Pamphlets
Allen, E.T. *Practical Forestry in the Pacific Northwest*. Portland: Western Forestry and Conser-
     vation Association 1911
Aronowitz, Stanley. *Science as Power: Discourse and Ideology in Modern Society*. Minneapolis:
     University of Minnesota Press 1988
Bailey, I.W. and H.A. Spoehr. *The Role of Research in the Development of Forestry in North
     America*. New York: Macmillan 1929
Baran, Paul A. and Paul M. Sweezy. *Monopoly Capital: An Essay on the American Economic and
     Social Order*. New York: Monthly Review Press 1966
Barman, Jean. *The West Beyond The West: A History of British Columbia*. Toronto: University
     of Toronto Press 1991
Beckam, Curt. *Gyppo Logging Days*. Myrtle Point: Hillside Book Company 1978
Binns, Archie. *The Roaring Land*. New York: Robert M. McBride 1942
Brandstrom, Axel J.F. *Analysis of Logging Costs and Operating Methods in the Douglas Fir Re-
     gion*. Seattle: Charles Lathrop Pack Forestry Foundation 1933
–. *Development of Industrial Forestry in the Pacific Northwest*. Seattle: University of Washing-
     ton College of Forestry 1957

Braverman, Harry. *Labor and Monopoly Capital: The Degradation of Work in the Twentieth Century*. New York: Monthly Review Press 1974

Bunting, Robert. *The Pacific Raincoast: Environment and Culture in an American Eden, 1778-1900*. Lawrence: University Press of Kansas 1997

Burawoy, Michael. *The Politics of Production: Factory Regimes Under Capitalism and Socialism*. London: Verso 1985

Burke, Doyle, C. Mann, and P. Schiess, eds. *Proceedings of the Fifth Northwest Skyline Logging Symposium*. Seattle: University of Washington College of Forest Resources 1982

Callahan, Raymond E. *Education and the Cult of Efficiency*. Chicago: University of Chicago Press 1962

Chandler, Alfred D. Jr. *The Visible Hand: The Managerial Revolution in American Business*. Cambridge: Harvard University Press 1977

Clark, Donald H. *Eighteen Men and a Horse*. Seattle: Metropolitan Press 1949

Clary, David A. *Timber and the Forest Service*. Lawrence: University Press of Kansas 1986

Cleary, Brian D., Robert D. Greaves, and Richard K. Hermann. *Regenerating Oregon's Forests: A Guide for the Regeneration Forester*. Corvallis: Oregon State University School of Forestry 1978

Clement, Wallace. *Hardrock Mining: Industrial Relations and Technological Change at Inco*. Toronto: McClelland and Stewart 1981

Clepper, Henry. *Professional Forestry in the United States*. Baltimore: Johns Hopkins University Press 1971

Coman, Edwin T. Jr., and Helen M. Gibbs. *Time, Tide and Timber: A Century of Pope and Talbot*. Stanford: Stanford University Press 1949

Cone, Joseph and Sandy Riddlington, eds. *The Northwest Salmon Crisis: A Documentary History*. Corvallis: Oregon State University Press 1996

Conklin, Paul K. *The New Deal*. Arlington Heights: AHM Publishing 1975

Cowan, Charles S. *The Enemy is Fire!* Seattle: Superior Publishing Company 1961

Cox, Thomas R., Robert S. Maxwell, Phillip Drennon Thomas, and Joseph J. Malone. *This Well-Wooded Land: Americans and Their Forests from Colonial Times to the Present*. Lincoln: University of Nebraska Press 1985

Cox, Thomas R. *Mills and Markets: A History of the Pacific Coast Lumber Industry to 1900*. Seattle: University of Washington Press 1974

Dana, Samuel Trask. *Forest and Range Policy: Its Development in the United States*. New York: McGraw-Hill 1956

DeBresson, Chris. *Understanding Technological Change*. Montreal: Black Rose Books 1987

Dickson, David. *The New Politics of Science*. New York: Pantheon Books 1984

Dietrich, William. *The Final Forest: The Battle for the Last Great Trees of the Pacific Northwest*. New York: Simon & Schuster 1992

Doig, Ivan. *Early Forestry Research: A History of the Pacific Northwest Forest and Range Experiment Station*. U.S. Department of Agriculture 1977

Drushka, Ken. *HR: A Biography of H.R. MacMillan*. Madeira Park: Harbour Publishing 1995

–. *Stumped: The Forest Industry in Transition*. Vancouver: Douglas & McIntyre 1985

–. *Working in the Woods: A History of Logging on the West Coast*. Madeira Park: Harbour Publishing 1992

Edwards, Richard. *Contested Terrain: The Transformation of the Workplace in the Twentieth Century*. New York: Basic Books 1979

Eichar, Douglas M. *Occupation and Class Consciousness in America*. New York: Greenwood Press 1989

Engstrom, Emil. *The Vanishing Logger*. New York: Vantage Press 1956

Ficken, Robert E. *Lumber and Politics: The Career of Mark E. Reed*. Seattle: University of Washington Press 1979

–. *The Forested Land: A History of Lumbering in Western Washington*. Seattle: University of Washington Press 1987

Fisher, Robin. *Duff Pattullo of British Columbia*. Toronto: University of Toronto Press 1991

Fox, Alan. *Beyond Contract: Work, Power and Trust Relations*. London: Faber and Faber 1974

Friedland, William H., Amy E. Barton, and Robert J. Thomas. *Manufacturing Green Gold: Capital, Labor, and Technology in the Lettuce Industry*. New York: Cambridge University Press 1981

Friedman, Andrew. *Industry and Labour: Class Struggle at Work and Monopoly Capitalism*. London: MacMillan Press 1977

Garner, Joe. *Never Chop Your Rope*. Nanaimo: Cinnibar Press 1988

Garratt, George A. *Forestry Education in Canada*. Vancouver: Evergreen Press 1971

Gibbons, William H. *Logging in the Douglas Fir Region*. Washington, DC: United States Department of Agriculture Bulletin No. 711, 1918

Gillis, R. Peter and Thomas R. Roach. *Lost Initiatives: Canada's Forest Industries, Forest Policy and Forest Conservation*. New York: Greenwood Press 1986

Greeley, William B. *Forests and Men*. Garden City: Doubleday and Company 1951

Griffiths, Bus. *Now You're Logging*. Madeira Park: Harbour Publishing 1978.

Grigg, D.H. *From One to Seventy*. Vancouver: Mitchell Printing and Publishing Company 1953

Hammond, Herb. *Seeing the Forest Among the Trees: The Case for Wholistic Forest Use*. Vancouver: Polestar 1991

Harris, Howell John. *The Right to Manage: Industrial Relations Policies of American Business in the 1940s*. Madison: University of Wisconsin Press 1982

Hawley, Ellis. *The New Deal and the Problem of Monopoly*. Princeton: Princeton University Press 1968

Hays, Samuel P. *American Political History as Social Analysis: Essays by Samuel P. Hays*. Knoxville: University of Tennessee Press 1980

–. *Beauty, Health and Permanence: Environmental Politics in the United States, 1955-1985*. New York: Cambridge University Press 1987

–. *Conservation and the Gospel of Efficiency: The Progressive Conservation Movement, 1880-1920*. Cambridge: Harvard University Press 1959

Heron, Craig and Robert Storey, eds. *On the Job: Confronting the Labour Process in Canada*. Montreal: McGill-Queen's University Press 1986

Hidy, Ralph W., Frank Ernest Hill, and Allan Nevins. *Timber and Men: The Weyerhaeuser Story*. New York: Macmillan 1963

Hirt, Paul W. *A Conspiracy of Optimism: Management of the National Forests Since World War Two*. Lincoln: University of Nebraska Press 1994

Hoffman, J.V. *Natural Regeneration of Douglas Fir in the Pacific Northwest*. Washington, DC: US Department of Agriculture 1924

Holbrook, Stewart. *Green Commonwealth*. Simpson Logging Company 1945

–. *Holy Old Mackinaw: A Natural History of the American Lumberjack*. New York: Macmillan 1945

Howard, Irene. *The Struggle for Social Justice in British Columbia: Helena Gutteridge, the Unknown Reformer*. Vancouver: UBC Press 1992

Howe, C.D. *The Reproduction of Commercial Species in the Southern Coastal Forests of British Columbia*. Ottawa: Commission on Conservation 1915

Isaac, Leo A. *Reproductive Habits of Douglas Fir*. Washington, DC: Charles Lathrop Pack Forestry Foundation 1943

Johansen, Dorothy O. *Empire of the Columbia: A History of the Pacific Northwest*. New York: Harper and Row 1967

Johnson, R.J. *Environmental Problems: Nature, Economy and the State*. New York: Belhaven Press 1989

Jones, Alden. *From Jamestown to Coffin Rock: A History of Weyerhaeuser Operations in Southwestern Washington*. Weyerhaeuser Company 1974

Kirkland, Burt P. and Axel J.F. Brandstrom. *Selective Timber Management in the Douglas Fir Region*. Seattle: Charles Lathrop Pack Forestry Foundation 1936

Kocka, Jurgen. *White Collar Workers in America, 1890-1940*. Beverly Hills: Sage Publications 1980

Kolko, Gabriel. *The Triumph of Conservatism: A Reinterpretation of American History, 1900-1916*. New York: Free Press 1963

Kusterer, Ken C. *Know How on the Job: The Important Working Knowledge of 'Unskilled' Workers*. Boulder: Westview Press 1978

Langston, Nancy. *Forest Dreams, Forest Nightmares: The Paradox of Old Growth in the Inland West*. Seattle: University of Washington Press 1995

Layton, Edwin T. *The Revolt of the Engineers: Social Responsibility and the American Engineering Profession*. Cleveland: Case Western Reserve University Press 1971

Leuchtenburg, William E. *A Troubled Feast: American Society Since 1945*. Boston: Little, Brown and Co. 1983

Lowitt, Richard. *The New Deal and the West*. Bloomington: Indiana University Press 1984

McConnell, Grant. *Private Power and American Democracy*. New York: Alfred A. Knopf 1966

McCulloch, W.F. *Forest Management Education in Oregon*. Corvallis: Oregon State College 1949

–. *Forest Practice in Oregon*. Salem: Oregon State Board of Forestry 1943

MacDaniels, E.H. *A Decade of Progress in Douglas Fir Forestry*. Seattle: Joint Committee on Forest Conservation 1943

MacKay, Donald. *Empire of Wood: The MacMillan Bloedel Story*. Vancouver: Douglas & McIntyre 1982

–. *The Lumberjacks*. Toronto: McGraw-Hill 1978

McKinnon, F.S. and T. Wells. *The Green Timbers Forestry Station and Forest Tree Nursery: A Brief Review of its Purpose and Development*. Victoria: King's Printer 1943

McQuaid, Kim. *Big Business and Presidential Power: From FDR to Reagan*. New York: William Morrow 1982

Mahood, Ian and Ken Drushka. *Three Men and a Forester*. Madeira Park: Harbour Publishing 1990

Marchak, Patricia. *Green Gold: The Forest Industry in British Columbia*. Vancouver: UBC Press 1983

–. *Logging the Globe*. Montreal: McGill-Queen's University Press 1995

Marshall, Robert. *The Social Management of American Forests*. New York: League for Industrial Democracy 1930

Merkle, Judith. *Management and Ideology: The Legacy of the International Scientific Management Movement*. Berkeley: University of California Press 1980

Millard, J. Rodney. *The Master Spirit of the Age: Canadian Engineers and the Politics of Professionalism, 1872-1922*. Toronto: University of Toronto Press 1988

Moltke, Alfred W. *Memoirs of a Logger*. College Place: College Press 1955

Morgan, George T. *William B. Greeley: A Practical Forester*. St. Paul: Forest History Society 1961

Morgan, Murray. *The Mill on the Boot: The Story of the St. Paul and Tacoma Lumber Company*. Seattle: University of Washington Press 1982

Mulholland, F.D. *The Forest Resources of British Columbia*. Victoria: King's Printer 1937

Nelles, H.V. *The Politics of Development: Forests, Mines and Hydro-Electric Power in Ontario, 1891-1941*. Toronto: MacMillan 1974

Nelson, Daniel. *Frederick W. Taylor and the Rise of Scientific Management*. Madison: University of Wisconsin Press 1980

–. *Managers and Workers: Origins of the New Factory System in the United States, 1880-1920*. Madison: University of Wisconsin Press 1975

Noble, David. *America by Design: Science, Technology and the Rise of Corporate Capitalism*. New York: Alfred A. Knopf 1977

–. *Forces of Production: A Social History of Industrial Automation*. New York: Alfred A. Knopf 1984

–. *Progress Without People: New Technology, Unemployment, and the Message of Resistance*. Toronto: Between the Lines 1995

Ormsby, Margaret. *British Columbia: A History*. Toronto: Macmillan 1958

Osberg, Lars, Fred Wien, and Jan Grude. *Vanishing Jobs: Canada's Changing Workplaces*. Toronto: James Lorimer and Company 1995

Paehlke, Robert C. *Environmentalism and the Future of Progressive Politics*. New Haven: Yale University Press 1989

Patterson, James T. *Congressional Conservatives and the New Deal*. Lexington: University of Kentucky Press 1967
–. *The New Deal and the States*. Princeton: Princeton University Press 1969
Paulik, Max. *The Truth About Our Forests*. Vancouver: Foresta Publishers 1937
Peavy, George W. *Oregon's Commercial Forests: Their Importance to the State*. Salem: State Printing Department 1922
Pinchot, Gifford. *The Fight for Conservation*. Seattle: University of Washington Press 1967
Pinkett, Harold T. *Gifford Pinchot: Private and Public Forester*. Chicago: University of Chicago Press 1970
Poulantzas, Nicos. *Classes in Contemporary Capitalism*. London: Verso 1978
Proceedings, Skyline Logging Symposium. Vancouver 1976
Prouty, Andrew Mason. *More Deadly Than War: Pacific Coast Logging, 1827-1981*. New York: Garland Publishing 1985
Radforth, Ian. *Bushworkers and Bosses: Logging in Northern Ontario, 1900-1980*. Toronto: University of Toronto Press 1987
Rajala, Richard. *The Legacy and the Challenge: A Century of the Forest Industry at Cowichan Lake*. Lake Cowichan Heritage Advisory Committee 1993
Raphael, Ray. *Tree Talk: The People and Politics of Timber*. Covelo: Island Press 1981
Rifkin, Jeremy. *The End of Work: The Decline of the Global Labour Force and the Dawn of the Post-Market Era*. New York: G.P. Putnam's Sons 1996
Robbins, William G. *American Forestry: A History of National, State, and Private Cooperation*. Lincoln: University of Nebraska Press 1985
–. *Hard Times in Paradise: Coos Bay, Oregon, 1850-1986*. Seattle: University of Washington Press 1988
–. *Lumberjacks and Legislators: Political Economy of the U.S. Lumber Industry, 1890-1941*. College Station: Texas A & M University Press 1982
Robin, Martin. *The Rush for Spoils: The Company Province, 1871-1933*. Toronto: McClelland and Stewart 1972
Robinson, Gordon. *The Forest and the Trees: A Guide to Excellent Forestry*. Covelo: Island Press 1988
Robson, Peter A. *The Working Forest of British Columbia*. Madeira Park: Harbour Publishing 1995
Rogers, Andrew D. *Bernard Edward Fernow: A Story of American Forestry*. Princeton: Princeton University Press 1951
Salaman, Graeme. *Class and the Corporation*. Glasgow: Fontana Paperbacks 1981
Sandberg, Anders L., ed. *Trouble in the Woods: Forest Policy and Social Conflict in Nova Scotia and New Brunswick*. Fredericton: Acadiensis Press 1992
Schmidt, Ralph. *The History of Cowichan Lake Research Station*. Victoria: British Columbia Ministry of Forests 1992
Schmitz, Henry. *The Long Road Travelled: An Account of Forestry at the University of Washington*. Seattle: Arboretum Foundation 1973
Schwantes, Carlos A. *The Pacific Northwest: An Interpretive History*. Lincoln: University of Nebraska Press 1989
Sloan, Gordon. *Report of the Commissioner Relating to the Forest Resources of British Columbia*. Victoria: King's Printer 1945
Smith, J. Harry G. *UBC Forestry, 1921-1990; An Informal History*. Vancouver: Faculty of Forestry, University of British Columbia 1990
Spector, Robert. *Family Trees: Simpson's Centennial Story*. Bellevue: Documentary Book Publishers Corporation 1990
Spulber, Nicolas. *Managing the American Economy From Roosevelt to Reagan*. Bloomington: Indiana University Press 1989
Steen, Harold K. *The U.S. Forest Service: A History*. Seattle: University of Washington Press 1976
Stevens, Victor. *The Powers Story*. North Bend: Wegford Publications 1979
Swift, Jamie. *Cut and Run: The Assault on Canada's Forests*. Toronto: Between the Lines 1983

Taylor, C.J. *The Heritage of the British Columbia Forest Industry: A Guide for Planning, Selection and Interpretation of Sites*. Ottawa: Environment Canada 1987

Taylor, G.W. *Timber: History of the Forest Industry in B.C.* Vancouver: J.J. Douglas 1975

Thompson, John Herd and Allen Seager. *Canada, 1922-1939: Decades of Discord*. Toronto: University of Toronto Press 1985

Thompson, Paul. *The Nature of Work: An Introduction to Debates on the Labour Process*. London: MacMillan Press 1983

Thompson, Paul and David McHugh. *Work Organizations: A Critical Introduction*. London: MacMillan 1990

Traves, Tom. *The State and Enterprise: Canadian Manufacturers and the Federal Government, 1917-1931*. Toronto: McClelland and Stewart 1979

Turner, Robert D. *Logging By Rail: The British Columbia Story*. Victoria: Sono Nis Press 1990

Twinning, Charles E. *Phil Weyerhaeuser: Lumberman*. Seattle: University of Washington Press 1985

Van Sickle, Edwin. *They Tried to Cut it All*. Seattle: Pacific Search Press 1980

Van Tassel, Alfred J. *Mechanization in the Lumber Industry: A Study of Technology in Relation to Resources and Employment Opportunity*. Philadelphia: Works Projects Administration 1940

Webster, Andrew. *Science, Technology and Society: New Directions*. New Brunswick: Rutgers University Press 1991

Weinstein, James. *The Corporate Ideal in the Liberal State, 1900-1918*. Boston: Beacon Press 1968

White, Richard. *Land Use, Environment, and Social Change: The Shaping of Island County, Washington*. Seattle: University of Washington Press 1992

Whitford, H.N. and R.D. Craig. *The Forests of British Columbia*. Ottawa: Commission on Conservation 1918

Widner, Henry, ed. *Forests and Forestry in the American States*. Washington, DC: National Association of State Foresters 1968

Williams, Michael. *Americans and Their Forests: A Historical Geography*. New York: Cambridge University Press 1989

Wood, Stephen, ed. *The Degradation of Work: Skill, Deskilling and the Labour Process*. London: Hutchinson & Co. 1982

Wynn, Graeme. *Timber Colony: A Historical Geography of Early Nineteenth Century New Brunswick*. Toronto: University of Toronto Press, 1981

Zimbalist, Andrew, ed. *Case Studies on the Labor Process*. New York: Monthly Review Press 1979

Articles

Abdill, George P. 'Bull Team Logger.' *True West* 21 (July-Aug. 1974): 6-12

Adler, Paul S. 'Marx, Machines, and Skill.' *Technology and Culture* 31 (Oct. 1990): 780-812

Akrigg Manning, Helen. 'Ernest C. Manning.' In *Manning Park Memories: Reflections of the Past*. Victoria: British Columbia Ministry of Lands and Parks 1991

Albo, Gregory and Jane Jensen. 'A Contested Concept: The Relative Autonomy of the State.' In *The New Canadian Political Economy*, ed. Wallace Clement and Glen Williams. Montreal: McGill-Queen's University Press 1989

Alexander, Tony. 'Early Day Logging.' In *The Willapa County History Report*, ed. Mrs. Nels Olsen. Raymond: Raymond Herald and Advertiser 1965

Anderson, Gordon B. 'Oregon's Forest Conservation Laws.' Part I *American Forests* 83 (Mar. 1977): 16-9, 52-6

Ashworth, Adam. 'Reckoning Schemes of Legitimation: On Commissions of Inquiry as Power/Knowledge Forms.' *Journal of Historical Sociology* 3 (Mar. 1990): 1-22

Attewell, Paul. 'The Deskilling Controversy.' *Work and Occupations* 14 (Aug. 1987): 323-46

Baikie, Wallace. 'Early Logging Days on Denman Island.' *British Columbia Forest History Newsletter* 5 (Apr. 1983): 3-5

–. 'Logging with Bulls.' *British Columbia Forest History Newsletter* 8 (Apr. 1984): 3-4

Benton, Ted. 'Marxism and Natural Limits: An Ecological Critique and Reconstruction.' *New Left Review* 178 (1989): 51-86

Bird, Elizabeth Ann. 'The Social Construction of Nature: Theoretical Approaches to the History of Environmental Problems.' *Environmental Review* 11 (Winter 1987): 225-64

Block, Fred. 'The Ruling Class Does Not Rule: Notes on a Marxist Theory of the State.' *Socialist Revolution* 33 (1977): 6-28

Bunting, Robert. 'Abundance and the Forests of the Douglas Fir Bioregion, 1840-1920.' *Environmental History Review* 18 (Winter 1994): 41-62

Burris, Val. 'Capital Accumulation and the Rise of the New Middle Class.' *Review of Radical Political Economics* 12 (Spring 1980): 17-34

Cameron, David A. 'The Silverton Nursery: An Early Experiment in Pacific Northwest Reforestation.' *Journal of Forest History* 23 (July 1979): 122-9

Carchedi, G. 'On the Economic Identification of the New Middle Class.' *Economy and Society* 4 (1975): 1-85

Carrothers, W.A. 'Forest Industries of British Columbia.' In *The North American Assault on Canadian Forest,* ed. Arthur M. Lower. Toronto: Ryerson Press 1938

Chandler, Alfred D. Jr. 'The Emergence of Managerial Capitalism.' *Business History Review* 58 (Winter 1984): 473-503

Clary, David A. 'What Price Sustained Yield? The Forest Service, Community Stability, and Timber Monopoly Under the 1944 Sustained-Yield Act.' *Journal of Forest History* 31 (Jan. 1987): 4-18

Clow, Michael. 'Alienation From Nature: Marx and Environmental Politics.' *Alternatives* 10 (Summer 1982): 36-40

Cohen, Sheila. 'A Labour Process to Nowhere?' *New Left Review* 165 (Sept.-Oct. 1987): 34-50

Cottell, Phillip L. 'Human Factors in Logging Productivity.' In *Manpower – Forest Industry's Key Resource,* ed. Lloyd C. Irving. New Haven: Yale University 1975

Cox, Thomas R. 'The Stewardship of Private Forests: Evolution of a Concept in the United States, 1864-1950.' *Journal of Forest History* 25 (Oct. 1981): 188-96

–. 'Trade, Development, and Environmental Change: The Utilization of North America's Pacific Coast Forests to 1914 and its Consequences.' In *Global Deforestation in the Nineteenth Century World Economy,* ed. Richard P. Tucker and J.F. Richards, 14-29. Durham: Duke University Press 1983

Cuff, Robert D. 'American Historians and the Organizational Factor.' *Canadian Review of American Studies* 4 (Spring 1973): 19-31

Dahlberg, Kenneth A. 'The Changing Nature of Natural Resources.' In *Natural Resources and People: Conceptual Issues in Interdisciplinary Research,* ed. Kenneth A. Dahlberg and John W. Bennett. Boulder: Westview Press 1986

Delorme, Ronald L. 'Rational Management Takes to the Woods: Frederick Weyerhaeuser and the Pacific Northwest Wood Products Industry.' *Journal of the West* 25 (Jan. 1986): 39-43

Dickson, David. 'Technology and the Construction of Social Reality.' In *Radical Science Essays,* ed. Les Levidow. London: Free Association Books 1986

Doig, Ivan. 'The Murky Annals of Clearcutting: A 40-Year Old Dispute.' *Pacific Search* 10 (Dec. 1975-Jan. 1976): 12-4

Drushka, Ken. 'The New Forestry: Middle Ground in the Debate Over the Region's Forests.' *The New Pacific* 4 (Fall 1990): 7-24

Du Boff, Richard B. and Edward S. Herman. 'Alfred Chandler's New Business History: A Review.' *Politics and Society* 10 (1980): 87-110

Dunk, Thomas. 'Talking About Trees: Environment and Society in Forest Workers' Culture.' *Canadian Review of Sociology and Anthropology* 31 (1994): 14-34

Ehrenreich, Barbara and John. 'The Professional-Managerial Class.' In *Between Labor and Capital,* ed. Pat Walker. Boston: South End Press 1979

Emerson, George H. 'Lumbering on Grays Harbor.' *The Coast* 14 (July 1907): 1-11

Enzenberger, H.M. 'A Critique of Political Ecology.' *New Left Review* 84 (Mar.-Apr. 1974): 3-31

Ficken, Robert E. 'Gifford Pinchot Men: Pacific Northwest Lumbermen and the Conservation Movement, 1902-1910.' *Western Historical Quarterly* 13 (Apr. 1982): 165-78

–. 'Pulp and Timber: Rayonier's Timber Acquisition Program on the Olympic Penninsula, 1937-1952.' *Journal of Forest History* 27 (1983): 4-14

–. 'Weyerhaeuser and the Pacific Northwest Timber Industry, 1899-1903.' *Pacific Northwest Quarterly* 70 (Oct. 1979): 146-54

Foster, John Bellamy. 'The Limits of Environmentalism Without Class: Lessons From the Ancient Forest Struggle in the Pacific Northwest.' *Capitalism, Nature, Socialism* 13 (Mar. 1993): 11-42

Friedman, Andrew. 'The Means of Management Control and Labour Process Theory: A Critical Note on Storey.' *Sociology* 21 (1987): 287-94

Galambos, Louis. 'The Emerging Organizational Synthesis in Modern American History.' *Business History Review* 44 (Autumn 1970): 279-90

Gillis, R. Peter and Thomas R. Roach. 'The American Influence on Conservation in Canada, 1899-1911.' *Journal of Forest History* 30 (Oct. 1986): 160-74

Gold, David A., Clarence Y.H. Lo, and Eric Olin Wright. 'Recent Developments in Marxist Theories of the Capitalist State.' *Monthly Review* 27, 5 (1975): 29-43; 6 (1975): 36-51

Goldman, Paul and Donald R. Van Houten. 'Managerial Strategies and the Worker: A Marxist Analysis.' *Sociological Quarterly* 18 (Winter 1977): 108-25

Golinski, Jan. 'Experiment in Scientific Practice.' *History of Science* 28 (1990): 203-9

Gray, Stephen. 'The Government's Timber Business: Forest Policy and Administration in British Columbia, 1912-1928.' *BC Studies* 81 (Spring 1989): 24-49

Hammond, Herb. 'Putting Wholistic Forest Use into Practice.' In *Touch Wood: B.C. Forests at the Crossroads*, ed. Ken Drushka, Box Nixon, and Ray Travers. Madeira Park: Harbour Publishing 1993

Hawley, Ellis. 'Herbert Hoover, the Commerce Secretariat, and the Vision of an Associative State.' *Journal of American History* 61 (June 1974): 116-40

–. 'Three Facets of Hooverian Associationalism: Lumber, Aviation and Movies, 1921-1930.' In *Regulation in Perspective: Historical Essays*, ed. Thomas K. McCraw. Cambridge: Harvard University Press 1981

Hoffman, J.V. 'The Establishment of a Douglas Fir Forest.' *Ecology* 1 (1920): 49-53

Holmes, Frederic L. 'Do We Understand Historically How Experimental Knowledge is Acquired?' *History of Science* 30 (1992): 119-35

Howe, C.D. 'Address Delivered Before B.C. Forest Club.'*Proceedings of the British Columbia Forest Club* 2 (1916): 83-7

Hull, James P. 'A Common Effort to Determine the Facts: The Sharing of Technical Knowledge in Canadian Industry, 1900-1939.' *Journal of Canadian Studies* 25 (Winter 1990-91): 50-63

Johnson, Terry. 'Work and Power.' In *The Politics of Work and Occupations*, ed. Geoff Esland and Graeme Salaman. Milton Keynes: Open University Press 1980

Kantor, Harvey. 'Vocationalism in American Education: The Economic and Political Context.' In *Work, Youth and Schooling: Historical Perspectives on Vocationalism in American Education*, ed. Harvey Kantor and David B. Tyack. Stanford: Stanford University Press 1982

Kapp, Karl W. 'Environmental Disruption and Protection.' In *Socialism and the Environment*, ed. Ken Coates. Nottingham: Spokesman Books 1972

Kennedy, Richard H. 'Logging Our Great Forests.' *Pacific Monthly* 13 (Jan. 1905): 24-34

Krimsky, Sheldon. 'The New Corporate Identity of the American University.' *Alternatives* 14 (May/June 1987): 20-9

Larson, Megali Sarfatti. 'The Production of Expertise and the Constitution of Expert Power.' In *The Authority of Experts*, ed. Thomas L. Haskell. Bloomington: Indiana University Press 1984

Lazonick, William H. 'Technical Change and the Control of Work: The Development of Capital-Labour Relations in U.S. Mass Production Industries.' In *Managerial Strategies and Industrial Relations: An Historical and Comparative Study*, ed. Howard F. Gospel and Craig R. Littler. London: Heinemann Books 1983

Leiss, William. 'Utopia and Technology: Reflections on the Conquest of Nature.' *International Social Science Journal* 22 (1970): 576-88

Long, Jack. 'The Quinsam Nursery.' *British Columbia Forest History Newsletter* 38 (Dec. 1993): 1-3

McCraw, Thomas K. 'The Challenge of Alfred D. Chandler, Jr.: Retrospect and Prospect.' *Reviews in American History* 15 (Mar. 1987): 160-78

McDonnell, Lawrence T. '"You Are Too Sentimental": Problems and Suggestions For a New Labor History.' *Journal of Social History* 17 (Summer 1984): 629-53

McGuire, Patrick. 'Instrumental Class Power and the Origin of Class-Based State Regulation in the U.S. Electric Utility Industry.' *Critical Sociology* 16 (Summer-Fall 1989): 181-203

McRoberts, Mary. 'When Good Intentions Fail: A Case of Forest Policy in the British Columbia Interior, 1945-1956.' *Journal of Forest History* 32 (July 1988): 138-49

Marchak, Patricia. 'A Global Contest for British Columbia.' In *Touch Wood: B.C. Forests at the Crossroads,* ed. Ken Drushka, Bob Nixon, and Ray Travers, 67-84. Madeira Park: Harbour Publishing 1993

–. 'Public Policy, Capital and Labour in the Forest Industry.' In *Workers, Capital and the State in British Columbia,* ed. Rennie Warburton and David Coburn. Vancouver: UBC Press 1988

Meiskins, Peter F. 'Science in the Labor Process: Engineers as Workers.' In *Professionals as Workers: Mental Labor in Advanced Capitalism,* ed. Charles Derber. Boston: G.K. Hall 1982

Morgan, George T. Jr. 'Conflagration as Catalyst: Western Lumbermen and American Forest Policy.' *Pacific Historical Review* 47 (1978): 167-87

Mulkay, M.J. 'Sociology of the Scientific Research Community.' In *Science, Technology and Society: A Cross Disciplinary Perspective,* ed. Ina Spiegel-Rosing and Derek de Solla-Price. Beverley Hills: Sage Publications 1977

Nokev, Joel and Karen Kampen. 'Sustainable or Unsustainable Development? An Analysis of an Environmental Controversy.' *Canadian Journal of Sociology* 17 (1992): 249-73

O'Connor, James. 'Socialism and Ecology.' *Our Generation* 22 (Fall 1990-Spring 1991): 75-87

Offe, Claus. 'The Theory of the Capitalist State and the Problem of Policy Formation.' In *Stress and Contradiction in Modern Capitalism: Public Policy and the Theory of the State,* eds. Leon N. Lindberg, Robert Alford, Colin Crouch, and Claus Offe. Toronto: D.C. Heath 1975

Orians, Gordon H. '"New Forestry" and the Old-Growth Forests of Northwestern North America: A Conversation with Jerry F. Franklin.' *Northwest Environmental Journal* 6 (1990): 446-61

O'Riordan, Timothy. 'Policy Making and Environmental Management: Some Thoughts on Processes and Research Issues.' In *Natural Resources for a Democratic Society: Public Participation in Decision-Making,* ed. Albert E. Utton, W.R. Sewell, and Timothy O'Riordan. Boulder: Westview Press 1976

Panitch, Leo. 'The Role and Nature of the Canadian State.' In *The Canadian State,* ed. Leo Panitch. Toronto: University of Toronto Press 1977

Pinckett, Harold T. 'Western Perception of Forest Conservation.' *Journal of the West* 18 (1977): 72-3

Pross, A.P. 'The Development of Professions in the Public Service: The Foresters in Ontario.' *Canadian Public Administration* 10 (Sept. 1967): 376-404.

Pursell, Carroll. 'Conservation, Environmentalism, and the Engineers: The Progressive Era and the Recent Past.' In *Environmental History: Critical Issues in Comparative Perspectives,* ed. Kendall E. Bailes. Lanham: University Press of America 1985

Rajala, Richard A. 'Bill and the Boss: Labor Protest, Technological Change, and the Transformation of the West Coast Logging Camp.' *Journal of Forest History* 33 (Oct. 1989): 168-79

–. 'A Dandy Bunch of Wobblies: Pacific Northwest Loggers and the Industrial Workers of the World, 1900-1930.' *Labor History* 37 (Spring 1996): 205-34

–. 'The Forest as Factory: Technological Change and Worker Control in the West Coast Logging Industry, 1880-1930.' *Labour/Le Travail* 32 (Fall 1993): 73-104

–. 'Managerial Crisis: The Emergence and Role of the West Coast Logging Engineer, 1900-1930.' In *Canadian Papers in Business History* 1 (1989), ed. Peter Baskerville, 101-28

–. 'The Receding Timber Line: Forest Practice, State Regulation, and the Decline of the Cowichan Lake Timber Industry.' In *Canadian Papers in Business History* 2 (1993), ed. Peter Baskerville, 179-210

Reavis, John. 'Logging on Puget Sound.' *Washington Magazine* (Sept. 1899): 13-7

Reed, Michael. 'The Labour Process Perspective on Management Organization: A Critique and Reformulation.' In *The Theory and Philosophy of Organizations: Critical Issues and New Perspectives*, ed. John Hassard and Denis Dym. New York: Routledge 1990

Reid, Keith and Don Weaver. 'Aspects of the Political Economy of the B.C. Forest Industry.' In *Essays in B.C. Political Economy*, ed. Paul Knox and Philip Resnick. Vancouver: New Star Books 1974

Roach, Thomas R. 'Stewards of the People's Wealth: The Founding of British Columbia's Forest Branch.' *Journal of Forest History* 28 (Jan. 1984): 14-23

Robbins, William G. 'Federal Forestry Cooperation: The Fernow-Pinchot Years.' *Journal of Forest History* 28 (Oct. 1984): 164-73

–. 'The Great Experiment in Industrial Self-Government: The Lumber Industry and the National Recovery Administration.' *Journal of Forest History* 25 (July 1981): 128-43

–. 'Lumber Production and Community Stability: A View From the Pacific Northwest.' *Journal of Forest History* 31 (Oct. 1987): 187-96

–. 'The "Luxuriant Landscape": The Great Douglas Fir Bioregion.' *Oregon Humanities* (Winter 1990): 1-5

–. 'The Social Context of Forestry: The Pacific Northwest in the Twentieth Century.' *Western Historical Quarterly* 16 (Oct. 1985): 413-28

Rutledge, Peter J. and Richard H. Tooker. 'Steam Power for Loggers: Two Views of the Dolbeer Donkey.' *Journal of Forest History* 14 (1970): 19-28

Scammon, C.M. 'Lumbering in Washington Territory.' *Overland Monthly* 5 (1870): 55-60

Schon, D.O.L. 'Unique British Columbia Pioneer.' *Forest History* 14 (Jan. 1971): 18-22

Schrecker, Ted. 'Resisting Environmental Regulation: The Cryptic Pattern of Business-Government Relations.' In *Managing Leviathan: Environmental Politics and the Administrative State*, ed. Robert Paehlke and Douglas Torgerson. Peterborough: Broadview Press 1990

Schwarz, Bill. 'Re-Assessing Braverman: Socialization and Dispossession in the History of Technology.' In *Science, Technology and the Labour Process*, vol. 2, ed. Les Levidow and Bob Young. London: Free Association Books 1985

Skocpol, Theda. 'Bringing the State Back In: Strategies of Analysis in Current Research.' In *Bringing the State Back In*, ed. Peter B. Evans, Dietrich Rueschmeyer, and Theda Skocpol. Cambridge: Cambridge University Press 1985

Smith, David M. 'Even-Age Management: Concept and Historical Development.' In *Even-Age Management: Proceedings of a Symposium Held August 1, 1922*, ed. Richard K. Hermann and Denis P. Lavender. Corvallis: Oregon State University School of Forestry.

Stacer, Thomas C. 'The Oregon Conservation Act.' *Willamette Law Journal* 2 (1962-1963): 268-84

Stark, David. 'Class Struggle and the Transformation of the Labour Process.' *Theory and Society* 9 (Jan. 1980): 89-130

Storey, John. 'The Means of Management Control.' *Sociology* 19 (1985): 193-211

Szymanski, Al. 'Braverman as a Neo-Luddite.' *Insurgent Sociologist* 8 (Winter 1978): 45-50

Taylor, Duncan and Jeremy Wilson. 'Environmental Health – Democratic Health: An Examination of Proposals for Decentralization of Forest Management in British Columbia.' *Forest Planning Canada* 9 (Mar./Apr. 1993): 34-45

Twinning, Charles E. 'Weyerhaeuser and the Clemons Tree Farm: Experimenting With a Theory.' In *History of Sustained-Yield Forestry: A Symposium*, ed. Harold K. Steen. Durham: Forest History Society Inc. 1984

Walker, K.J. 'Ecological Limits and Marxian Thought.' *Politics* 14 (May 1979): 29-46

Wall, Louise H. 'Hauling Logs in Washington.' *Northwest Magazine* (Apr. 1893): 20-1

White, Richard. '"Are You an Environmentalist or Do You Work for a Living?": Work and Nature.' In *Uncommon Ground: Rethinking the Human Place in Nature*, ed. William Cronon. New York: W.W. Norton 1995

Williams, Glen. 'Greening the Canadian Political Economy.' *Studies in Political Economy* 37 (Spring 1992): 5-30

Wilson, Jeremy. 'Forest Conservation in British Columbia, 1935-1985: Reflections on a Barren Political Debate.' *BC Studies* 76 (Winter 1987-1988): 3-32

Woodrow, R. Brian. 'Resources and Policy-Making at the National Level: The Search for Focus.' In *Resources and the Environment: Policy Perspectives for Canada,* ed. O.P. Dwivedi. Toronto: McClelland and Stewart 1980

Worster, Donald. 'Transformations of the Earth: Toward an Agroecological Perspective in History.' *Journal of American History* 76 (March 1990): 1087-106.

Wright, Erik Olin. 'Varieties of Marxist Conceptions of Class Structure.' *Politics and Society* 9 (1980): 323-70

Zussman, Robert. 'The Middle Levels: Engineers and the "Working Middle Class."' *Politics and Society* 13 (1984): 217-52

Theses and Dissertations

Anderson Craig, Claudia. 'Forest Practices, Legislation and Social Valuation of Forested Land in Three Western States.' M.Sc. thesis, University of Washington 1977

Aylen, Peter G. 'Sustained Yield Forestry Policy in B.C. to 1956: A Deterministic Analysis.' M.A. thesis, University of Victoria 1979

Garvey, Clarence Ross. 'Overhead Systems of Logging in the Northwest.' M.Sc. in Forestry thesis, University of Washington 1914

Griffin, Robert B. 'The Shawnigan Lake Lumber Company, 1899-1943.' M.A. thesis, University of Victoria 1979

Hamill, Louise. 'A Preliminary Study of the Status and Use of the Forest Resources of Western Oregon in Relation to Some Objectives of Public Policy.' Ph.D. thesis, University of Washington 1963

Lawrence, Joseph C. 'Markets and Capital: A History of the Lumber Industry of British Columbia, 1778-1952.' M.A. thesis, University of British Columbia 1957

Legendre, Camille Georges. 'Organizational Technology, Structure and Environment: The Pulp and Paper Industry of Quebec.' Ph.D. thesis, Michigan State University 1977

Parenteau, William M. 'Forest and Society in New Brunswick: The Political Economy of the Forest Industries.' Ph.D. thesis, University of New Brunswick 1994

Salazar, Debra Jennifer. 'Political Processes and Forest Practice Legislation.' Ph.D. thesis, University of Washington 1985

Shull, Josiah T. 'Overhead Logging on the Pacific Coast.' M.Sc. in Forestry thesis, University of Washington 1926

Steen, Harold K. 'Forestry in Washington to 1925.' Ph.D. thesis, University of Washington 1969

Taylor, Joseph E., III. 'Making Salmon: Economy, Culture, and Science in the Oregon Fisheries, Precontact to 1960.' Ph.D. thesis, University of Washington 1996

Unpublished Papers and Manuscripts

Cowlin, Robert W. 'Federal Forest Research in the Pacific Northwest: The Pacific Northwest Research Station.' Unpublished manuscript, Pacific Northwest Research Station

Gilbert John. 'Logging and Railroad Building on Puget Sound, Washington Territory.' University of Washington Libraries 1878

Hobi, Frank. 'The Story of a Logger.' Unpublished manuscript, University of Washington Libraries

Irwin, E.J. 'Logging in British Columbia.' Unpublished manuscript, British Columbia Legislative Library

Oakley, Philip. 'Development of the Nitinat Division.' Qualifying thesis, Association of British Columbia Foresters 1962

Rajala, Richard A. 'Timber and Fish: Resource Agencies, Forest Practices, and Salmon Habitat in British Columbia, 1900-1965.' Paper presented to the BC Studies Conference, Nanaimo 1997

Interviews

Drinkwater, Albert. Interview by Imbert Orchard, 1964

Frink, Francis. Interview by Elwood R. Maunder, Forest History Foundation, 1957. University of Washington Libraries

Fry, Amelia R. *Thornton T. Munger: Forest Research in the Pacific Northwest, An Interview Conducted by Amelia R. Fry*. Berkeley: University of California Regional Oral History Office 1967

–. *Leo A. Isaac: Douglas Fir Research in the Pacific Northwest, 1920-1956*. Berkeley: University of California Regional Oral History Office 1967

Lund, Walter H. *Timber Management in the Pacific Northwest Region, 1927-1965. An Interview Conducted by Amelia R. Fry*. Berkeley: University of California Regional Oral History Office 1967

Meece, Elijah M. Interview by Michael A. Runestrand, Washington State Oral/Aural History Project 16 June 1976

Murray, L.T. Interview by Elwood R. Maunder, Forest History Foundation, 1957. University of Washington Libraries

Rogers, Lloyd C. Interview by C.D. Orchard, 1956, C.D. Orchard Collection, BCA

Stuart, R.V. Interview by C.D. Orchard, 1960, C.D. Orchard Collection, BCA

Index

selective logging, 149; support for regulation at state level, 90, 105, 180; and Timber Conservation Board, 125; and timber industry public relations, 146; on tractor logging, 128; on Tree Farm programs, 182. *See also* US Forest Service
Green Timbers Tree Nursery, 120
Greenman, Judd, 57, 62, 126-7
Gregg, E.E., 199
Griggs, Everett G., 67, 104
'Ground-lead' logging, 18-9
'Gyppo' system, 38

H.J. Andrews Experimental Forest, 215
H.R. MacMillan Export Company, 73, 74
Haefner, H.E., 143
Hagenstein, William, 186, 187, 210
Hall, J.A., 205
Hammerquist, Don, 148
Hammond Lumber Company, 62
Hanzlik, E.J., 147
Hanzlik formula, 199
Harding, Warren G., 102
Harris, Howell, 6
Harrison, Benjamin, 54
Hart, John, 168, 190, 191, 192, 194
Harter, Lee, 189
Hawley Pulp and Paper Company, 74
Hays, Samuel P., 61
Hemlock, increase in value of, xvii, 205
Herbicides, and inhibition of brush encroachment, 210
High-lead logging: 'aerial interlocking skidder,' 21; 'cold deck,' 21, 22, 26, 36, 39; and forest regeneration, 112; and spar tree, 20
'High rigger,' 26, 27, 44, 50
Higher education. *See* Engineers, logging; Foresters; names of specific universities; Vocational training, for timber industry
Hirt, Paul, xx
Hoar, Jim, 63
Hobi, Frank, 39, 208
Hodgins, Hugh, 211
Hoffman, B.E., 140, 144
Hoffman, J.V., 96, 101-3, 108, 110, 112, 113, 218
Hoisting equipment, 17
Holbrook, Stewart, 30, 50
Homestead Act (US), xvii
Hook Bill, 1946 (US), 185
'Hooktender,' 12, 16, 17, 19, 20, 25
Horses, in logging, 13, 14, 15, 16, 17, 19
Hough, Franklin B., 53
Howe, C.D., 101, 112, 189
Hughes, W.G., 201, 203

Hunt, Nils, 44

Ickes, Harold L., 149
Imperial Order Daughters of the Empire, 165
Imperial Preferential Agreement, 1932 (BC), 156
Industrial foresters. *See* Foresters
Industrial Workers of the World (IWW), 6, 29-30
Information-gathering: aerial photography, 74, 75; and computer technology, 76-7; topographic maps, 61-4, 74-5
Internal combustion engine, 31, 36-40
International Business Machines (IBM), 76
International Woodworkers of America (IWA), 6, 34, 183
Isaac, Leo: appointment at Wind River Experimental Forest Nursery, 113; disproval of 'seed storage' theory, 102, 115; and 'Reproductive Habits of Douglas Fir,' 1943, 179, 193; research on direct seeding, 210; research on selective logging and forest regeneration, 150, 168, 206; on seed trees per acre, 188
'Isaacson Logging Tower,' 42
Isaacson Steel Works, 42
IWA. *See* International Woodworkers of America (IWA)
IWW. *See* Industrial Workers of the World (IWW)

Jacobson, Norman, 67, 72, 148, 149-50, 177, 208
Jerome, Tiff, 23, 29
Jewett, George, 180
Johnson, Byron, 198
Johnson, Hugh S., 133
Johnson, R.J., xxi
Joint Committee on Forest Conservation (of WCLA and PNLA), 66-7, 134, 136, 138, 144-5, 146, 152, 169, 173, 176-7, 179, 180, 184. *See also* Forest Conservation Committee of the Pacific Northwest Forest Industries
Joint Congressional Committee on Forestry (US), 124, 146, 151, 172
Jones, Alden, 44

Keith, Charles S., 126
Kellogg, Royal S., 104, 107, 131
Kenney, E.T., 197-8
Kerry Mill Company, 21, 22
Kirkland, Burt, 94, 95, 105, 127, 128, 140, 205

industry, 124, 137, 142, 145, 146, 150-1; inspection of selective logging operations, 149. *See also* US Forest Service
Silen, Roy, 210
Silvicultural measures. *See* Reforestation
Simpson, Sol, 15, 16
Simpson Logging Company, 56-7, 72, 73, 76, 129, 134, 142, 147, 148, 171, 174, 181, 185, 196, 206
Sitka spruce, xvii
Skagit Corporation, 46
Skagit Steel and Iron Works, 37, 42
Skidder systems, 20
'Skidroad,' 12, 17
Skinner, R.J., 99
Slash burning: and Douglas fir reproduction, 93, 112, 116-7; and forest regeneration, in BC, 162; requirement of, in BC, 163
Sloan, Gordon, 70, 191, 192-3, 196, 197
Sloan Commission. *See* Royal Commission on Forest Resources (BC)
Small operators, survival of, xviii
Smith, David, 207
Smith, J.H.G., 76-7
Smith, Sid, 25, 194
Smoot-Hawley tariff, 1930, 125, 155
Snell, Bertrand, 106, 107
Snell Bill (US), 107, 108, 109, 110
'Sniper,' 24
'Sniping,' 12
Social Credit Party, 197
The Social Management of American Forests (Marshall), 130
Society of American Foresters (SAF), 54-5, 104, 130, 131
Sommers, Charles, 200
Soundview Pulp Company, 42
South Saanich Farmers' Institute, 165
Spar tree: and 'high rigger,' 26, 27; single, 20, 21; two-tree system, 20, 21, 22
Sparhawk, William, 130
'Splitter,' 37
'Spool tender,' 17
'Spotter,' for grapple operator, 47
'Springboards,' 10-1
St. Clair, R.C., 199
St. Paul and Tacoma Lumber Company, 39, 67, 72, 104, 148, 149, 150, 171, 174, 187, 207-8
St. Regis Paper Company, xix, 69, 76
Stamm, E.P., 187-8
Stamp, Edward, xvii
Standard Oil, xviii
Steam 'donkey': and clearcutting, 89; effect on forest regeneration, 91-3; and

factory regime, 88; increase in logging production, 14-20, 217; multi-gear, 25-6; replacement of, by motorized vehicles, 31; replacement of animals by, 7, 16, 17, 19
Steam engine. *See* Steam 'donkey'
Steel-spar: and automatic grapple, 46; diesel-powered, 42; portable, 40-9, 221; skidders, 26-9
Steen, Harold, xx
Stevens, H.H., 192
Stihl chain saw, 32
Stokes, J.S., 202, 214
Stoodley, G.E., 113
Streams, damage by early logging techniques, 91
Strip clearcutting. *See* Patch clearcutting
Stuart, R.Y., 18, 101, 121-2, 129, 133, 158-9
'Stump roller,' 17
Sustained-yield cutting: cooperative, 180; costs of, 131; and forest management, 127; policy, BC, 86, 166, 167-8, 189-204, 220, 223; and timber industry compliance, 143
Sustained-Yield Forest Management Act, 1944 (US), 72, 168, 180
Suzzallo, Henry, 59
'Swamper,' 12, 17, 24

Taft, William, 98
Talbot, E.C., xvii
Tannhaeuser, R., 203
Tariffs: Imperial Preferential Agreement, 1932, (BC), 156; Smoot-Hawley tariff, 125, 155
Taxes, on cut timber, 103-4, 190
Taylor, D.B., 201
Taylor, Frederick W., 3, 51, 64, 78, 79, 80
'Teamster,' 12-4, 16
Technology, production. *See* Mechanization
Telford, R.C., 197, 200
Tennant, J.D., 136
Tetramine, seed treatment by, 210
TFL. *See* Tree Farm Licences (BC)
Thomas and Meservey Inc., 62
Thompson, Paul, 50, 79
Tilton, Warren, 39, 136, 144, 152
Timber and Stone Act (US), xviii
Timber Conservation Board (US), 125
Timber Growing and Logging Practice in the Douglas Fir Region (Munger), 117
Timber industry: from 1880-1930, 88-122; during 1930s, xix, 67, 123-53; from 1940-65, 167-216; and Article X,

Set in Stone by Artegraphica Design Co. Ltd.

Copy editor: Andy Carroll

Indexer: Annette Lorek

Printed and bound in Canada by Friesens